Fourth SIGHAN Workshop on Chinese Language Processing

(IJCNLP 2005)

Jeju Island, Korea
14-15 October 2005

ISBN: 978-1-62748-367-4

Printed from e-media with permission by:

Curran Associates, Inc.
57 Morehouse Lane
Red Hook, NY 12571

Some format issues inherent in the e-media version may also appear in this print version.

Printed by Curran Associates, Inc. (2013)

For permission requests, please contact the Association for Computational Linguistics at the address below.

Association for Computational Linguistics
209 N. Eighth Street
Stroudsburg, Pennsylvania 18360

Phone: 1-570-476-8006
Fax: 1-570-476-0860

acl@aclweb.org

Additional copies of this publication are available from:

Curran Associates, Inc.
57 Morehouse Lane
Red Hook, NY 12571 USA
Phone: 845-758-0400
Fax: 845-758-2634
Email: curran@proceedings.com
Web: www.proceedings.com

IJCNLP-05

Fourth SIGHAN Workshop on Chinese Language Processing

Proceedings of the Workshop

14-15 October 2005
Jeju Island, Korea

Preface

We would like welcome you to the Fourth SIGHAN Workshop on Chinese Language Processing held on Jeju Island, Republic of Korea, October 14-15, 2005. Building on previous workshops in Sapporo and Barcelona, SIGHAN4 brings together researchers from Asia and around the world to report recent developments in many aspects of Chinese language processing. This year for the first time the workshop is being held under the auspices of the Asia Federation of Natural Language Processing, in conjunction with the Second International Joint Conference on Natural Language Processing. We hope that this collaboration will encourage the participation of a broad group of researchers.

This year's workshop has assembled a diverse general technical program. With ten regular papers and six poster presentations, the general session spans topics from segmentation and part-of-speech tagging to semantics, discourse, and dialogue. Presenters represent institutions in Asia, North America, and Europe. We hope that these papers will engage the participants and promote wide-ranging discussion.

This year's workshop also presents the results of the Second International Chinese Word Segmentation Bakeoff sponsored by SIGHAN. The First Bakeoff, held in conjunction with SIGHAN2 at ACL 2003 in Sapporo, quickly became the standard evaluation for segmentation systems, and we hope this new evaluation will prove to be a worthy successor. Twenty-three groups from eight countries participated in the evaluation, and their results as well as an overview comprise the Bakeoff section of the workshop.

We thank all who submitted papers. We greatly appreciate the time and insightful reviews provided by the members of the Program Committee. We also thank Tom Emerson for his great efforts in bringing together the Segmentation Bakeoff and all the bakeoff participants for their contribution to the success of the event. Finally, we would also like to thank the SIGHAN Board, the IJCNLP-05 workshop chairs, Yuji Matsumoto and Laurent Romary, and the publications chairs, Olivia Kwong and Jian Su, for their guidance and support.

Chu-Ren Huang, Gina-Anne Levow , SIGHAN4 Co-chairs

Organizers

Co-Chairs:

Chu-Ren Huang - Academia Sinica, Taiwan
Gina-Anne Levow - University of Chicago, USA

Segmentation Bakeoff Organizer:

Tom Emerson - Basis Technology Corp, USA

Program Committee

Joyce Chai - Michigan State Univ, USA
Keh-Jiann Chen - Academia Sinica, Taiwan
Zheng Chen - Microsoft Research Asia, China
Tom Emerson - Basis Technology Corp, USA
Pascale Fung - Hong Kong University of Science and Technology, Hong Kong
Tingting He - Huazhong Normal University, China
Chu-Ren Huang - Academia Sinica, Taiwan
K.L.Kwok - Queens College, USA
Tom Lai - City Univ. of Hong Kong, Hong Kong
Gina-Anne Levow - University of Chicago, USA Mingjing Li - Microsoft Research Asia, China
Mu Li - Microsoft Research Asia, China
Qin Lu - The Hong Kong Polytechnic University, Hong Kong
Qing Ma - Ryukoku University, Japan
Masaki Murata - Communications Research Laboratory, Japan
Shimei Pan - IBM, USA
Richard Sproat - University of Illinois, Urbana-Champaign, USA
Keh-Yih Su - Behavior Design Corporation, Taiwan
Maosong Sun - Tsinghua University, China
Shu-chuan Tseng - Academia Sinica, Taiwan
Benjamin Tsou - City University of Hong Kong, Hong Kong
Dekai Wu - Hong Kong University of Science and Technology, Hong Kong
Yunfang Wu - Peking University, China
Nianwen Xue - University of Pennsylvania, USA
Qiang Zhou - Tsinghua University, China

Further Information

Gina-Anne Levow
Department of Computer Science
University of Chicago
1100 E 58th St.
Chicago, IL 60637 USA

Fourth SIGHAN Workshop on Chinese Language Processing
Workshop Program

October 14

08:30 Opening Remarks

Session I: Segmentation, Input, and Parsing

08:35 *Detecting Segmentation Errors in Chinese Annotated Corpus*
Chengjie Sun, Chang-Ning Huang, Xiaolong Wang, and Mu Li

08:55 *Using Word-Pair Identifier to Improve Chinese Input System*
Jia-Lin Tsai

09:15 *Chinese Deterministic Dependency Analyzer: Examining Effects of Global Features and Root Node Finder*
Yuchang Cheng, Masayuki Asahara, and Yuji Matsumoto

09:35 *Break*

Session II: Part-of-Speech and Named Entity Recognition

09:45 *Chinese Classifier Assignment Using SVMs*
Hui Guo and Huayan Zhang

10:05 *Morphological features help POS tagging of unknown words across language varieties*
Huihsin Tseng, Daniel Jurafsky, and Christopher Manning

10:25 *Product Named Entity Recognition Based on Hierarchical Hidden Markov Model*
Feifan Liu, Jun Zhao, Bibo Lv, Bo Xu and Hao Yu

10:45 *Break*

Session III: Semantics and Dialogue

11:00 *Chinese Sketch Engine and the Extraction of Grammatical Collocations*
Chu-Ren Huang, Adam Kilgarriff, Yiching Wu, Chih-Ming Chiu, Simon Smith, Pavel Rychly, Ming-Hong Bai and Keh-Jiann Chen

11:20 *Word Meaning Inducing via Character Ontology: A Survey on the Semantic Prediction of Chinese Two-Character Words*
Shu-Kai Hsieh

11:40 *Domain Specific Word Extraction from Hierarchical Web Documents: A First Step Toward Building Lexicon Trees from Web Corpora*
Jing-Shin Chang

12:00 *Turn-Taking in Mandarin Dialogue: Interactions of Tone and Intonation*
Gina-Anne Levow

12:20 *Lunch*

Session IV: General Session Posters

14:00 *Poster Briefings* (5 minutes each)

Learning a Log-Linear Model with Bilingual Phrase-Pair Features for Statistical Machine Translation
Bing Zhao and Alex Waibel

Integrating Collocation Features in Chinese Word Sense Disambiguation
Wanyin Li, Qin Lu, and Wenjie Li

NIL Is Not Nothing: Recognition of Chinese Network Informal Language Expressions
Yunqing Xia, Kam-Fai Wong and Wei Gao

The Robustness of Domain Lexico-Taxonomy: Expanding Domain Lexicon with CiLin
Chu-Ren Huang, Xiang-Bing Li and Jia-Fei Hong

Some Studies on Chinese Domain Knowledge Dictionary and Its Application to Text Classification
Jingbo Zhu and Wenliang Chen

Resolving Pronominal References in Chinese with the Hobbs Algorithm
Susan Converse

14:30 *Poster Viewing*

15:40 *Break*

Session V: Bakeoff Overview and Presentations

16:00 *The Second International Chinese Word Segmentation Bakeoff*
Thomas Emerson

16:20 *Combination of Machine Learning Methods for Optimum Chinese Word Segmentation*
Masayuki Asahara, Kenta Fukuoka, Ai Azuma, Chooi-Ling Goh, Yotaro Watanabe, Yuji Matsumoto, and Takashi Tsuzuki

16:35 *Unigram Language Model for Chinese Word Segmentation*
Aitao Chen, Yiping Zhou, Anne Zhang, and Gordon Sun

16:50 *Report To BMM-based Chinese Word Segmentor with Context-based Unknown Word Identifier for the Second International Chinese word Segmentation Bakeoff*
Jia-Lin Tsai

October 15

Session VI: Bakeoff Presentations

09:30 *An Example-Based Chinese Word Segmentation System for CWSB-2*
Chunyu Kit and Xiaoyue Liu

09:45 *Chinese Word Segmentation in FTRD Beijing*
Heng Li, Yuan Dong, Xinnian Mao, Haila Wang, and Wu Liu

10:00 *Perceptron Learning for Chinese Word Segmentation*
Yaoyong Li, Chuanjiang Miao, Kalina Bontcheva, and Hamish Cunningham

10:15 *Data-driven Language Independent Word Segmentation Using Character-Level Information*
Dong-Hee Lim and Seung-Shik Kang

10:35 *Break*

Session VII: Bakeoff Presentations

11:00 *A Maximum Entropy Approach to Chinese Word Segmentation*
Jin Kiat Low, Hwee Tou Ng, and Wenyuan Guo

11:15 *Description of the HKU Chinese Word Segmentation System for Sighan Bakeoff 2005*
Guohong Fu, Kang-Kwong Luke, and Percy Ping-Wai Wong

11:30 *A Conditional Random Field Word Segmenter for Sighan Bakeoff 2005*
Huihsin Tseng, Pichuan Chang, Galen Andrew, Daniel Jurafsky, and Christopher Manning

11:45 *Chinese Word Segmentation with Multiple Postprocessors in HIT-IRLab*
Huipeng Zhang, Ting Liu, Jinshan Ma, and Xiantao Liao

12:00 *SIGHAN Business Meeting*

Table of Contents

Detecting Segmentation Errors in Chinese Annotated Corpus

Chengjie Sun* Harbin Institute of Technology, Harbin, 150001, China

Chang-Ning Huang Microsoft Research, Asia, Beijing, 100080, China

Xiaolong Wang Harbin Institute of Technology, Harbin, 150001, China

Mu Li Microsoft Research, Asia, Beijing, 100080, China

{cjsun, wangxl}@insun.hit.edu.cn cnhuang@msrchina.research.microsoft.com

muli@microsoft.com

Abstract

This paper proposes a semi-automatic method to detect segmentation errors in a manually annotated Chinese corpus in order to improve its quality further. A particular Chinese character string occurring more than once in a corpus may be assigned different segmentations during a segmentation process. Based on these differences our approach outputs the segmentation error candidates found in a segmented corpus and then on which the segmentation errors are identified manually. Segmentation error rate of a gold standard corpus can be given using our method. In Peking University (PK) and Academic Sinica (AS) test corpora of Special Interest Group for Chinese Language Processing (SIGHAN) Bakeoff1, 1.29% and 2.26% segmentation error rates are detected by our method. These errors decrease the F-measure of SIGHAN Bakeoff1 baseline test by 1.36% in PK test data and 1.93% in AS test data respectively.

* This work was done while Chengjie Sun was visiting Microsoft Research Asia.

1 Introduction

SIGHAN Bakeoff1[1] proposed an automatic method to evaluate the performance of different Chinese word segmentation systems on four distinct data sets. This method makes the performance of different Chinese word segmentation systems comparable and greatly promotes the technology of Chinese Word Segmentation. However, the quality of the reference corpora in the evaluation should be paid more attention because they provide training material for participants and they serve as a gold standard for evaluating the performance of participant systems.

This paper presents a semi-automatic method to detect segmentation errors in a manually annotated Chinese corpus in order to improve its quality further. Especially a segmentation error rate of a gold standard corpus could be obtained with our approach. As we know a particular Chinese character string occurring more than once in a corpus may be assigned different segmentations. Those differences are considered as segmentation inconsistencies by some researchers (Wu, 2003; Chen, 2003). Segmentation consistency is also considered as one of the quality criteria of an annotated Chinese corpus (Sun, 1999). But in order to provide a more clearer description of those segmentation differences we define a new

[1] http://www.sighan.org/bakeoff2003/

term, segmentation variation, to replace the original one, segmentation inconsistency.

Our approach of spotting segmentation errors within an annotated corpus consists of two steps: (1) automatically listing the segmentation error candidates with segmentation variations found in an annotated corpus, (2) spotting segmentation errors within those candidates manually. The target of this approach is to count the number of error tokens in the corpus and give the segmentation error rate of the corpus, which is not given for any gold standard corpus in Bakeoff1.

The remainder of this paper is structured as follows. In section 2, we discriminate the kinds of segmentation inconsistencies in test sets of SIGHAN Bakeoff1. In section 3, segmentation variation is defined and our approach to detect segmentation errors in a manually annotated corpus is proposed. In section 4 we conduct baseline experiments of PK and AS corpora with revised test sets in order to show exactly the impact of segmentation errors in the test sets of Bakeoff1. Section 5 is a brief conclusion.

2 Segmentation inconsistency

In the close test of Bakeoff1, participants could only use training material from the training data for the particular corpus being testing on. No other material was allowed (Sproat and Emerson, 2003). As we know that the test data should be consistent with the training data based on a general definition of Chinese words. That is if we collect all words seen in the training data and store them into a lexicon, then each word in a test set is either a lexicon word or an OOV (out of vocabulary) word (Gao et al., 2003). In another word, if a character string has been treated as one word, i.e. a lexicon word, in the training data, the same occurrence should be taken in the corresponding test data unless it is a CAS (combination ambiguity string) and vice versa.

As we all know that a CAS like "才能 [cai2-neng2]" may be segmented into one word or two words depending on different contexts. Thus segmentation inconsistency like "才能" (talent) and "才 能" (only can) could both be correct segmentations in a text. Therefore "segmentation inconsistency" should not be regarded as incorrect segmentations in general and should be clarified further. If one wants to discuss the segmentation errors based on segmentation inconsistencies, then from which those CAS instances should be excluded.

If we exclude CAS words in our investigation temporary then for a non-CAS character string, there are four kinds of situations violating the general definition of Chinese word, also called lexicon driven principle in automatic word segmentation technology:

S1. A character string is segmented inconsistently within a training data;

S2. A character string is segmented inconsistently within a test data;

S3. A character string is segmented inconsistently between a test data and its training data. This situation could be divided into the following two cases further:

S3.1 A word identified in a training data has been segmented into multiple words in corresponding test data;

S3.2 A word identified in a test data has been segmented into multiple words in corresponding training data.

Chen (2003) describes inconsistency problem found in cases S1, S2 and S3.1 of PK corpora. For example, he gives the amount of unique text fragments that have two or more segmentations within PK training data, within PK test data and also between PK training data and PK test data.

But those CAS words have not been excluded in his description. Ignoring the content of inconsistencies the influence about the number of segmentation inconsistencies of a particular corpus will be exaggerated greatly. In addition, Chen didn't consider the case of S3.2 which could also affect the evaluation significantly according to the lexicon driven principle. 53 word types found in case 3.2 (refer to Appendix part 2) were totally treated as OOV words in Bakeoff1 which impacts the identification of those authentic new words in the task. So the issue of segmentation inconsistency in reference corpora needs further investigation.

As mentioned before, in common knowledge "segmentation inconsistency" is a derogatory term. But our investigation shows that most of segmentation inconsistencies found in an annotated corpus turned out to be correct segmentations of CASs. Therefore it is not an appropriate technique term to assess the quality of an annotated corpus. Besides, with the concept of "segmentation inconsistency" it is hard to distinguish the different inconsistent components within an annotated corpus and finally count up the number of segmentation errors exactly. In the next section we propose a new term "segmentation variation" to replace the original one, "segmentation inconsistency".

3 Segmentation variation

3.1 Definition

Definition 1: In annotated corpora *C*, a set of f(*W*, *C*) is defined as: f(*W*, *C*) = {all possible segmentations that word *W* has in corpora *C*}.

Definition 2: *W* is a **segmentation variation type (segmentation variation** in short, hereafter) with respect to *C* iff |f(*W*, *C*)|>1.

Definition 3: An instance of element in f(*W*, *C*) is called a **variation instance**. Thus a segmentation variation (type) consists of more than one variation instances in corpora *C*. And a variation instance may include one or more than one **tokens**.

Definition 4: If a variation instance is an incorrect segmentation, it is called an **error instance** (**EI**).

The definitions of segmentation variation, variation instance and error instance (EI) clearly distinguish those inconsistent components, so we can count the number of segmentation errors (in tokens) exactly.

The term variation is also used to express other annotation inconsistency in a corpus by other researchers. For example, Dickinson and Meurers (2003) used variation to describe POS (Part-of-Speech) inconsistency in an annotated corpus.

Example 1: Segmentation variations (Bakeoff1 PK corpus):
Word "等同[deng3-tong2]" is segmented as "等同" (equal) and "等 同" (et al. with).
Word "黄金周[huang2-jin1-zhou1]" is segmented as "黄金周" (golden week) and "黄金 周" (gold week).
Word "冰清玉洁[bing1-qing1-yu4-jie2]" is segmented as "冰清玉洁" (pure and noble) and "冰 清 玉 洁" (ice clear jade clean).

In example 1, Words like "等同", "黄金周" and "冰清玉洁" are segmentation variation types. Segmentations "等同" and "等 同" are two variation instances of segmentation variation "等同". Besides, the variation instance "等 同" consists of two tokens "等" and "同". While the variation instance "冰 清 玉 洁" consists of four tokens "冰", "清", "玉" and "洁".

The existence of segmentation variations in corpora lies in two reasons: 1) ambiguity: variation type *W* has multiple possible segmentations in different contexts, or 2) error: *W* has been wrongly segmented which could be judged by a given lexicon.

Example 2: A segmentation variation caused by ambiguity (Bakeoff1 PK corpus):
Segmentation variation: "国都[guo2-du1]"
Variation instances: "国都" (capital) and "国[guo2] 都[dou1]" (countries all). They are both correct segmentations in following sentences:
君士坦丁堡 成为 拜占庭 国都 。
(Constantinople became the capital of Byzantium.)
两 国 都 主张 通过 对话 和 谈判 来 解决 分歧 。
(Both countries all advocate solving disagreements by conversation and negotiation.)

Example 3: Segmentation variations caused by error (Bakeoff1 PK corpus):
Segmentation variation: "尽管如此[jin4-guan3-ru2-ci4]"
Variation instances: "尽管如此" (still) and "尽管 如此" (despite so).
Segmentation variation: "冰清玉洁"
Variation instances: "冰清玉洁" and "冰 清 玉 洁".

In the rest of the paper, a segmentation variation caused by ambiguity is called a CAS variation and a segmentation variation caused by error is called a non-CAS variation. Each kind of segmentation variations may include error instances (EIs).

Situation	Within test data	Between: One-to-Mult	Between: Mult-to-One
# of variation type	21	92	228
# of variation instances	87	129	506
# of EIs*	12(3)	68(4)	77
# of error tokens*	28(6)	142(8)	77

*: The number in the bracket is the amount caused by CAS.

Table 1 segmentation variations types, instances and EIs in PK test data

3.2 Finding error instances (EIs)

How to find the segmentation variations in corpora? Following is the algorithm of finding segmentation variations. According to our definition, the algorithm is quite straightforward. It takes two segmented Chinese corpora (reference corpus and corpus to be checked) and outputs a list of segmentation variation instances between the two corpora[2].

Algorithm steps:

1. Extract all the multi-character words in reference corpus and store their positions in reference corpus respectively;
2. Find the words that be segmented into N parts (N is from 2 to the length of current word) in the corpus to be checked. Store the positions of those segmentations found in the corpus to be checked;
3. Output a list of variation instances with their contexts between two corpora.

We use "AutoCheck" to stand for the processing using the algorithm above. In order to find the segmentation variations within one corpus, we can also make the reference corpus and the corpus to be checked be the same corpus. Data in Table 1 are obtained through "AutoCheck + manual

[2] These two corpora could be also regarded as one unique corpus: the corpus to be checked. A large scale reference corpus is always helpful in spotting more variations in the corpus to be checked.

checking". That is firstly running "AutoCheck" 3 times as shown in Table 2 to get the list of variation types and instances in each situation respectively, and then EIs are found through manual checking.

In Table 1, situations "within test data", "Between: One-to-Mult" and "Between: Mult-to-One" correspond to the Situations S2, S3.1 and S3.2 described in Section 2. Here we still include CAS segmentations in order to take a close look at the distribution of EIs in each kind of segmentation variation. We can see that in situation "Between: One-to-Mult", there are only 4 EIs caused by CAS among 68 EIs. It is a very small fraction, so most of CAS variation instances are correct segmentations in a manually checked corpus.

Situation	Reference corpus	Corpus to be checked
Within test data	PK test data	PK test data
Between: One-to-Mult	PK training data	PK test data
Between: Mult-to-One	PK test data	PK training data

Table 2 Inputs of different AutoCheck runs

Except "黄金　周" (gold week) most of the EIs in S2: "within test data" are also found in S3.1: "Between one-to-mult"[3]. This is because in S3.1 the size of the reference corpus (training set) is much greater than the corpus to be checked (test set) so variations found in this case almost cover all of those found in S2 (test set only). EIs in S3.2: "between: mult-to-one" are such strings that they are never considered as one word in PK training data while always identified as one word in PK test data. For example, the segmentation variation (type) "上图 [shang4-tu2]" occurs four times as one word "上图" (above picture) in test data, but three of its variation instances "上　图" (upper picture) have been found in the training set. Thus, variation type "上图" should be identified as a segmentation error rather than an OOV word as in Bakeoff1. From Table 1, we can find 221 error tokens in all error instances (EIs) after removing the 26 redundant ones in PK test data (17194 tokens). So, the error rate of PK test data is 1.29%.

Using the same method, we also find out the 139 error instances (271 error tokens) in AS test data. The error rate of AS test data is 2.26% as shown in table 3.

Table 3 shows the error rate of AS test set is 2.26% and it is higher than PK test data which is 1.29%. So we believe that the reason why the evaluation result on AS corpus are higher than those on PK corpus of Bakeoff1 is not due to the segmentation quality of AS test data but because of the OOV rate (0.022) in AS test data which is much lower than PK test data (0.069).

data	PK test data	AS test data
Total tokens	17194	11985
Error tokens	221	271
Error rate	1.29%	2.26%

Table 3 Segmentation errors in PK and AS test data

"AutoCheck" outputs a list of all variation instances found in the corpus but it can not judge whether a variation instance is EI or not. Besides, the output of "AutoCheck" doesn't include those segmentation errors which are not instances of any segmentation variation in a corpus. Two examples are given in Example 4. It

[3] "黄金　周" is considered as a segmentation error according to its variation instance "黄金周" (golden week).

means that "AutoCheck+manual checking"[4] can not spot all segmentation errors in a corpus. Despite of these disadvantages of "AutoCheck", it is still a necessary assistant to find out almost all of the segmentation errors in an annotated corpus for its effective in finding segmentation error candidates.

Example 4: Segmentation errors which are not instances of any segmentation variation (Bakeoff1 PK corpus):

1）执政官 路易吉・马扎 和 马里诺・扎诺蒂 １６日 上午 举行 仪式

(Archon Marino Zanotti held a ceremony on the morning of 16th)

2）已 发展 成为 世界 上规模 最 大 的 代理 系统

(…has become the largest scale agency system in the world)

AutoCheck has been applied in preparing the MSRA (Microsoft Research Asia) annotated corpora of Chinese word segmentation (MS corpora, hereafter) that were submitted to SIGHAN Bakeoff2 as one of the data sets. "AutoCheck+manual checking" is applied as the principal way of quality control on MS corpora. Even only taking a manual check on those variations output by the AutoCheck could provide an approximate assessment about the quality of the annotated corpus. The lower the number of error instances (EIs) found in the output list the lower the segmentation error rate the annotated corpus reaches. For example, there are 37 variation instances output by AutoCheck in an annotated document #25 with 26K tokens in MS Corpora, in which no EIs has been found manually. Then the whole document was reviewed thoroughly by a person in which only two segmentation errors (shown in Example 5) have been found. Our practice shows that with the quality control method above the segmentation error rate of MS corpora reaches 0.1% in average at the worst cases.

Example 5: Segmentation errors in #25

Error 1: 已 有 三百六十多名 军师 职领导干部 深入 部队 或 院校 。

(There are more than 360 leaders of corps and division working in grass roots of army and college.)

The string "军师[jun1-shi1]" (military counselor) should be corrected as "军 师" (corps and division).

Error 2: 它 似 一面 六 棱镜 ，折射 出 时代 的 风貌 ，

(It is like a prism reflecting the style and features of the age)

The string "一面[yi1-mian4] (at the same time) should be corrected as "一 面" (a).

4 The impact to the evaluation caused by segmentation errors in corpora of Bakeoff1

In order to show the impact to the evaluation result caused by EIs existing in test data of Bakeoff1, we conduct the baseline close test with PK and AS corpora, i.e. we compile lexicons only containing words in their training data and then use the lexicons with a forward maximum matching algorithm to segment their test data respectively (Sproat and Emerson, 2003). Original and modified test data are used as gold standard in our baseline test.

In table 4, reference data PK1 and AS1 are the original PK test data and AS test data. Reference data PK2 and AS2 are obtained after correcting all segmentation errors found in their original data (Table 3).

Results in Table 4 are the output of Bakeoff1 evaluation program. Word count is the number of tokens in reference data and the change in word count is caused by our modification. Table 4 shows the impact of EIs in test data to the evaluation results. We

[4] "manual checking" is restricted on the output list only. Therefore it is a very effective way to assess approximately the quality of an annotated corpus.

can see the F measure increase to 0.879 (0.933) from 0.867 (0.915) and the OOV ratio is decrease to 0.065 (0.020) from 0.069 (0.022) when all EIs are corrected in PK (AS) test data.

Reference data	Word count	R	P	F	OOV	R_{OOV}	R_{IV}
PK1	17,194	0.909	0.829	0.867	0.069	0.050	0.972
PK2	17,200	0.920	0.841	0.879	0.065	0.053	0.980
AS1	11,985	0.917	0.912	0.915	0.022	0.000	0.938
AS2	11.886	0.939	0.926	0.933	0.020	0.000	0.958

Table 4 Baseline test results with original and revised PK and AS test data

5 Conclusion

A semi-automatic method to detect segmentation errors in a manually annotated Chinese corpus is presented in this paper. The main contributions of this research are:

- Offer an effective way to spot the segmentation errors in a manually annotated corpus and give the segmentation error rate of the corpus.
- Point out that segmentation inconsistency is not an appropriate technique term to assess the segmentation quality of an annotated corpus and define the concept of segmentation variation instead to get the segmentation error rate of a gold standard corpus.
- Show the influence to the evaluation result caused by the segmentation errors in a gold standard corpus. 1.29% error rate of PK test data and 2.26% error rate of AS test data decrease the F-measure of the SIGHAN Bakeoff1 baseline test by 1.36% and 1.93% respectively.

Acknowledgements

We would like to thank the members of the Natural Language Computing Group at Microsoft Research Asia, especially to acknowledge Jianfeng Gao, John Chen, and the two anonymous reviewers for their insightful comments and suggestions.

References

Aitao Chen. 2003. Chinese word segmentation using minimal linguistic knowledge. In Proceedings of the Second SIGHAN Workshop on Chinese Language Processing, July 11-12, 2003, Sapporo, Japan.

Andi Wu. 2003. Chinese word segmentation in MSR-NLP. In Proceedings of the Second SIGHAN Workshop on Chinese Language Processing, July 11-12, 2003, Sapporo, Japan.

Jianfeng Gao, Mu Li and Chang-Ning Huang. 2003. Improved source-channel models for Chinese word segmentation. In Proceedings of ACL-2003. July 7-12, 2003. Sapporo, Japan.

Markus Dickinson, W. Detmar Meurers. 2003. Detecting errors in Part-of-Speech annotation. In Proceedings of the 11th Conference of the European Chapter of the Association for

Computational Linguistics (EACL-03), 2003, Budapest, Hungary

Richard Sproat, Thomas Emerson. 2003. The first international Chinese word Segmentation Bakeoff. In Proceedings of the Second SIGHAN Workshop on Chinese Language Processing, July 11-12, 2003, Sapporo, Japan.

Sun Maosong. 1999. On the consistency of word-segmented Chinese corpus. (In Chinese) Applied Linguistics, (2):88-91, 1999.

Appendix: Modified EIs in PK test data

1) EI found in CAS variations:
Original: 李 长春 、 罗 干 等同 首都 各界 人士
Modified: 李 长春 、 罗 干 等 同 首 都 各界 人士

2) Some EIs in S3.2 which are considered as new words in Bakeoff1:
如果说 交通部门 问明 大世界 看着 全城 区内 换上 庆春节 没想到 踏上 文化村 老同志 迎春花市 守岛 喜迁 全过程 全天 双眼 双腿 族人 上图 共商 走入 领到 代为 一方 年味 岁岁 率兵 送往 前南 节节高 设在 驶过 工商部门 跳进 较大 翻看 惊呆 院团 外资金 下图 冰上 回老家 见到 县市区 极端分子 带回 这栋 办厂 小包 留在

3) Some EIs in S3.1 in which their variation types should be lexicon words

Original	Modified
科教 兴 国	科教兴国
火树银花 不 夜 天	火树银花不夜天
大 酒店	大酒店
集团 公司	集团公司
留学 人员	留学人员
尽管 如此	尽管如此
冰 清 玉 洁	冰清玉洁
羽毛 球队	羽毛球队
高等 学校	高等学校
直 指	直指
吐 翠	吐翠
报 春	报春
贺 岁	贺岁

Using Word-Pair Identifier to Improve Chinese Input System

Jia-Lin Tsai
Tung Nan Institute of Technology, Department of Information Management
Taipei 222, Taiwan, R.O.C.
tsaijl@mail.tnit.edu.tw

Abstract

This paper presents a word-pair (WP) identifier that can be used to resolve homonym/segmentation ambiguities and perform syllable-to-word (STW) conversion effectively for improving Chinese input systems. The experiment results show the following: (1) the WP identifier is able to achieve tonal (syllables with four tones) and toneless (syllables without four tones) STW accuracies of 98.5% and 90.7%, respectively, among the identified word-pairs; (2) while applying the WP identifier, together with the Microsoft input method editor 2003 and an optimized bigram model, the tonal and toneless STW improvements of the two input systems are 27.5%/18.9% and 22.1%/18.8%, respectively.

1 Introduction

More than 100 Chinese input methods have been developed in the past (Becker 1985, Huang 1985, Gu *et al.* 1991, Chung 1993, Kuo 1995, Fu *et al.* 1996, Lee *et al.* 1997, Hsu *et al.* 1999, Chen *et al.* 2000, Tsai and Hsu 2002, Gao *et al.* 2002, Lee 2003). Their underlying approaches can be classified into four types: (1) Optical character recognition (OCR) based (Chung 1993), (2) Online handwriting based (Lee *et al.* 1997), (3) Speech based (Fu *et al.* 1996, Chen *et al.* 2000), and (4) Keyboard based consists of phonetic and pinyin based (Chang *et al.* 1991, Hsu *et al.* 1993, Hsu 1994, Hsu *et al.* 1999, Kuo 1995, Lua and Gan 1992); arbitrary codes based [Fan *et al.* 1988]; and structure scheme based (Huang 1985).

Currently, the most popular method for Chinese input is phonetic and pinyin based, because Chinese people are taught to write the corresponding phonetic and pinyin syllables of each Chinese character and word in primary school. In Chinese, each Chinese character corresponds to at least one syllable; and each Chinese word can be a mono-syllabic word, such as "鼠(mouse)", a bi-syllabic word, such as "袋鼠(kangaroo)", or a multi-syllabic word, such as "米老鼠(Mickey mouse)." Although there are more than 13,000 distinct Chinese characters (of which 5,400 are commonly used), there are only about 1,300 distinct syllables. As per (Qiao *et al.* 1984), each Chinese syllable can be mapped from 3 to over 100 Chinese characters, with the average number of characters per syllable being 17. According to our computation, the minimum, maximum and average numbers f Chinese words per syllable-word in MOE-MANDARIN dictionary "教育部國語辭典" (one of most commonly-used Chinese dictionaries published by the Ministry of Education in Taiwan, its online dictionary is at (MOE)) are 1, 22 and 1.5, respectively. Since the size of problem space for syllable-to-word conversion is much less than that of syllable-to-character conversion, the most existing Chinese input systems (Hsu 1994, Hsu *et al.* 1999, Tsai and Hsu 2002, Gao *et al.* 2002, MSIME) are addressed on syllable-to-word conversion, not syllable-to-character conversion. To the research field of Chinese speech recognition, the STW conversion is the main task of Chinese language processing in typical Chinese speech recognition systems (Fu *et al.* 1996, Lee *et al.* 1993, Chien *et al.* 1993, Su *et al.* 1992).

Conventionally, there are two approaches for syllable-to-word (STW) conversion: (1) the **linguistic approach** based on syntax parsing, semantic template matching and contextual information (Hsu 1994, Fu *et al.* 1996, Hsu *et al.* 1999, Kuo 1995, Tsai and Hsu 2002); and (2) the **statistical approach** based on the n-gram models where n is usually 2 or 3 (Lin and Tsai 1987, Gu *et al.* 1991, Fu *et al.* 1996, Ho *et al.* 1997, Sproat 1990, Gao *et al.* 2002, Lee 2003). Although the linguistic approach requires considerable effort in designing effective syntax rules, semantic templates or contextual information, it is more user-friendly than the statistical approach on understanding why such a system makes a mistake (Hsu 1994, Tsai and Hsu 2002). On the other hand, the statistical language model (SLM) used in the statistical approach requires less effort and has been widely adopted in commercial Chinese input systems.

According to previous studies (Chung 1993, Fong and Chung 1994, Tsai and Hsu 2002, Gao *et al.* 2002, Lee 2003), *homophone selection* and *syllable-word segmentation* are two critical problems to the STW conversion in Chinese. Incorrect homophone selection and failed syllable-word segmentation will directly influence the STW conversion rate. For example, consider the syllable sequence "yi1 du4 ji4 yu2 zhong1 guo2 de5 niang4 jiu3 ji4 shu4" of the sentence "一度(once)覬覦(covet)中國(China)的(of)釀酒(making-wine)技術(technique)." As per the MOE-MANDARIN dictionary, the two possible syllable-word segmentations (in pinyin) are:

(F)"yi1/du4ji4/yu2/zhong1guo2/de5/niang4jiu3/ji4shu4"; and

(B)"yi1/du4/ji4yu2/zhong1guo2/de5/niang4jiu3/ji4shu4."

(We use the forward (F) and the backward (B) longest syllable-word first strategies (Chen *et al.* 1986, Tsai and Hsu 2002), and "/" to indicate a syllable-word boundary).

Among the above syllable-word segmentations, there is an ambiguous syllable-word section: /du4ji4/yu2/ (/{妒忌}/{于,圩,余,於,盂,俞,娛,魚,愉,渝,腴,萸,隅,畲,愚,榆,瑜,虞,逾,漁,諛,餘,輿}/); and /du4/ji4yu2/ (/{妒,杜,肚,度,渡,鍍,蠹}/{覬覦,鯽魚}/), respectively. For the ambiguous syllable-word section, the set of word-pairs comprised of two multi-syllabic Chinese words (including bi-syllabic words in the following) and their corresponding word-pair frequencies found in the UDN2001 corpus are: {一度-覬覦(1), 一度-中國(1), 一度-技術(4), 覬覦-中國(1), 覬覦-技術(1), 中國-技術(26), 釀酒-技術(19)}. The UDN2001 corpus (Tsai and Hsu 2002) is a collection of 4,539,624 Chinese sentences extracted from whole 2001 articles on the United Daily News Website (UDN) in Taiwan. For this case, if the word-pair "中國(China)-技術(technique)" with the maximum frequency 26 is used to be the key word-pair, the set of co-occurrence word-pairs with the key word-pair found in the UDN2001 will be {一度-覬覦, 一度-中國, 一度-技術, 覬覦-中國, 覬覦-技術}. Then, by the key word-pair "中國-技術" and its co-occurrence word-pair set {一度-覬覦, 一度-中國, 一度-技術, 覬覦-中國, 覬覦-技術}, the mentioned ambiguous syllable-word section (/du4ji4/yu2/ and /du4/ji4yu2/) and the homophone selection of syllable-word /ji4 shu4/ (/{技術(technique),計數(count)}/) of this case can be resolved, simultaneously. Thus, the Chinese words "一度(once)", "覬覦(covet)", "中國(China)" and "技術(technique)" in the syllable sequence "yi1 du4 ji4 yu2 zhong1 guo2 de5 niang4 jiu3 ji4 shu4" can then be correctly identified. If we use the Microsoft Input Method Editor 2003 for Traditional Chinese (MSIME) to translate the syllables, it will be converted into "一度(once)繼(continue)於(to)中國(China)的(of)釀酒(making-wine)技術(technique)." As per (Gao *et al.* 2002), MSIME is a trigam-like Chinese input system. The two error converted words "繼(continue)" and "於(to)" are widely recognized that unseen event (覬覦-中國) and over-weighting (於-中國) the two major problems of SLM systems (Fu *et al.* 1996, Gao *et al.* 2002).

The objective of this study is to illustrate the effectiveness of word-pairs for resolving the STW conversion for improving the Chinese input systems. We also conduct STW experiments to show the tonal and toneless STW accuracies of a commercial input product and a bigram model can be improved by our word-pair identifier without a tuning process. Here, the "tonal" is to indicate the syllables input with four tones, such as "niang4(釀) jiu3(酒) ji4(技) shu4(術)" and the "toneless" is to indicate the syllables input without four tones, such as "niang(釀) jiu(酒) ji(技) shu(術)."

The remainder of this paper is arranged as follows. In Section 2, we present a method for auto-generating word-pair (AUTO-WP) database from Chinese sentences. Then, we develop a word-pair identifier with the WP database to effectively resolve homonym and segmentation ambiguities of STW conversion on the WP-related portion in Chinese syllables. In Section 3, we present our STW experiment results. Finally, in Section 4, we give our conclusions and suggest some future research directions.

2 Development of Word-Pair Identifier

The system dictionary of our word-pair identifier is comprised of 155,746 Chinese words taken from the MOE-MANDARIN dictionary (MOE) and 29,408 unknown words auto-found in UDN2001 corpus by a Chinese word auto-confirmation (CWAC) system (Tsai *et al.* 2003). The system dictionary provides the knowledge of words and their corresponding pinyin syllable-words. The pinyin syllable-words were translated by phoneme-to-pinyin mappings, such as "ㄐㄧˋ"-to-"ji4."

2.1 Generating the Word-Pair Database

The steps of our AUTO-WP to auto-discovery word-pairs from a given Chinese sentence are as below:

Step 1. **Segmentation**: Generate the word segmentation for a given Chinese sentence by backward maximum matching (BMM) techniques (Chen *et al.* 1986) with the system dictionary. Take the Chinese sentence "將軍用零件帶來(bring the military component parts here)" as an example. Its BMM word-segmentation is "將(get)/軍用(military)/零件(component parts)/ 帶來(bring)" and its forward maximum matching (FMM) word-segmentation is "將軍(a general)/用(use)/ 零件(component parts)/ 帶來(bring)." According to our previous work (Tsai *et al.* 2004), the word segmentation precision of BMM is about 1% greater than that of FMM.

Step 2. **Initial WP set**: Extract all the combinations of word-pairs from the word segmentations of Step 1 to be the initial WP set. For the above case, there are six combinations of word-pairs extracted: {"將/軍用", "將/零件", "將/帶來", "軍用/零件", "軍用/帶來", "零件/帶來"}.

Step 3. **Final WP set**: Select out the word-pairs comprised of two multi-syllabic Chinese words to be the finial WP set. For the final WP set, if the word-pair is not found in the WP database, insert it into the WP database and set its frequency to 1; otherwise, increase its frequency by 1. In the above case, the final WP set includes three word-pairs: {"軍用/零件", "軍用/帶來", "零件/帶來"}.

By applying our AUTO-WP to the UDN2001 corpus (the training corpus), totally 25,439,679 word-pairs were generated. From the generated WP database, the frequencies of word-pairs "軍用/零件", "軍用/帶來" and "零件/帶來" are 1, 1 and 2, respectively. The frequency of a word-pair is the number of sentences that contain the word-pair with the same word-pair order in the training corpus.

2.2 Word-Pair Identifier

The algorithm of our WP identifier for a given Chinese syllables is as follows:

Step 1. Input tonal or toneless syllables.

Step 2. Generate all possible word-pairs comprised of two multi-syllabic Chinese words for the input syllables to be the input of Step 3.

Step 3. Select out the word-pairs that match a word-pair in the WP database to be the initial WP set, firstly. Then, from the initial WP set, select the word-pair with maximum frequency as the key word-pair. Finally, find the co-occurrence word-pairs with the key word-pair in the training corpus to be the final WP set. If there are two or more word-pairs with the same maximum frequency, one of them is randomly selected as the key word-pair.

Step 4. Arrange all word-pairs of the final WP set into a WP-sentence. If no word-pairs can be identified in the input syllables, a NULL WP-sentence is produced.

Table 1 is a step by step example to show the details of applying our WP identifier on the Chinese syllables "yi1 ge5 wen2 ming2 de5 shuai1 wei2 guo4 cheng2(一 個 [a] 文 明 [civilization]的[of]衰微[decay]過程[process])." For this case, we have a WP-sentence "一個文明 de5shuai1wei2 過程." As we have mentioned in Section 1, we found this WP-sentence can also be used to correct the MSIME converted errors in its output "一個[a]聞名[famous]的[of]衰微[decay]過程[process]."

Table 1. An illustration of a WP-sentence generation for the Chinese syllables "yi1 ge5 wen2 ming2 de5 shuai1 wei2 guo4 cheng2(一個[a]文明[civilization]的[of]衰微[decay]過程[process])"

Step #	Results
Step.1	yi1 ge5 wen2 ming2 de5 shuai1 wei2 guo4 cheng2 (一 個 文 明 的 衰 微 過 程)
Step.2	The found word-pair / word-pair frequency: 一個(yi1 ge5)-文明(wen2 ming2) / 9 一個(yi1 ge5)-聞名(wen2 ming2) / 1 一個(yi1 ge5)-衰微(shuai1 wei2) / 0 **一個(yi1 ge5)-過程(guo4 cheng2) / 65** 文明(wen2 ming2)- 衰微(shuai1 wei2) / 0 文明(wen2 ming2)-過程(guo4 cheng2) / 3 衰微(shuai1 wei2) -過程(guo4 cheng2) / 0
Step.3	The key word-pair: **一個(yi1 ge5)-過程(wen2 ming2)** The co-occurrence word-pairs: 一個(yi1 ge5)-文明(wen2 ming2) 文明(wen2 ming2)-過程(guo4 cheng2)
Step.4	WP-sentence: 一 個 文 明 de5 shuai1 wei2 過 程

3 The STW Experiments

To evaluate the STW performance of our WP identifier, we define the STW accuracy, identified character ratio (ICR) and STW improvement, by the following equations:

STW accuracy = # of correct characters / # of total characters. (1)

Identified character ratio (ICR) = # of characters of identified WP / # of total characters in testing sentences. (2)

STW improvement (i.e. STW error reduction rate) = (accuracy of STW system with WP – accuracy of STW system)) / (1 – accuracy of STW system). (3)

3.1 Generation of the Word-Pair Database

To conduct the STW experiments, firstly, use the inverse translator of phoneme-to-character (PTC) provided in GOING system to convert testing sentences into their corresponding syllables. Then, all the error PTC translations of GOING were corrected by post human-editing. Then, apply our WP identifier to convert these testing syllables back to their WP-sentences. Finally, calculate its STW accuracy and identified character ratio by Equations (1) and (2). Note that all test sentences are composed of a string of Chinese characters in this study.

The training/testing corpus, closed/open test sets and the testing WP database used in the STW experiments are described as below:

(1) Training corpus: We used the UDN2001 corpus mentioned in Section 1 as our training corpus. All knowledge of word frequencies, word-pairs, word-pair frequencies was auto-generated and computed by this corpus.

(2) Testing corpus: The UDN2002 corpus was selected as our testing corpus. It is a collection of 3,321,504 Chinese sentences that were extracted from whole 2002 articles on the United Daily News Website (UDN).

(3) Closed test set: 10,000 sentences were randomly selected from the UDN2001 corpus as the closed test set. The {minimum, maximum, and mean} of characters per sentence for the closed test set were {4, 37, and 12}.

(4) Open test set: 10,000 sentences were randomly selected from the UDN2002 corpus as the open test set. At this point, we checked that the selected open test sentences were not in the closed test set as well. The {minimum, maximum, and mean} of characters per sentence for the open test set were {4, 43, and 13.7}.

(5) Testing WP database: By applying our AUTO-WP on the UDN2001 corpus, we created 25,439,679 word-pairs as the testing WP database.

We conducted the STW experiment in a progressive manner. The results and analysis of the experiment are described in Sub-sections 3.2 and 3.3.

3.2 STW Experiment of the WP Identifier

The purpose of this experiment is to demonstrate the tonal and toneless STW accuracies among the identified word-pairs by using the WP identifier with the testing WP database.

From Table 2, the average tonal and toneless STW accuracies of the WP identifier for the closed and open test sets are 98.5% and 90.7%, respectively. Between the closed and the open test sets, the differences of the tonal and toneless STW accuracies of the WP identifier are 0.5% and 1.4%, respectively. These results strongly support that the WP identifier can be used to effectively perform Chinese STW conversion on the WP-related portion.

Table 2. The results of the tonal and toneless STW experiment for the WP identifier on the identified word-pairs

	Closed	Open	Average (ICR)
Tonal	98.7%	98.2%	98.5% (47%)
Toneless	91.4%	90.0%	90.7% (39%)

3.3 A Commercial IME System and A Bigram Model with WP Identifier

We selected Microsoft Input Method Editor 2003 for Traditional Chinese (MSIME) as our experimental commercial Chinese input system. In addition, an optimized bigram model called BiGram was developed. The BiGram STW system is a bigram-based model developing by SRILM (Stolcke 2002) with Good-Turing backoff smoothing (Manning and Schuetze, 1999), as well as forward and backward longest syllable-word first strategies (Chen *et al.* 1986, Tsai *et al.* 2004). The training corpus and system dictionary of the BiGram system are same with that of the WP identifier. All the bigram probabilities were calculated by the UDN2001 corpus.

Table 3a compares the results of MSIME and MSIME with the WP identifier on the closed and open test sentences. Table 3b compares the results of BiGram and BiGram with the WP identifier on the closed and open test sentences. In this experiment, the STW output of the MSIME with the WP identifier, or the BiGram with the WP identifier, was collected by directly replacing the identified word-pairs (WP-sentences) from the corresponding STW output of MSIME or BiGram.

Table 3a. The results of the tonal and toneless STW experiment for the MSIME and the MSIME with the WP identifier

	MSIME	MSIME+WP [a]	Improvement
Tonal	94.9%	96.3%	27.5%
Toneless	86.9%	89.8%	22.1%

[a] STW accuracies of the words identified by the MSIME with the WP identifier

Table 3b. The results of the tonal and toneless STW experiment for the BiGram and the BiGram with the WP identifier

	BiGram	BiGram+WP [a]	Improvement
Tonal	96.3%	97.0%	18.9%
Toneless	86.2%	88.8%	18.8%

[a] STW accuracies of the words identified by the BiGram with the WP identifier

From Table 3a, the tonal and toneless STW improvements of MSIME by using the WP identifier are 27.5% and 22.1%, respectively. Meanwhile, from Table 3b, the tonal and toneless STW improvements of BiGram by using the WP identifier are 18.9% and 18.8%, respectively. (Note that we also developed a TriGram STW system with the same source and techniques of BiGram. However, the differences between the tonal and toneless STW accuracies of BiGram and TriGram are only about 0.2%)

To sum up the results of this experiment, we conclude that the WP identifier can achieve a better STW accuracy than that of the MSIME and BiGram systems on the WP-related portion. The results of Tables 3a and 3b indicate that the WP identifier can effectively improve the tonal and toneless STW accuracies of MSIME and BiGram without tuning processing. Appendix A presents two cases of STW results that were obtained from the experiment.

3.4 Error Analysis of the STW Conversion

We examine the Top 300 cases in the *tonal* and *toneless* STW conversion errors, respectively, from the open testing results of BiGram with the WP identifier. As per our analysis, the problems of STW conversion errors can be classified into three major types:

(1) ***Unknown word problem***: For any Chinese NLP system, unknown word extraction is one of the most difficult problems and a critical issue (Tsai *et al.* 2003). When an error is caused only by the lack of words in the system dictionary, we call it *unknown*

word problem.

(2) ***Inadequate syllable segmentation problem***: When an error is caused by syllable-word overlapping (or say ambiguous syllable-word segmentation), instead of an unknown word problem, we call it *inadequate syllable segmentation.*

(3) ***Homophones problem***: These are the remaining STW conversion errors.

Table 4. The coverage of three problems caused the tonal and toneless STW conversion errors

Problems	Coverage (%)	
	Tonal	Toneless
Unknown Word	12%	11%
Inadequate Syllable Segmentation	36%	51%
Homophone	53%	39%

[a] STW accuracies of the words identified by the BiGram with the WP identifier

Table 4 is the coverage of the three problems. From Table 4, we have two observations:

(1) **The *coverage* of unknown word problem for tonal and toneless STW systems is similar**. Since the unknown word problem is not specifically a STW problem, it can be easily taken care of through manual editing or semi-automatic learning during input. In practice, therefore, the tonal and toneless STW accuracies could be raised to 98% and 91%, respectively. Although some of unknown words have been incorporated in the system dictionary by a CWCA system (Tsai *et al.* 2004), they could still face the problems: *inadequate syllable segmentation* and *failed homophone disambiguation*.

(2) **The major problem caused error conversions in tonal and toneless STW systems is different**. To improve tonal STW systems, the major targets should be the cases of failed homophone selection (53% coverage). For toneless STW systems, on the other hand, the cases of inadequate syllable segmentation (51% coverage) should be the focus for improvement.

To sum up the above two observations, the bottlenecks of the STW conversion lie in the second and third problems. To resolve these issues, we believe one simple and effective approach is to extend the size of WP database, because our experiment results show that the WP identifier can achieve better tonal and toneless STW accuracies than those of MSIME and BiGram on the WP-related portion.

4 Conclusion and Future Directions

In this paper, we have applied a WP identifier to support the Chinese language processing on the STW conversion and obtained a high STW accuracy on the identified word-pairs. All of the WP data can be generated fully automatically by applying the AUTO-WP on the system and user corpus. We are encouraged by the fact that WP knowledge can achieve tonal and toneless STW accuracies of 98.5% and 90.7%, respectively, for the WP-related portion on the testing syllables. The WP identifier can be easily integrated into existing Chinese input systems by identifying word-pairs in a post-processing step. Our experimental results show that, by applying the WP identifier together with MSIME (a trigram-like model) and BiGram (an optimized bigram model), the tonal and toneless STW improvements of the two Chinese input systems are 27.5%/22.1% and 18.9%/18.8%, respectively. For adaptation STW approach, we have tried to apply the AUTO-WP to extract the word-pairs from the 10,000 open testing sentences into the testing WP database, the tonal and toneless STW accuracies of the MSIME with the adaptation WP identifier and the BiGram with the adaptation WP identifier will become 97.0%/97.2% and 91.1%/90.0%, respectively.

Currently, our approach is quite basic when more than one WP occurs in the same sentence. Although there is room for improvement, we believe it would not produce a noticeable effect as far as the STW accuracy is concerned. However, this issue will become important as we want to apply the WP knowledge to speech recognition. According to our computations, the collection of testing WP knowledge can cover approximately 50% and 40% of the characters in the UDN2001 and UDN2002 corpus, respectively.

We will continue to expand our collection of WP knowledge to cover more characters in the UDN2001 and UDN2002 corpus with Web corpus (search engine results) for improving our STW system. In other directions, we will try to improve our WP-based STW conversion with other statistical language models, such as HMM, and extend it to other areas of NLP, especially word segmentation and speech recognition.

Acknowledgement

We thank the Mandarin Promotion Council of the Ministry of Education in Taiwan for providing us the MOE-MANDARIN dictionary.

References

Becker, J.D. 1985. Typing Chinese, Japanese, and Korean, *IEEE Computer* 18(1):27-34.

Chang, J.S., S.D. Chern and C.D. Chen. 1991. Conversion of Phonemic-Input to Chinese Text Through Constraint Satisfaction, *Proceedings of ICCPOL'91*, 30-36.

Chen, B., H.M. Wang and L.S. Lee. 2000. Retrieval of broadcast news speech in Mandarin Chinese collected in Taiwan using syllable-level statistical characteristics, *Proceedings of the 2000 International Conference on Acoustics Speech and Signal Processing*.

Chen, C.G., Chen, K.J. and Lee, L.S. 1986. A model for Lexical Analysis and Parsing of Chinese Sentences, *Proceedings of 1986 International Conference on Chinese Computing*, 33-40.

Chien, L.F., Chen, K.J. and Lee, L.S. 1993. A Best-First Language Processing Model Integrating the Unification Grammar and Markov Language Model for Speech Recognition Applications, *IEEE Transactions on Speech and Audio Processing*, 1(2):221-240.

Chung, K.H. 1993. *Conversion of Chinese Phonetic Symbols to Characters*, M. Phil. thesis, Department of Computer Science, Hong Kong University of Science and Technology.

Fong, L.A. and K.H. Chung. 1994. Word Segmentation for Chinese Phonetic Symbols, *Proceedings of International Computer Symposium*, 911-916.

Fu, S.W.K, C.H. Lee and Orville L.C. 1996. A Survey on Chinese Speech Recognition, *Communications of COLIPS*, 6(1):1-17.

Gao, J, Goodman, J., Li, M. and Lee K.F. 2002. Toward a Unified Approach to Statistical Language Modeling for Chinese, *ACM Transactions on Asian Language Information Processing*, 1(1):3-33.

Gu, H.Y., C.Y. Tseng and L.S. Lee. 1991. Markov modeling of mandarin Chinese for decoding the phonetic sequence into Chinese characters, *Computer Speech and Language* 5(4):363-377.

Ho, T.H., K.C. Yang, J.S. Lin and L.S. Lee. 1997. Integrating long-distance language modeling to phonetic-to-text conversion, *Proceedings of ROCLING X International Conference on Computational Linguistics*, 287-299.

Hsu, W.L. and K.J. Chen. 1993. The Semantic Analysis in GOING - An Intelligent Chinese Input System, *Proceedings of the Second Joint Conference of Computational Linguistics*, Shiamen, 1993, 338-343.

Hsu, W.L. 1994. Chinese parsing in a phoneme-to-character conversion system based on semantic pattern matching, *Computer Processing of Chinese and Oriental Languages* 8(2):227-236.

Hsu, W.L. and Chen, Y.S. 1999. On Phoneme-to-Character Conversion Systems in Chinese Processing, *Journal of Chinese Institute of Engineers*, 5:573-579.

Huang, J.K. 1985. The Input and Output of Chinese and Japanese Characters, *IEEE Computer* 18(1):18-24.

Kuo, J.J. 1995. Phonetic-input-to-character conversion system for Chinese using syntactic connection table and semantic distance, *Computer Processing and Oriental Languages*, 10(2):195-210.

Lee, L.S., Tseng, C.Y., Gu, H..Y., Liu F.H., Chang, C.H., Lin, Y.H., Lee, Y., Tu, S.L., Hsieh, S.H., and Chen C.H. 1993. Golden Mandarin (I) - A Real-Time Mandarin Speech Dictation Machine for Chinese Language with Very Large Vocabulary, *IEEE Transaction on Speech and Audio Processing*, 1(2).

Lee, C.W., Z. Chen and R.H. Cheng. 1997. A perturbation technique for handling handwriting variations faced in stroke-based Chinese character classification, *Computer Processing of Oriental Languages*, 10(3):259-280.

Lee, Y.S. 2003. Task adaptation in Stochastic Language Model for Chinese Homophone Disambiguation, *ACM Transactions on Asian Language Information Processing*, 2(1):49-62.

Lin, M.Y. and W.H. Tasi. 1987. Removing the ambiguity of phonetic Chinese input by the relaxation technique, *Computer Processing and Oriental Languages*, 3(1):1-24.

Lua, K.T. and K.W. Gan. 1992. A Touch-Typing Pinyin Input System, *Computer Processing of Chinese and Oriental Languages*, 6:85-94.

Manning, C. D. and Schuetze, H. 1999. *Fundations of Statistical Natural Language Processing*, MIT Press: 191-220.

Microsoft Research Center in Beijing, "http://research.microsoft.com/aboutmsr/labs/beijing/"

MOE, MOE-MANDARIN online dictionary,

"http://140.111.34.46/dict/?open"

UDN, On-Line United Daily News, "http://udnnews.com/NEWS/"

Qiao, J., Y. Qiao and S. Qiao. 1984. Six-Digit Coding Method, *Commun. ACM* 33(5):248-267.

Sproat, R. 1990. An Application of Statistical Optimization with Dynamic Programming to Phonemic-Input-to-Character Conversion for Chinese, *Proceedings of ROCLING III*, 379-390.

Stolcke A. 2002. SRILM - An Extensible Language Modeling Toolkit, *Proc. Intl. Conf. Spoken Language Processing, Denver*.

Su, K.Y., Chiang, T.H. and Lin, Y.C. 1992. A Unified Framework to Incorporate Speech and Language Information in Spoken Language Processing, *ICASSP-92*, 185-188.

Tsai, J.L. and W.L. Hsu. 2002. Applying an NVEF Word-Pair Identifier to the Chinese Syllable-to-Word Conversion Problem, *Proceedings of 19th COLING 2002*, 1016-1022.

Tsai, J,L, Sung, C.L. and Hsu, W.L. 2003. Chinese Word Auto-Confirmation Agent, *Proceedings of ROCLING XV*, 175-192.

Tsai, J.L, Hsieh, G. and Hsu, W.L. 2004. Auto-Generation of NVEF knowledge in Chinese, *Computational Linguistics and Chinese Language Processing*, 9(1):41-64.

Appendix A. Two STW results used in this study (The frequencies and English words in parentheses are included for explanatory purposes only)

Case I.

Tonal STW results for the Chinese tonal syllable input "ji2fu4qi2min2zu2te4se4" of the Chinese sentence "極富(abundance)其(it)民族(folk)特色(characteristic)"

Methods	STW results
	民族/特色(13) (Key WP)
	極富/特色(11) (Co-occurrence WP)
WP-sentence	極富 qi2 民族特色
MSIME	及復其民族特色
MSIME+WP	**極富**其**民族特色**
BiGram	極富期民族特色
BiGram+WP	**極富**期**民族特色**

Toneless STW results for the Chinese toneless syllable input "jifuqiminzutese" of the Chinese sentence "極富(abundance)其(it)民族(folk)特色(characteristic)"

Methods	STW results
	民族/特色(13) (Key WP)
	極富/特色(11) (Co-occurrence WP)
WP-sentence	極富 qi 民族特色
MSIME	及夫妻民族特色
MSIME+WP	**極富**妻**民族特色**
BiGram	及夫妻民族特色
BiGram+WP	**極富**妻**民族特色**

Case II.

Tonal STW results for the Chinese tonal syllable input "cong2qian2shui3diao4yu2chong1lang4yang2fan2chu1hai3you2yong3" of the Chinese sentence "從(from)潛水(dive)釣魚(fishing)衝浪(surfing)揚帆(driving sail)出海(outward bound)游泳(swim)"

Methods	STW results
	出海/游泳(2) (Key WP)
	潛水/釣魚(1) (Co-occurrence WP)
	潛水/游泳(1) (Co-occurrence WP)
	釣魚/游泳(1) (Co-occurrence WP)
	揚帆/出海(1) (Co-occurrence WP)
WP-sentence	cong2 潛水釣魚 chong1lang4 揚帆出海游泳
MSIME	從前水釣魚衝浪揚帆出海游泳
MSIME+WP	從**潛水釣魚**衝浪**揚帆出海游泳**
BiGram	從前水釣魚衝浪揚帆出海游泳
BiGram+WP	從**潛水釣魚**衝浪**揚帆出海游泳**

Tonal STW results for the Chinese tonal syllable input "congqianshuidiaoyuchonglangyangfanchuhaiyouyong" of the Chinese sentence "從(from)潛水(dive)釣魚(fishing)衝浪(surfing)揚帆(driving sail)出海(outward bound)游泳(swim)"

Methods	STW results
	出海/游泳(2) (Key WP)
	潛水/釣魚(1) (Co-occurrence WP)
	潛水/游泳(1) (Co-occurrence WP)
	釣魚/游泳(1) (Co-occurrence WP)
	揚帆/出海(1) (Co-occurrence WP)
WP-sentence	cong2 潛水釣魚 chong1lang4 揚帆出海游泳
MSIME	從前水釣魚衝浪揚帆出海游泳
MSIME+WP	從**潛水釣魚**衝浪**揚帆出海游泳**
BiGram	從前水釣魚衝浪揚帆出海游泳
BiGram+WP	從**潛水釣魚**衝浪**揚帆出海游泳**

Chinese Deterministic Dependency Analyzer: Examining Effects of Global Features and Root Node Finder

Yuchang CHENG, Masayuki ASAHARA and Yuji MATSUMOTO
Nara Institute of Science and Technology
8916-5 Takayama, Ikoma, Nara 630-0192, Japan
{yuchan-c, masayu-a, matsu}@is.naist.jp

Abstract

We present a method for improving dependency structure analysis of Chinese. Our bottom-up deterministic analyzer adopt Nivre's algorithm (Nivre and Scholz, 2004). Support Vector Machines (SVMs) are utilized to determine the word dependency relations. We find that there are two problems in our analyzer and propose two methods to solve them. One problem is that some operations cannot be solved only using local feature. We utilize the global features to solve this. The other problem is that this bottom-up analyzer doesn't use top-down information. We supply the top-down information by constructing SVMs based root node finder to solve this problem. Experimental evaluation on the Penn Chinese Treebank Corpus shows that the proposed extensions improve the parsing accuracy significantly.

1 Introduction

Many syntactic analyzers for English have been implemented and have demonstrated good performance (Charniak, 2000; Collins, 1997; Ratnaparkhi, 1999). However, implementation of Chinese syntactic structure analyzers is still limited, since the structure of the Chinese language is quite different from other languages. Therefore the experience in processing western languages cannot be guaranteed that it can apply to Chinese language directly (Lee, 1991). Chinese language has many special syntactic phenomena substantially different from western languages. Discussions about such characteristics of Chinese language can be found in the literature (Chao 1968; Li and Thompson 1981; Huang 1982).

About the previous work of Chinese dependency structure analysis, Zhou proposed a rule based approach (Zhou, 2000). Lai et al. proposed a span-based statistical probability approach (Lai, 2001). Ma et al. proposed a statistic dependency parser by using probabilistic model (Ma, 2004). Using machine learning-based approaches for dependency analysis of Chinese is still limited. In this paper, we propose a deterministic Chinese syntactic structure analyzer by using global features and a root node finder.

Our analyzer is a dependency structure analyzer. We utilize a deterministic method for dependency relation construction. First, a dependency relation matrix is constructed, in which each element corresponds to a pair of tokens. A likelihood value is assigned to the dependency relation of each pair of tokens. Second, the optimal dependency structure is estimated using the likelihood of the whole sentence, provided there is no crossing between dependencies. A bottom-up algorithm proposed by (Nivre and Scholz, 2004) is use for a deterministic dependency structure analysis. Our dependency relations are composed by machine learners. SVMs (Vapnik, 1998) deterministically estimate if there is a dependency relation between a pair of words in the methods.

However, this method has two problems. First, some operations in the algorithm needs long distance information. However, the long distance information cannot be available if we assume a context of a fixed size in all operations.

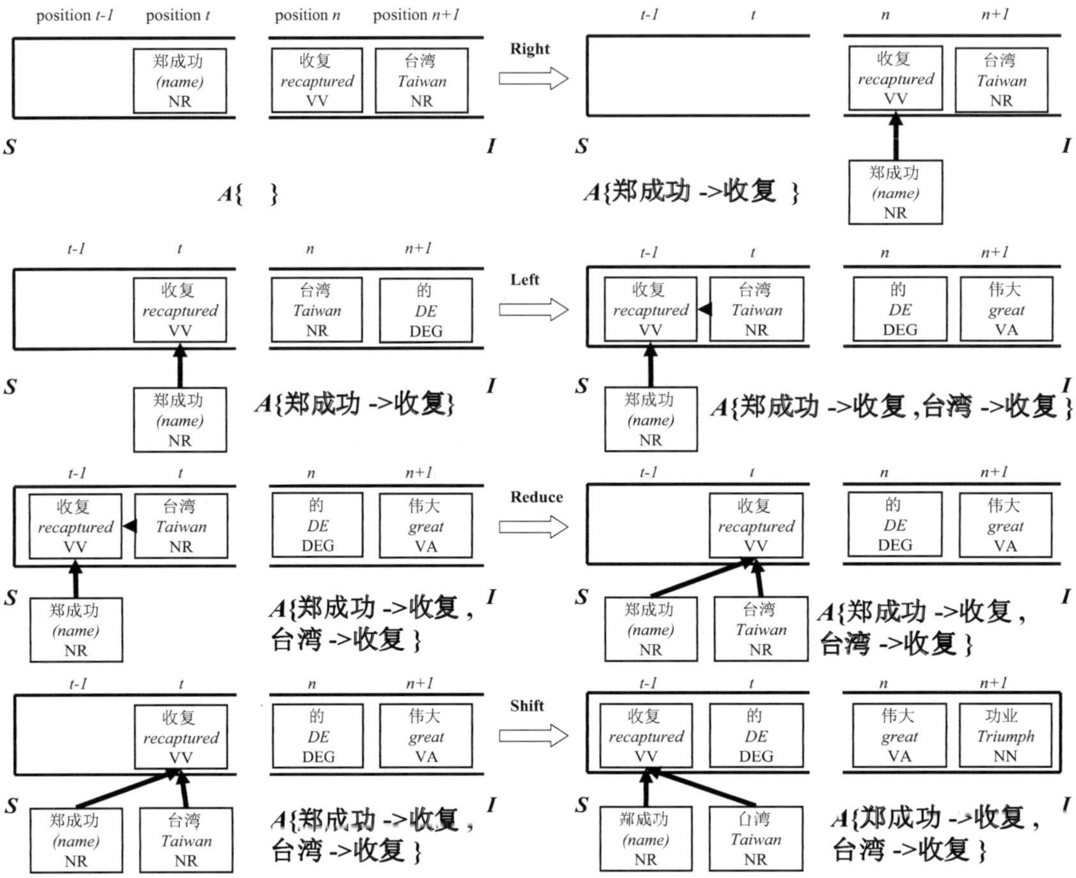

Example: 郑成功收复台湾的伟大功业 (*The great triumph that Cheng Cheng-Kung recaptured Taiwan.*)

Fig. 1. The operations of the Nivre algorithm

The second problem is that the top-down information isn't used in the bottom-up approach. We use the global features to solve the first problem and we construct a SVM-based root node finder in our system to supplement the top-down information.

Our analyzer is trained on the Penn Chinese Treebank 5.0 (Xue et al., 2002), which is a phrase structure annotated corpus. The phrase structure is converted into a dependency structure according to the head rules. We perform experimental evaluation in several settings on this corpus.

In the next section, we describe our deterministic dependency structure analysis algorithm. Section 3 shows the global features and the two-step process. Section 4 describes the use of the root node finder. Section 5 describes the experimental setting and the results. Finally, we summarize our findings in the conclusion.

2 Parsing method

This chapter presents a basic parsing algorithm proposed by (Nivre and Scholz, 2004). The algorithm is the base of our dependency analyzer. This algorithm is based on a deterministic approach, in which the dependency relations are constructed by a bottom-up deterministic schema. While Nivre's method uses memory-based learning, we use SVMs instead. The algorithm consists of two major procedures:

(i) Extract the surrounding features for the focused node (or node pair).

(ii) Estimate the dependency relation operation for the focused node by a machine learning method.

2.1 Algorithm

We utilize a bottom-up deterministic algorithm proposed by (Nivre and Scholz, 2004) in our analyzer. In the algorithm, the states of analyzer are represented by a triple $\langle S, I, A \rangle$. S and I are stacks, S keeps the words being in consideration, and I keeps the words to be processed. A is a list of dependency relations decide during the algorithm. Given an input word sequence W, the analyzer is initialized by the triple $\langle nil, W, \phi \rangle$. The analyzer estimates the dependency relation between two words (the top elements of stack S and stack I). The algorithm iterates until the list I becomes empty. Then, the analyzer outputs the word dependency relations A.

There are four possible operations for the configuration at hand:

Right: Suppose the current triple is $\langle t \mid S, n \mid I, A \rangle$ (t and n are the top elements, S and I are the remaining elements in the stacks), if there is a dependency relation that the word t depends on word n, add the new dependency relation $(t \rightarrow n)$ into A, remove t from S. The configuration now becomes $\langle S, n \mid I, A \cup \{(t \rightarrow n)\} \rangle$.

Left: In the current triple is $\langle t \mid S, n \mid I, A \rangle$, if there is a dependency relation that the word n depends on the word t, adds the new dependency relation $(n \rightarrow t)$ into A, push n onto the stack S. The configuration now becomes $\langle n \mid t \mid S, I, A \cup \{(n \rightarrow t)\} \rangle$.

Suppose the current triple is $\langle t \mid S, n \mid I, A \rangle$, if there is no dependency relation between n and t, check the following conditions.

Reduce: If there are no more words n' ($n' \in I$) which may depend on t, and t has a parent on its left side, the analyzer removes t from the stack S. The configuration now becomes $\langle S, n \mid I, A \rangle$.

Shift: If there is no dependency between n and t, and the triple doesn't satisfy the conditions for **Reduce**, then push n onto the stack S. The configuration now becomes $\langle n \mid t \mid S, I, A \rangle$.

These operations are depicted in **Fig. 1**. Given an input sentence of length N (words), the analyzer is guaranteed to terminate after at most $2N$ actions. The dependency structure given at the termination is well-formed if and only if the relations in A constitute a single connected tree. This means that the algorithm produces a well-formed dependency graph.

2.2 Machine learning method

A classification task usually involves with training and testing data which consist of annotated data instances. Each instance in the training set contains one "target value" (class label) and several "attributes" (features). The goal of a classifier is to produce a model which predicts target value of data instances in the testing set which only give the attributes.

SVMs are binary classifiers based on the maximal margin strategy. Suppose we have a set of training data for a binary classification problem: $(\boldsymbol{x}_1, y_1)...(\boldsymbol{x}_n, y_n)$, where $\boldsymbol{x}_i \in R^n$ is the feature vector of the i-th sample in the training data and $y_i \in \{+1, -1\}$ is the class label of the sample. The goal is to find a decision function $f(x) = sign(\sum_{\mathbf{z}_i \in SV} a_i y_i K(\boldsymbol{x}, \boldsymbol{z}_i) + b)$ for an input vector $\boldsymbol{x}$. The vectors $\boldsymbol{z}_i \in SV$ are called support vectors, which are representative examples. Support vectors and other constants are determined by solving a quadratic programming problem. $K(\mathbf{x}, \mathbf{z})$ is a kernel function which maps vectors into a higher dimensional space. We use the polynomial kernel: $K(\mathbf{x}, \mathbf{z}) = (1 + \mathbf{x} \cdot \mathbf{z})^d$. The performance of SVMs is better than using other machine learning methods, such as memory based learning or maximum entropy method, in our analyzer. This is because that SVMs can adopt combining features automatically (using the polynomial kernel), whereas other method cannot. To extend binary classifiers to multi-class classifiers, we use the pair-wise method, which utilizes ${}_nC_2$ binary classifiers between all pairs of the classes (Kreel, 1998). We use Libsvm (Lin et al., 2001) in our experiments.

2.3 Features (Local features)

It should be noted that we use a different machine learner from the original method (Nivre, 2004). Nivre's work used memory based learning in their analyzer, we utilize SVMs in our analyzer. Therefore, the features of our analyzer are different from the original Nivre's method.

In our method, the analyzer considers the dependency of two nodes (n,t) which are in current triple. The nodes include the word, the POS-tag and the information of its children. The context features we use are 2 preceding nodes of node *t* (and *t* itself), 2 succeeding nodes of node *n* (and *n* itself), and their child nodes. The distance between nodes *n* and *t* is also used as a feature. We call these features as local features.

3 Global features and two-step process

In the algorithm, the operation **Reduce** needs the condition that the node *n* should have no child in *I*. However, it is difficult to check this condition. In a long sentence, the modifier of the focused node *n* may be far away from *n*. Moreover, some non-local dependency may cause this kind of error. In this section, we will describe this problem and a solution to it.

3.1 Global features

The analyzer selects features for deciding the optimum operation, and then gives these features to machine learner. The machine learner uses the same information to decide the optimum operation even when these operations essentially disagree. However, the different operation consists of different condition. In the deterministic bottom-up dependency analysis, we can generally consider the process as two tasks:

Task 1: Does the focused word depend on a neighbor node?

Task 2: Does the focused word may have a child in the remaining token sequence?

In the Task 1, the problem can be resolved by using the information of the neighbor nodes. This information is possibly the same as the features that we described in section 2.3. However, these features may not be able to resolve the problem in task 2. For resolving the problem in task 2, we need the information of long distance dependency. In **Fig. 2,** for example, the analyzer is considering the relation between focused words "告诉 (*tell*)" and "他 (*he*)". The features used in this original analysis are the information of words "请 (*please*)", "告诉 (*tell*)", "他(*he*)", "何时 (*what time*)" and "准备 (*prepare*)". These features are "local features". The correct answer in this situation is the operation "**Shift**". It is because the word "告诉 (*tell*)" has a child "出发 (*start*)" which is not yet analyzed and the focused words don't depend on each other. However, the local features do not include the information of word "出发 (*start*)". Therefore, the analyzer possibly estimates the answer as the operation "**Reduce**". The results make a mistake in this situation because of the lack of long distance information. To resolve this problem, we should refer some information of long distance dependency in machine learning. The information about long distance relations is defined as "global features". In this paper, we select the words which remain in stack *I* but don't be consider in local features as global features.

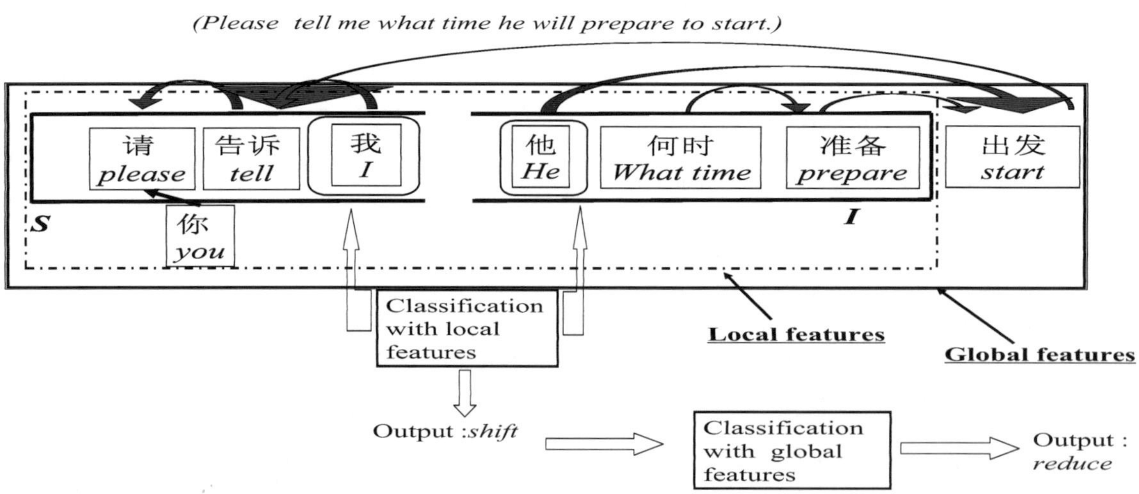

Fig. 2. An example of the ambiguity of deciding the long distance dependency relation and using two-steps classification dependency relation

3.2 two-step process

To use the global features, we cannot use them immediately because the global features are not effective in all operations. For using global features efficiently, we propose a two-step process in our analyzer. The analysis processes are divided to two processes. First, the analyzer uses only the local features (as described in Section 2.3) to decide the optimum operation. If the result is "**Reduce**" or "**Shift**", it means that the focused words do not have any dependency relation. The analyzer leaves the decision to another machine learner that makes use of global features. The analyzer will select global features for analyzing the Task 2. Then the analyzer outputs the final answer of this analysis process.

Fig. 2 describes an example of using two-step classification for analyzing dependency relation. In this example, the focused words are "我 (*I*)" and "他 (*He*)". The word "我 (*I*)" depends on the word "告诉 (*tell*)". The local features are surrounded by dotted line and the global features are surrounded by solid line. The analyzer used local features to analyze the operation of this situation. The result is the operation "***shift***". The analyzer then selected the global features to analyze again and the output is the operation "***reduce***". The final result of this situation is the operation "***reduce***".

4 The root node finder

In Isozaki's work (Isozaki et. al, 2004), they adopted a root finder in their system to find the root word of the input sentence. Their method used the information of the root word as a new feature for machine learning. Their experiments showed that information of root word was a beneficial feature. However, we think the information of root word can be used not only as the feature of machine learning, but also can be used to divide the sentence. Therefore, the complexity of the sentence can be alleviated by dividing the input sentence.

4.1 Root node and dividing sentence by using root finder

In the fundamental definition of dependency structure, there is one and only one head word in a dependency structure. An element cannot have dependents lying on the other side of its own governor.

These peculiarities imply that the head word divides the phrase into two independent parts and each part does not cross the head word. As in **Fig. 3**, the original input sentence has a root word (the head word of phrase) "与 (*and*)". There are not any dependency relation which crosses the root word. Therefore we can divide this sentence into two sub-sentence "出国 (*exodus*) / 去 (*do*) / 进修 (*study*) / 与 (*and*)" and "与 (*and*) / 到 (*go*) / 国外 (*foreign country*) / 去(*do*) / 旅行 (*visit*)". Both these sub-sentences have their root word and the root word is "与(and)". We can conceive that to analyze the dependency structure of the full sentence is to analyze the dependency structure of two sub-sentences. Combining structures of two sub-sentences, we can get the full structure of original sentence. Our dependency analyzer is a bottom-up deterministic analyzer. Instinctively, the accuracy of analyzing short sentence is significantly better than analyzing long sentence. Thus the performance of the dependency analyzer can be improved by this method.

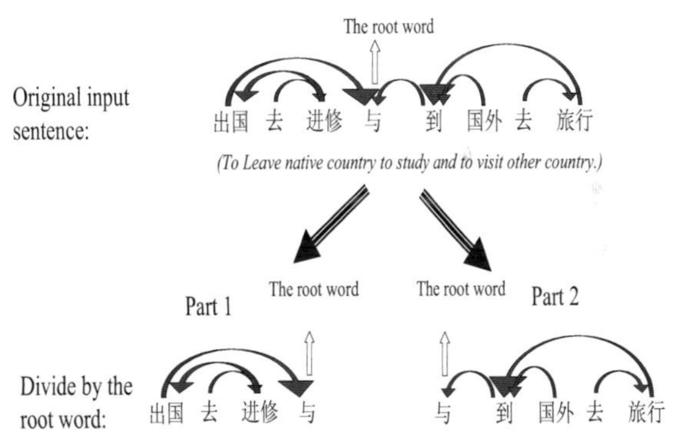

Fig. 3. Dividing the phrase as two phrases by the root word

4.2 Constructing a root finder

To use the root node, we should construct the root finder. Similarly to Isozaki's work, we use machine learner (SVMs) to construct the root finder. We refer to the features which are used in Isozaki's work and investigate other effective features. The performance of our root node finder is 90.71%. This is better than the root accuracy of our analyzer (86.22%, see **Table 2**).

Therefore, using the root finder can give the dependency analyzer more top-down information.

The tags and features of the root finding are shown in **Fig. 4**. We extract all root words in the training data and tagging every word to show that it is root word or not. For example, the root word in **Fig. 4** is "得到 (*get*)". The root finder analyzes each word in the sentence and gives the tag "true" or "false" to indicate the root word. The features for machine learning of root finder include the contextual features (the information about the focused word, the two preceding words, and two succeeding words) and the word relation features (the words which are in the outside of the window). Other effectual features include the Boolean features "root word is found" and "the focus word is the first/last word of sentence". For example, the contextual features of the word "经济 (*economic*)" include information of the focused (*n*) word "经济 (*economic*)", the "*n*-1"th word "宏观 (*wide*)", the "*n*-2"th word "的 (*DE*)", the "*n*+1"th word" 环境 (*environment*)" and the "*n*+2"th word "将 (*will*)". The word relation features include the preceding word set {中国 (*China*)}, the succeeding word set {得到, 进一步, 的, 改善} and the Boolean features are: "root_word_is_found=false", "first_word=false" ,"last_word=false".

When we use the root finder to analyze the root word of the sentence, we do not know the structure of input sentence (either the phrase structure or the dependency structure). It may look odd that the root finder can analyzes the root word without any information of the structure. However, this analysis is practicable. Naturally, the root word of a sentence is usually a verb (about 61% of sentences have a verb as the root word in our testing corpus). For example, in the example 1 of **Fig. 5** "我 / 去 / 学校 (*I go to school*)", we know the POS-tags are "noun, verb, noun" thus we can find that the root word is "去 (go)". However, many sentences include more then one verb or the root word is not verb (in NP or PP…etc.). We can not only choose the verbs as root word directly. To decide the root word of complex sentences, there are some special word/POS relations that can be used to estimate the root node of a sentence. Considering the root finder in **Fig. 4**, the root finder gives the root tag to each word of the sentence.

The processes of analyzing the root word can be thought as two tasks:

Task 1: Does the focus word depend on a neighbor word?

Task 2: Are there any special relation in the sentence?

In **Fig. 4**, the contextual features (two preceding words and two succeeding words) can be used to process the **Task 1**, and the word relation features can be used to process the **Task 2**. If the focused word possibly depends on neighbor words, it is impossible that the focused word is the root word. Therefore these words will be tagged as "false".

Alternately, considering the example 2 in **Fig. 5**, the sentence has a verb "收复 (*recapture*)", but the special word "的 (*DE*)" is in the right side of the verb "收复 (*recapture*)". Therefore, the verb "收复 (*recapture*)" is possibly in the 的 (*DE*)-phrase and the verb cannot be the root word. The special word "的 (*DE*)" resembles a preposition and it is always the last word of DE-phrase. Therefore, although we do not know the structure of sentence, we can identify which words can be the root word by the relation and position of the features. If the features of the focused word include the special word relations

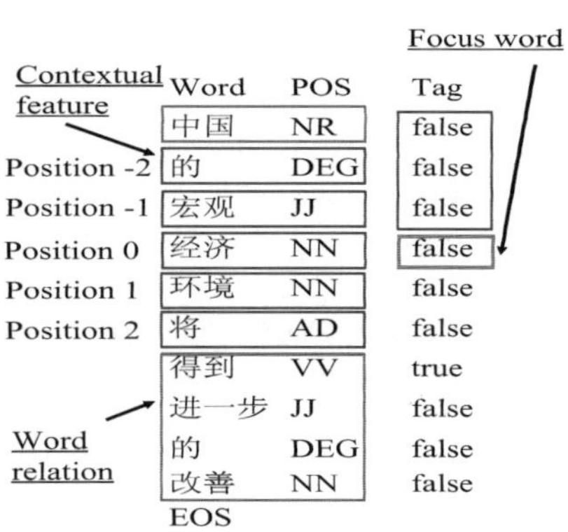

Fig. 4. The features and tag of root finder

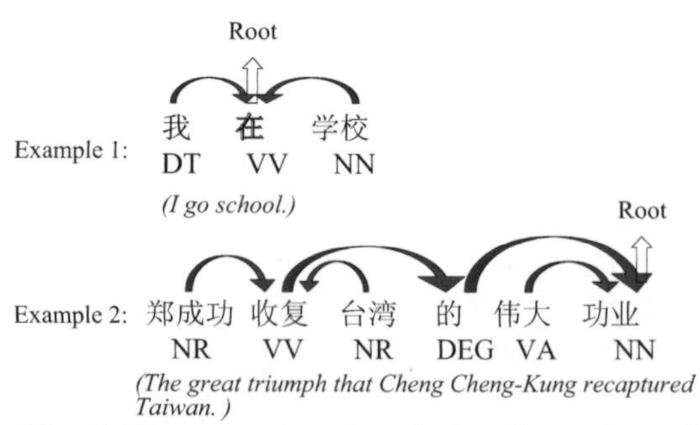

Fig. 5: The examples of analyzing the root word of sentences

(for example, the focused word is in the prepositional phrase), it isn't the root word. The features "word relations" in **Fig. 5** can consider this situation.

5 Experiments

5.1 Corpus and estimation

We use Penn Chinese Treebank 5.0 (Xue et al., 2002) in our experiments. This Treebank is represented by phrase structure and doesn't include the head information of each phrase. The first step of using Penn Chinese Treebank is to derive the head rules for deciding the head word of each phrase. Some examples of head rules are shown in **Table 1.** We convert the Treebank by using these head rules. The training corpus includes about 377,408 words for learning and 63,886 words for testing. It should be noted that the punctuation mark "。" marks the end of a sentence in the Treebank. However, the punctuation mark "," also can be the end of a sentence. It is hard to determine the dependency rule of the clauses on the both side of comma. Therefore, to decide the dependency relation which crosses a punctuation mark "," is difficult. We do not deal with the ambiguity of commas and divide the sentence by the punctuation mark ",".

Phrase	The order of deciding the head of phrase (from left)
ADJP	CC PZ ADJP JJ
ADVP	CC PZ AD
CLP	PZ CLP M LC
DP	DP CLP QP DT
DVP	DEV DEC DEG
VCP	VC VV

Table 1. Some examples of head rules

The performance of our dependency structure analyzer is evaluated by the following three measures:

Dependency Accuracy:

$$= \frac{\textit{number of correctly analyzed dependency relations}}{\textit{number of dependency relations}}$$

Root Accuracy:

$$= \frac{\textit{number of correctly analyzed root nodes}}{\textit{number of clauses}}$$

Sentence Accuracy:

$$= \frac{\textit{number of fully correctly analyzed clause}}{\textit{number of clauses}}$$

5.2 Results and discussion

Our experimental results are shown in **Table. 2**. First row in the table is the result of our basic analyzer (Nivre algorithm with SVMs), second and third row show the effects of the proposed extensions. The last row is the result of combining the two extensions. We had used McNemar test to confirm the significance of the methods. The McNemar test proves that using the proposed methods improve the analyzers significantly. Comparing the results of our basic analyzer to related works, our analyzer (dep. Accuracy: 87.64) is better than (Ma et al., 2004, dep. Accuracy: 80.38) and (Zhou, 2000, dep. Accuracy of newspaper: 67.7). However, these researches used different corpus. We cannot compare the performances directly.

According to the second row of **Table. 2**, dividing the process of classification as two steps can improve the performance of dependency analyzer. However, the improvement of using this method is limited. This is because that long distance relations are not many in the corpus. The absence of global information does not occur in the sentences without long distance relations. Another reason is the distribution of operations. The instances of operations in our experimental corpus are not balanced. The operation "***reduce***" is the least (7.8%) and it is far less than other operations. Therefore the instances for creating the model of operation "***reduce***" are not satisfactory. These facts result in that our experiment of using two step classification cannot improve the analyzer remarkably.

About the experiment of utilizing root finder in our analyzer, we tried to adopt the root information to the analyzer (using the information as features for machine learning). However, the performance is worse than the baseline (the fundamental analyzer "Nivre+SVMs"). Therefore, we use our method to improve the analyzer by using root information (dividing the sentence according to root node).

According to the third row of **Table. 2**, dividing the sentence into two sub-sentences can improve the performance of dependency analyzer. However, the sentence accuracy cannot increase reliably. This result shows that using root finder and dividing sentence can reconstruct some mistakes in sentences. Certainly, the performance of the root finder influences the analyzer strongly. If we use a perfect root node finder into our analyzer, the performance will improve significantly.

The last row of **Table. 2** shows the results of combining the two proposed methods (using global features and root node finder) to improve our analyzer. Combining two methods can increase the dependency accuracy better than using either one of the methods. It means that some analysis errors of fundamental analyzer can be resolved by using both improvement methods. Therefore using combined method cannot supply higher improvement.

	Dep. Acc.	Root Acc.	Sent. Acc.
Baseline (Nivre with SVMs)	85.25	86.18	59.98
Baseline with two-step process	85.44	86.22	60.1
Baseline with root node finder	86.13	**90.94**	**61.33**
Baseline with two-step process and root node finder	**86.18**	**90.94**	**61.33**

Table 2. The experimental results

6 Conclusion and future work

In this paper, we present two methods to improve a deterministic dependency structure analyzer for Chinese. This basic analyzer implements a bottom-up deterministic algorithm with SVMs. We convert a phrase structure annotated corpus (Penn Chinese Treebank) to dependency tagged corpus by using head rules. According to the properties of Chinese language and dependency structure, we try to add a root finder in our dependency analyzer to improve the analyzer. Moreover, considering the machine learning process of our analyzer, we divide the process into two processes to improve the performance of analyzer. The improving methods (using root finder and dividing machine learning process) showed to improve the analyzer.

Future work includes three points. First, we should improve the performance of the root finder. Second, we should construct a useful prepositional phrase chunker, because the prepositional phrase is a major error source of our basic analyzer. The original analyzer tends to let the preposition governing a partial subtree of the full phrase. According to the properties of Chinese language, the prepositional phrases in Chinese are head-initial. Intuitively, if we can extract the prepositional phrases from sentence, the complexity of the sentence will decrease. Thus an important task is how to chunk the prepositional phrase in the sentence.

Finally, we should deal with the ambiguity of the meaning of punctuation mark "，". The definition of "sentence" is ambiguous in Chinese. In Chinese articles, the normal ending mark of a sentence is the punctuation mark "。". However, the mark "，" is often used at the end of a sentence. To distinguish the meaning of the punctuation mark "，" is difficult. Therefore, we should adopt semantic analysis in our analyzer.

References

1. Eugene Charniak, 2001. Immediate-Head Parsing for Language Models. pages 124-131, NAACL-2001.
2. Yuen Ren Chao, 1968. A Grammar of Spoken Chinese. Berkeley, CA: University of California Press.
3. Michael Collins, Brian Roark, 2004, Incremental parsing with the Perceptron algorithm. Pages 112-119, ACL-2004.
4. J. Huang, 1982. Logical relations in Chinese and the theory of grammar Doctoral dissertation, Massachusetts Institute of Technology, Cambridge.
5. Ulrich. H.-G. Kreβel, 1998. Pairwise classification and support vector machines. In Advances in Kernel Methods, pages 255–268. The MIT Press.
6. Chih Jen Lin, 2001. A practical guide to support vector classification, http://www.csie.ntu.edu.tw/~cjlin/libsvm/.
7. Lai, Bong Young Tom, Huang, Changning, 1994. Dependency Grammar and the Parsing of Chinese Sentences. PACLIC 1994
8. Hideki Isozaki, Hideto Kazawa, Tsutomu Hirao, 2004. A Deterministic Word Dependency Analyzer Enhanced With Preference Learning, pages 275-281, COLING-2004
9. Charles Li, and Thompson Sandra A., 1981. Mandarin Chinese. University of California Press.
10. Lin-Shan Lee, Long-Ji Lin, Keh-Jiann Chen, and James Huang, 1991. An Efficient Natural Language Processing System Specially Designed for the Chinese Language. Computational Linguistics, Volume 17, Number 4.
11. Ma Jinshan, Zhang yu, Liu ting, and Li sheng, 2004. A Statistical Dependency Parser of Chinese-under Small Training Data. IJCNLP 2004 Workshop: Beyond shallow analyses, Formalisms and statistical modeling for deep analyses.
12. Joakim Nivre and Mario Scholz, 2004. Deterministic Dependency Parsing of English Text. Pages 64-70, COLING-2004.
13. Adwait Ratnaparkhi, 1999. Learning to parse natural language with maximum entropy models. Machine Learning, 34(1-3) pages151–175.
14. Vladimir N. Vapnik, 1998. Statistical Learning Theory. A Wiley-Interscience Publication.
15. Nianwen Xue, Fu-Dong Chiou, Martha Stone Palmer, 2002. Building a Large-Scale Annotated Chinese Corpus. COLING 2002
16. Ming Zhou, 2000. A block-based robust dependency parser for unrestricted Chinese text. The second Chinese Language Processing Workshop attached to ACL-2000.

Chinese Classifier Assignment Using SVMs

Hui Guo and Huayan Zhong
Department of Computer Science
Stony Brook University
Stony Brook, NY 11794-4400, USA
{huguo, huayan}@cs.sunysb.edu

Abstract

In Chinese, nouns need numeral classifiers to express quantity. In this paper, we explore the relationship between classifiers and nouns. We extract a set of lexical, syntactic and ontological features and the corresponding noun-classifier pairs from a corpus and then train SVMs to assign classifers to nouns. We analyse which features are most important for this task.

1 Introduction

In English, numbers directly modify count nouns, as in 'two apples' and 'five computers'. Numbers cannot directly modify mass nouns; instead, an embedded noun phrase must be formed, e.g. 'five slices of bread'. However, in Chinese all nouns need numeral classifiers to express quantity[1]. When translating from English to Chinese, we may need to choose Chinese classifiers to form noun phrases. We can see the difference between the two languages in the following two examples:

两*[liang]* 个*[***ge***]* 苹果*[pingguo] (Chinese)*
two apples (English)

and

五*[wu]* 片*[***pian***]* 面包*[mianbao] (Chinese)*
five slices of bread (English)

Noun classifer combinations appear with high frequency in Chinese. There are more than 500 classifiers although fewer than 200 of them are frequently used. Each classifier can only be used with certain classes of noun. Nouns in a class usually have similar properties. For example, nouns that can be used with the classifier '根[gen]' are: '稻草'(straw), '筷子'(chopstick), '管子'(pipe), etc. All these objects are long and thin. However, sometimes nouns with similar properties are in different classes. For example, '牛'(cow), '马'(horse) and '羊'(lamb) are all livestock, but they associate with different classifiers. This means that classifier assignment is not totally rule-based but partly idiomatic.

In this paper, we explore the relationship between classifiers and nouns. We extract a set of features and the corresponding noun-classifier attachments from a corpus and then train SVMs to assign classifers to nouns. In Section 4 we describe our data set. In Section 5 we describe our experiments. In Section 6 we present our results.

2 Related Work

Many Asian languages (e.g. Chinese, Korean, Japanese and Thai) have numeral classifier systems. Previous work on noun-classifier matching has been done in these languages. (Sornlertlamvanich et al., 1994) present an algorithm for selecting an appropriate classifier for a noun in Thai. The general idea is to extract noun-classifier collocations from a corpus, and output a list of noun-classifier pairs with frequency information. During noun phrase generation, the most frequently co-occurring classifier for a given noun is selected. However, no evaluation is reported for this algorithm.

The algorithm described in (Paik and Bond, 2001) generates Japanese and Korean numeral

[1] Proper nouns and bare noun phrases do not need classifiers.

classifiers using semantic classes from an ontology. The authors assigned classifiers to each of the 2,710 semantic classes in the ontology by hand. During generation, nouns in each semantic class are assigned the associated classifier. The classifier assignment accuracy is 81% for Japanese classifiers and 62% for Korean classifiers. However, the evaluation set contains only 90 noun phrases, which is pretty small. Furthermore, it is hard work to attach classifiers to an ontology by hand, and with this approach it is hard to deal with cases like the cattle example mentioned earlier.

(Paul et al., 2002) present a method for extracting classifier information from a bilingual (Japanese-English) corpus based on phrasal correspondences in the sentential context. Bilingual sentence pairs are compared to find noun-classifier collocations. The evaluation was done by a human. The precision is high (84.2%) but the recall is only about 40% because the algorithm does not give output for half of the nouns.

In contrast to these algorithms, our approach: is based on a large data set; uses machine learning; and does not require the attachment of classifiers to an ontology by hand.

3 Support Vector Machines

Support Vector Machines (SVMs) are a type of classifier first introduced in (Boser et al., 1992). In the last few years SVMs have become an important and active field in machine learning research. The SVM algorithm detects and exploits complex patterns in data.

A binary SVM is a *maximum margin classifier*. Given a set of training data $\{x_1, x_2, ..., x_k\}$, with corresponding labels $y_1, y_2, ..., y_k \in \{+1, -1\}$, a binary SVM divides the input space into two regions at a *decision boundary*, which is a separating hyperplane $\langle w, x\rangle + b = 0$ (Figure 1). The decision boundary should classify all points correctly, that is:

$$y_i(\langle w, x_i\rangle + b) > 0, \forall i$$

Also, the decision boundary should have the maximum separating margin with respect to the two classes. If we rescale w and b to make the closest point(s) to the hyperplane satisfy

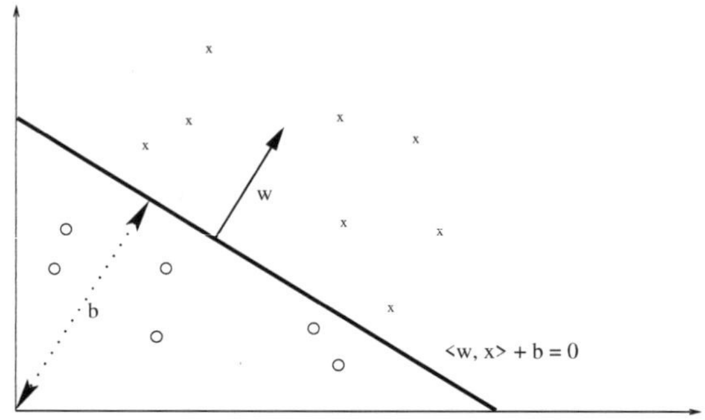

Figure 1: The input space and hyperplane

$|\langle w, x_i\rangle + b| = 1$, then the margin equals $1/||w||$ and the problem can be formulated as:

$$\text{minimize} \quad \frac{1}{2}||w||^2$$

$$\text{subject to} \quad y_i(\langle w, x_i\rangle + b) \geq 1, \forall i$$

The generalized Lagrange Function is:

$$L(w, b, \alpha) = \frac{1}{2}\langle w, w\rangle - \sum_{i=1}^{l} \alpha_i[y_i(\langle w, x_i\rangle + b) - 1]$$

So we can transform the problem to its dual: maximize

$$W(\alpha) = \sum_{i=1}^{n} \alpha_i - \frac{1}{2}\sum_{i=1,j=1}^{n} \alpha_i\alpha_j y_i y_j\langle x_i, x_j\rangle$$

$$\text{subject to} \quad \alpha_i \geq 0, \sum_{i=1}^{n} \alpha_i y_i = 0$$

This is a quadratic programming (QP) problem and we can always find the global maximum of α_i. We can recover w and b for the hyperplane by:

$$w = \sum_{i=1}^{n} \alpha_i y_i x_i$$

$$b = -\frac{\max_{y_i=-1}(\langle w, x_i\rangle) + \min_{y_i=+1}(\langle w, x_i\rangle)}{2}$$

If the points in the input space are not linearly separable, we allow 'slack variables' ξ_i in the classification. We need to find a soft margin hyperplane, e.g.:

$$\text{minimize} \quad \frac{1}{2}||w||^2 + C\sum_{i=1}^{n} \xi_i$$

subject to $y_i(\langle w, x_i \rangle + b) \geq 1 - \xi_i, \forall i$

Once again, a QP solver can be used to find the solution.

For our task we need multi-class SVMs. To get multi-class SVMs, we can construct and combine several binary SVMs (one-against-one), or we can directly consider all data in one optimization formula (one-against-all).

Many SVM implementations are available on the web. We chose LIBSVM (Chang and Lin, 2001), which is an efficient multi-class implementation. LIBSVM uses the "one-against-one" approach in which $k(k-1)/2$ classifiers are constructed and each one trains on data from two different classes (Hsu and Lin, 2002).

4 Data and Resources

We use the Penn Chinese Treebank (Xue et al., 2002) as our corpus and the ontology/lexicon HowNet (Dong and Dong, 2000) to get ontological features for nouns. We train SVMs on different feature sets to see which set(s) of features are important for noun-classifier matching.

4.1 Penn Chinese Treebank

The Penn Chinese Treebank is a 500,000 word Chinese corpus annotated with both part-of-speech (POS) tags and syntactic brackets.

We automatically extract noun phrases that contain classifiers from the corpus. An example noun phrase (translation: 'a major commercial waterway') is:

```
(IP
....
 (NP (QP (CD 一) (CLP (M 条)))
   (NP (NN 水运)) (ADJP (JJ 大))
     (NP (NN 动脉)))
...
)
```

The word in (CLP (M 条[tiao])) is the classifier and the head noun of the noun phrase is (NN 动脉). In Section 5.3 we describe a set of features we obtain from each noun phrase and the sentence in which it is embedded.

In our corpus, there are 61587 noun occurrences (12225 unique nouns) and 3940 classifier-noun co-occurrences (212 unique classifiers). However, there is a trival rule determining whether a noun needs a classifier. If a noun is preceded by a quantifier or a determiner, then a classifier is needed, otherwise it is not. Hence, we only focus on noun-classifier pairs. The most frequently occurring classifier in this corpus is '个[ge]', which occurs with 497 unique nouns. In this corpus, 87 classifiers occur in only one noun-classifier pair.

4.2 HowNet

We get ontological features of nouns from HowNet. HowNet is a bilingual Chinese-English lexicon and ontology. Each word sense is assigned to a concept containing ontological features. HowNet uses basic meaning units named sememes to construct concepts.

Table 1 shows an example entry in HowNet. The entry in Table 1 is for the word '作家'(writer). The sememe at the first position, 'human(人)', is the **categorical attribute**, which describes the general category of the concept. The sememes following the first sememe are **additional attributes**, which give additional specific features. There are two types of pointer, '#' and '*', in the definition. '#' means 'related', so '#occupation' shows that the concept has a relationship with 'occupation'. '*' means 'agent', so '*compile' shows that 'writer' is the agent of 'compile'. The sememes '#readings' and 'literature' show that the job of 'writer' is to compile 'readings' about 'literature'.

We use HowNet 2000, which contains 120,496 entries for about 65,000 Chinese words defined with a set of 1503 sememes. It is big enough for our task and we can get ontological features for 94.71% of the nouns from the Penn Chinese Treebank. For the nouns that are not in HowNet, we just leave the ontological features blank.

5 Experiments

We use six different feature sets to assign classifiers to nouns. To evaluate each feature set, we perform 10-fold cross validation. We report our results in Section 6.

5.1 Baseline Algorithm

In the training data, we count the number of times each classifier appears with a given noun. We assign to each noun in the testing data its most fre-

No.: 114303 W_C (word in Chinese): 作家 E_C (example in Chinese): G_C (POS tag in Chinese): N W_E (word in English): writer E_E (example in English): G_E (POS tag in English): N DEF (concept definition): human(人),#occupation(职位),*compile(编辑), #readings(读物),literature(文)

Table 1: An entry in HowNet

Lexical Features	**Syntactic Features**
noun	POS of noun
first premod	POS of first premod
second premod	POS of second premod
main verb	POS of main verb
total number of premodifiers	sentType
	embedded in vp or pp
	quoted or not

Table 2: Features extracted from training data

quently co-occurring classifier (c.f. (Sornlertlamvanich et al., 1994)). If a noun does not appear in the training data, we assign the classifier '个[ge]', the classifier which appears most frequently overall in the corpus.

5.2 Noun Features

Since classifiers are assigned mostly based on the noun, the most important features for classifier prediction should be features of the nouns. We ran four different experiments for noun features:

- **(1)** The feature set includes only the *noun* itself.
- **(2)** The feature set includes *ontological features* of the noun only. If classifiers are associated with semantic categories (c.f. (Paik and Bond, 2001)), we should be able to assign classifiers based on the ontological features of nouns.
- **(3)** The feature set includes the *noun* and *ontological features*.
- **(4)** Two SVMs are trained: one on the *noun* only, and one on *ontological features* only. During testing, nouns in the training set are assigned classifiers using the first SVM; other nouns are assigned classifiers using the second SVM.

5.3 Context Features

In this set of experiments, we used features from both the noun and the context. The features we used can be categorized into two groups: lexical features and syntactic features. They are shown in Table 2.

We ran two experiments using this set of features:

- **(5)** The feature set includes the noun, lexical and syntactic features only.
- **(6)** The feature set includes the noun, lexical, syntactic and ontological features.

6 Results and Discussion

We built SVMs using all the feature sets described in Section 5 and tested using 10-fold cross validation. We tried the four types of kernel function in LIBSVM: linear, polynomial, radial basis function (RBF) and sigmoid, then selected the RBF kernal $K(x, y) = e^{-\gamma||x-y||^2}$, which gives the

Algorithm	**All nouns**	**Nouns occuring 2+ times**
Baseline	50.76%	50.69%
(1) noun only	57.81% (c = 4, $\gamma = 0.5$)	59.34% (c = 16, $\gamma = 0.125$)
(2) ontology only	58.69% (c = 4, $\gamma = 0.5$)	60.68% (c = 256, $\gamma = 0.125$)
(3) noun **and** ontology	57.81% (c = 16, $\gamma = 0.5$)	59.46% (c = 16, $\gamma = 0.125$)
(4) noun **or** ontology	58.71%	60.55%
(5) noun, syntactic and lexical features	52.14% (c = 1024, $\gamma = 0.5$)	53.51% (c = 16, $\gamma = 0.5$)
(6) all features	52.06% (c = 1024, $\gamma = 0.075$)	53.55% (c = 16, $\gamma = 0.5$)

Table 3: Accuracy of different algorithms

	Most common noun	位[**wei**]	次[**ci**]	个[**ge**]	名[**ming**]	届[**jie**]	项[**xiang**]
位[**wei**]	官员 (official)			24.1 (57.1)	14.7 (34.7)		
次[**ci**]	大会 (convention)			22.3 (53.3)		1.1 (2.6)	7.6 (18.2)
个[**ge**]	项目 (project)	1.0 (7.0)			0.7 (5.2)	0.2 (1.7)	3.3 (24.4)
名[**ming**]	人员 (person)	31.7 (55.2)		23.8 (41.4)			
届[**jie**]	运动会 (sports tournament)	1.9 (2.1)	29.6 (34.0)	31.5 (36.2)			
项[**xiang**]	成果 (achievement)		6.6 (11.3)	35.2 (60.4)		1.1 (1.9)	

Table 4: Most commonly misclassified classifiers; Cell shows percentage of total occurrences of row value misclassified as column value and (percentage of total misclassifications of row value misclassified as column value)

highest accuracy. For each feature set, we systematically varied the values for the parameters C (range from 2^{-5} to 2^{15}) and γ (range from 2^{3} to 2^{-15}); we report the best results with corresponding values for C and γ. Finally, for each feature set, we ran once on all nouns and once only on nouns occurring twice or more in the corpus.

Classifier assignment accuracy is reported in Table 3. The performance of all the SVMs is significantly better than baseline (paired t-test, $p < 0.005$). There is no significant difference between the performance with the 1st, 2nd, 3rd and 4th feature sets. But the performance of the SVMs using lexical and syntactic features (experiments 5 and 6) is significantly worse than the performance on feature sets 1-4 (df = 17.426, $p < 0.05$).

These results show that lexical and syntactic contextual features do not have a positive effect on the assignment of classifiers. They confirm the intuition that the noun is the single most important predictor of the classifier; however, the semantic class of the noun works as well as the noun itself. In addition, a combination approach that uses semantic class information when the noun is previously unseen does not perform better.

We also computed the confusion matrix for the most commonly misclassified classifiers. The results are reported in Table 4.

For these experiments we used automatic evaluation (cf. (Paul et al., 2002)). A classifier is only judged to be correct if it is exactly the same as that in the original test set. For some noun phrases, there are multiple valid classifiers. For example, we can say

'一[yi] 块[**kuai**] 金牌[jinpai]'

or

'一[yi] 枚[**mei**] 金牌[jinpai]'

(a golden medal).

We did a subjective evaluation on part of our data to evaluate how many automatically generated classifiers are acceptable to human readers. We randomly selected 241 noun-classifier pairs from our data. We presented the sentence containing each pair to a human judge who is a native speaker of Mandarin Chinese. We asked the judge to rate all the classifiers generated by our

Algorithm	Number rated 1 or higher	Percent rated 1 or higher	Average rating
Baseline	209	86.7%	1.59
(1) noun only	224	92.9%	1.76
(2) ontology only	226	93.8%	1.78
(3) noun **and** ontology	226	93.8%	1.77
(4) noun **or** ontology	227	94.2%	1.80
(5) noun, syntactic and lexical features	218	90.5%	1.67
(6) all features	218	90.5%	1.67
Original	241	100%	1.95

Table 5: Human evaluation: Ratings of classifiers

algorithms as well as the original classifier by indicating whether each is good (2), acceptable (1) or bad (0) in that sentence context. The classifiers were presented in random order; the judge was blind to the source of the classifiers.

The results for our human evaluation are reported in Table 5. Although our automatic evaluation indicates relatively poor accuracy, 94.2% of generated classifiers using feature set 4) are rated acceptable or good in our subjective evaluation. Also, the performance of SVMs with the 1st, 2nd, 3rd and 4th feature sets is significantly better than baseline (paired t-test, $p < 0.005$). There is no significant difference between the performance with the 1st, 2nd, 3rd and 4th feature sets. But the performance of the SVMs using lexical and syntactic features (experiments 5 and 6) is significantly worse than those without ($p < 0.05$). The ratings of the classifiers generated by all our algorithms are significantly worse than the original classifiers in the corpus. In future work, we plan to extend this evaluation using more judges.

Which classifier to select also depends on the emotional background of the discourse (Fang, 2003). For example, we can use different classifiers to express different affect for the same noun (e.g. if a government official is in favor or disgrace). However, we cannot get this kind of information from our corpus.

7 Conclusions and Future Work

Our machine learning approach to classifier assignment in Chinese performs better than previously published rule-based approaches and works for bigger data sets. The noun is clearly the most important feature (experiment 1). However, we still think ontological features may be useful in classifier assignment, for example for previously unseen nouns, and our experimental results show a trend in this direction, although not a statistically significant one (experiments 2 and 4).

We used the Chinese Treebank for these experiments because it is the only available corpus of parsed Chinese text. Now that we have isolated the relevant features for this task, we plan to conduct further experiments using larger corpora, such as the Chinese Gigaword (Graf and Chen, 2003).

Our use of ontological features could be improved in several ways. First, the ontological features we get from HowNet do not fit our purpose well. For example, the definitions of '猫' (cat) and '牛' (cow) are both 'livestock'; however, they should use different classifiers. In order to improve the performance of our approach, we need an ontology that correctly groups nouns into classes according to their semantic properties (e.g. type, shape, color, size).

For another knowledge-rich approach, we could use a complex ontology plus a Chinese classifier dictionary that describes the properties of the objects each classifier can modify. By comparing noun properties and classifier characteristics, classifier assignment could be improved as long as the nouns are in the ontology. However, there are many idiomatic noun-classifier matchings that can not be categorised by dictionaries. Therefore, a combination of rule-based and machine-learning approaches seems most promising.

Third, we can classify Chinese classifers into groups and focus on those that modify single objects. Certain Chinese classifiers can be used before all plural nouns. Some classifiers specify the container of the objects, for example, '一[yi] 篮子[**lanzi**] 苹果[pingguo]' (a basket of apples). The classifier changes when the container changes. These can be treated differently from sortal and anaphoric classifiers.

Acknowledgements

We thank the anonymous reviewers for their helpful feedback, HowNet for giving us permission to download their knowledge base, and Chih-Chung Chang and Chih-Jen Lin for the implementation of LIBSVM.

This material is based upon work supported by the Defense Advanced Research Projects Agency (DARPA), through the Department of the Interior, NBC, Acquisition Services Division, under Contract No. NBCHD030010.

References

B. Boser, I. Guyon, and V. Vapnik. 1992. A training algorithm for optimal margin classifiers. In *Proceedings of the Fifth Annual ACM Conference on Computational Learning Theory (COLT 1992)*.

Chih-Chung Chang and Chih-Jen Lin, 2001. *LIBSVM: a library for support vector machines*. Software available at http://www.csie.ntu.edu.tw/ cjlin/libsvm.

Z. Dong and Q. Dong. 2000. Introduction to HowNet - Chinese message structure base. http://www.keenage.com.

L. Fang. 2003. Research of Chinese lexicon teaching - quantities. *Journal of Secondary Education*.

D. Graf and K. Chen. 2003. Chinese gigaword. LDC Catalog Number LDC2003T09.

C. Hsu and C. Lin. 2002. A comparison of methods for multi-class support vector machines. In *IEEE Transactions on Neural Networks*.

K. Paik and F. Bond. 2001. Multilingual generation of numeral classifiers using a common ontology. In *Proceedings of the 19th International Conference on Computer Processing of Oriental Languages*.

M. Paul, E. Sumita, and S. Yamamoto. 2002. Corpus-based generation of numeral classifier using phrase alignment. In *Proceedings of the 19th International Conference on Computational Linguistics*.

V. Sornlertlamvanich, W. Pantachat, and S. Meknavin. 1994. Classifier assignment by corpus-based approach. In *Proceedings of the 15th Conference on Computational Linguistics*.

N. Xue, F. Chiou, and M. Palmer. 2002. Building a large-scale annotated Chinese corpus. In *Proceedings of the 19th International Conference on Computational Linguistics*.

Morphological features help POS tagging of unknown words across language varieties

Huihsin Tseng
Dept. of Linguistics
University of Colorado
Boulder, CO 80302
tseng@colorado.edu

Daniel Jurafsky
Dept. of Linguistics
Stanford University
Stanford, CA 94305
jurafsky@stanford.edu

Christopher Manning
Dept. of Computer Science
Stanford University
Stanford, CA 94305
manning@stanford.edu

Abstract

Part-of-speech tagging, like any supervised statistical NLP task, is more difficult when test sets are very different from training sets, for example when tagging across genres or language varieties. We examined the problem of POS tagging of different varieties of Mandarin Chinese (PRC-Mainland, PRC-Hong Kong, and Taiwan). An analytic study first showed that unknown words were a major source of difficulty in cross-variety tagging. Unknown words in English tend to be proper nouns. By contrast, we found that Mandarin unknown words were mostly common nouns and verbs. We showed these results are caused by the high frequency of morphological compounding in Mandarin; in this sense Mandarin is more like German than English. Based on this analysis, we propose a variety of new morphological unknown-word features for POS tagging, extending earlier work by others on unknown-word tagging in English and German. Our features were implemented in a maximum entropy Markov model. Our system achieves state-of-the-art performance in Mandarin tagging, including improving unknown-word tagging performance on unseen varieties in Chinese Treebank 5.0 from 61% to 80% correct.

1 Introduction

Part-of-speech tagging is an important enabling task for natural language processing, and state-of-the-art taggers perform quite well, when training and test data are drawn from the same corpus. Part-of-speech tagging is more difficult, however, when a test set is drawn from a corpus that includes significantly different varieties of the language. One factor that may play a role in this cross-variety difficulty is the presence of test-set words that were unseen in cross-variety training sets.

We chose Mandarin Chinese to study this question of cross-variety and unknown-word POS tagging. Mandarin is both a spoken and a written language; as a written language, it is the official written language of the PRC (Mainland and Hong Kong), and Taiwan. Thus regardless of which dialect people speak at home, they write in Mandarin. But the varieties of Mandarin written in the PRC (Mainland and Hong Kong) and Taiwan differ in orthography, lexicon, and even grammar about as much as the British, American, and Australian varieties of English (or more in some cases). The corpus we use, Chinese Treebank 5.0 (Palmer et al., 2005), contains data from the three language varieties as well as different genres within the varieties. It thus provides a good data set for the impact of language variation on tagging performance.

Previous work on POS tagging of unknown words has proposed a number of features based on prefixes and suffixes and spelling cues like capitalization (Toutanova et al. 2003, Brants 2000, Ratnaparkhi 1996). For example, these systems followed Samuelsson (1993) in using n-grams of letter sequences ending and starting each word as unknown word features. But these features have mainly been tested on inflectional languages like English and German, whose derivational and inflectional affixes tend to be a strong indicator of word classes; Brants (2000), for example, showed that an English word ending in the suffix *-able* was very likely to be an adjective. Chinese, by contrast, has more than 4000 frequent affix characters. The amount of training data for each affix is thus quite sparse and (as we will show later) Chinese affixes are quite ambiguous in their part-of-speech identity. Furthermore, it is possible that n-gram features may not be suited to Chinese at all, since Chinese words are much shorter than English (averaging 2.4 characters per word compared with 7.7 for English, for unknown words in CTB 5.0 and Wall Street Journal (Marcus et el., 1993)).

In order to deal with these difficulties, we first performed an analytic study with the goal of understanding the morphological properties of unknown words in Chinese. Based on this analysis, we then propose new morphological features for addressing the unknown word problem. We also showed how these features could make use of a non-CTB corpus that had been labeled with very different POS tags, by converting those tags into features.

The remainder of the paper is organized as follows. The next section is concerned with a corpus analysis of cross language variety differences and introduces Chinese morphology. In Section 3, we evaluate a number of lexical, sequence, and linguistic features. Section 4 reviews related work and summarizes our contribution.

2 Data

Chinese Treebank 5.0 (CTB) contains 500K words of newspaper and magazine articles annotated with segmentation, part-of-speech, and syntactic constituency information. It includes data from three major media sources, XH[1] from PRC, HKSAR[2] from Hong Kong, and SM[3] from Taiwan. In terms of genre, both XH and HKSAR focus on politics and economic issues, and SM more on topics such as culture, health, education and travel. All of the files in CTB are encoded using Guo Biao (GB) and use simplified characters.

We did some cleanup of character encoding errors in CTB before running our experiments. Taiwan and Hong Kong still use the traditional forms of characters, while PRC-Mainland has adopted simplified forms of many characters, which also collapse some distinctions between characters. Additionally a different character set encoding is standardly used. The articles in HKSAR and SM originally used traditional characters and Big 5 encoding, but prior to inclusion in the CTB corpus they had been converted into simplified characters and GB. Some errors seem to have crept into this conversion process, accidentally leaving traditional characters such as 後 instead of simplified 后 (after), 於 for 于 (for), 甚麼 and 什麼 and 什么 (what), all of which we fixed. We also normalized half width numbers, alphabets, and punctuation to full width. Finally we removed the -NONE- traces left over from CTB parse trees.

3 Corpus analysis

We begin with an analytic study of potential problems for POS tagging on cross language variety data.

3.1 More unknown words across varieties?

We first test our hypothesis that a test set from a different language variety will contain more unknown words. Table 1 has the number of words in our devset that were unseen in the XH-only training set (we describe our training/dev/test split more fully in the next section). The devset contains equal amounts of data from all three varieties (XH, HKSAR, and SM). As table 1 shows, in data taken from the same source as the training data (XH), 4.63% of the words were unseen in training, compared to the much larger numbers of unknown words in the cross-variety datasets (14.3% and 16.7%). Some of this difference is probably due to genre as well, especially for the outlier-genre SM set.

Table 1 Percent of words in devset that were unseen in an XH-only training set. See Table 4 for more details.

Data Set	*Lang Variety*	*Source*	*Genre*	*% unk*
XH	Mainland Mandarin	Xinhua	News	4.6
HKSAR	Hong Kong Mandarin	HKSAR	News	14.2
SM	Taiwan Mandarin	Sino-rama	Magazine	16.7
Devset	Mix	Mix	Mix	12.0

3.2 What are the unknown words?

In this section, we analyze the part-of-speech characteristics of the unknown words in our devset.

Table 2 Word class distribution of unknown words in devset, XH, HKSAR, SM. Devset represents the conjunction of the three varieties. CC, DT, LC, P, PN, PU, and SP are considered as closed classes by CTB.

Word class	*Devset*	*XH*	*HKSAR*	*SM*
AD (adverb)	74	2	23	49
CC (coordinating conj.)	7	-	-	7
CD (cardinal number)	151	108	23	20
DT (determiner)	10	-	6	4
FW (foreign words)	2	2	-	-
JJ (other noun modifier)	79	14	38	27
LC (localizer/postposit)	1	-	1	-
M (measure word)	12	2	4	6
NN (common noun)	1128	131	520	477
NR (proper noun)	400	92	156	152
NT (temporal noun)	53	3	38	12
OD (ordinal number)	4	-	4	-
P (preposition)	16	1	8	7
PN (pronoun)	10	-	3	7
PU (punctuation)	361	-	110	251
SP(sentence final particle)	1	-	-	1
VA(predicative adjective)	43	1	19	23
VV (other verbs)	497	25	215	257
Total	2849	381	1168	1300

Table 2 shows that the majority of Chinese unknown words are common nouns (NN) and verbs (VV). This holds both within and across different varieties. Beyond the content words, we find that 10.96% and 21.31% of unknown words are function words in HKSAR and SM data. Such unknown function words include the determiner *gewei* ("everybody"), the conjunction *huoshi* ("or"), the preposition *liantong* ("with"), the pronoun *nali* ("where"), and symbols used as quotes "「" and "」" (punctuation). XH does contain words with similar function (*huozhe*

[1] Xinhua Agency
[2] Information Services Department of Hong Kong Special Administrative Region
[3] Sinorama magazine

"or", *yu* "with", *dajia* "everybody", quotation marks "『"and "』"). Our result thus suggests that each Mandarin variety may have characteristic function words.

3.3 Cross language comparison

A key goal of our work is to understand the way that unknown words differ across languages. We thus compare Chinese, German, and English. Following Brants (2000), we extracted 10% of the data from the Penn Treebank Wall Street Journal (WSJ[4]) and NEGRA[5] (Brants et al., 1999) as observation samples to compare to the rest of the corpora.

In these observation samples, we found that Chinese words are more ambiguous in POS than English and German; 29.9% of tokens in CTB have more than one POS tag, while only 19.8% and 22.9% of tokens are ambiguous in English and German, respectively.

Table 3 shows that 40.6% of unknown words are proper nouns[6] in English, while both Chinese and German have less than 15% of unknown words as proper nouns. Unlike English, 60% of the unknown words in Chinese and German are verbs and common nouns. In the next section we investigate the cause of this similarity between Chinese and German unknown word distribution.

Table 3 Comparison of unknown words in English, German and Mandarin. The English and German data are extracted from WSJ and NEGRA. Chinese data is our CTB devset.

Language	*English%*	*German%*	*Chinese%*
Proper nouns	40.6	12.2	14.0
Other nouns	24.0	53.0	41.5
Verbs	6.8	11.4	19.0
ALL	100.0	100.0	100.0

4 Morphological analysis

In order to understand the causes of the similarity of Chinese and German, and to help suggest possible features, we turn here to an introduction to Chinese morphology and its implications for part-of-speech tagging.

[4] WSJ unknown words are those in WSJ 19-21 but unseen in WSJ 0-18; these are the devset and training set from Toutanova et al. (2003).

[5] The unknown words of NEGRA are words in a 10% randomly extracted set that were unseen in the rest of the corpus.

[6] We treat NNP (proper noun) and NNPS(proper noun plural) as proper nouns, NN(noun) and NNS(noun plural) as other nouns, and V* as verbs in WSJ. We treat NE (Eigennamen) as proper nouns, NN (Normales Nomen) as other nouns, and V* as verbs in NEGRA. We treat NR as proper nouns, NN and NT as other nouns, and V* as verbs in CTB.

4.1 Chinese morphology

Chinese words are typically formed by four morphological processes: affixation, compounding, idiomization, and reduplication, as shown in Table 4.

In affixation, a bound morpheme is added to other morphemes, forming a larger unit. Chinese has a small number of prefixes and infixes[7] and numerous suffixes (Chao 1968, Li and Thompson 1981). Chinese prefixes include items such as *gui* ("noble") in *guixing* ("your name"), *bu* ("not") in *budaode* ("immoral"), and *lao* ("senior") in *laohu* ("tiger") and *laoshu* ("mouse"). There are a number of Chinese suffixes, including *zhe* ("marks a person who is an agent of an action") in *zuozhe* ("author"), *shi* ("master") in *laoshi* ("teacher"), *ran* (-ly) in *huran* ("suddenly"), and *xin* (-ity or –ness) in *kenengxin* ("possibility").

Compound words are composed of multiple stem morphemes. Chao (1968) describes a few of the different compounding rules in Mandarin, such as coordinate compound, subject predicate compound, noun noun compound, adj noun compound and so on. Two examples of coordinate compounds are *anpai* ARRANGE-ARRANGE ("to arrange, arrangement") and *xuexi* STUDY-STUDY ("to study").

Table 4 Chinese morphological rules and examples

	Examples
Prefix	*lao* ("senior") in *laohu* ("tiger")
Suffix	*shi* ("master") in *laoshi* ("teacher")
Compounding	*xuexi* ("to study", "study")
Idiomization	*wanshiruyi* ("everything is fine")
Reduplication	*changchang* ("taste a bit")

Compounding is extremely common in both Chinese and German. The phrase "income tax" is treated as an NP in English, but it is a word in German, *Einkommensteuer*, and in Chinese, *suodesui*. We suggest that it is this rich use of compounding that causes the wide variety of unknown common nouns and verbs in Chinese and German. However, there are still differences in their compound rules. German compounds can compose with a large number of elements, but Chinese compounds normally consist of two bases. Most German compounds are nouns, but Chinese has both noun and verb compounds.

Two final types of Chinese morphological processes that we will not focus on are idiomization (in which a whole phrase such as *wanshiruyi* ("everything is fine") functions as a word, and reduplication, in which a morpheme or word is repeated to form a new word such as the formation of *changchang* ("taste a

[7] Chinese only has two infixes, which are *de* and *bu* (not). We do not discuss infixes in the paper, because they are handled phrasally rather than lexically in CTB.

bit"), from *chang* "taste". (Chao 1968, Li and Thompson 1981).

4.2 Difficulty

The morphological characteristics of Chinese create various problems for part-of-speech tagging. First, Chinese suffixes are short and sparse. Because of the prevalence of compounding and the fact that the morphemes are short (1 character long), there are more than 4000 affixes. This means that the identity of an affix is often a sparsely-seen feature for predicting POS. Second, Chinese affixes are poor cues to POS because they are ambiguous; for example 63% of Chinese suffix tokens in CTB have more than one possible tag, while only 31% of English suffix tokens in WSJ have more than one tag. Most English suffixes are derivational and inflectional suffixes like *-able*, *-s* and *-ed*. Such functional suffixes are used to indicate word classes or syntactic function. Chinese, however, has no inflectional suffixes and only a few derivational suffixes and so suffixes may not be as good a cue for word classes. Finally, since Chinese has no derivational morpheme for nominalization, it is difficult to distinguish a nominalization and a verb.

These points suggest that morpheme identity, which is the major feature used in previous research on unknown words in English and German, will be insufficient in Chinese. This suggests the need for more sophisticated features, which we will introduce below.

5 Experiments

We evaluate our tagger under several experimental conditions: after showing the effects of data cleanup we show basic results based on features found to be useful by previous research. Next, we introduce additional morphology-based unknown word features, and finally, we experiment with training data of variable sizes and different language varieties.

5.1 Data sets

To study the significance of training on different varieties of data, we created three training sets: training set I contains data only from one variety, training set II contains data from 3 varieties, and is similar in total size to training set I. Training set III also contains data from 3 varieties and has twice much data as training set I. To facilitate comparison of performance both between and within Mandarin varieties, both the devset and the test set we created are composed of three varieties of data. The XH test data we selected was identical to the test set used in previous parsing research by Bikel and Chiang (2000). For the remaining data, we included HKSAR and SM data that is similar in size to the XH test set. Table 5 details characteristics of the data sets.

Table 5 Data set splits used. The unknown word tokens are with respect to Training I.

Data set	*Sect'ns*	*Token*	*Unknown*
Training I	26-270, 600-931	213986	-
Training II	600-931, 500-527, 1001-1039	204701	-
Training III	001-270, 301-527, 590-593, 600-1039, 1043-1151	485321	-
Devset		23839	2849
XH	001-025	7844	381
HKSAR	500-527	8202	1168
SM	590-593, 1001-1002	7793	1300
Test set		23522	2957
XH	271-300	8008	358
HKSAR	528-554	7153	1020
SM	594-596, 1040-1042	8361	1579

5.2 The model

Our model builds on research into loglinear models by Ng and Low (2004), Toutanova et al., (2003) and Ratnaparkhi (1996). The first research uses independent maximum entropy classifiers, with a sequence model imposing categorical valid tag sequence constraints. The latter two use maximum entropy Markov models (MEMM) (McCallum et al., 2000), that use log-linear models to obtain the probabilities of a state transition given an observation and the previous state, as illustrated in Figure 1 (a).

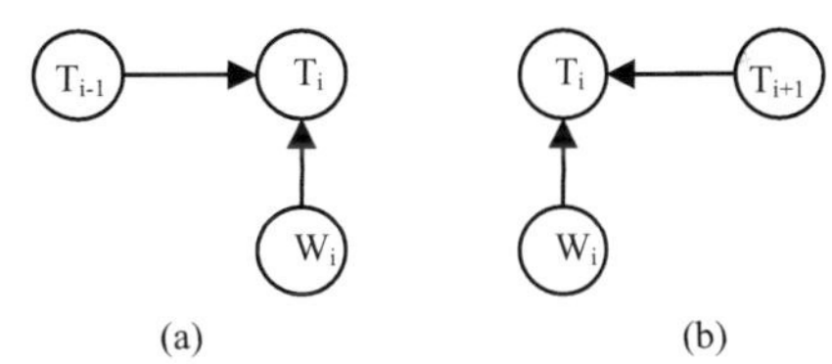

Figure 1 Graphical representation of transition probability calculation used in maximum entropy Markov models. (a) The previous state and the current word are used to calculate the transition probabilities for the next state transition. (b) Same as (a), but when model is run right to left.

Using left-to-right transition probabilities, as in Figure 1 (a), the equation for the MEMM can be formally stated as the following, where by d_i represents the set of features the transition probabilities are conditioned on:

$$P(t,w) = \prod_i P(t_i \mid d_i)$$

Maximum entropy is used to calculate the probability $P(t_i| d_i)$ using the equation below. Here, $f_j(t_i,d_i)$ represents a feature derived from the available contextual information (e.g. current word, previous tag, next word, etc.)

$$P(t_i \mid d_i) = \frac{\exp(\sum_j \lambda_j f_j(t_i, d_i))}{\sum_{t' \in T} \exp(\sum_j \lambda_j f_j(t', d_i))}$$

We also used Gaussian prior to prevent overfitting. This technique allows us to utilize a large number of lexical and MEMM state sequence based features and also provides an intuitive framework for the use of morphological features generated from unknown word models.

5.3 Data cleanup

Before investigating the effect of our new features, we show the effects of data cleanup. Table 6 illustrates the .46 (absolute) performance gain obtained by cleaning character encoding errors and normalizing half width to full width.

We also clustered punctuation symbols, since training set I has too many (36) variety of punctuations, compared to 9 in WSJ. We clustered punctuations, for example grouping "《" and "〈" together. This mapping renders an overall improvement of .08%. All models in the following sections are then trained on font-normalized and punctuation clustered data.

Table 6 Improvement of tagging accuracy after data cleanup. The features used by all of the models are the identity of the two previous words, the current word and the two following word. No features based on the sequence of tags were used.

Models	*Token A[8] %*	*Δ Token A%*	*Unk A %*
$2R_w$+$2L_w$	87.11	-	47.03
+Cleanup	87.57	0.46	48.54
+PU	87.65	0.08	49.26

5.4 Sequence features

We examined several tag sequence features from both left and right side of the current word. We use the term *lexical features* to refer to features derived from the identity of a word, and *tag sequence features* refer to features derived from the tags of surrounding words.

These features have been shown to be useful in previous research on English (Toutanova et al, 2003, Brants 2000, Thede and Harper 1999)

The models[9] in Table 7 list the different tag sequence features used; they also use the same lexical features from the model $2R_w$+$2L_w$ shown in Table 6. The table shows that Model L_t+LL_t conditioning on the previous tag and the conjunction of the two previous tags yields 88.27%. As such, using the sequence features $\langle t_{i-1}, t_{i-1}t_{i-2}\rangle$ achieves the current best result.

So far, there are no features specifically tailored toward unknown words in the model.

Table 7 Tagging accuracy of different sequence feature sets.

Models	*Feature sets*	*Token A %*	*Unk A %*
R_t+RR_t +$2R_w$+$2L_w$	$\langle t_i,t_{i+1}\rangle$,$\langle t_i,t_{i+1},t_{i+2}\rangle$ + lexical features	88.10	50.11
L_t+LL_t +$2R_w$+$2L_w$	$\langle t_i,t_{i-1}\rangle$,$\langle t_i,t_{i-1},t_{i-2}\rangle$ +lexical features	88.27	51.16

5.5 Unknown word model

Starting with Model L_t+LL_t from the last section, we introduce 8 features to improve the performance of the tagger on unknown words. In the sections that follow, the model using affixation in conjunction with the basic lexical features described above is considered to be our baseline.

We considered words that occur less than 7 times in the training set I as rare; if W_i is rare, an unknown word feature is used in place of a feature based on the actual word's identity. During evaluation, unknown word features are used for all words that occurred zero to 7 times in the training data. In addition, when tagging such rare and unknown words, we restrict the set of possible tags to just those tags that were associated with one or more rare words in the training data.

5.5.1 Affixation

Our affixation feature is motivated by similar features seen in inflectional language models. (Ng and Low 2004, Toutanova et al, 2003, Brants 2000, Ratnaparkhi 1996, Samuelsson 1993). Since Chinese also has affixation, it is reasonable to incorporate this feature into our model. For this feature, we use character *n*-gram prefixes and suffixes for *n* up to 4.[10] An example is:

资料袋 INFORMATION-BAG "folder"
W_i=资料袋 "a folder"
F_{AFFIX}={(prefix1,资), (prefix2,资料), (prefix3,资料袋), (suffix1,袋), (suffix2,料袋), (suffix3,资料袋)}

5.5.2 CTBMorph (CTBM)

While affix information can be very informative, we showed earlier that affixes in Chinese are sparse, short, and ambiguous. Thus as our first new feature we used a POS-vector of the set of tags a given affix could have. We used the training set to build a morpheme/POS dictionary with the possible tags for each

[8] We abbreviate accuracy as "A".

[9] Except where otherwise stated, during training, a count cutoff of 3 is applied to all features found in the training set. If a feature occurs fewer than 3 times, it is simply removed from the training data. All models are trained on training set I and evaluated on the devset.

[10] Despite the short average word length, we found that affixes up to size 4 worked better than affixes only up to size 2, perhaps mainly because they help with long proper nouns and temporal expressions.

morpheme. Thus for each prefix and suffix that occurs with each CTB tag in the training set I, we associate a set of binary features corresponding to each CTB tag. In the example below the prefix 资 occurred in both NN and VV words, but not AD or AS.

Prefix1=资, suffix1=袋
$F_{CTBM\text{-}pre}$= {(AD,0),(AS,0),...(NN,1),...(VV,1)}
$F_{CTBM\text{-}suf}$= {(AD,0),(AS,0),...(NN,1),...(VV,0)}

This model smoothes affix identity and the quantity of active CTBMorph features for a given affix expresses the degree of ambiguity associated with that affix.

Figure 2 Pseudo-code for CTBMorph

```
GenCTBMorphFeatureSet (Word W)
  FeatureSet f;
  for each t in CTB tag set:
    for each single-character prefix or suffix k of W
          if t.affixList contain k f.appendPair(t, 1)
      else f.appendPair(t, 0)
```

5.5.3 ASBC

One way to deal with robustness is to add more varied training data. For example the Academic Sinica Balanced Corpus[11] contains POS-tagged data from a different variety (Taiwanese Mandarin). But the tags in this corpus are not easily converted to the CTB tags. This problem of labeled data from very different tagsets can happen more generally. We introduce two alternative methods for making use of such a corpus.

5.5.3.1 ASBCMorph (ASBCM)

The ASBCMorph feature set is generated in an identical manner to the CTBMorph feature set, except that rather than generating the morpheme table using CTB, another corpus is used. The morpheme table is generated from the Academic Sinica Balanced Corpus, ASBC (Huang and Chen 1995), a 5 M word balanced corpus written in Taiwanese Mandarin. As the CTB annotation guide[12] states, the mapping between the tag sets used in the two corpora is nontrivial. As such, the ASBC data can not be directly used to augment the training set. However, using our ASBCMorph feature, we are still able to derive some benefit out of such an alternative corpus.

5.5.3.2 ASBCWord (ASBCW)

The ASBCWord feature is identical to the ASBCMorph feature, except that instead of using a table of tags that occur with each affix, we use a table of tags that a word occurs with in the ASBC data. Thus, a rare word in the CTB training/test set is augmented with features that correspond to all of the tags that the given word occurred with in the ASBC corpus, i.e. in this case, the pos tag of the identical word in ASBC, 资料袋.

W_i=资料袋
$F_{ASBCWord}$={(A,0),(Caa,0),(Cab,0)...(V_2,0)}

5.5.4 Verb affix

This feature set contains only two feature values, based on whether a list of verb affixes contains the prefix or suffix of an unknown word. We use the verb affix list created by the Chinese Knowledge Information Processing Group[13] at Academia Sinica. It contains 735 frequent verb prefixes and 282 frequent verb suffixes. For example,

Prefix1=资, suffix1=袋
F_{verb}={(verb prefix, 1), (verb suffix, 0)}

5.5.5 Radicals

Radicals are the basic building blocks of Chinese characters. There are over 214 radicals, and all Chinese characters contain one or more of them. Sometimes radicals reflect the meaning of a character. For example, the characters 猴 (monkey), 猪 (pig) 猫 (kitty cat) all contain the radical 犭 that roughly means "something that is an animal". For our radical based feature, we use the radical map from the Unihan database.[14] The radicals associated with the characters in the prefix and suffix of unknown words were incorporated into the model as features, for example:

Prefix1=资, suffix1=袋
$F_{RADICAL}$={(radical prefix, 贝), (radical suffix,衣)}

5.5.6 Named Entity Morpheme (NEM)

There is a convention that the suffix of a named entity points out the essential meaning of the named entity. For example, the suffix *bao* (newspaper) appears in Chinese translation of "WSJ", *huaerjierebao*. The suffix *he* (river) is used to identify rivers, for example in *huanghe* (yellow river).
To take advantage of this fact, we made 3 tables of named entity characters from the Chinese English Named Entity Lists (CENEL) (Huang 2002). These lists consist of a table of Chinese first name characters, a table of Chinese last name characters, and a

[11] The ASBC was originally encoded in traditional Big5 character, and we converted it to simplified GB.
[12] http://www.cis.upenn.edu/~chinese/posguide.3rd.ch.pdf
[13] http://turing.iis.sinica.edu.tw/affix/
[14] Unihan database is downloadable from their website: http://www.unicode.org/charts/unihan.html.

Table 8 Devset performance of the cumulatively rare word models, starting with the baseline. The second and third columns show the change in token accuracies and unknown word accuracies from the baseline for each feature introduced cumulatively. The fourth column shows the improvement from each feature set. The six columns on the right side of the table shows the error rate for the 5 most frequent tagsets of unknown words and the rest of unknown words.

				Error analysis: error rate % of unknown words in each POS					
Feature (add one in)	Token	Unk A%	Δ Unk A%	NN	VV	NR	PU	CD	Others
L_t+LL_t	88.27	51.16	-	16.67	57.14	68.25	100.00	16.56	60.86
+Suffix	89.70	60.74	9.58	12.50	41.65	44.75	100.00	5.30	37.25
+Prefix → **baseline**	90.03	63.66	2.92	10.55	36.62	40.00	100.00	3.97	34.76
+CTBM	91.48	76.13	12.47	13.74	31.99	36.00	1.99	0.00	20.58
+ASBCM	91.69	77.36	1.23	14.01	28.37	33.75	1.99	0.66	19.57
+ASBCW	91.85	78.84	1.48	13.30	23.54	33.50	1.42	0.00	17.93
+Verb affix	91.82	79.05	0.21	12.59	24.14	32.75	0.85	0.00	17.76
+Radical	91.85	79.09	0.04	11.88	24.75	33.50	0.85	0.00	18.78
+NEM	91.91	79.61	0.53	12.23	23.54	31.00	0.85	0.00	18.39
+Length→**best**	91.97	79.86	0.25	12.15	22.94	30.25	0.85	0.00	18.21

table of named entity suffixes such as organization, place, and company names in CENEL. Our named entity feature set contains 3 features, each corresponding to one of the three tables just described. To generate these features, first, we check if the prefix of an unknown is in the Chinese last name table. Second, we check if the suffix is in the Chinese first name table. Third, we check if the suffix of an unknown word is in the table of named entity suffixes. In Chinese last names are written in front of a first name, and the whole name is considered as a word, for example:

Prefix1=资, suffix1=袋
F_{NEM}={(last name, 0), (first name, 0), (NE suffix, 1)}

5.5.7 Length of a word

The length of a word can be a useful feature, because the majority of words in CTB have less than 3 characters. Words that have more than 3 characters are normally proper nouns, numbers, and idioms. Therefore, we incorporate this feature into the system. For example:

W_i=资料袋, F_{length}={(length , 3)}

5.5.8 Evaluation

Table 8 shows our results using the standard maximum entropy forward feature selection algorithm; at each iteration we add the feature family that most significantly improves the log likelihood of the training data given the model. We seed the feature space search with the features in Model L_t+LL_t. From this model, adding suffix information gives a 9.58% (absolute) gain on unknown word tagging. Subsequently adding in prefix makes unknown word accuracy go up to 63.66%. Our first result is that Chinese affixes are indeed informative for unknown words. On the right side of Table 8, we can see that this performance gain is derived from better tagging of common nouns, verbs, proper nouns, numbers and others. Because earlier work in many languages including Chinese uses these simple prefix and suffix features (Brants 2000, Ng and Low 2004) we consider this performance (63.66% on unknown words) as our baseline.

Adding in the feature set CTBM gives another 12.47% (absolute) improvement on unknown words. With this feature, punctuation shows the largest tagging improvement. The CTBM feature helps to identify punctuation since all other characters have been seen in different morpheme table made from the training set. That is, for a given word the lack of CTBM features cues that the word is a punctuation mark. Also, while this feature set generally helps all tagsets, it hurts a bit on nouns.

Adding in the ASBC feature sets yields another 1.23% and 1.48% (absolute) gains on unknown words. These two feature sets generally improve performance on all tagsets. Including the verb affix feature helps with common nouns and proper nouns, but hurts the performance on verbs. Overall, it yields 0.21% gain on unknown words. Finally, adding the radical feature helps the most on nouns, while subsequently adding in the name entity morphemes help to reduce the error on proper nouns by 2.50%. Finally, adding in feature length renders a 0.25% gain on unknown words. Commutatively, applying the feature sets results in an overall accuracy of 91.97% and an unknown word accuracy of 79.86%.

5.6 Experiments with the training sets of variable sizes and varieties

In this section, we compare our best model with the baseline model using different corpora size and language varieties in the training set. All the evaluations are reported on the test set, which has roughly equal amounts of data from XH, HKSAR, and SM.

The left column of Table 9 shows that when we train a model only on a single language variety and test on a mixed variety data, our unknown word accuracy is 79.50%, which is 18.48% (absolute) better than the baseline. The middle column shows when the training set is composed of different varieties and hence looks like the test set, performance of both the baseline and our best model improves.

Table 9 Comparison of the baseline and our best model. Using different training sets to evaluate on the test set. (McNemar's Test $p < .001$)

	Training I		*Training II*		*Training III*	
	Token	Unk	Token	Unk	Token	Unk
Base-line	89.17	61.02	92.54	74.78	93.51	81.11
Best	*91.34*	*79.50*	*93.00*	*81.62*	*93.74*	*86.33*

The right column shows the effect of doubling the training set size, using mixed varieties. As expected, using more data benefits both models.

These results show that having training data from different varieties is better than having data from one source. But crucially, our morphological-based features improve the tagging performance on unknown words even when the training set includes some data that resembles the test set.

How good are our best numbers, i.e. 93.7% on POS tagging in CTB 5.0? Unfortunately, there are no clean direct comparisons in the literature. The closest result in the literature is Xue et al. (2002), who re-train the Ratnaparkhi (1996) tagger and reach accuracies of 93% using CTB-I. However CTB-I contains only XH data and furthermore the data split is no longer known for this experiment (Xue p.c.) so a comparison is not informative. However, our performance on tagging when trained on Training I and tested on just the XH part of the test set is 94.44%, which might be a more relevant comparison to Xue et al. (2002).

6 Conclusion

Previous research in part-of-speech tagging has resulted in taggers that perform well when the training set and test set are both drawn from the same corpus. Unfortunately, for many potential real world applications, such an arrangement is just not possible.

Our results show that using sophisticated morphological features can help solve this robustness problem. These features would presumably also be applicable to other languages and NLP tasks that could benefit from the use of morphological information

Besides these tagging results, our research provides valuable analytic results on understanding the nature of unknown words cross-linguistically. Our results that unknown words in Chinese are not proper nouns like in English, but rather common nouns and verbs, suggest a similarity to German. We suggest this is because both German and Chinese, despite their huge differences in genetic, area, and other typological characteristics, tend to form unknown words through a similar word formation rule, compounding.

7 Acknowledgement

Thanks to Kristina Toutanova and Galen Andrew for their generous help and to the anonymous reviewers. This work was partially funded by ARDA AQUAINT and by NSF award IIS-0325646.

8 References

Bikel, Daniel and David Chiang. 2000. Two statistical parsing models applied to the Chinese Treebank. In *CLP* 2.

Brants, Thorsten. 2000. TnT: a statistical part-of-speech tagger. In *ANLP* 6.

Brants, Thorsten Wojciech Skut, Hans Uszkoreit. 1999. Syntactic Annotation of a German Newspaper Corpus In: *Anne Abeillé: ATALA sur le Corpus Annotés pour la Syntaxe Treebanks*.

Chao, Yuen Ren. 1968. *A Grammar of Spoken Chinese*. Berkeley: University of California Press.

Huang, Chu-ren. and Keh-Jiann Chen. 1995. Academic Sinica Balanced Corpus. Technical Report 95-02/98-04. Academic Sinica.

Huang, Shudong. 2002. Chinese <-> English Name Entity Lists Version 1.0 beta. Catalog number: LDC2003E01.

Li, Charles and Sandra A Thompson. 1981. *Mandarin Chinese: A Functional Reference Grammar*. Berkeley: University of California Press.

McCallum, Andrew, Dayne Freitag, Fernando Pereira. 2000. Maximum Entropy Markov Models for Information Extraction and Segmentation. In *ICML* 17.

Marcus, Mitchel, Beatrice Santorini and Mary Ann Marcinkiewicz. 1993. Building a large annotated corpus of English: The Penn Treebank. In *Computational Linguistics*, 19.

Ng, Hwee Tou and Jin Kiat Low. 2004. Chinese Part-of-Speech Tagging: One-at-a-Time or All-at-Once? Word-Based or Character-Based? In *EMNLP* 9.

Martha Palmer, Fu-Dong Chiou, Nianwen Xue, Tsan-Kuang Lee. 2005. Chinese Treebank 5.0. Catalog number: LDC2005T01.

Ratnaparkhi, Adwait. 1996. A maximum entropy model forpart-of-speech tagging. In *EMNLP* 1.

Thede, Scott and Mary P. Harper. 1999. Second-order hidden Markov model for part-of-speech tagging. In *ACL 37*.

Toutanova, Kristina, Dan Klein, Christopher Manning, and Yoram Singer. 2003. Feature-Rich Part-of-Speech Tagging with a Cyclic Dependency Network. In *HLT-NAACL* 2003.

Samuelsson, Christer. 1993. Morphological tagging based entirely on bayesian inference. In *NCCL* 9.

Xue, Nianwen, Fu-dong Chiou and Martha Palmer. 2002. Building a large-scale annotated Chinese corpus. In *COLING*.

Product Named Entity Recognition Based on Hierarchical Hidden Markov Model*

Feifan Liu, Jun Zhao, Bibo Lv, Bo Xu
National Laboratory of Pattern Recognition
Institute of Automation Chinese Academy of Sciences
Beijing P.O. Box 2728, 100080
{ffliu,jzhao,bblv,xubo}@nlpr.ia.ac.cn

Hao Yu
FUJITSU R&D
Xiao Yun Road No.26
Chao Yang District, Beijing, 100016
yu@frdc.fujitsu.com

Abstract

A hierarchical hidden Markov model (HHMM) based approach of product named entity recognition (NER) from Chinese free text is presented in this paper. Characteristics and challenges in product NER is also investigated and analyzed deliberately compared with general NER. Within a unified statistical framework, the approach we proposed is able to make probabilistically reasonable decisions to a global optimization by leveraging diverse range of linguistic features and knowledge sources. Experimental results show that our approach performs quite well in two different domains.

1 Introduction

Named entity recognition(NER) plays a significantly important role in information extraction(IE) and many other applications. Previous study on NER is mainly focused either on the proper name identification of person(*PER*), location(*LOC*), organization(*ORG*), time(*TIM*) and numeral(*NUM*) expressions almost in news domain, which can be viewed as general NER, or other named entity (NE) recognition in specific domain such as biology.

As far as we know, however, there is little prior research work conducted by far on product named entity recognition which can be crucial and valuable in many business IE applications, especially with the increasing research interest in Market Intelligence Management(MIM), Enterprise Content Management (ECM) [Pierre 2002] and *etc.*

This paper describes a prototype system for product named entity recognition, ProNER, in which a HHMM-based approach is employed. Within a unified statistical framework, the approach based on a mixture model is able to make probabilistically reasonable decisions to a global optimization by exploiting diverse range of linguistic features and knowledge sources. Experimental results show that ProNER performs quite well in two different domains.

2 Related Work

Up to now not much work has been done on product named entity recognition, nor systematic analysis of characteristics for this task. [Pierre 2002] developed an English NER system capable of identifying product names in product views. It employed a simple Boolean classifier for identifying product name, which was constructed from the list of product names. The method is similar to token matching and has a limitation for product NER applications. [Bick *et al.* 2004] recognized named entities including product names based on constraint grammar based parser for Danish. This rule-based approach is highly dependent on the performance of Danish parser and suffers from its weakness in system portability. [C. Niu *et al.* 2003] presented a bootstrapping approach for English named entity recognition using successive learners of parsing-based decision

[0]This work was supported by the Natural Sciences Foundation of China(60372016,60272041) and the Natural Science Foundation of Beijing(4052027).

System	*Statistical Model*	*Linguistic Feature*	*Combinative Points*
[Zhang *et al.* 2003]	HMM	semantic role, tokens	pattern rules
[Sun *et al.* 2002]	class-based LM	word form, NE category	cue words list
[Tsai *et al.* 2004]	ME model	tokens	knowledge representation

Table 1: Comparison between several Chinese NER systems[1]

list and HMM, and promising experiment results (F-measure: 69.8%) on product NE (corresponding to our *PRO*) were obtained. Its main advantage lies in that manual annotation of a sizable training corpus can be avoided, but it suffers from two problems, one is that it is difficult to find sufficient concept-based seeds needed in bootstrapping for the coverage of the variations of *PRO* subcategories, another it is highly dependent on parser performance as well.

Research on product NER is still at its early stage, especially in Chinese free text collections. However, considerable amount of work has been done in the last decade on the general NER task and biological NER task. The typical machine learning approaches for English NE are transformation-based learning[Aberdeen *et al.* 1995], hidden Markov model[Bikel *et al.* 1997], maximum entropy model[Borthwick, 1999], support vector machine learning[Eunji Yi *et al.* 2004], unsupervised model[Collins *et al.* 1999]and *etc.*

For Chinese NER, the prevailing methodology applied recently also lie in machine learning combining other knowledge base or heuristic rules, which can be compared on the whole in three aspects showed in Table 1.

In short, the trend in NER is to adopt a statistical framework which try to exploit some knowledge base as well as different level of text features within and outside NEs. Further those ideas, we present a hybrid approach based on HHMM [S. Fine *et al.* 1998] which will be described in detail.

3 Problem Statements and Analysis

3.1 Task Definition

3.1.1 Definition of Product Named Entity

In our study, only three kinds of product named entities are considered, namely *Brand Name(BRA)*, *Product Type(TYP)*, *Product Name(PRO)*, and *BRA* and *TYP* are often embedded in *PRO*. In the following two examples, there are two BRA NEs, one TYP NE and one PRO NE all of which belong to the family of product named entities.

Exam 1: 明基*(Benq)/**BRA*** 品牌(brand)市场占有率(market shares)稳步(steadily)上升(ascend)。

Exam 2: 公司(corporation)即将(will)推出(deliver) *[Canon/**BRA** 334万(ten thousand)像素(pixels)数码(digital)相机(camera) Pro90IS/**TYP**]/**PRO*** 。

Brand Name refer to proper name of product trademark such as "明基(Benq)" in Exam 1.

Product Type is a kind of product named entities indicating version or series information of product, which can consist of numbers, English characters, or other symbols such as "+" and "-" *etc.*In our study, two principles should be followed.

(1) Chinese characters are not considered to be *TYP*, nor subpart of *TYP* although some of them can contain version or series information. For instance, in "2005新年贺岁(happy new year)版(version)手机(cell phone)", here "新年贺岁(happy new year)版(version)"should not be considered as a *TYP*.

(2) Numbers are essential elements in product type entity. For instance, in "PowerShot 系列(series)数码(digital)相机(camera)", "PowerShot" is not considered as a *TYP*, however, in "PowerShot S10 数码(digital)相机(camera)", "PowerShot S10" can make up of a *TYP*.

Product Name, as showed above in Exam 2, is a kind of product named entities expressing self-contained proper name for some specified product in real world compared to *BRA* and *TYP* which only express one attribute of product. *i.e.* a *PRO* NE must be assigned with distinctly discriminative information which can not shared with other general product-related expressions.

[1]Note: LM(language model); ME(maximum entropy).

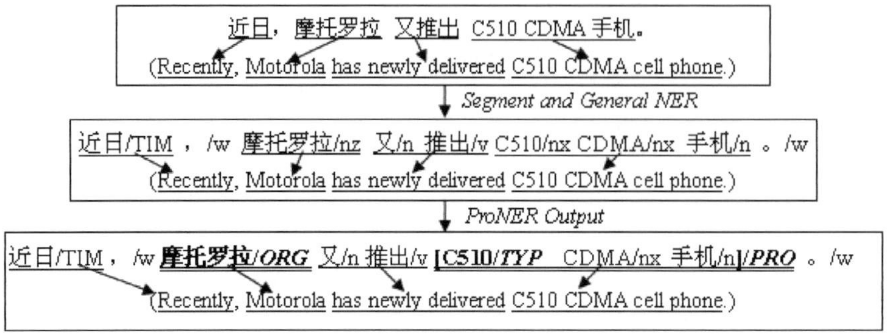

Figure 1 An Example of Product Named Entity Recognition Task

(1) Product-related expressions which are embedded with either *BRA* or *TYP* can be qualified to be a *PRO* entity. *e.g.* "BenQ闪存(flash)盘(disk)" is a *PRO* entity, but the general product-related expression "闪存(flash)市场(market)调查(investigation)" cannot make up of a *PRO* entity.

(2) Product-related expressions indicating some specific version or series information which is unique for a *BRA* can also be considered as a *PRO* entity. *e.g.* "DIGITAL IXUS系列(series)数码(digital)相机(camera)" is a *PRO* because "DIGITAL IXUS" series is unique for Canon product, but "智能(intelligent)型(version)手机(cell phone)" is not a *PRO* because the attribute of "intelligent version" can be assigned to any cell phone product.

3.1.2 Product Named Entity Recognition

Product named entity recognition involves the identification of product-related proper names in free text and their classification into different kinds of product named entities, referring to *PRO*, *TYP* and *BRA* in this paper.In comparison with general NER, nested product NEs should be tagged separately rather than being tagged just as a single item, shown as Figure 1.

3.2 Challenges for Product Named Entity Recognition

①For general named entities, there are some cues which are very useful for entity recognition, such as "市"(city), "公司"(Inc.), and *etc.* In comparison, product named entities have no such named conventions and cues, resulting in higher boundary ambiguities and more complex NE candidate triggering difficulties.

②In comparison with general NER, more challenges in product NER result from miscellaneous classification ambiguities. Many entities with identical form can be a kind of general named entity, a kind of product named entity, or just common words.

③In comparison with general named entities, product named entities show more flexible variant forms. The same entity can be expressed in several different forms due to spelling variation, word permutation and *etc.* This also compounds the difficulties in product named entity recognition.

④In comparison with general named entities, it is more frequent that product named entities are nested as *Figure* 1 illustrates. More efforts have to be made to identify such named entities separately.

3.3 Our Solutions

We adopt the following strategies in triggering and disambiguating process respectively.

(1) As to product NER, it's pivotal to control the triggering candidates efficiently for the balance between precision and recall. Here we use the knowledge base such as brand word list, and other heuristic information which can be easily acquired.

(2)After triggering candidates, we try to employ a statistical model to make the most of multi-level context information mentioned above in disambiguation. We choose hierarchical hidden Markov model (HHMM) [S. Fine et al. 1998] for its more powerful ability to model the multiplicity of length scales and recursive nature of sequences.

4 Hybrid Approach for Product NE Recognition

4.1 Overall Workflow of ProNER

①***Preprocessing:*** Segment, POS tagging and general NER is primarily conducted using our off-shelf SegNer2.0 toolkit on input text.

②***Generating Product NE Candidates:*** First, *BRA* or *ORG* and *TYP* are triggered by brand word list and some word features respectively. Here we categorize the triggering word features into six classes: alphabet string, alphanumeric string, digits, alphabet string with fullwidth, digits with fullwidth and other symbols except Chinese characters. Then *PRO* are triggered by *BRA* and *TYP* candidates as well as some clue words indicating type information to some extent such as "版"(version), "系列"(series). In this step the model structure(topology) of HHMM[S. Fine *et al.* 1998] is dynamically constructed, and some conjunction words or punctuations and specified maximum length of product NE are used to control it.

③***Disambiguating Candidates:*** In this module, boundary and classification ambiguities between candidates are resolved simultaneously. And Viterbi algorithm is applied for most-likely state sequences based on the HHMM topology.

4.2 Integration with Heuristic Information

To get more efficient control in triggering process above, we try to integrate some heuristic information. The heuristic rules we used are as domain-independent as possible in order that they can be integrated with statistical model systematically rather than just some tricks on it.

(1) Stop Word List:

Common English words, English brand word, and some punctuations are extracted automatically from training set to make up of stop word list for *TYP*; by co-occurrence statistics between *ORG* and its contexts, some words are extracted from the contexts to make up of stop word list for *PRO* in order to overcome the case that brand word is prone to bind its surroundings to be a *PRO*.

(2) Constrain Rules:

Rule 1: For the highly frequent pattern "数字+英文量词"(number + English quantifier word), all the corresponding *TYP* candidates triggered by categorized word features(CWF) should be removed.

Rule 2: Product NE candidates in which some binate symbols don't match each other should be removed.

Rule 3: Unreasonable symbols such as "-" or ":" should not occur in the beginning or end of product NE candidates.

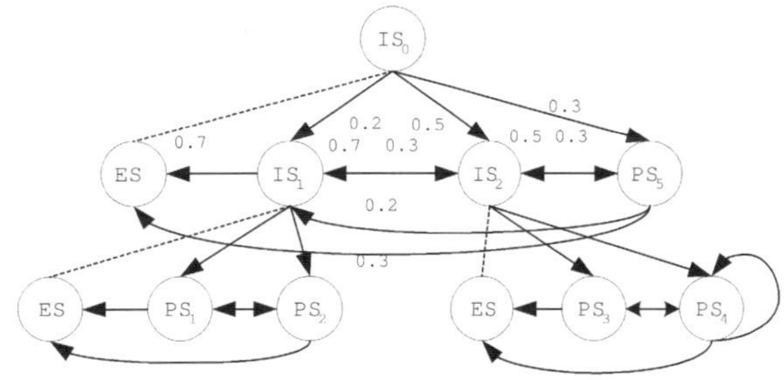

Figure 2 Structure of Hierarchical Hidden Markov Model (HHMM)

4.3 HHMM for product NER application

By HHMM [S. Fine *et al.* 1998] the product NER can be formulated as a tagging problem using Viterbi algorithm. Unlike traditional HMM in POS tagging, here the topology of HHMM is not fixed and internal states can be also a similar stochastic model on themselves, called internal states compared to production states which will emit only observations.

Our HHMM structure actually consists of three level approximately illustrated as figure 2 in which *IS* denotes internal state, *PS* denotes production state and *ES* denote end state at every level. For our application, an input sequence from our SegNer2.0 toolkit can be formalized as $w_1/t_1 w_2/t_2 \ldots w_i/t_i \ldots w_n/t_n$, among which w_i and t_i is the *i*th word and its part-of-speech, n is the number of words. The POS tag set here is the combination of tag set from Peking University(***PKU-POS***) and our general NE categories(***GNEC***) including *PER*(person), *LOC*(location), *ORG*(organization), *TIM*(time expression), *NUM*(numeric expression). Therefore we can construct our HHMM model by the state set {S} consisting of {***GNEC***}, {*BRA*, *PRO*, *TYP*}, and {***V***} as well as the observation set {O} consisting of {V} which is the word set from training data. That is to say, the word forms in {V} which are not included in NEs are also viewed as production states.

In our model, only *PRO* are internal state which may activate other production states such as *BRA* and *TYP* resulting in recursive HMM. In consistence with S. Fine's work, q_i^d ($1 \leq d \leq D$) is used to indicate the *i*th state in the *d*th level of hierarchy. So, the product NER problem is to find the most-likely state activation sequence Q*, a multi-scale list of states, based on the dynamic topology of HHMM given a observation sequence W = $w_1 w_2 \ldots w_i \ldots w_n$, formulated as follows based on Bayes rule ($P(W)$=1).

$$Q^* = \arg\max_Q P(Q|W) = \arg\max_Q P(Q)P(W|Q) \quad (1)$$

From the root node of HHMM, activity flows to all other nodes at different levels according to their transition probability. For description convenience, we take the *k*th level as example(activated by the *m*th state at the *k-1*th level).

$$P(Q) \cong \underbrace{p(q_1^k|q_m^{k-1})}_{vertical\ transition} \overbrace{p(q_2^k|q_1^k)\prod_{j=3}^{|q^k|} p(q_j^k|q_{j-1}^k, q_{j-2}^k)}^{horizontal\ transition} \quad (2)$$

$$P(W|Q) = \begin{cases} \cong \prod_{j=1}^{|q_{PS}^k|} p([w_{q_j^k-begin} \cdots w_{q_j^k-end}]|q_j^k) \\ \qquad if\ q_j^k \notin \{IS\} \\ activate\ other\ states\ recursively \\ \qquad if\ q_j^k \in \{IS\} \end{cases} \quad (3)$$

Where $|q^k|$ is the number of all states and $|q_{PS}^k|$ is the number of production states in the kth level; $w_{q_j^k-begin} \cdots w_{q_j^k-end}$ indicates the word sequence corresponding to the state q_j^k.

(1) In equation (3), if $q_j^k \in$ {{***GNEC***},{***V***}}, $p([w_{q_j^k-begin} \cdots w_{q_j^k-end}]|q_j^k)$=1, because we assume that the general NER results from the preceding toolkit are correct;

(2) If $q_j^k = PRO$, production states in the (k+1)th level will be activated by this internal state through equation (2),(3) and go back when arriving at an end state, thus hierarchical computation is implemented;

(3) If $q_j^k = BRA$, we assign equation (3) a constant value in that *BRA* candidates consist of only a single brand word in our method. In addition brand word can also generate *ORG* candidates, thus we can assign equation (3) as follows.

$$p([w_{q_j^k-begin} \cdots w_{q_j^k-end}]|q_j^k = BRA) = 0.5 \quad (4)$$

(4) If $q_j^k = TYP$, categorized word features(CWFs) defined in section 4.1 are applied, *i.e.* the words associated with the current state are replaced with their CWFs (WC) acting as observations. Then we can compute the emission probability of this *TYP* production state as the following equation, among which $|q_j^k|$ is the length of observation sequence associated with the current state.

$$p([w_{q_j^k-begin} \cdots w_{q_j^k-end}]|q_j^k = TYP)$$
$$\cong p(wc_1|begin)p(end|wc_{|q_j^k|}) \prod_{m=2}^{|q_j^k|} p(wc_m|wc_{m-1})$$

All the parameters in every level of HHMM can be acquired using maximum likelihood method with smoothing from training data.

4.4 Mixture of Two Hierarchical Hidden Markov Models

Now we have implemented a simple HHMM for product NER. Note that in the above model(HHMM-1), we exploit both internal and external features of product NEs only at levels of simply semantic classification and just word form. To achieve our motivation in section 3.3, we construct another HHMM(HHMM-2) for exploiting multi-level contexts by mixing with HHMM-1.

In HHMM-2, the difference from HHMM-1 lies in the state set S_{II} and observation set O_{II}. Because the input text will be processed by segment, POS tagging and general NER, as a alternative, we can also take T=$t_1 t_2 \ldots t_i \ldots t_n$ as observation sequence, *i.e.* O_{II}={PKU-POS}. Accordingly, S_{II}= {{PKU-POS}, {GNEC}, BRA, TYP,

Data Sets	PRO	BRA	TYP	PER	LOC	ORG
DataSetPRO1.2	12,432	5,047	10,606	424	1,733	4,798
OpenTestSet	1800	803	1364	39	207	614
CloseTestSet	1553	513	1296	55	248	619

Table 2: Overview of Data Sets

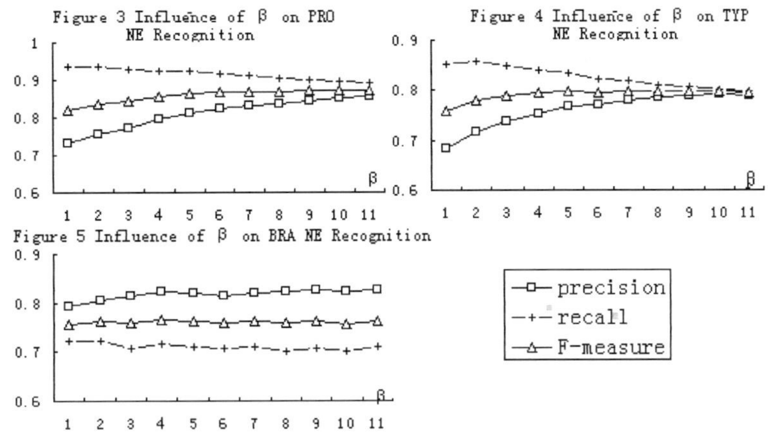

PRO}, among which *PRO* is internal state. Similarly, the problem is formulated as follows with HHMM-2.

$$\begin{aligned} Q^*_{II} &= \arg\max_{Q_{II}} P(Q_{II}|T) \\ &= \arg\max_{Q_{II}} P(Q_{II})P(T|Q_{II}) \end{aligned} \quad (5)$$

The description and computation of HHMM-2 is similar to HHMM-1 and is omitted here.

We can see that besides making use of semantic classification of NEs in common, HHMM-1 and HHMM-2 exploit word form and part-of-speech (POS) features respectively. Word form features make the model more discriminative, while POS features result in robustness. Intuitively, the mixture of these two models is desirable for higher performance in product NER by balancing the robustness and discrimination which can be formulated in logarithmic form as follows.

$$\begin{aligned} &(Q^*, Q^*_{II}) \\ &= \arg\max_{Q,Q_{II}} \{\log(P(Q)) + \log(P(W|Q)) \\ &+ \beta[\log(P(Q_{II})) + \log(P(T|Q_{II}))]\} \end{aligned} \quad (6)$$

Where β is a tuning parameter for adjusting the weight of two models.

5 Experiments and analysis

5.1 Data Set Preparation

A large number of web pages in mobile phone and digital domain are compiled into text collections, DataSetPRO, on which multi-level processing were performed. Our final version, DataSetPRO1.2, consists of 1500 web pages, roughly 1,000,000 Chinese characters. Randomly selected 140 texts (digital 70, mobile phone 70) are separated from DataSetPRO1.2 as our OpenTestSet, the rest as TrainingSet, from which 160 texts are extracted as CloseTestSet. Table 2 illustrates the overview of them.

5.2 Experiments

Due to various and flexible forms of product NEs, though some boundaries of recognized NEs are inconsistent with manual annotation, they are also reasonable. So soft evaluation is also applied in our experiments to make the evaluation more reasonable. The main idea is that a discount score will be given to recognized NEs with wrong boundary but correct detection and classification. However, strict evaluation only score completely correct ones.

All the results is conducted on OpenTestSet unless it is particularly specified. Also, the evaluation scores used below are obtained mainly by

Digital Domain (β=8)						
Product NEs	Close Test			Open Test		
	Precision	Recall	F-measure	Precision	Recall	F-measure
PRO	0.864	0.799	0.830	0.762	0.744	0.753
TYP	0.903	0.906	0.905	0.828	0.944	0.882
BRA	0.824	0.702	0.758	0.723	0.705	0.714
Mobile Phone Domain (β=8)						
Product NEs	Close Test			Open Test		
	Precision	Recall	F-measure	Precision	Recall	F-measure
PRO	0.917	0.935	0.926	0.799	0.856	0.827
TYP	0.959	0.976	0.967	0.842	0.886	0.864
BRA	0.911	0.741	0.818	0.893	0.701	0.785

Table 3: Experimental Results in Digital and Mobile Phone Domain

soft metrics, and strict scores are also given for comparison in experiment 3.

1. Evaluation on the Influence of β in the Mixture Model.

In the mixture model denoted as equation (6), the β value reflects the different contribution of two individual models to the overall system performance. The larger β, the more contribution made by HHMM-2. Figure 3, 4, 5 illustrate the varying curves of recognition performance with the β value on *PRO*, *TYP*, *BRA* respectively.

Note that, if β equal to 1 then two models are mixed with equivalent weight. We can see that, as β goes up, the F-measures of *PRO* and *TYP* increase obviously firstly, and begin to go down slightly after a period of growing flat. It can be explained that HHMM-2 mainly exploits part-of-speech and general NER features which can relieve the sparseness problem to some extent, which is more serious in HHMM-1 due to using lower level of contextual information such as word form. However, as β becomes larger, the problem of imprecise modeling in HHMM-2 will be more salient and begin to illustrate a side-effect in the mixture model. Whereas, the influence of β on *BRA* is negligible because its candidates are triggered by the relatively reliable knowledge base and its sub-model in HHMM is assigned a constant as shown in equation(4).

Summings-up:

(1) Mixture with HHMM-2 can make up the weakness of HHMM-1.

(2) HHMM-2 can make more contributions to the mixture model under the conditions that limited annotated data is available at present. In our system, β is assigned to 8 based on above experimental results.

2. Evaluation on the portability of ProNER in two domains.

First, we can see from Table 3 that ProNER have achieved fairly high performance in both digital and mobile phone domain. This can validate to some extent the portability of our system, which is consistent with our initial motivation.

Second, the results also show that our system performs slightly better in mobile phone domain for both close test and open test. This can be explained that there are more challenging ambiguities in digital domain due to more complex product taxonomy and more flexible variants of product NEs.

Summings-up: *The results provide promising evidence on the portability of our system to different domains though there are some differences between them.*

3. Evaluation on the efficiency of the mixture model and the improvement of the triggering control with heuristics.

In table 4, "1" denotes HHMM-1; "2" denotes HHMM-2; "+" means the mixture model; "*" means integrating with heuristics mentioned in section 4.2.

The results reveal that the mixture model outperforms each individual model with both soft and strict metrics. Also, the results show that heuristic information can increase the F-measure of *PRO* and *TYP* by 10 points or so for both indi-

HHMM	*BRA*		*TYP*		*PRO*	
	strict score	soft score	strict score	soft score	strict score	soft score
1	0.68	0.72	0.57	0.66	0.52	0.61
1*	0.70	0.74	0.70	0.80	0.63	0.72
2	0.67	0.73	0.66	0.74	0.61	0.68
2*	0.70	0.74	0.76	0.85	0.70	0.76
1+2	0.70	0.75	0.67	0.77	0.67	0.72
1+2*	0.72	0.76	0.76	0.87	0.75	0.80

Table 4: Improvement results (F-measure) with heuristics and model mixture

vidual model and the mixture model. Additionally we can see that HHMM-2 performs better on the whole than HHMM-1, which is consistent with experiment 1 that heavier weights should be assigned to HHMM-2 in the mixture model.

Summings-up:

(1) Either HHMM-1 or HHMM-2 can not perform quite well independently, but systematical integration of them can achieve obvious performance improvement due to the leverage of diverse levels of linguistic features by their efficient interaction.

(2) Heuristic information can highly enhance the performance for both individual model and the mixture model.

6 Conclusions and Future Work

This paper presented a hierarchical HMM (hidden Markov model) based approach of product named entity recognition from Chinese free text. By unifying some heuristic rules into a statistical framework based on a mixture model of HHMM, the approach we proposed can leverage diverse range of linguistic features and knowledge sources to make probabilistically reasonable decisions for a global optimization. The prototype system we built achieved the overall F-measure of 79.7%, 86.9%, 75.8% corresponding to *PRO*, *TYP*, *BRA* respectively, which also provide experimental evidence to some extent on its portability to different domains.

Our future work will focus on the following:

(1) Using long dependency information;

(2) Integrating segment, POS tagging, general NER and product NER to avoid error spread.

References

John M. Pierre. (2002) Mining Knowledge from Text Collections Using Automatically Generated Metadata. In: *Procs of Fourth International Conference on Practical Aspects of Knowledge Management.*

Michael Collins and Yoram Singer. (1999) Unsupervised Models for Named Entity Classification. In: *Proc. of EMNLP/VLC-99.*

Eunji Yi, Gary Geunbae Lee, and Soo-Jun Park. (2004) SVM-based Biological Named Entity Recognition using Minimum Edit-Distance Feature Boosted by Virtual Examples. In: *Proceedings of the First International Joint Conference on Natural Language Processing (IJCNLP-04).*

Bick, Eckhard (2004) A Named Entity Recognizer for Danish. In: *Proc. of 4th International Conf. on Language Resources and Evaluation*,pp:305-308.

Jian Sun, Jianfeng Gao, Lei Zhang, Ming Zhou, Changning Huang. (2002) Chinese Named Entity Identification Using Class-based Language Model. In: *COLING 2002*. Taipei, Taiwan.

Huaping Zhang, Qun Liu, Hongkui Yu, Xueqi Cheng, Shuo Bai. Chinese Named Entity Recognition Using Role Model. *Special Iissue "Word Formation and Chinese Language processing" of the International Journal of Computational Linguistics and Chinese Language Processing*, 8(2),2003, pp:29-60

Aberdeen, John *et al.* (1995)MITRE: Description of the ALEMBIC System Used for MUC-6. *Proc. of MUC-6*, pp. 141-155

D.M. Bikel, S. Miller, R. Schwartz, R. Weischedel. (1997) Nymble: a High-Performance Learning Name-finder. In: *Fifth Conference on Applied Natural Language Processing*, pp 194-201.

Borthwick. A. (1999) A Maximum Entropy Approach to Named Entity Recognition. PhD Dissertation.

Tzong-Han Tsai, S.H. Wu, C.W. Lee, Cheng-Wei Shih, and Wen-Lian Hsu. (2004) Mencius: A Chinese Named Entity Recognizer Using the Maximum Entropy-based Hybrid Model. *International Journal of Computational Linguistics and Chinese Language Processing*, Vol. 9, No 1.

Cheng Niu, W. Li, J.h. Ding and R.K. Srihari. (2003) A Bootstrapping Approach to Named Entity Classification Using Successive Learners. In: *Proceedings of the 41st ACL*, Sapporo, Japan, pp:335-342.

S. Fine, Y. Singer, N. Tishby. (1998) The Hierarchical Hidden Markov Model: Analysis and Applications. *Machine Learning*. 32(1), pp:41-62

Chinese Sketch Engine and

the Extraction of Grammatical Collocations

Chu-Ren Huang	Adam Kilgarriff	Yiching Wu	Chih-Ming Chiu
Inst. of Linguistics	Lexicography MasterClass	Inst. of Linguistics	Inst. of Information Science
Academia Sinica	Information Technology	Tsing Hua University	Academia Sinica
churen@sinica.edu.tw	adam@lexmasterclass.com	d898702@oz.nthu.edu.tw	henning@hp.iis.sinica.edu.tw

Simon Smith	Pavel Rychly	Ming-Hong Bai	Keh-Jiann Chen
Dept. of Applied English	Faculty of Informatics	Inst. of Information Science	Inst. of Information Science
Ming Chuan University	Masaryk University.	Academia Sinica	Academia Sinica
ssmith@mcu.edu.tw	pary@textforge.cz	mhbai@sinica.edu.tw	kchen@iis.sinica.edu.tw

Abstract. This paper introduces a new technology for collocation extraction in Chinese. Sketch Engine (Kilgarriff et al., 2004) has proven to be a very effective tool for automatic description of lexical information, including collocation extraction, based on large-scale corpus. The original work of Sketch Engine was based on BNC. We extend Sketch Engine to Chinese based on Gigaword corpus from LDC. We discuss the available functions of the prototype Chinese Sketch Engine (CSE) as well as the robustness of language-independent adaptation of Sketch Engine. We conclude by discussing how Chinese-specific linguistic information can be incorporated to improve the CSE prototype.

1. Introduction

The accessibility to large scale corpora, at one billion words or above, has become both a blessing and a challenge for NLP research. How to efficiently use a gargantuan corpus is an urgent issue concerned by both users and corpora designers. Adam Kilgarriff et al. (2004) developed the Sketch Engine to facilitate efficient use of corpora. Their claims are two folded: that genuine linguistic generalizations can be automatically extracted from a corpus with simple collocation information provided that the corpus is large enough; and that such a methodology is easily adaptable for a new language. The first claim was fully substantiated with their work on BNC. The current paper deals with the second claim by adapting the Sketch Engine to Chinese.

2. Online Chinese Corpora: The State of the Arts

2.1 Chinese Corpora

The first online tagged Chinese corpus is Academia Sinica Balanced Corpus of Modern Chinese (Sinica Corpus), which has been web-accessible since November, 1996. The current version contains 5.2028 million words (7.8927 million characters). The corpus data was collected between 1990 and 1996 (CKIP, 1995/1998). Two additional Chinese corpora were made available on line in 2003. The first is the Sinorama Chinese-English Parallel Text Corpus (Sinorama Corpus). The Sinorama Corpus is composed of 2,373 parallel texts in both Chinese and English that were published between 1976 and 2000. There are 103,252 pairs of sentences, composed of roughly 3.2 million

English words and 5.3 million Chinese characters[1]. The second one is the modern Chinese corpus developed by the Center for Chinese Linguistics (CCL Corpus) at Peking University. It contains eighty-five million (85,398,433) simplified Chinese characters which were published after 1919 A.D.

2.2 Extracting Linguistic Information from Online Chinese Corpora: Tools and Interfaces

The Chinese corpora discussed above are all equipped with an online interface to allow users to extract linguistic generalizations. Both Sinica Corpus and CCL Corpus offer KWIC-based functions, while Sinorama Corpus gives sentence and paragraph aligned output.

2.2.1 String Matching or Word Matching

The basic unit of query that a corpus allows defines the set of information that can be extracted from that corpus. While there is no doubt that segmented corpus allows more precise linguistic generalizations, string-based collocation still afford a corpus of the robustness that is not restricted by an arbitrary word-list or segmentation algorithm. This robustness is of greatest value when extracting neologism or sub-lexical collocations. Since CCL Corpus is not segmented and tagged, string-based KWIC is its main tool for extracting generalizations. This comes with the familiar pitfall of word boundary ambiguity. For instance, a query of *ci.yao* 次要 'secondary' may yield the intended result (la), as well as noise (1b).

1a. 但这是次要的
dan zhe shi ci.yao de
but this is secondary DE
'But this is secondary'

b. 他几次要求她答复
ta ji ci yao.qiu ta da.fu
he several time ask her answer
'He had asked her to answer for several times'

[1]http://cio.nist.gov/esd/emaildir/lists/mt_list/msg00033.html

Sinica Corpus, on the other hand, is fully segmented and allows word-based generalizations. In addition, Sinica Corpus also allows wildcards in its search. Users specify a wildcard of arbitrary length (*), or fixed length (?). This allows search of a class of words sharing some character strings.

2.2.2 Display of Extracted Data

Formal restriction on the display of extracted data also constraints the type of information that can be obtained from that corpus. Sinica Corpus allows users to change window size from about 25 to 57 Chinese characters. However, since a Chinese sentence may be longer than 57 characters, Sinica Corpus cannot guarantee that a full sentence is displayed. CCL Corpus, on the other hand, is able to show a full output sentence, which may be up to 200 Chinese characters. However, it does not display more than a full sentence. Thus it cannot show discourse information. Sinorama Corpus with TOTALrecall interface is most versatile in this respect. Aligned bilingual full sentences are shown with an easy link to the full text.

In terms of size and completeness of extracted data, Sinica Corpus returns all matched examples. However, cut and paste must be performed for the user to build his/her dataset. CCL Corpus, on the other hand, limits data to 500 lines per page, but allows easy download of output data. Lastly, Sinorama/TOTALrecall provides choices of 5 to 100 sentences per page.

2.2.3 Refining Extracted Information: Filter and Sorter

Both Sinica Corpus and CCL corpus allows users to process extracted information, using linguistic and contextual filter or sorter. The CCL corpus requires users to remember the rules, while Sinica Corpus allows users to fill in blanks and/or choose from pull-down menu. In particular, Sinica Corpus allows users to refine their generalization by quantitatively characterizing the left and right contexts. The quantitative sorting functions allowed include both word and POS frequency, as well as word mutual information.

2.2.4 Extracting Grammatical Information

Availability of grammatical information depends on corpus annotation. CCL and Sinorama Corpus do not have POS tags. Sinica Corpus is the only Chinese corpus allowing users to access an overview of a keyword's syntactic behavior. Users can obtain a list of types and distribution of the keyword's syntactic category. In addition, users can find possible collocations of the keyword from the output of Mutual Information (MI).

The most salient grammatical information, such as grammatical functions (subject, object, adjunct etc.) is beyond the scope of the traditional corpus interface tools. Traditional corpora rely on the human users to arrive at these kinds of generalizations.

3. Sketch Engine: A New Corpus-based approach to Grammatical Information

Several existing linguistically annotated corpus of Chinese, e.g. Penn Chinese Tree Bank (Xia et al., 2000), Sinica Treebank (Chen et al., 2003), Proposition Bank (Xue and Palmer, 2003, 2005) and Mandarin VerbNet (Wu and Liu, 2003), suffer from the same problem. They are all extremely labor-intensive to build and typically have a narrow coverage. In addition, since structural assignment is theory-dependent and abstract, inter-annotator consistency is difficult to achieve. Since there is also no general consensus on the annotation scheme in Chinese NLP and linguistics, building an effective interface for public use is almost impossible.

The Sketch Engine offers an answer to the above issues.

3.1 Initial Implementation and Design of the Sketch Engine

The Sketch Engine is a corpus processing system developed in 2002 (Kilgarriff and Tugwell, 2002; Kilgarriff et al., 2004). The main components of the Sketch Engine are KWIC concordances, word sketches, grammatical relations, and a distributional thesaurus. In its first implementation, it takes as input basic BNC (British National Corpus, (Leech, 1992)) data: the annotated corpus, as well as list of lemmas with frequencies. In other words, the Sketch Engine has a relatively low threshold for the complexity of input corpus.

The Sketch Engine has a versatile query system. Users can restrict their query in any sub-corpus of BNC. A query string may be a word (with or without POS specification), or a phrasal segment. A query can also be performed using Corpus Query Language (CQL). The output display format can be adjusted, and the displayed window of a specific item can be freely expanded left and right. Most of all, the Sketch Engine produces a Word Sketch (Kilgarriff and Tugwell, 2002) that is an automatically generated grammatical description of a lemma in terms of corpus collocations. All items in each collocation are linked back to the original corpus data. Hence it is similar to a

Linguistic Knowledge Net anchored by a lexicon (Huang et al., 2001).

A Word Sketch is a one-page list of a keyword's functional distribution and collocation in the corpus. The functional distribution includes: subject, object, prepositional object, and modifier. Its collocations are described by a list of linguistically significant patterns in the language. Word Sketch uses regular expressions over POS-tags to formalize rules of collocation patterns, e.g. (2) is used to retrieve the verb-object relation in English:

2. 1:"V" "(DET|NUM|ADJ|ADV|N)"* 2:"N"

The expression in (2) says: extract the data containing a verb followed by a noun regardless of how many determiners, numerals, adjectives, adverbs and nouns preceding the noun. It can extract data containing *cook meals* and *cooking a five-course gala dinner*, and *cooked the/his/two surprisingly good meals* etc.

The Sketch Engine also produces thesaurus lists, for an adjective, a noun or a verb, the other words most similar to it in their use in the language (Kilgarriff et al. 2004). For instance, the top five synonym candidates for the verb *kill* are *shoot* (0.249), *murder* (0.23), *injure* (0.229), *attack* (0.223), and *die* (0.212).[2] It also provides direct links to the Sketch Difference which lists the similar and different patterns between a keyword and its similar word. For example, both *kill* and *murder* can occur with objects such as *people* and *wife*, but *murder* usually occurs with personal proper names and seldom selects animal nouns as complement whereas *kill* can take *fox, whale, dolphin*, and *guerrilla,* etc. as its object.

The Sketch Engine adopts Mutual Information (MI) to measure the salience of a collocation. Salience data are shown against each collocation in Word Sketches and other Sketch Engine output. MI provides a measure of the degree of association of a given segment with others. Pointwise MI, calculated by Equation 3, is what is used in lexical processing to return the degree of association of two words x and y (a **collocation**).

3. $$I(x;y) = \log\frac{P(x \mid y)}{P(x)}$$

3.2 Application to Chinese Corpus

In order to show the cross-lingual robustness of the Sketch Engine as well as to propose a powerful tool for collocation extraction based on a large scale corpus with minimal pre-processing; we constructed Chinese Sketch Engine (CSE) by loading the Chinese Gigaword to the Sketch Engine (Kilgarriff et al., 2005). The Chinese Gigaword contains about 1.12 billion Chinese characters, including 735 million characters from Taiwan's Central News Agency, and 380 million characters from China's Xinhua News Agency[3]. Before loading Chinese Gigaword into Sketch Engine, all the simplified characters were converted into traditional characters, and the texts were segmented and POS tagged using the Academia Sinica segmentation and tagging system (Huang et al., 1997). An array of machine was used to process the 1.12 million characters, which took over 3 days to perform. All components of the Sketch Engine were implemented, including Concordance, Word Sketch, Thesaurus and Sketch Difference.

In our initial in-house testing of this prototype of the Chinese Sketch Engine, it does

[2] The similarity is measured and ranked adopting Lin's (1998) mathematics.

[3] http://www.ldc.upenn.edu/Catalog/CatalogEntry.jsp?catalogId=LDC2003T09

produce the expected results with an easy to use interface. For instance, the Chinese Word Sketch correctly shows that the most common and salient object of *dai.bu* 逮捕 'to arrest' is *xian.fan* 嫌犯 'suspect'; the most common subject *jing.fang* 警方 'police'; and the most common modifier *dang.chang* 當場.

The output data of Thesaurus correctly verify the following set of synonyms from the Chinese VerbNet Project: that *ren.wei* 認為 'to think' behaves most like *biao.shi* 表示 'to express, to state' (salience 0.451), while *yi.wei* 以為 'to take somebody/something as' is more like *jue.de* 覺得 'to feel, think' (salience 0.488). The synonymous relation can be illustrated by (4) and (5).

4a. 他認為到海外投資有一個觀念很重要，就是要知道當地的遊戲規則，接受這些條件。

ta ren.wei dao hai.wai tou.zi you yi ge guan.nian hen zhong.yao, jiu shi yao zhi.dao dang.di de you.xi gui.ze

'He believes that for those investing overseas, there is a very important principle-one must know the local rules of the game, and accept them.'

b. 執政黨也表示，由於公視爭議太大，恐怕無法全力支持。

zhi.zheng.dang ye biao.shi, you.yu gong.shi zheng.yi tai da, kong.pa wu.fa quan.li zhi.chi

'The KMT also commented that due to the many controversies surrounding PTV, it could not wholeheartedly support it either.'

5a. 何家駒就認為：「電視有基本語言和文法，要講究賣點和市場。」

he.jia.ju jiu ren.wei：「dian.shi you ji.ben yu.yan he wen.fa, yao jiang.jiu mai.dian he shi.chang。」

'Ho Chia-chu says, "Television has its own fundamental language and grammar. You must consider selling points and the market."'

b. 她表示：「我希望佛教徒能瞭解，父權社會與覺悟的社會是不相合的。」

ta biao.shi：「wo xi.wang fuo.jiao.tu neng liao.jie, fu.quan she.hui yu jue.wu de she.hui shi bu xiang.he de。」

'She says "I hope that followers of Buddhism can realize that a patriarchal society is incompatible with an enlightened society."'

The above examples show that *ren.wei* and *biao.shi* can take both direct and indirect quotation. *Yi.wei* and *jue.de*, on the other hand, can only be used in reportage and cannot introduce direct quotation.

Distinction between near synonymous pairs can be obtained from Sketch Difference. This function is verified with results from Tsai et al.'s study on *gao.xing* 高興 'glad' and *kuai.le* 快樂 'happy' (Tsai et al., 1998). *Gao.xing* 'glad' specific patterns include the negative imperative *bie* 別 'don't'. It also has a dominant collocation with the potentiality complement marker *de* 得 (e.g. *ta gao xing de you jiao you tiao* 她高興得又叫又跳 'she was so happy that she cried and danced'). In contrast, *kuai.le* 'happy' has the specific collocation with holiday nouns such as *qiu.jie* 秋節 'Autumn Festival'. The Sketch Difference result is consistent with the account that *gao.xing/kuai.le* contrast is that inchoative state vs. homogeneous state.

4. Evaluation and Future Developments

An important feature of the prototype of the Chinese Sketch Engine is that, in order to test the robustness of the Sketch Engine design, the original regular expression patterns were adopted with minimal modification for Chinese. Even though both are SVO languages with similar surface word order, it is obvious that they differ substantially in terms of assignment of grammatical functions. In addition, the Sinica tagset is different from the BNC tagset and actually has much richer functional information. These are the two main directions that we will pursue in modification and improvement of the Chinese Sketch Engine.

4.1 Word Boundary Representation

Word breaks are not conventionalized in Chinese texts. This poses a challenge in Chinese language processing. The Chinese Sketch Engine inserted space after segmentation, which helps to visualize words. In the future, it will be trivial to allow the conventional alternative of no word boundary markups. However, it will not be trivial to implement fuzzy function to allow searches for non-canonical lemmas (i.e. lemmas that are segmented differently from the standard corpus).

4.2 Sub-Corpora Comparison

The Chinese Gigaword corpus is marked with two different genres, story and non-story. A still more salient sub-corpus demarcation is the one between Mainland China corpus and Taiwan corpus. Sketch Difference between lemmas form two sub-corpora is being planned. This would allow future comparative studies and would have wide applications in the localization adaptations of language related applications.

4.3 Collating Frequency Information with POS

One of the convenient features of Sketch Engine that a frequency ranked word list is linked to all major components. This allows a very easy and informative reference. Since cross-categorical derivation with zero morphology is dominant in Chinese, it would help the processing greatly if POS information is added to the word list. Adding such information would also open the possibility of accessing the POS ranked frequency information.

4.5 Fine-tuning Collocation Patterns

The Sketch Engine relies on collocation patterns, such as (2) above, to extract collocations. The regular expression format allows fast processing of large scale corpora with good results. However, these patterns can be fine-tuned for better results. We give VN collocates with object function as example here. In (6), verbs are underlined with a single line, and the collocated nouns identified by English Word Sketch are underlined with double lines. Other nominal objects that the Sketch Engine misses are marked with a dotted line.

6.a. In addition to encouraging kids to ask, think and do, parents need to be tolerant and appreciative to avoid **killing** a **child**'s creative sense.

b. Children are taught to **love** their **parents**, classmates, animals, nature . . . . in fact they are taught to love just about everything except to love China, their mother country.

c. For example, the government deliberately chose not to **teach** Chinese **history** and culture, nor civics, in the schools.

d. At the game there will be a lottery drawing for a motorcycle! And perhaps you'll **catch** a foul **ball** or a home run.

The sentences in (6) show that the current Sketch Engine tend to only identify the first object when there are multiple objects. The resultant distributional information thus obtained will be valid given a sufficiently large corpus. However, if the collocation patterns are fine-tuned to allow treatment of coordination, richer and more precise information can be extracted.

A regular expression collocation pattern also runs the risk of mis-classification. For instance, speech act verbs often allow subject to occur in post-verbal positions, and intransitive verbs can often take temporal nouns in post-verbal positions too.

7. a. …you can **say goodbye** to your competitive career.
   b. `No,' **said Scarlet**, `but then I don't notice much.'
8. a. Where did you **sleep** last **night**?
   b. …it **arrived** Thursday **morning**.
   c. From Arty's room **came** the **sound** of an accordion.
9. `I'll look forward to that.' `So **will I**.'

Such non-canonical word orders are even more prevalent in Chinese. Chinese objects often occur in pre-verbal positions in various pre-posing constructions, such as topicalization.

10. 全穀麵包，**吃**了很健康。
    quan.gu mian.bao, ***chi*** *le hen jian.kang*
    whole-grain bread, **eat** LE very healthy
    'Eating whole-grain bread is very healthy.'

11a. 有人嘗試要**將**這荷花**分類**，卻越分越累。
    you ren chang.shi yao ***jiang*** *zhe he.hua* ***fen.lei,*** *que yue fen yue lei*
    someone try to **JIANG** the lotus **classify**, but more classify more tired
    'People have tried to decide what category the lotus belongs in, but have found the effort taxing.'
   b. 我一定要**把**老大**除掉**。
    wo yi.ding yao ***ba*** *lao.da* ***chu.diao***
    I must want **BA** the oldest (son) **get rid of**
    'I really want to get rid of the older son.'

When objects are pre-posed, they tend to stay closer to the verb than the subject. Adding object marking information, such as *ba* 把, *jiang* 將, *lian* 連 would help correctly identify collocating pre-posed objects. However, for those unmarked pre-posed structures, closeness to the verb may not provide sufficient information. Several rules will need to be implemented jointly.

The above example underlines a critical issue. That is, whether relative position alone is enough to identify positional information. The Sketch Engine is in essence a powerful tool extracting generalizations from annotated corpus data. We have shown that it can extract useful grammatical information with POS tag alone. If the corpus is tagged with richer annotation, the Sketch Engine should be able to extract even richer information.

The Sinica Corpus tagset adapts to the fact that Chinese has a freer word order than English by incorporating semantic information with the grammatical category. For instance, locational and temporal nouns, proper nouns, and common nouns each are assigned a different tag. Verbs are sub-categorized according to activity and transitivity. Such information is not available in the BNC tagset and hence not used in the original Sketch Engine design. We will enrich the collocation patterns with the annotated linguistic information from the Sinica Corpus tagset. In particular, we are converting ICG lexical subcategorization frames (Chen and Huang 1990) to Sketch Engine collocation patters. These ICG frames, called Basic Patterns and Adjunct Patterns, have already been fully annotated lexically and tested on the Sinica Corpus. We expect their incorporation to improve Chinese Sketch Engine results markedly.

6. Conclusion

In this paper, we introduce a powerful tool for extraction of collocation information from large scale corpora. Our adaptation proved the cross-lingual robustness of the Sketch Engine. In particular, we show the robustness of the Sketch Engine by achieving better results through fine-tuning of the collocation patterns via integrating available grammatical knowledge.

References

Chen, Keh-Jiann and Huang, Chu-Ren. 1990. Information-based Case Grammar. *Proceedings of the 13th COLING*. Helsinki, Finland. 2:54-59.

Chen, Keh-Jiann, Chu-Ren Huang, Feng-Yi Chen, Chi-Ching Luo, Ming-Chung Chang, and Chao-Jan Chen. 2003. Sinica Treebank: Design Criteria, Representational Issues and Implementation. In Anne Abeill´e, (ed.): *Building and Using Parsed Corpora. Text, Speech and Language Technology,* 20:231-248. Dordrecht: Kluwer.

CKIP (Chinese Knowledge Information Processing Group). 1995/1998. *The Content and Illustration of Academica Sinica Corpus. (Technical Report no 95-02/98-04).* Taipei: Academia Sinica

Huang, Chu-Ren, Feng-Ju Lo, Hui-Jun Hsiao, Chiu-Jung Lu, and Ching-chun Hsieh. 2001. From Language Archives to Digital Museums: Synergizing Linguistic Databases. Presented at the IRCS workshop on linguistic Databases. University of Pennsylvania.

Huang, Chu-Ren, Keh-Jiann Chen, and Lili Chang. 1997. Segmentation Standard for Chinese Natural Language Processing. *Computational Linguistics and Chinese Language Processing.* 2(2):47-62.

Kilgarriff, Adam and Tugwell, David. Sketching Words. 2002. In Marie-Hélène Corréard (ed.): *Lexicography and Natural Language Processing. A Festschrift in Honour of B.T.S. Atkins*. 125-137. Euralex.

Kilgarriff, Adam, Chu-Ren Huang, Pavel Rychlý, Simon Smith, and David Tugwell. 2005. Chinese Word Sketches. ASIALEX 2005: Words in Asian Cultural Context. Singapore.

Kilgarriff, Adam, Pavel Rychlý, Pavel Smrz and David Tugwell. 2004. The Sketch Engine. *Proceedings of EURALEX*, Lorient, France. (http://www.sketchengine.co.uk/)

Leech, Geoffrey. 1992. 100 million words of English: the British National Corpus (BNC). *Language Research* 28(1):1-13

Lin, Dekang. 1998. An Information-Theoretic Definition of Similarity. *Proceedings of International Conference on Machine Learning.* Madison, Wisconsin. (http://www.cs.umanitoba.ca/~lindek/publication.htm)

Tsai, Mei-Chih, Chu-Ren Huang, Keh-Jiann Chen, and Kathleen Ahrens. 1998. Towards a Representation of Verbal Semantics--An Approach Based on Near Synonyms. *Computational Linguistics and Chinese Language Processing.* 3(1): 61-74.

Wu, Yiching and Liu, Mei-Chun. 2003. The Construction and Application of Mandarin Verbnet. *Proceedings of the Third International Conference of Internet Chinese Education*. 39-48. Taipei, Taiwan.

Xia, Fei, Martha Palmer, Nianwen Xue, Mary Ellen Okurowski, John Kovarik, Fu-Dong Chiou, Shizhe Huang, Tony Kroch, and Mitch Marcus. 2000. Developing Guidelines and Ensuring Consistency for Chinese Text Annotation. *Proceedings of the second International Conference on Language Resources and Evaluation (LREC 2000),* Athens, Greece. (http://www.cis.upenn.edu/~chinese/ctb.html)

Xue, Nianwen and Palmer, Martha. 2003. Annotating Propositions in the Penn Chinese Treebank. *Proceedings of the Second Sighan Workshop*. Sapporo, Japan. (http://www.cis.upenn.edu/~xueniwen/)

Xue, Nianwen and Palmer, Martha. 2005. Automatic Semantic Role Labeling for Chinese Verbs. *Proceedings of the 19th International Joint Conference on Artificial Intelligence*. Edinburgh, Scotland. (http://www.cis.upenn.edu/~xueniwen/)

Websites

Sinica Corpus.
http://www.sinica.edu.tw/SinicaCorpus/

British National Corpus (BNC).
http://www.natcorp.ox.ac.uk/

Center for Chinese Linguistics, PKU.
http://ccl.pku.edu.cn/#

Corpora And NLP (Natural Language Processing) for Digital Learning of English (CANDLE).
http://candle.cs.nthu.edu.tw/candle/

FrameNet.
http://www.icsi.berkeley.edu/~framenet/

Penn Chinese Treebank.
http://www.cis.upenn.edu/~chinese/ctb.html

Proposition Bank.
http://www.cis.upenn.edu/~ace/

Sinica Treebank.
http://treebank.sinica.edu.tw/

Sketch Engine (English).
http://www.sketchengine.co.uk/

Sketch Engine (Chinese).
http://corpora.fi.muni.cz/chinese/

Sou Wen Jie Zi-A Linguistic KnowledgeNet.
http://words.sinica.edu.tw/

Word Meaning Inducing via Character Ontology: A Survey on the Semantic Prediction of Chinese Two-Character Words

Shu-Kai Hsieh
Seminar für Sprachwissenschaft
Abt. Computerlinguistik
Universität Tübingen
72074, Germany
kai@hanzinet.org

Abstract

This paper presents a semantic class prediction model of Chinese two-character compound words based on a character ontology, which is set to be a feasible conceptual knowledge resource grounded in Chinese characters. The experiment we conduct yields satisfactory results which turn out to be that the task of semantic prediction of two-character words could be greatly facilitated using Chinese characters as a knowledge resource.

1 Introduction

This paper describes the theoretical consideration concerning with the interaction of ontology and morpho-semantics, and an NLP experiment is performed to do semantic class prediction of unknown two-character words based on the ontological and lexical knowledge of Chinese morphemic components of words (i.e., characters). The task that the semantic predictor (or classifier) performs is to automatically assign the (predefined) semantic thesaurus classes to the unknown two-character words of Chinese.

Among these types of unknown words, Chen and Chen (2000) pointed out that *compound words* constitute the most productive type of unknown words in Chinese texts. However, the caveat at this point should be carefully formulated, due to the fact that there are no unequivocal opinions concerning with some basic theoretical settings in Chinese morphology. The notion of *word*, *morpheme* and *compounding* are not exactly in accord with the definition common within the theoretical setting of Western morphology. To avoid unnecessary misunderstanding, the pre-theoretical term *two-character* words will be mostly used instead of *compound* words in this paper.

2 Word Meaning Inducing via Character Meaning

2.1 Morpho-Semantic Description

As known, "bound roots" are the largest classes of *morpheme* types in Chinese morphology, and they are very productive and represent lexical rather than grammatical information (Packard 2000). This morphological phenomena leads many Chinese linguists to view the word components (i.e., characters) as building blocks in the *semantic composition* process of dis- or multisyllabic words. In many empirical studies (Tseng and Chen (2002); Tseng (2003); Lua (1993); Chen (2004)), this view has been confirmed repeatedly.

In the semantic studies of Chinese word formation, many descriptive and cognitive semantic approaches have been proposed, such as argument structure analysis (Chang 1998) and the frame-based semantic analysis (Chu 2004). However, among these qualitative explanation theoretical models, problems often appear in the *lack of predictability* on the one end of spectrum, or *overgeneration* on the other.[1] Empirical data have

[1] For example, in applying Lieber's (1992) analysis of argument structure and theta-grid in Chinese V-V compounds, Chang (1998) found some examples which may satisfy the semantic and syntactic constraints, but they may not be ac-

also shown that in many cases, – e.g., the abundance of phrasal lexical units in any natural language, – the principle of *compositionality* in a strict sense, that is, "the meaning of a complex expression can be *fully* derivable from the meanings of its component parts, and from the schemas which sanction their combination"(Taylor 2002), which is taken to be a fundamental proposition in some of *morpho-semantically motivated* analysis, is highly questionable.

This has given to the consideration of the embeddedness of linguistic meanings within broader *conceptual structures*. In what follows, we will argue that an *ontology-based* approach would provide an interesting and efficient prospective toward the *character-triggered* morpho-semantic analysis of Chinese words.

2.2 Conceptual Aggregate in *Compounding*: A Shift Toward Character Ontology

In prior studies, it is widely presumed that the category (be it syntactical or semantic) of a word, is somehow strongly associated with that of its composing characters. The *semantic compositionality* underlying two-character words appears in different terms in the literature.[2]

Word semantic similarity calculation techniques have been commonly used to retrieve the similar compositional patterns based on semantic taxonomic thesaurus. However, one weak point in these studies is that they are unable to separate *conceptual* and *semantic* levels. Problem raises when words in question are *conceptually* correlated are not necessarily *semantically* correlated, viz, they might or might not be physically close in the CILIN thesaurus (Mei et al 1998). On closer observations, we found that most synonymic words (i.e., with the same CILIN semantic class) have characters which carry similar conceptual information. This could be best illustrated by examples. Table 1 shows the *conceptual distribution* of the *modifiers* of an example of VV compound by presuming the second character 取 as a *head*. The first column is the semantic class of CILIN (middle level), the second column lists the instances with lower level classification number, and the third column lists their conceptual types adopted from a character ontology we will discuss later. As we can see, though there are 12 resulting semantic classes for the * 取 compounds, the modifier components of these compounds involve only 4 concept types as follows:

11000 (SUBJECTIVE → EXCITABILITY → ABILITY → ORGANIC FUNCTION) 吸、攝,

11010 (SUBJECTIVE → EXCITABILITY → ABILITY → SKILLS) 摘、榨、拾、拔、提、攝、選,

11011 (SUBJECTIVE → EXCITABILITY → ABILITY → INTELLECT) 牟、謀、考、選、錄、記、聽,

11110 (SUBJECTIVE → EXCITABILITY → SOCIAL EXPERIENCE → DEAL WITH THINGS) 收、獲、領、換、奪、竊、詐、獵、掠、爭、剽、襲、攻、進

We defined these patterns as *conceptual aggregate pattern* in compounding. Unlike statistical measure of the co-occurrence restrictions or association strength, a *concept aggregate pattern* provides a more knowledge-rich scenario to represent a specific manner in which concepts are aggregated in the ontological background, and how they affect the compounding words. We will propose that the semantic class prediction of Chinese two-character words could be improved by making use of their *conceptual aggregate pattern* of head/modifier component.

3 Semantic Prediction of Unknown Two-Character Words

The practical task intended to be experimented here involves the automatic classification of Chinese two-character words into a predetermined number of semantic classes. Difficulties encountered in previous researches could be summarized as follows:

First, many models (Chen and Chen 1998;2000) cannot deal with the issue of "incompleteness" of characters in the lexicon, for these models depend heavily on CILIN, a Chinese Thesaurus containing only about 4,133 monosyllabic morphemic components (characters). As a result, if unknown words contain characters that are not listed in CILIN, then the prediction task cannot be performed automatically. Second, the ambiguity of characters is often shunned by

ceptable to native speakers.

[2]Using statistical techniques, Lua (1993) found out that each Chinese two-character word is a result of 16 types of *semantic transformation patterns*, which are extracted from the meanings of its constituent characters. In Chen (2004), the combination pattern is referred to as *compounding semantic template*.

SC	VV compounds	Concept types of modifier component
Ee	37 進取	11110
Fa	05 榨取 08 摘取 15 拾取	11010
Fc	05 聽取	11011
Gb	07 記取	11011
Ha	06 奪取	11110
Hb	08 襲取 12 攻取 12 奪取 12 襲取	11110
Hc	07 收取 23 拔取 25 錄取	{11110;11011}
Hi	27 領取 27 提取	{11010;11110}
Hj	25 選取 25 摘取	{11010;11110}
Hn	03 掠取 10 剽取 12 榨取	11110
If	09 考取	11011
Je	12 爭取 12 詐取 12 吸取 12 攝取 12 竊取 12 牟取 12 謀取 12 掠取 12 獵取 12 截取 12 獲取 12 換取 12 奪取	{11000;11110;11011;11110}

Table 1: Conceptual aggregate patterns in two-character VV (compound) words: An example of ＊取

manual pre-selection of character meaning in the training step, which causes great difficulty for an automatic work. Third, it has long been assumed (Lua 1997; Chen and Chen 2000) that the overwhelming majority of Chinese compounds are more or less *endocentric*, where the compounds denote a hyponym of the *head* component in the compound. E.g, 電郵 ("electric-mail"; e-mail) is a kind of mail. So the process of identifying semantic class of a *compound* boils down to find and to determine the semantic class of its *head* morpheme. However, there is also an amount of *exocentric* and appositional compounds[3] where no straightforward criteria can be made to determine the head component. For example, in a case of VV compound 訓斥 ("denounce-scold", drop-on), it is difficult (and subjective) to say which character is the head that can assign a semantic class to the compound.

To solve above-mentioned problems, Chen (2004) proposed a non head-oriented character-sense association model to retrieve the *latent* senses of characters and the *latent* synonymous compounds among characters by measuring similarity of semantic template in compounding by using a MRD. However, as the author remarked in the final discussion of classification errors, the performance of this model relies much on the productivity of compounding semantic templates of the target compounds. To correctly predict the semantic category of a compound with an unproductive semantic template is no doubt very difficult due to a sparse existence of the template-similar compounds. In addition, the statistical measure of sense association does not tell us any more about the constraints and knowledge of conceptual combination.

In the following, we will propose that a knowledge resource at the morpheme (character) level could be a straightforward remedy to these problems. By treating characters as instances of conceptual primitives, a character ontology thereof might provide an interpretation of *conceptual grounding* of word senses. At a coarse grain, the character ontological model does have advantages in efficiently defining the *conceptual space* within which character-grounded concept primitives and their relations, are *implicitly* located.

4 A Proposed Character Ontology-based Approach

In carrying out the semantic prediction task, we presume the *context-freeness* hypothesis, i.e., without resorting to any contextual information. The consideration is taken based on the observation that native speaker seems to reconstruct their new conceptual structure *locally* in the processing of unknown compound words. On the other hand, it has the advantage especially for those unknown words that occur only once and hence have limited context.

In general, the approach proposed here differs in some ways from previous research based on the following presuppositions:

[3] Lua reports a result of 14.14% (Z3 type).

4.1 Character Ontology as a Knowledge Resource

The new model that we will present below will rely on a coarsely grained upper-level ontology of characters.[4] This character ontology is a tree-structured conceptual taxonomy in terms of which only two kinds of relations are allowed: the *INSTANCE-OF* (i.e., certain characters are instances of certain concept types) and *IS-A* relations (i.e., certain concept type is a kind of certain concept type).

In the character ontology, monosyllabic characters [5] are assigned to *at least* [6] one of 309 consets (concept set), a new term which is defined as a type of concept sharing a given putatively primitive meaning. For instance, 說 (speak), 道 (chatter), 曰 (say), 云 (say), 告 (tell), 訴 (inform), 講 (explain), 敘 (narrate), 謂 (be called), 述 (state), these characters are assigned to the same conset.

Following the basic line of *OntoClear* methodology (Guarino and Welty (2002)), we use *simple monotonic inheritance*, which means that each node inherits properties only from a single ancestor, and the inherited value cannot be overwritten at any point of the ontology. The decision to keep the relations to one single parent was made in order to guarantee that the structure would be able to grow indefinitely and still be manageable, i.e. that the transitive quality of the relations between the nodes would not degenerate with size. Figure 1 shows a snapshot of the character ontology.

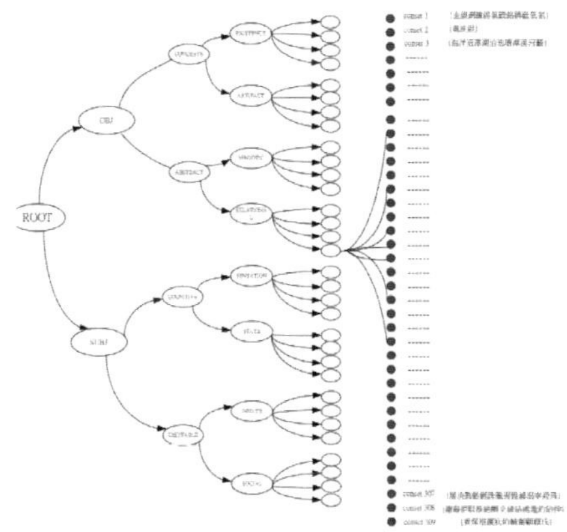

Figure 1: The character ontology: a snapshot

4.2 Character-triggered Latent Near-synonyms

The rationale behind this approach is that similar conceptual primitives - in terms of characters - probably participate in similar context or have similar *meaning-inducing* functions. This can be rephrased as the following presumptions: (1). Near-synonymic words often overlap in senses, i.e., they have same or close semantic classes. (2). Words with characters which share similar conceptual information tend to form a *latent* cluster of synonyms. (2). These similar conceptual information can be formalized as *conceptual aggregate patterns* extracted from a character ontology. (3). Identifying such *conceptual aggregate patterns* might thus greatly benefit the automatically acquired near-synonyms, which give a set of good candidates in predicting the semantic class of previously unknown ones.

The proposed semantic classification system retrieves at first a set of near-synonym candidates using *conceptual aggregation patterns*. Considerations from the view of lexicography can winnow the *overgenerated* candidates, that is, a final decision of a list of near-synonym candidates is formed on the basis of the CILIN's verdict as to what latent near-synonyms are. Thus the semantic class of the target unknown two-character words will be assigned with the semantic class of the top-ranked near-synonym calculated by the similarity measurement between them. This method has advantage of avoiding the snag of apparent multiplicity of semantic usages (ambiguity) of a character.

Take for an example. Suppose that the semantic class of a two-character word 保護 (protect; `Hi37`) is unknown. By presuming the leftmost character 保 the *head* of the word, and the rightmost character 護 as the *modifier* of the word,

[4] At the time of writing, about 5,600 characters have been finished in their information construction. Please refer to [4]

[5] In fact, in addition to monosyllabic morpheme, it also contains a few dissyllabic morphemes, and *borrowed polysyllabic morphemes*.

[6] This is due to the homograph.

we first identify the conset which the modifier 護 belongs to. Other instances in this conset are 保, 袒, 戌, 衛, 庇, 佑, 顧, 輔, 佐, 守, 養, etc. So we can retrieve a set of possible *near-synonym* candidates by substitution, namely, NS_1: {保保, 保袒, 保戌, 保衛, 保庇, 保佑, 保顧, 保輔, 保佐, 保守, 保養}; in the same way, by presuming 護 as the *head*, we have a second set of possible *near-synonym* candidates, NS_2: {護護, 袒護, 戌護, 衛護, 庇護, 佑護, 顧護, 輔護, 佐護, 守護, 養護}[7]. Aligned with CILIN, those candidates which are also listed in the CILIN are adopted as the final two list of the near-synonym candidates for the unknown word 保護: NS'_1: {袒護(Hi41), 衛護(Hb04;Hi37), 庇護(Hi47), 守護(Hi37),養護(Hd01)}, and NS'_2: {保佑(Hl33),保養(Hj33), 保守(Ee39)}.

4.3 Semantic Similarity Measure of Unknown Word and its Near-Synonyms

Given two sets of character-triggered near-synonyms candidates, the next step is to calculate the semantic similarity between the unknown word (UW) and these near-synonyms candidates.

CILIN Thesaurus is a tree-structured taxonomic semantic structure of Chinese words, which can be seen as a special case of semantic network. To calculate semantic similarity between nodes in the network can thus make use of the structural information represented in the network.

Following this information content-based model, in measuring the semantic similarity between unknown word and its candidate near-synonymic words, we use a measure metric modelled on those of Chen and Chen (2000), which is a simplification of the Resnik algorithm by assuming that the occurrence probability of each leaf node is equal. Given two sets (NS'_1, NS'_2) of candidate near synonyms, each with m and n near synonyms respectively, the similarity is calculated as in equation (1) and (2), where sc_{uwc1} and sc_{uwc2} are the semantic class(es) of the first and second morphemic component (i.e., character) of a given unknown word, respectively. sc_i and sc_j are the semantic classes of the first and second morphemic components on the list of candidate near-synonyms NS'_1 and NS'_2. f is the frequency of the semantic classes, and the denominator is the total value of numerator for the purpose of normalization. β and $1-\beta$ are the weights which will be discussed later. The *Information Load* (IL) of a semantic class sc is defined in Chen and Chen (2004):

$$IL(sc) = Entropy(system) - Entropy(sc) \quad (3)$$

$$\simeq (-\frac{1}{q}\sum \log_2 \frac{1}{q}) - (-\frac{1}{p}\sum \log_2 \frac{1}{p})$$

$$= \log_2 q - \log_2 p$$

$$= -\log_2(\frac{p}{q}),$$

if there is q the number of the minimal semantic classes in the system,[8] p is the number of the semantic classes subordinate sc.

4.4 Circumventing "Head-oriented" Presupposition

As remarked in Chen (2004), the previous research concerning the automatic semantic classification of Chinese compounds (Lua 1997; Chen and Chen 2000) presupposes the *endocentric* feature of compounds. That is, by supposing that compounds are composed of a *head* and a *modifier*, determining the semantic category of the *target* therefore boils down to determine the semantic category of the *head* compound.

In order to circumventing the strict "head-determination" presumption, which might suffer problems in some borderline cases of V-V compounds, the weight value (β and $1-\beta$) is proposed. The idea of weighting comes from the discussion of *morphological productivity* in Baayen (2001). We presume that, within a given two-character words, the more productive, that is, the more numbers of characters a character can combine with, the more possible it is a *head*, and the more weight should be given to it. The weight is defined as $\beta = \frac{C(n,1)}{N}$, viz, the number of candidate *morphemic components* divided by the total number of N. For instance, in the above-mentioned example, NS_1 should gain more weights than NS_2, for 護 can combine with more characters (5 near-synonyms candidates) in

[7]Note that in this case, 保 and 護 are happened to be in the same conset.

[8]In CILIN, $q = 3915$.

$$sim_{\mu}(UW, NS'_1) = \arg^{max}_{i=1,m} \frac{IL(LCS(sc_{uwc1}, sc_i)) * f_i}{\sum_{i=1}^{m} IL(LCS(sc_{uwc1}, sc_i)) * f_i}(\beta) \quad (1)$$

$$sim_{\nu}(UW, NS'_2) = \arg^{max}_{j=1,n} \frac{IL(LCS(sc_{uwc2}, sc_j)) * f_j}{\sum_{j=1}^{n} IL(LCS(sc_{uwc2}, sc_j)) * f_j}(1-\beta) \quad (2)$$

NS_1 than 保 does in NS_2 (3 near-synonyms candidates). In this case, $\beta = \frac{5}{8} = 0.625$. It is noted that the weight assignment should be character and position independent.

4.5 Experimental Settings

4.5.1 Resources

The following resources are used in the experiments: (1)Sinica Corpus[9], (2) CILIN Thesaurus (Mei et al 1998) and (3) a Chinese character upper-level ontology.[10] (1) is a well known balanced Corpus for modern Chinese used in Taiwan. (2) CILIN Thesaurus is a Chinese Thesaurus widely accepted as a semantic categorization standard of Chinese word in Chinese NLP. In CILIN, a collection of about 52,206 Chinese words are grouped in a Roget's Thesaurus-like structure based on *categories* within which there are several 3 levels of finer clustering (12 major, 95 minor and 1428 minor semantic classes).(3) is an on-going project of Hanzi-grounded Ontology and Lexicon as introduced.

4.5.2 Data

We conducted an open test experiment, which meant that the training data was different from the testing data. 800 two-character words in CILIN were chosen at random to serve as test data, and all the words in the test set were assumed to be unknown. The distribution of the grammatical categories of these data is: NN (200, 25%), VN (100, 12.5%) and VV (500, 62.5%).

4.5.3 Baseline

The baseline method assigns the semantic class of the randomly picked head component to the semantic class of the unknown word in question. It is noted that most of the morphemic components (characters) are ambiguous, in such cases, semantic class is chosen at random as well.

[9]http://www.sinica.edu.tw/SinicaCorpus/

[10]http://www.hanzinet.org/HanziOnto/

Compound types	Baseline	Our algorithm
V-V	12.20%	42.00%
V-N	14.00%	37.00%
N-N	11.00%	72.50%

Table 2: Accuracy in the test set (level 3)

4.5.4 Outline of the Algorithm

Briefly, the strategy to predict the semantic class of a unknown two-character word is, to measure the semantic similarity of unknown words and their candidate near-synonyms which are retrieved based on the character ontology. For any unknown word UW, which is the character sequence of C_1C_2, the $RANK(sim_{\mu}(\beta), sim_{\nu}(1-\beta))$ is computed. The semantic category sc of the candidate synonym which has the value of $MAX(sim_{\mu}(\beta), sim_{\nu}(1-\beta))$, will be the top-ranked guess for the target unknown word.

4.6 Results and Error Analysis

The correctly predicted semantic class is the sematic class listed in CILIN. In the case of ambiguity, when the unknown word in question belongs to more than one semantic classes, any one of the classes of an ambiguous word is considered correct in the evaluation.

The SC prediction algorithm was performed on the test data for outside test in level-3 classification. The resulting accuracy is shown in Table 2. For the purpose of comparison, Table 3 also shows the more shallow semantic classification (the 2nd level in CILIN).

Generally, without contextual information, the classifier is able to predict the meaning of a Chinese two-character words with satisfactory accu-

Compound types	Baseline	Our algorithm
V-V	13.20%	46.20%
V-N	16.00%	42.00%
N-N	12.50%	76.50%

Table 3: Accuracy in the test set (level 2)

racy against the baseline. A further examination of the bad cases indicates that error can be grouped into the following sources:

- Words with no semantic transparency:
  Like "proper names", these types have no semantic transparency property, i.e., the word meanings can not be derived from their morphemic components. Loan words such as 沙發 (/shāfā/; "sofa") are typical examples.

- Words with weak semantic transparency:
  These can be further classified into four types:

  - Appositional compounds: words whose two characters stand in a coordinate relationship, e.g. 東西 ("east-west", thing).
  - Lexicalized idiomatic usage: For such usage, each word is an indivisible construct and each has its meaning which can hardly be computed by adding up the separate meaning of the components of the word. The sources of these idiomatic words might lie in the *etymological past* and are at best meaningless to the modern native speaker. e.g, 薪水 ("salary-water", salary).
  - Metaphorical usage: the meaning of such words are therefore different from the literal meaning. Some testing data is not semantically transparent due to their metaphorical uses, For instance, 喉舌 (Aj) is assigned to the 喉頭 (Bk).

- Derived words:
  Such as 進去 (enter). These could be filter out using syntactical information.

- The quality and coverage of CILIN and character ontology:
  Since our SC system's test and training data are gleaned from CILIN and the character ontology, the quality and coverage play a crucial role. For example, for the unknown compound word 慅慅 (/sāo-sāo/; "be in tumult"), there not even an example which has 慅 as the first character or as the second character. the same problem such as falling short on coverage and data sparseness goes to the character ontology, too. For instance, there are some dissyllabic morphemes which are not listed in ontology, such as 覬覦 (/jìyú/;"covet").

Compound types	Our model	Current best model
V-V	42.00%	39.80% (Chen 2004)
N-N	72.50%	81.00% (Chen and Chen 2000)

Table 4: Level-3 performance in the outside test: a comparison

4.7 Evaluation

So far as we know, no evaluation in the previous works was done. This might be due to many reasons: (1) the different scale of experiment (how many words are in the test data?), (2) the selection of syntactic category (VV, VN or NN?) of morphemic components, and (3) the number of morphemic components involved (two or three-character words?).. etc. Hence it is difficult to compare our results to other models. Among the current similar works, Table 4 shows that our system outperforms Chen(2004) in VV compounds, and approximates the Chen and Chen(2000) in NN compounds.

5 Conclusion

In this paper, we propose a system that aims to gain the possible semantic classes of unknown words via similarity computation based on character ontology and CILIN thesaurus. In general, we approach the task in a hybrid way that combines the strengths of ontology-based and example-based model to achieve at better result for this task.

The scheme we use for automatic semantic class prediction takes advantage of the presumptions that the conceptual information *wired* in Chinese characters can help retrieve the near-synonyms, and the near-synonyms constitute a key indicator for the semantic class guess of unknown words in question.

The results obtained show that, our SC prediction algorithm can achieve fairly high level of performance. While the work presented here in still in progress, a first attempt to analyze a test set of 800 examples has already shown a 43.60% correctness for VV compounds, 41.00% for VN compounds, and 74.50% for NN compounds at the level-3 of CILIN. If shallow semantics is taken into consideration, the results are even better.

Working in this framework, however, one point as suggested by other similar approach is that, human language processing is not limited to an abstract ontology alone (Hong et al. 2004). In practical applications, ontologies are seldom used as the only knowledge resources. For those unknown words with very weak semantic transparency, it would be interesting to show that an ontology-based system can be greatly boosted when other information sources such as metaphor and etymological information integrated. Future work is aimed at improving this accuracy by adding other linguistic knowledge sources and extending the technique to WSD (Word Sense Disambiguation).

Acknowledgements

I would like to thank Erhard Hinrichs and Lothar Lemnitzer for their useful discussions. I also thank the anonymous referees for constructive comments. Thanks also go to the institute of linguistics of Academia Sinica for their kindly data support.

References

Baayen, Harald. (2001). Word frequency distributions. Kluwer Academic Publishers.

Chen, Keh-Jiann and Chao-Jan Chen. (2000). Automatic semantic classification for Chinese unknown compound nouns. COLING 2000, Saarbrücken, Germany.

Chen, Chao-Ren. (2004). Character-Sense association and compounding template similarity: Automatic semantic classification of Chinese compounds. *The 3rd SIGHAN Workshop.*

Chu, Yan. (2004). *Semantic wordformation of Chinese compound words*. Peking University Press.

HanziNet Project: `http://www.hanzinet.org`.

Guarino, Nicola and Chris Welty. (2002). Evaluating ontological decisions with OntoClean. In: *Communications of the ACM*. 45(2):61-65.

Hong, Li and Huang (2004). Ontology-based Prediction of Compound Relations: A study based on SUMO. *PACLIC 18*.

Hsieh, Shu-Kai. (2005). HanziNet: An enriched conceptual network of Chinese characters. *The 5rd workshop on Chinese lexical semantics*, China: Xiamen.

Lin, Dekang. (1998). A information-theoretic definition of similarity. In:*Proceeding of 15th International Conference of Machine Learning.*.

Lua, K. T. (1993). A study of Chinese word semantics and its prediction. *Computer Processing of Chinese and Oriental Languages*, Vol 7. No 2.

Lua, K.T. (1997). Prediction of meaning of bisyllabic Chinese words using back propagation neural network. In:*Computer Processing of Oriental Languages. 11(2).*

Lua, K. T. (2002). The Semantic Transformation of Chinese Compound Words (漢語造詞過程的語意轉換). *The 3rd workshop on Chinese lexical semantics*, Taipei.

Packard, J. L. (2000). *The morphology of Chinese*. Cambridge, UK: Cambridge University Press.

Mei et al (1998). 同義詞詞林. Dong-Hua Bookstore: Taipei.

Domain Specific Word Extraction from Hierarchical Web Documents: A First Step Toward Building Lexicon Trees from Web Corpora

Jing-Shin Chang
Department of Computer Science & Information Engineering
National Chi-Nan University
1, University Road, Puli, Nantou, Taiwan 545, ROC.
jshin@csie.ncnu.edu.tw

Abstract

Domain specific words and ontological information among words are important resources for general natural language applications. This paper proposes a statistical model for finding domain specific words (DSW's) in particular domains, and thus building the association among them. When applying this model to the hierarchical structure of the web directories node-by-node, the document tree can potentially be converted into a large semantically annotated lexicon tree. Some preliminary results show that the current approach is better than a conventional TF-IDF approach for measuring domain specificity. An average precision of 65.4% and an average recall of 36.3% are observed if the top-10% candidates are extracted as domain-specific words.

1 Domain Specific Words and Lexicon Trees as Important NLP Resources

Domain specific words (DSW's) are important "anchoring words" for natural language processing applications that involve word sense disambiguation (WSD). It is appreciated that multi-sense words appearing in the same document tend to be tagged with the same word sense if they belong to the same common domain in the semantic hierarchy (Yarowsky, 1995). The existence of some DSW's in a document will therefore be a strong evidence of a specific sense for words within the document. For instance, the existence of "basketball" in a document would strongly suggest the "sport" sense of the word "活塞" ("Pistons"), rather than its "mechanics" sense. It is also a personal belief that DSW-based sense disambiguation, document classification and many similar applications would be easier than sense-based models since sense-tagged documents are rare while domain-aware training documents are abundant on the Web. DSW identification is therefore an important issue.

On the other hand, the semantics hierarchy among words (especially among sets of domain specific words) as well as the membership of domain specific words are also important resources for general natural language processing applications, since the hierarchy will provide semantic links and ontological information (such as "is-A" and "part-of" relationships) for words, and, domain specific words belonging to the same domain may have the "synonym" or "antonym" relationships. A hierarchical lexicon tree (or a network, in general) (Fellbaum, 1998; Jurafsky and Martin, 2000), indicative of sets of highly associated domain specific words and their hierarchy, is therefore invaluable for NLP applications.

Manually constructing such a lexicon hierarchy and acquiring the associated words for each node in the hierarchy, however, is most likely unaffordable both in terms of time and cost. In addition, new words (or new usages of words) are dynamically produced day by day. For instance, the Chinese word "活塞" (pistons) is more frequently used as the "sport" or "basketball" sense (referring to the "Detroit

Pistons") in Chinese web pages rather than the "mechanics" or "automobile" sense. It is therefore desirable to find an automatic and inexpensive way to construct the whole hierarchy.

Since the hierarchical web pages provide semantic tag information (explicitly from the HTML/XML tags or implicitly from the directory names) and useful semantic links, it is desirable that the lexicon construction process could be conducted using the web corpora. Actually, the directory hierarchy of the Web can be regarded as a kind of classification tree for web documents, which assigns an implicit hidden tag (represented by the directory name) to each document and hence the embedded domain specific words. Converting such a hierarchy into a lexicon tree is therefore feasible, provided that we can remove non-specific terms from the associated document sets.

For instance, the domain-specific words for documents under the "sport" hierarchy are likely to be tagged with a "sport" tag. These tags, in turn, can be used in various word sense disambiguation (WSD) tasks and other hot applications like anti-spamming mail filters. Such rich annotation provides a useful knowledge source for mining various semantic links among words.

We therefore will explore a non-conventional view for constructing a lexicon tree from the web hierarchy, where domain-specific word identification turns out to be a key issue and the first step toward such a construction process. An inter-domain entropy (IDE) measure will be proposed for this purpose.

2 Conventional Clustering View for Constructing Lexicon Trees

One conventional way to construct the lexicon hierarchy from web corpora is to collect the terms in all web documents and measure the degree of word association between word pairs using some well-known association metrics (Church and Hanks, 1989; Smadja et al., 1996) as the distance measure. Terms of high association are then clustered bottom-up using some clustering techniques to build the hierarchy. The clustered hierarchy is then submitted to lexicographers to assign a semantic label to each sub-cluster. The cost will be reduced in this way, but could still be unaffordable. Besides, it still depends on the lexicographers to assign appropriate semantic tags to the list of highly associated words.

There are several disadvantages with this approach. Firstly, the hierarchical relationship among the web documents, and hence the embedded DSW's, is lost during the document collection process, since the words are collected without considering where they come from in the document hierarchy. The loss of such hierarchical information implies that the clustered one will not match human perception quite well. Secondly, the word association metric and the clustering criteria used by the clustering algorithm are not directly related to human perception. Therefore, the lexicographers may not be able to adjust the clustered hierarchy comfortably. Thirdly, most clustering algorithms merge terms in a binary way; this may not match human perception as well. As far as the computation cost is concerned, computation of word association based on *pairwise* word association metrics will be time consuming.

Actually, such an approach may not be the only option today, thanks to the large number of web documents, which are natively arranged in a *hierarchical* manner.

3 Lexicon Tree Construction as Domain Specific Word Detection from Web Hierarchy

Since the web documents virtually form an extremely huge document classification tree, we propose here a simple approach to convert it into a lexicon tree, and assign implicit semantic tags to the domain specific words in the web documents automatically.

This simple approach is inspired by the fact that most text materials (webpages) in websites are already classified in a hierarchical manner; the hierarchical directory structures implicitly suggest that the domain specific terms in the text materials of a particular subdirectory are closely related to a common subject, which is identified by the name of the subdirectory.

If we can detect domain specific words within each document, and remove words that are non-specific, and tag the DSW's thus acquired with the directory name (or any appropriate tag), then we virtually get a hierarchical lexicon tree. In such a tree, each node is semantically linked by the original web document hierarchy, and each node has a set of domain specific words associated with it.

For instance, a subdirectory entitled 'entertainment' is likely to have a large number of web pages containing domain specific terms like 'singer', 'pop songs', 'rock & roll', 'Ah-Mei' (nickname of a pop song singer), 'album', and so on. Since these words are highly associated with the 'entertainment' domain, we will be able to collect the domain specific words of the 'entertainment' domain from such a directory.

In the extraction process, the directory names can be regarded as *implicit sense labels* or *implicit semantic tags* (which may be different from linguistically motivated semantic tags), and the action to put the web pages into properly named directories can be regarded as an *implicit tagging* process by the webmasters. And, the hierarchical directory itself provides information on the hierarchy of the semantic tags.

From a well-organized web site, we will then be able to acquire an implicitly tagged corpus from that site. Thanks to the webmasters, whose daily work include the implicit tagging of the corpora in their websites, there is almost no cost to extract DSW's from such web corpora. This idea actually extends equally well for other Internet resources, such as news groups and BBS articles, that are associated with hierarchical group names. Extending the idea to well organized book chapters, encyclopedia and things like that would not be surprised too.

The advantages of such a construction process, by removing non-specific terms, are many folds. First, the original hierarchical structure reflects human perception on document (and term) classification. Therefore, the need for adjustment may be rare, and the lexicographers may be more comfortable to adjust the hierarchy even if necessary. Second, the directory names may have higher correlation with linguistically motivated sense tags than those assigned by a clustering algorithm, since the web hierarchy was created by a human tagger (i.e., the webmaster). As far as the computation cost is concerned, pairwise word association computation is now replaced by the computation of "domain specificity" of words against domains. The reduction is significant, from $O(|W|x|W|)$ to $O(|W|x|D|)$, where $|W|$ and $|D|$ represent the vocabulary size and number of domains, respectively.

4 Domain Specific Word Extraction as the Key Technology: An Inter-Domain Entropy Approach

Since the terms (words or compound words) in the documents include general terms as well as domain-specific terms, the only problem then is an effective model to exclude those domain-independent terms from the implicit tagging process. The degree of domain independency can be measured with the inter-domain entropy (IDE) as will be defined in the following **DSW (Domain-Specific Word) Extraction Algorithm**. Intuitively, a term that distributes evenly in all domains is likely to be independent of any domain. We therefore weight such terms less probable as DSW's. The method can be summarized in the following algorithm:

Domain-Specific Word Extraction & Lexicon Tree Construction Algorithm:

<u>Step1 (Data Collection)</u>: Acquire a large collection of web documents using a web spider while preserving the directory hierarchy of the documents. Strip unused markup tags from the web pages.

<u>Step2 (Word Segmentation or Chunking)</u>: Identify word (or compound word) boundaries in the documents by applying a word segmentation process, such as

(Chiang et al., 1992; Lin et al., 1993), to Chinese-like documents (where word boundaries are not explicit) or applying a compound word chunking algorithms to English-like documents (where word boundaries are clear) in order to identify interested word entities.

Step3 (Acquiring Normalized Term Frequencies for all Words in Various Domains): For each subdirectory d_j, find the number of occurrences n_{ij} of each term w_i in all the documents, and derive the normalized term frequency $f_{ij} = n_{ij} / N_j$ by normalizing n_{ij} with the total document size, $N_j \equiv \sum_i n_{ij}$, in that directory. The directory is then associated with a set of $< w_i, d_j, f_{ij} >$ tuples, where w_i is the i-th words of the complete word list for all documents, d_j is the j-th directory name (refer to as the domain hereafter), and $f_{ij} = n_{ij} / N_j$ is the normalized relative frequency of occurrence of w_i in domain d_j.

Step4 (Identifying Domain-Independent Terms): Domain-independent terms are identified as those terms which distributed evenly in all domains. That is, terms with large **Inter-Domain Entropy** (IDE) defined as follows:

$$H_i \equiv H(w_i) \equiv -\sum_j P_{ij} \log P_{ij}$$

$$P_{ij} \equiv \frac{f_{ij}}{\sum_j f_{ij}}$$

Terms whose IDE's are above a threshold are likely to be removed from the lexicon tree since such terms are unlikely to be associated with any particular domain. Terms with a low IDE, on the other hand, may be retained in a few domains with high normalized frequencies.

To appreciate the fact that a high frequency term may be more important in a domain, the IDE is further weighted by the term frequency in the particular domain when deciding whether a term should be removed. Currently, the weighting method is the same as the conventional TF-IDF method (Baeza-Yates and Ribeiro-Neto, 1998; Jurafsky and Martin, 2000) for information retrieval. In brief, a word with entropy *Hi* can be think of as a term that spreads in *2**Hi* domains on average. The equivalent number of domains a term could be found then can be equated to $Nd_i = 2^{H_i}$. The term weight for w_i in the *j-th* domain can then be estimated as:

$$W_{ij} = n_{ij} \times \log_2\left(\frac{N}{Nd_i}\right)$$

where N is the total number of domains. Unlike the conventional TF-IDF method, however, the expected number of domains that a term could be found is estimated by considering its probabilistic distribution, instead of simple counting.

Step5 (Output): Sort the words in each domain by decreasing weights, W_{ij}, and output the top-k% candidates as the domain specific words of the domain. The percentage (k) can be determined empirically, or based on other criteria, such as their classification performance in a DSW-based text classifier (Chang, 2005). The directory tree now represents a hierarchical classification of the domain specific terms for different domains.

Since the document tree may not be really perfect, we have the option to adjust the hierarchy or the sets of words associated with each node, after eliminating domain-independent terms from the directory tree. The terms can be further clustered into highly associated word lists, with other association metrics. On the other hand, we can further move terms that are less specific to the current domain upward toward the root. This action will associate such terms with a slightly more general domain. All these issues will be left as our future works.

However, the current method is independent of the source web hierarchy. Given a web organized as an encyclopedium of biology, the current method is likely to find out the living species associated with each node of the underlying taxonomy automatically. With more and more well organized web sites of various kinds of knowledge online, the problems with imperfect web hierarchy will hopefully become a less important issue.

5 Evaluation

To see how the above algorithm could be useful as a basis for building a large lexicon tree from web pages, some preliminary results will be examined in this section.

A large collection of Chinese web pages was collected from a local news site. The size of the HTML web pages amounts to about 200M bytes in 138 subdomains (including the most specific domains at the leaf nodes and their ancestor domains). About 16,000 unique words are identified after word segmentation is applied to the text parts.

It was observed, from some small sample domains, that only around 10% of the words in each subdomain are deemed domain specific. (The percentages, however, may vary from domain to domain.) The large vocabulary size and the small percentage of DSW's suggest that the domain specific word identification task is not an easy one.

Table 1 shows a list of highly associated domain-specific words of low inter-domain entropies and their domain names. (Literal English translation for each term is enclosed in the parenthesis.) They are sampled from 4 out of 138 subdomains. The domain names virtually act as the semantic tags for such word lists. The tags, being extracted from manually created directory, well reflect the senses of the words in each subdomains.

Table 1 shows that many domain-specific words can really be extracted with the proposed approach in their respect domains. For instance, the word "pitcher" ("投手") is specifically used in the "baseball" domain. The domain specific words and their domain tags are well associated.

As a result of such association, low inter-domain entropy words in the same domain are also highly correlated. For instance, the term "部長" for calling a *Japanese* baseball team "manager" is specifically used with "日本職棒" (Japanese professional baseball team), instead of a *Chinese* team, where "manager" is called differently.

In addition, new usages of words, such as "活塞 (Pistons)" with the "basketball" sense, could also be identified by the current approach. Furthermore, it was also observed that many irrelevant words (such as those words in the webmasters' advertisement) are rejected as the DSW candidates automatically since they have very high inter-domain entropies.

One can also find interesting lexical relations (Fellbaum, 1998) among the domain tags and domain specific words, form Table 1, such as:

Hypernym/Hyponym: athlete (運動) *vs.* baseball game (棒球賽); car (汽車) *vs.* small car (小型車).

Has-Member/Member-Of: baseball team (球團) *vs.* manager (部長), pitcher (投手).

Has-Part/Part-Of: car (汽車) *vs.* engine cover (引擎蓋), tank (水箱), safety system (安全系統), trunk (行李箱).

Antonym: shot (投籃) *vs.* defense (防守).

Such lexical relations are, in general, interesting to lexical database builders. Furthermore, for data driven applications, such fine details are unlikely to be listed in a general purpose lexical database. Extracting DSW's with the inter-domain entropy (IDE) metric is therefore well founded.

Baseball	Broadcast-TV	Basketball	Car
日本職棒 (Japanese professional baseball)	有線電視 (cable TV)	一分 (one minute)	千西西 (Kilo-c.c.)
棒球賽 (baseball games)	東風 (the Dong Fong TV Station)	三秒 (three seconds)	小型車 (small car)
熱身 (warm up)	開工 (start to work)	女子組 (girl's teams)	中古 (used car)
運動 (athlete)	節目中 (on air)	包夾 (fold; clip)	引擎蓋 (engine cover)
場次 (time table)	廣電處 (radio-tv office)	外線	水箱 (tank)
價碼 (cost)	收視	犯規 (foul)	加裝
球團 (baseball team)	和信 (Ho-Hsin TV Station)	投籃 (shot)	市場買氣 (market atmosphere)
部長 (manager)	新聞局 (government information office)	男子組 (male team)	目的地 (destination)
練球 (practicing)	開獎	防守 (defense)	交車 (car delivery)
興農 (Hsin-Lung team)	頻道 (channel)	冠軍戰(championship)	同級 (of the same grade)
球場(course; diamond)	電視 (TV)	後衛 (fullback)	合作開發 (co-development)
投手 (pitcher)	電影(movie)	活塞 (Pistons team)	安全系統 (safety system)
球季 (season)	熱門 (hot)	國男 (national male team)	行李 (luggage)
賽程 (schedule)	影視 (video)	華勒(Wallace)	行李廂 (trunk)
太陽 (the Sun team)	娛樂 (entertainment)	費城 (Philadelphia)	西西 (c.c.)

Table 1. Sampled domain specific words with low entropies.

In order to have a quantitative evaluation, we have inspected a few domains of small sizes (each containing about 300 unique words or less) for a preliminary estimation. The top-10% candidates with lowest inter-domain entropy, weighted by their term frequencies in their respect domains, are evaluated. (The 10% threshold is selected arbitrarily.) Table 2 shows the results in terms of precision (P), recall (R) and F-measure (F). The column with the '#Words' label shows the numbers of unique words used in the 5 domains.

Since it is difficult sometimes to have a consistent judgment on "domain specificity", the estimation could vary drastically on other domains by other persons. For this reason, the degree of domain specificity is ranked from 0 (irrelevant) to 5 (absolutely specific to the domain) points. Therefore, when computing the precision and recall measures, a completely "correct" answer should have a grading point '5'. Fortunately, most terms are assigned the grading point 5, with a few less certain cases assigned '3' or '4'.

Domain	#Words	R	P	F
Baseball	149	29.7	68.0	41.3
Basketball	277	26.2	60.7	36.6
Broadcast -TV	161	47.6	50.0	48.8
Education	255	40.0	81.5	53.7
Health -care	263	38.2	66.9	48.6
(Average)		36.3	65.4	45.8

Table 2. Performance of the Top-10% DSW candidate lists in 5 sample domains.

Table 2 shows that, by only gathering the first 10% of the word lists, we can identify about 36% of the embedded domain specific words, and the precision is as high as 65%. Therefore, we can identify significant amount of DSW's about every 1.5 entries from the top-10% list of low entropy words.

Since the TF-IDF (term frequency-inverse document frequency) approach (Baeza-Yates and Ribeiro-Neto, 1998; Jurafsky and Martin 2000) is widely used in information retrieval applications for indexing important terms within documents, it can also be applied to identify domain specific words in various domains. To make a comparison, the TF-IDF term weighting method is also applied to the same corpus. The "baseball" domain is then inspected for their differences. It turns out that the top-10% candidate lists of both methods show the *same* performance. However, the IDE measure appears to reach the highest precision faster than the TF-IDF approach. Furthermore, the IDE measure has a better top-20% performance than that of the TF-IDF approach as listed in Table 3.

Model	R	P	F
IDE	48.3	55.3	51.6
TF-IDF	44.8	51.3	47.8

Table 3. Comparison of the top-20% candidate list performance between IDE and TFIDF -based approaches.

Although it is not sure whether the superiority of the IDE approach will retain when examining larger corpora, it does have its advantages in indicating the "degree of specificity". In particular, the degree of domain specificity of a term is estimated by considering the cross-domain *probability distribution* of the term in the current IDE-based approach. Instead, the TF-IDF approaches only count the number of domains a term was found as a measure of randomness. The IDE approach is therefore gaining a little bit performance than a TF-IDF model.

The results partially confirm our expectation to build a large semantically annotated lexicon tree from the web pages using the implicit tags associated with the web directory hierarchy and removing non-specific words from web documents.

6 Error Sources and Future Works

In spite of some encouraging results, we also observed some adverse effects in using the single inter-domain entropy metric to identify domain specific words. For instance, some non-specific words may also have low entropy simply because they appear in only one domain (IDE=0). Since such words cannot be distinguished from real "domain-specific" words, there should be other knowledge sources to reduce false alarms of this kind (known as the Type II errors.)

On the other hand, some multiple sense words may have too many senses such that they are considered non-specific in each domain (although the sense is unique in each respect domain). This is a typical Type I error we have observed.

As a result, further refinement of the purely statistical model is required to improve the precision of the current approach. Currently, we prefer a co-training approach inspired by the works in (Chang and Su, 1997; Chang, 1997), which is capable of augmenting a single IDE-like metric with other information sources.

We have also assumed that the directories of all web sites are well organized in the sense that the domain labels (directory names) are appropriate representatives of the documents under the directories. This assumption is not always satisfied since it depends on the site owners' views on the documents. There are good chances that the hierarchies differ from site to site. Therefore, we may need some measures of site similarity, and approaches to unify the different hierarchies and naming policies as well. The answers to such problems are not yet clear. However, we believe that the hierarchy of the directories (even though not well named) had substantially reduces the cost for lexicogrophers who want to build a large semantically annotated lexicon tree. And the whole process will become more and more automatic as we refine the above model against more and more data.

7 Concluding Remarks

The major contribution of the proposed model is to extract highly associated sets of domain-specific words, and keeping their hierarchical links with other sets of domain specific words at low cost. These sets of highly associated domain specific words can thus be used directly for sense disambiguation and similar applications. The proposed model takes advantages of the rich web text resources and the implicit semantic tags implied in the directory hierarchy for web documents. Therefore, the requirement for manual tagging is negligible. The extracted lists of DSW's are not only useful for word sense disambiguation but also useful as a basis for constructing lexicon databases with rich semantic links. So far, an average precision of 65.4% and an average recall of 36.3% are observed if the top-10% candidates are extracted as domain-specific words. And it outperforms the TF-IDF method for term weighting in the current task.

Acknowledgements

Part of the work was supported by the National Science Council (NSC), ROC, under the contract NSC 90-2213-E-260-015-.

References

Christiane Fellbaum (Ed.). 1998. *WordNet: An Electronic Lexical Database.* MIT Press, Cambridge, MA.

Daniel Jurafsky and James H. Martin. 2000. *Speech and Language Processing: An Introduction to Natural Language Processing, Computational Linguistics, and Speech Recognition*, Prentice-Hall, NJ, USA.

David Yarowsky. 1995. "Unsupervised Word Sense Disambiguation Rivaling Supervised Methods," in *Proceedings of the 33rd Annual Meeting of the Association for Computational Linguistics*, pp. 189-196, MIT, MA, USA.

Frank Smadja, Kathleen R. McKeown, and Vasileios Hatzivassiloglou. 1996. "Translating Collocations for Bilingual Lexicons: A Statistical Approach," *Computational Linguistics*, 22(1):1-38.

Jing-Shin Chang and Keh-Yih Su. 1997. "An Unsupervised Iterative Method for Chinese New Lexicon Extraction", *International Journal of Computational Linguistics and Chinese Language Processing (CLCLP)*, 2(2):97-148.

Jing-Shin Chang. 1997. *Automatic Lexicon Acquisition and Precision-Recall Maximization for Untagged Text Corpora*, Ph.D. dissertation, Department of Electrical Engineering, National Tsing-Hua University, Hsinchu, Taiwan, R.O.C.

Jing-Shin Chang. 2005. "Web Document Classification into a Hierarchical Document Tree Based on Domain Specific Words", submitted.

Ken Church and Patrick Hanks. 1989. "Word Association Norms, Mutual Information, and Lexicography," *Proc. 27th Annual Meeting of the ACL*, pp. 76-83, University of British Columbia, Vancouver, British Columbia, Canada.

Ming-Yu Lin, Tung-Hui Chiang and Keh-Yih Su. 1993. "A Preliminary Study on Unknown Word Problem in Chinese Word Segmentation," *Proceedings of ROCLING VI*, pp. 119-142.

Ricardo Baeza-Yates and Berthier Ribeiro-Neto. 1999. *Modern Information Retrieval,* Addison Wesley, New York.

Tung-Hui Chiang, Jing-Shin Chang, Ming-Yu Lin and Keh-Yih Su. 1992. "Statistical Models for Word Segmentation and Unknown Word Resolution," *Proceedings of ROCLING-V*, pp. 123-146, Taipei, Taiwan, R.O.C.

Turn-taking in Mandarin Dialogue: Interactions of Tone and Intonation

Gina-Anne Levow
Computer Science Department
University of Chicago
Chicago, IL 60637 USA
levow@cs.uchicago.edu

Abstract

Fluent dialogue requires that speakers successfully negotiate and signal turn-taking. While many cues to turn change have been proposed, especially in multi-modal frameworks, here we focus on the use of prosodic cues to these functions. In particular, we consider the use of prosodic cues in a tone language, Mandarin Chinese, where variations in pitch height and slope additionally serve to determine word meaning. Within a corpus of spontaneous Chinese dialogues, we find that turn-unit final syllables are significantly lower in average pitch and intensity than turn-unit initial syllables in both smooth turn changes and segments ended by speaker overlap. Interruptions are characterized by significant prosodic differences from smooth turn initiations. Furthermore, we demonstrate that these contrasts correspond to an overall lowering across all tones in final position, which largely preserves the relative heights of the lexical tones. In classification tasks, we contrast the use of text and prosodic features. Finally, we demonstrate that, on balanced training and test sets, we can distinguish turn-unit final words from other words at $\approx 93\%$ accuracy and interruptions from smooth turn unit initiations at 62% accuracy.

1 Introduction

Fluent dialogues require effective turn transitions between speakers. Research in turn-taking, typified by (Duncan, 1974), posits several key signals for turn-taking, including a turn-change signal which offers to cede the floor, speaker-state signal which indicates taking the floor, within-turn signal, and continuation signals. This process fundamentally requires cooperation between participants both to produce the contextually appropriate signals and to interpret those of their interlocutor. These analyses have proposed a wide range of cues to turn status, ranging from gaze and gesture in a multi-modal context to prosodic cues including pitch, intensity, and duration as well as lexical and syntactic cues.

Much of this fundamental research as well as computational implementations have focused on English, a language with well-studied intonational sentence and discourse structure. A substantial body of work has identified sentence-like units as well as fragments and repairs in conversational speech, including (Ostendorf, forthcoming; Liu et al., 2004; Shriberg et al., 2001) These approaches have employed lexical and prosodic cues in diverse frameworks, including Hidden Markov Models employing decision trees and hidden state language models, neural networks, and maximum entropy models. (Shriberg et al., 2001) identified jump-in points and jump-in words in multi-party meeting speech using prosodic and language model features at accuracies of 65 and 77% under equal priors. Furthermore, (Ward and Tsukahara, 2000) demonstrated that backchannels occurred at predictable points with specific prosodic characteristics in both English and Japanese.

In the current paper, we consider the interaction of potential prosodic intonational cues related to turn-taking with the realization of lexical tone in a tone language, Putonghua or Mandarin Chinese. Mandarin employs four canonical lexical tones distinguished by pitch height and pitch contour: high level, mid-rising, low falling-rising, and high falling. We explore whether prosodic features are also employed in turn-taking behavior in this language and whether the forms are comparable to those employed in languages with lexical tone. We demonstrate that intonational cues quite similar to those in English are also employed in Chinese with lower pitch and intensity at ends of turn units than at the beginnings of those turn units. Interruptions likewise are distinguished from smooth turn transitions by prosodic means, including greater pitch elevation. We demonstrate how these changes interact with lexical tone by substantial lowering of average pitch height across all tones in final positions and contrast pitch contours in final and non-final positions. Finally, these cues in conjunction with silence and durational features can be employed to distinguish turn-unit final words from non-final words in the dialogue and words that initiate interruptions from those which start smoother turn transitions.

In the remainder of the paper we will briefly describe the data set employed in these experiments and the basic extraction of prosodic features (Section 2). We then present acoustic analyses contrasting turn unit final and turn unit initial syllables under different turn transition types (Section 3). We will describe the impact of these intonational cues on the realization of lexical tone (Section 4). Finally we will apply these prosodic contrasts to enable classification of words for finality and interruption status (Section 5).

2 Experimental Data

The data in this study was drawn from the Taiwanese Putonghua Speech Corpus[1]. The materials chosen include 5 spontaneous dialogues by Taiwanese speakers of Mandarin, seven females and three males. The dialogues, averaging 20 minutes in duration, were recorded on two channels, one per speaker, in a quiet room and digitized at 16KHz sampling. The recordings were later manually transcribed and segmented into words; turn-beginnings and overlaps were time-stamped. The manual word segmentation was based on both syntax and phonology according to a methodology described in detail in (Duanmu, 1996).

2.1 Prosodic Features

For the subsequent analysis, the conversations were divided into chunks based on the turn and overlap time-stamps. Using a Chinese character-to-pinyin dictionary and a hand-constructed mapping of pinyin sequences to ARPABET phonemes, the transcribed text was then force-aligned to the corresponding audio segments using the language porting mechanism in the University of Colorado Sonic speech recognizer (Pellom et al., 2001). The resulting alignment provided phone, syllable, and word durations as well as silence positions and durations.

Pitch and intensity values for voiced regions were computed using the functions "To Pitch" and "To Intensity" in the freely available Praat acoustic analysis software package(Boersma, 2001). We then computed normalized pitch and intensity values based on log-scaled z-score normalization of each conversation side. Based on the above alignment, we then computed maximum and mean pitch and intensity values for each syllable and word for all voiced regions. Given the presence of lexical tone, we extracted five points evenly distributed across the "final" region of the syllable, excluding the initial consonant, if any. We then estimated the linear syllable slope based on the latter half of this region in which the effects of tonal coarticulation are likely to be minimized under the pitch target approximation model(Xu, 1997).

3 Acoustic Analysis of Turn-taking

Each of the turn units extracted above was tagged based on its starting and ending conditions as one of four types: smooth, rough, intersmooth, and interrough. "Smooth" indicates a segment-ending transition from one speaker to another, not caused

[1] Available from `http://www.ldc.upenn.edu`

Position	Start −Overlap or −Spkr Change	Start +Overlap +Spkr Change
End −Overlap	Smooth 1413	Intersmooth 289
End +Overlap	Rough 407	Interrough 68

Table 1: Types of turn units

by the start of overlap with another speaker. By contrast, a rough transition indicates the end of a chunk at the start of overlap with another speaker. The prefix "inter" indicates the turn began with an interruption, identified by overlap with the previous speaker and change of speaker holding the floor. In this class, the new speaker continues to hold the floor after the period of overlap.

We contrast turn unit initial and turn unit final syllables for each type of transition and across all turns. We compare mean pitch and mean intensity in each case. We find in all cases highly significant differences between mean pitch of turn unit initial syllables and mean pitch of final syllables ($p < 0.0001$) as illustrated in Figure 1. Syllables in initial position have much higher log-scaled mean pitch in all conditions. For intensity, we find highly significant differences across all conditions ($p < 0.005$), with initial syllables having higher amplitude than final syllables. These contrasts appear in Figure 2. Furthermore, comparing final intensity of transitions not marked by the start of overlap with the intensity of the final pre-overlap syllable in a transition caused by overlap, we find significantly higher normalized mean intensity in all rough transitions relative to others. In contrast, comparable differences in pitch do not reach significance.

Finally we compare smooth turn unit initiations ("smooth") to successful interruptions ("interrough","intersmooth"), contrasting initial syllables in each class. Here we find that both normalized mean pitch (Figure 3) and normalized mean intensity (Figure 4) in turn unit initial syllables are significantly higher in interruptions than in "smooth" turn transitions.[2] Speakers use these

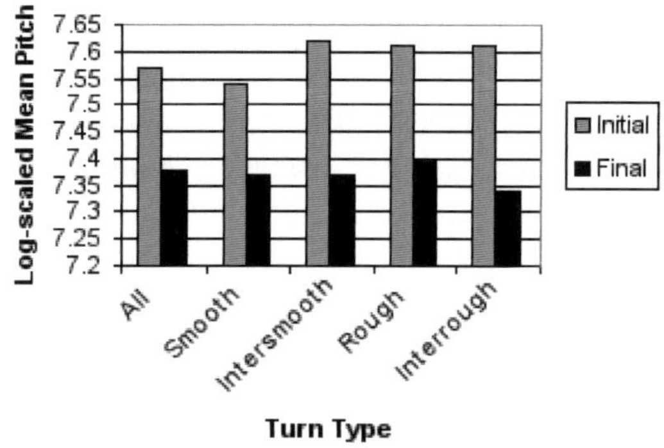

Figure 1: Pitch contrasts between syllables in initial and final position across turn types. Values for initial position are in grey, final position in black.

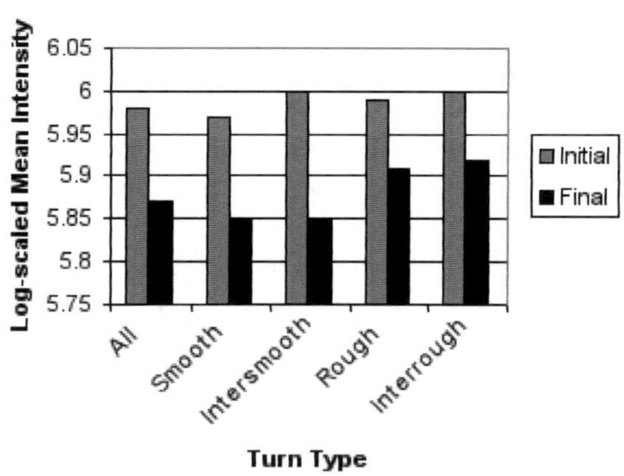

Figure 2: Intensity contrasts between syllables in initial and final position across turn types. Values for initial position are in grey, final position in black.

[2] If one compares both "smooth" and "rough" transitions to "intersmooth" and "interrough" transitions, initial syllables are significantly higher in pitch for the interruption

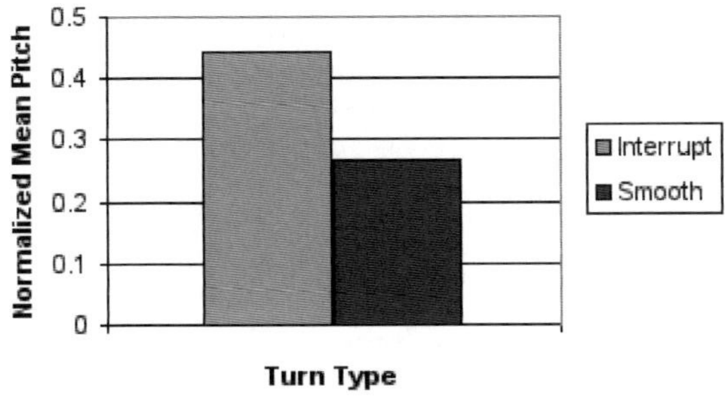

Figure 3: Pitch contrasts between initial syllables in smooth turn transitions and interruptions. Values for smooth transitions are in black, interruptions in grey.

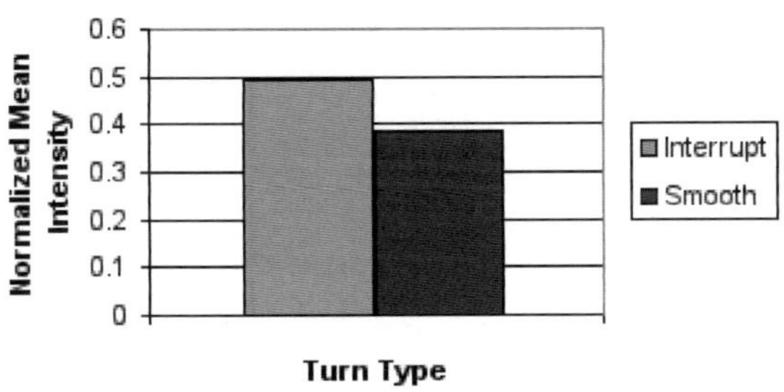

Figure 4: Intensity contrasts between initial syllables in smooth turn transitions and interruptions. Values for smooth transitions are in black, interruptions in grey.

prosodic cues to take the floor by interruption.

These descriptive analyses demonstrate that intonational cues to turn-taking do play a role in a tone language. Not only does intensity play a significant role, but pitch also is employed to distinguish initiation and finality, in spite of its concurrent use in determining lexical identity. In the following section, we describe the effects on tone height and tone shape caused by these broader intonational phenomena.

4 Tone and Intonation

We have determined that syllables in turn unit final position have dramatically reduced average pitch relative to those in turn unit initial position, and these contrasts can serve to signal turn-change and speaker change as suggested by (Duncan, 1974). How do these changes interact with lexical identity and lexical tone? Since tone operates on a syllable in Chinese, we consider the average pitch and tone contours of syllables in final and non-final position. We find that average pitch for all tones is reduced, and relative tone height is largely preserved.[3] Thus a final high tone is readily distinguishable from a final low tone, if the listener can interpret the syllable as turn-final. The contrasts appear in Figure 5.

classes, but differences for intensity do not reach significance ($p = 0.053$)

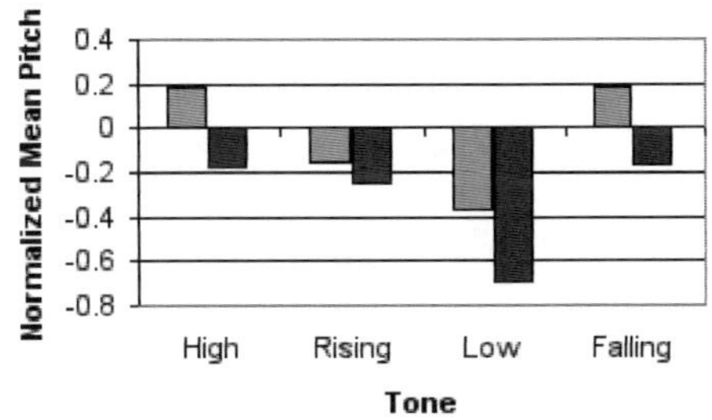

Figure 5: Contrasts in average pitch for the four canonical tones in turn non-final and final positions. Values for non-final positions are in grey, final positions in black.

Turning to tone contour, we find likewise little change between non-final and final contours, with the contours running parallel, but at a much lower pitch.[4] For illustration, mid-rising and high falling tones are shown in Figure 6. Comparable behavior has been observed at other discourse boundaries such as story boundaries in newswire speech. (Levow, 2004).

5 Recognizing Turn Unit Boundaries and Interruptions

Based on the salient contrasts in pitch and intensity observed above, we employ prosodic features both to identify turn boundaries and to distinguish between the start of interruptions and smooth transitions. We further contrast the use of prosodic features with text n-gram features.

[3]This analysis excludes exclamatory and interjective particles.

[4]It is also true that contours do not always match their canonical forms even in non-final position. This variation may be attributed to a combination of tonal coarticulatory effects and the presence of other turn-internal boundaries.

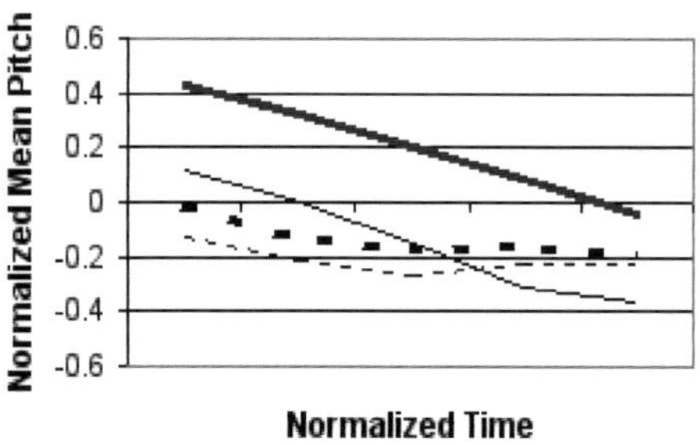

Figure 6: Contrasts in pitch contour for mid-rising and high falling tones in turn non-final and final positions. Values for non-final positions are in heavy lines, final positions in thin lines. Mid-rising tone is in black, dashed lines, high falling in solid lines.

5.1 Classifier Features: Prosodic

The features used in the classifier trained to recognize turn boundaries and turn types fall into two classes: local and contextual. The local features describe the words or syllables themselves, while the contextual features capture contrasts between adjacent words or syllables. The first set of features thus includes the mean pitch and mean intensity for the current word and syllable, the word duration, and the maximum pitch and intensity for the syllable. The second set of features include the length of any following silence and the differences in mean pitch and mean intensity between the current word or syllable and the following word or syllable.

5.2 Classifier Features: Text

For contrastive purposes, we also consider the use of textual features for turn boundary and boundary type classification.[5] Here we exploit syllable and word features, as well as syllable n-gram features. We use the toneless pinyin representation of the current word and the final syllable in each word. Such features aim to capture, for example, question particles that signal the end of a turn. In addition, we extracted the five preceding and five following syllables in the sequence around the current syllable. We then experimented with different window widths for n-gram construction, ranging from one to five, as supported by the classifier described below.

[5]All text features are drawn from the ground truth manual text transcripts.

5.3 Classifiers

We performed experiments with several classifiers: Boostexter (Schapire and Singer, 2000), a well-known implementation of boosted weak learners, multi-class Support Vector Machines with linear kernels (C-C.Cheng and Lin, 2001), an implementation of a margin-based discriminative classifier, and decision trees, implemented by C4.5(Quinlan, 1992). All classifiers yielded comparable results on this classification task. Here we present the results using Boostexter to exploit its support for text features and automatic n-gram feature selection as well as its relative interpretability. We used downsampled balanced training and test sets to enable assessment of the utility of these features for classification and employed 10-fold cross-validation, presenting the average over the runs.

5.3.1 Recognizing Turn Unit Ends

Using the features above we created a set of 1610 turn unit final words and 1610 non-final words. Based on 10-fold cross-validation, using combined text and prosodic features, we obtain an accuracy of 93.1% on this task. The key prosodic features in this classification are silence duration, which is the first feature selected, and maximum intensity. The highest lexical features are preceding 'ta', preceding 'ao', and following 'dui'. If silence features are excluded, classification accuracy drops substantially to 69%, still better than the 50% chance baseline for this set. In this case, syllable mean intensity features become the first selected for classification.

We also consider the relative effectiveness of classifiers based on text, with silence, or prosodic features alone. We find that, when silence duration features are available, both text- and prosodic-based classifiers perform comparably at 93.5% and 93.7% accuracy respectively, near the effectiveness of the combined text and prosodic classifier. However, when silence features are excluded, a greater difference is found between classification based on text features and classification based on prosodic features. Specifically, without silence information, classification based on text features alone reaches only 59.5%. However, classification based on prosodic features remains somewhat more robust, though still with a substantial drop in accuracy, at 66.5% for prosody only. This finding suggests that although the presence of a longer silence interval is the best cue to finality, additional prosodic features, such as differences in pitch and intensity, concurrently signal the opportunity for another speaker to start a turn. Text features, especially in highly disfluent conversational speech, provide less clear evidence. Results appear in Table 5.3.1.

5.3.2 Recognizing Interruptions

In order to create a comparable context for initial words in interruption and smoothly initiated turns, we reversed the direction of the contextual comparisons, comparing the preceding word features to those of the current word and measuring pre-word silences rather than following silences. Using this configuration, we created a set of 218 interruption initial words and 218 smooth transition initial words, following smooth transitions without overlap. Based on 10-fold cross-validation for this downsampled balanced case, we obtain an accuracy of 62%, relative to a 50% baseline. The best classifiers employed only prosodic features with silence duration and normalized mean word pitch. Addition of text features degrades test set performance as the classifier rapidly overfits to the training materials. If we exclude silence related features, accuracy drops to almost chance.

6 Discussion and Conclusion

We have demonstrated that even in a language that employs lexical tone, cues to turn and speaker status are still carried by prosodic means, including pitch. Specifically, turn unit initial syllables have significantly higher mean pitch and intensity than do final syllables in different turn transition types. The elevation of initial pitch is further enhanced in interruptions, when a new speaker seizes the floor beginning with an overlap of the current speaker. These contrasts are similar to those observed for English, and consistent with signals described in the literature. These changes result in an overall reduction in pitch for syllables in final position across all tones, but relative pitch height employed by lexical tone is preserved in most cases. Finally, we employed these cues to train classifiers to distinguish turn unit final words from other words in the dialogue and to distinguish interruption initial words from initial words in smooth transitions with no overlap.

We further contrasted the utility of text and prosodic features for the identification of turn boundary position and type. We find that silence is the most reliable cue both to identify final turn boundaries and to distinguish types of turn transitions. In conjunction with silence features, text, prosodic, and joint text-prosodic features can fare comparably. However, for turn unit boundaries, the availability of a variety of prosodic features proves to be essential for relatively better classification in the absence of silence information.

In future work, we plan to enhance tone recognition by better contextual modeling that will compensate for the effects of a variety of discourse boundaries, including turn and topic, on tone realization. We also plan to embed turn-based classification in a sequential discriminative model to further facilitate integration of prosodic and lexical features as well as sequence constraints on turn structure.

Acknowledgments

We would like to thank the developers of the Taiwanese Putonghua corpus and the Linguistic Data Consortium for the provision of these resources. This work was supported by NSF Grant 0414919.

References

P. Boersma. 2001. Praat, a system for doing phonetics by computer. *Glot International*, 5(9–10):341–345.

C-C.Cheng and C-J. Lin. 2001. LIBSVM:a library for support vector machines. Software available at: http://www.csie.ntu.edu.tw/ cjlin/libsvm.

San Duanmu. 1996. Notes on word boundaries. Taiwanese Putonghua Corpus Documentation.

S. Duncan, 1974. *Some signals and rules for taking speaking turns in conversations*, pages 298–311.

Gina-Anne Levow. 2004. Prosody-based topic segmentation for mandarin broadcast news. In *Proceedings of HLT-NAACL 2004, Companion Volume*, pages 137–140.

	Prosody Only	Text	Prosody + Text
With silence	93.7%	93.5%	93.1%
Without silence	66.5%	59.5%	69%

Table 2: Recognition of turn unit final vs. non-final words

Y. Liu, A. Stolcke, E. Shriberg, and M. Harper. 2004. Comparing and combining generative and posterior probability models: Some advances in sentence boundary detection in speech. In *Proceedings of Conf. on Empirical Methods in Natural Language Processing*.

M. Ostendorf. forthcoming. Prosodic boundary detection. In M. Horne, editor, *Prosody: Theory and Experiment. Studies Presented to Gosta Bruce*. Kluwer.

B. Pellom, W. Ward, J. Hansen, K. Hacioglu, J. Zhang, X. Yu, and S. Pradhan. 2001. University of Colorado dialog systems for travel and navigation.

J.R. Quinlan. 1992. *C4.5: Programs for Machine Learning*. Morgan Kaufmann.

Robert E. Schapire and Yoram Singer. 2000. Boostexter: A boosting-based system for text categorization. *Machine Learning*, 39(2–3):135–168.

E. Shriberg, A. Stolcke, and D. Baron. 2001. Can prosody aid the automatic processing of multi-party meetings? evidence from predicting punctuation, disfluencies, and overlapping speech. In *Proc. of ISCA Tutorial and Research Workshop on Prosody in Speech Recognition and Understanding*.

N. Ward and W. Tsukahara. 2000. Prosodic features which cue back-channel responses in English and Japanese. *Journal of Pragmatics*, 23:1177–1207.

Yi Xu. 1997. Contextual tonal variations in Mandarin. *Journal of Phonetics*, 25:62–83.

Learning a Log-Linear Model with Bilingual Phrase-Pair Features for Statistical Machine Translation

Bing Zhao and **Alex Waibel**
School of Computer Science
Carnegie Mellon University
{bzhao, waibel}@cs.cmu.edu

Abstract

We propose a set of informative feature functions together with a log-linear model framework for bilingual phrase-pair extraction to improve phrase-based statistical machine translation. The base feature functions investigated are phrase length model, phrase-level centers' distortion, lexicon translation equivalence, bracketing constraints and word alignment links. Two generative models show strong baselines with these base features, illustrating the effectiveness of the proposed feature functions. Strategies of extending the features and a log-linear model of learning the weighted combination of them are proposed to effectively extract phrase-pairs from parallel data. Experimental results of TIDES'03 Chinese-English small data track show improved translation qualities.

1 Introduction

Bilingual phrase-pair extraction from parallel data becomes a key component in today's state of the art phrase-based statistical machine translation systems. The significant advantages of using phrase-pairs over word level mixture models (Brown et al., 1993) are that both fertilities and distortions above phrase level are simpler to model and phrase-based approaches have flexibilities of modeling local word-reordering and are less sensitive to the preprocessing errors such as word segmentations (e.g., for Chinese and Japanese) and tokenization. These advantages are observed and supported by the positive evidences from many previous works such as (Wu, 1997; Och and Ney, 2004; Koehn et al., 2003; Zens and Ney, 2004; Vogel et al., 2003).

In practice, a phrase-pair extraction based on word alignment (Koehn, 2004; Tillmann, 2003; Och and Ney, 2004) works quite well given simple heuristics and millions of parallel sentences to cover enough instances needed for translation. However, it is more or less difficult to extend the heuristics to include more informative clues for better phrase-pair extractions. We propose a principled framework of combining a set of informative feature functions via a log-linear model for bilingual phrase-pair extraction. In particular, we introduce a few informative feature functions in keeping the philosophy of phrase translations. The base feature functions are designed to model three diverse aspects of a *block* (a phrase pair): a phrase-level length model to approximate phrasal length relevance, a center distortion model to model relative positions' differences for phrases in a given sentence pair and a generative phrase level lexical model to model translational equivalence. Furthermore, we extend the base feature functions by symmetrizing with noisy-channel models in two directions: source-to-target and target-to-source. The utilities of the proposed features are demonstrated using two generative models establishing strong baselines; together with constraints from word alignments, these feature functions are combined in a log-linear model to extract phrase pairs effectively; improved translation qualities are achieved over a state of the art system on TIDES'03 Chinese-English small data tack.

The remainder paper is structured as follows: in Section 2, statistical machine translation is briefly reviewed with notations for Blocks; in Section 3, base feature functions are explained; Section 4 contains two novel generative models as our baselines; our proposed log-linear model with extended feature functions are in Section 5; in Section 6, our experimental results; conclusions and discussions are given in Section 7.

2 Statistical Machine Translation

Generally speaking, the task of statistical machine translation (SMT) is to translate one sentence in a source language F into a target language E. For example[1], given a French sentence **f** with J words denoted as $f_1^J = f_1 f_2 ... f_J$, an SMT system automatically translates it into an English sentence **e** with I words denoted by $e_1^I = e_1 e_2 ... e_I$. The SMT system first proposes English hypotheses in its model space. Among all the hypotheses, the system selects the one with the highest conditional probability according to Bayes's decision rule as follows:

$$\hat{e}_1^I = \arg\max_{\{e_1^I\}} P(e_1^I|f_1^J) = \arg\max_{\{e_1^I\}} P(f_1^J|e_1^I)P(e_1^I), \quad (1)$$

where $P(f_1^J|e_1^I)$ is called *translation model* and $P(e_1^I)$ is the *language model*. For most of the phrase based machine translation systems, the translation model are essentially a collection of bilingual phrase-pairs extracted from parallel sentence pairs. This paper focus on how to extract high quality phrase-pairs from parallel data.

Each phrase pair is represented as a *Block*:X in a given parallel sentence pair:

$$X \rightarrow (f_j^{j+l}, e_i^{i+k}), \quad (2)$$

where f_j^{j+l} is the source phrase with $(l+1)$ French words; its projection is e_i^{i+k} in the target sentence with left boundary at the position of i and right boundary at $(i+k)$. We view the *phrase-pair extraction* as a local search algorithm: given a source phrase f_j^{j+l}, search for the projected boundaries of candidate target phrase e_i^{i+k} according to a weighted combination of diverse feature functions in a log-linear model. The log linear model then servers as a performance measure to guide a local search (i.e., a stochastic hill-climbing) to extract bilingual phrase pairs from the parallel data.

3 Base Feature Functions

We introduce several informative base feature functions, some of which are shown to be helpful in our previous works (Zhao and Vogel, 2005). They'll be briefly summarized here to be more self-contained. Each of the feature functions corresponds to one special aspect of the block embedded in the context of a given sentence pair. These aspects are then quantified by the proposed sub-models or our designed feature functions.

3.1 A Phrase-Level Length Model

Given the word fertility defined as in (Brown et al., 1993), we can compute a probability to predict *phrase length* relevance between a pair of phrases: given the candidate target phrase (English) e_1^I and a source phrase (French) f_1^J of length J, the model gives the probabilistic estimation of $P(J|e_1^I)$ via a dynamic programming algorithm using the English word fertilities models $P(\phi|e_i)$. Figure 1 shows an example fertility

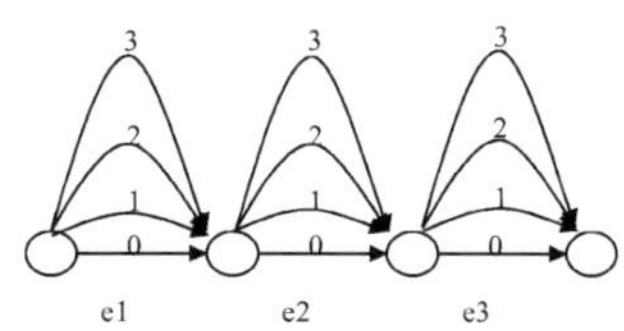

Figure 1: A trellis of an English trigram with maximum fertility of 4 for dynamic programming

trellis of an English trigram, where each edge between two nodes represents one English word e_i. The arc between two nodes represents one candidate non-zero fertility for word e_i. The fertility of zero (i.e., generating a Null word) corresponds to the direct edge between two nodes and thus, the Null word is incorporated into this model's representation. Each arc is associated with a English word fertility probability $P(\phi_i|e_i)$. A path ϕ_1^I through the trellis represents the number of French words ϕ_i generated by the English trigram. Thus, the probability of generating J words from the English phrase along the Viterbi path is:

$$P(J|e_1^I) = \max_{\{\phi_1^I, J=\sum_{i=1}^I \phi_i\}} \prod_{i=1}^{I} P(\phi_i|e_i) \quad (3)$$

The Viterbi path is inferred via dynamic programming as follows:

$$\phi[j,i] = max \begin{cases} \phi[j, i-1] + \log P_{Null}(0|e_i) \\ \phi[j-1, i-1] + \log P_\phi(1|e_i) \\ \phi[j-2, i-1] + \log P_\phi(2|e_i) \\ \phi[j-3, i-1] + \log P_\phi(3|e_i) \end{cases}$$

[1]We follow the notations used in (Brown et al., 1993)

where $P_{Null}(0|e_i)$ is the probability of generating a Null word from e_i; $P_\phi(k = 1|e_i)$ is the usual word fertility model of generating one French word from the word e_i; $\phi[j, i]$ is the cost so far for generating j words from $e_1^i : e_1, \cdots, e_i$. After computing the cost of $\phi[J, I]$, we can trace back the Viterbi path, along which the probability $P(J|e_1^I)$ of generating J French words from the English phrase e_1^I as shown in Eqn. 3.

Thus, for each block, one can compute a fertility based score Eqn. 3 to estimate to how relevant the phrase pairs' lengths are to each other.

3.2 A Center-Distortion Model

As introduced in Section 1, the distortion model above phrase level is usually easier to model. Empirical observations show that most high quality blocks are located close to the diagonal or the inverse diagonal in the alignment matrix of a sentence pair. A simple distortion model is designed to estimate how far away the phrase pairs are from each other.

The *center* $\odot_{f_j^{j+l}}$ of the phrase f_j^{j+l} is a normalized *relative position* in the source sentence defined as follows:

$$\odot_{f_j^{j+l}} = \frac{1}{J} \sum_{j'=j}^{j'=j+l} \frac{j'}{l+1} \tag{4}$$

The center of the English phrase is computed accordingly. Figure 2 shows histograms of the differences between the centers: $(\odot_{f_j^{j+l}} - \odot_{e_i^{i+k}})$ of $30.8K$ oracle phrase pairs extracted from 627 human word-aligned sentence pairs: for each source phrase, find the left-most and right-most projected positions in the target sentence according to both word alignment and the coherence constraint (Fox, 2002).

For phrase-pair extraction, the expected center of the phrase e_i^{i+k} is estimated for a given French phrase's center and then a local search starting around it is carried out to get candidate target phrases. The expected relative center for every French word $f_{j'}$ is first computed as follows:

$$\odot_{e_i^{i+k}}(f_{j'}) = \frac{1}{I} \cdot \frac{\sum_{i'=i}^{(i+k)} i' \cdot P(f_{j'}|e_{i'})}{\sum_{i'=i}^{(i+k)} P(f_{j'}|e_{i'})}, \tag{5}$$

where $P(f_{j'}|e_i)$ is the word translation lexicon estimated in IBM Models. i is the position index, which is weighted by the word level translation probabilities; the term of $\sum_{i=1}^{I} P(f_{j'}|e_i)$ provides a normalization so that the expected center is within the range of target sentence length. After this, the expected center of e_i^{i+k} is simply a average of $\odot_{e_i^{i+k}}(f_{j'})$:

$$\odot_{e_i^{i+k}} = \frac{1}{l+1} \sum_{j'=j}^{j+l} \odot_{e_i^{i+k}}(f_{j'}) \tag{6}$$

Given the estimated centers of $\odot_{f_j^{j+l}}$ and $\odot_{e_i^{i+k}}$, we can compute how close they are by the probability of $P(\odot_{f_j^{j+l}}|\odot_{e_i^{i+k}})$. To estimate $P(\odot_{f_j^{j+l}}|\odot_{e_i^{i+k}})$, one can start with a flat gaussian model to enforce the point of $(\odot_{e_i^{i+k}}, \odot_{f_j^{j+l}})$ not too far off the diagonal and build an initial list of phrase pairs and then compute the histogram to approximate $P(\odot_{f_j^{j+l}}|\odot_{e_i^{i+k}}) \simeq P(\odot_{f_j^{j+l}} - \odot_{e_i^{i+k}})$. As shown in Figure 2, this probability can be approximated as a gaussian distribution.

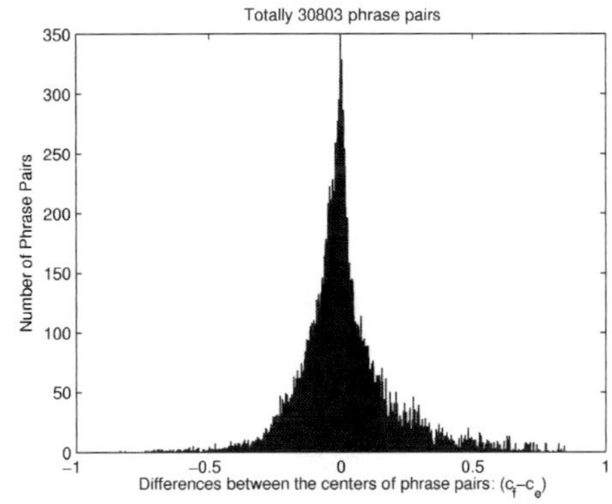

Figure 2: Histogram of relative centers' differences between oracle phrase pairs (blocks) extracted from 627 human word-aligned parallel sentence pairs.

3.3 A Phrase-Level Lexicon Model

Similar to IBM Model-1 (Brown et al., 1993), we use a bag-of-word generative model within the block. According to Bayes rule:

$$P(f_j^{j+l}|e_i^{i+k}) = \prod_{j' \in [j,j+l]} \sum_{i' \in [i,i+k]} P(f_{j'}|e_{i'}) P(e_{i'}|e_i^{i+k}), \tag{7}$$

where $P(e_{i'}|e_i^{i+k}) \simeq 1/(k+1)$ is approximated by a unigram bag-of-word language model. Because phrase-pairs are usually very short, this assumption works very well in practice (Koehn et al., 2003; Brown et al., 1993).

The parameters used by the three feature functions are estimated using IBM Model-4.

4 Two Generative Models

We here present two generative models of $Pr(f_j^{j+l}|e_i^{i+k})$ for phrase-pair extraction. The first one models three aspects of a phrase pair, i.e., the phrase level lexical translation equivalence, positions' distortion and length relevance. The second one takes into consideration of bracketing a sentence pair at a block level and generate sub-blocks synchronously.

4.1 Generative Model-1

To model $Pr(f_j^{j+l}|e_i^{i+k})$, *Model-1* first proposes how many words of f_j to generate according to $P(l+1|e_i^{i+k})$; then it proposes the location of the source phrases f_j^{j+l} by predicting the center $\odot_{f_j^{j+l}}$ of the phrase; and then the model generates the words f_j according to a lexicon model $P(f|e)$. The model is summarized in Eqn. 8.

$$\begin{aligned} Pr(f_j^{j+l}|e_i^{i+k}) = \max_{\{f_j^{j+l}\}} P(l+1|e_i^{i+k}) \cdot \\ P(\odot_{f_j^{j+l}}|\odot_{e_i^{i+k}}) P(f_j^{j+l}|e_i^{i+k}), \end{aligned} \quad (8)$$

where the three components $P(l+1|e_i^{i+k})$, $P(\odot_{f_j^{j+l}}|\odot_{e_i^{i+k}})$ and $P(f_j^{j+l}|e_i^{i+k})$ control three different aspects of a bilingual phrase pair: phrase level fertility, center distortion and translation equivalence as explained in the previous section. A variation of this model is applied in a ACL05 shared task for phrase-based statistical machine translation (Zhao and Vogel, 2005).

4.2 Generative Model-2: Bracketing

Instead of modeling the three aspects individually as in Model-1, we propose to model the brackets induced by the segmentation of the parallel sentence pair given a block. Shown in Figure 3, a phrase pair (block A) split the sentence pairs into five shaded parts A, B, C, D, E, which are the valid parts to be generated in our Model-2.

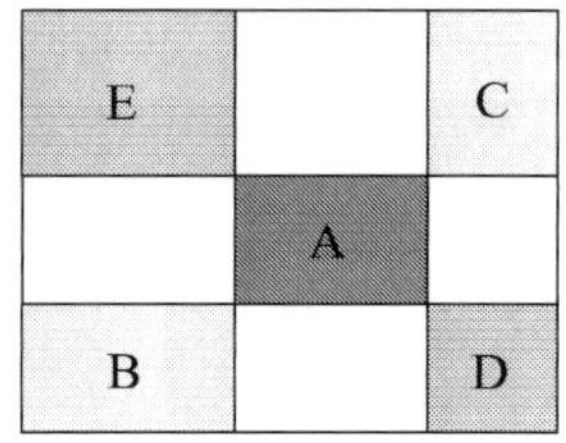

Figure 3: Ngram Bracketing Model

We enforce the following bracketing constraints so that one can only bracket the sentence pair in the following two ways:

$$\begin{aligned} \delta^{[]}(\mathbf{f},\mathbf{e}) &\rightarrow [B, A, C] \\ \delta^{<>}(\mathbf{f},\mathbf{e}) &\rightarrow <D, A, E>, \end{aligned} \quad (9)$$

where $\delta^{[]}$ indicates the bracketing along the diagonal and $\delta^{<>}$ indicates the inverse bracketing. Each bracketing direction is associated with a probability under the same assumption of "bag-of-words" generation as in Eqn. 7. In a way, this model relates to the bilingual bracketing (Wu, 1997) as it requires the other two brackets (either (B, C) or (D, E)) to be generated synchronously. However, the model is a flat one because it requires only one level bracketing for any given block A. The model is summarized as follows:

$$Pr(f_j^{j+l}, e_i^{i+k}|\mathbf{e},\mathbf{f}) = \max_{\{\delta^{[]},\delta^{<>}\}} P(\delta|\mathbf{e},\mathbf{f}), \quad (10)$$

where $P(\delta^{[]}|\mathbf{e},\mathbf{f}) \simeq P(A)P(B)P(C)$; and $P(A)$, $P(B)$ and $P(C)$ are defined similarly as in Eqn. 7 using the lexicon of $P(f|e)$.

The parameters $P(f|e)$ are from IBM Model-4. Using the constraints from the bracketing in Eqn. 9, this model gives quite good performance shown in our experiments.

4.3 A Local Search for Blocks

Both Eqn. 8 and Eqn. 10 involve some local search within a sentence pair: given a source phrase f_j^{j+l}, search for the candidate phrase translation e_i^{i+k} in the target sentence according to the score computed in Eqn. 8 or Eqn. 10. In practice, only the phrase pairs to be used in decoding are searched, i.e., we only search phrase pairs in which the source phrase f_j^{j+l} is seen in a pre-defined list to save computations and disk space. With Eqn. 8 or Eqn. 10 as the performance measures, we employ a twisted stochastic hill-climbing, in which several down-hill moves are accepted to allow one or two left or right functional words to be attached to e_i^{i+k}.

To make the local search more effective, we normalize the lexicon model $P(f|e)$ within the parallel sentence pair in Eqn. 11

$$\hat{P}(f|e) = \frac{P(f|e)}{\sum_{j'=1}^{J} P(f_{j'}|e)}. \quad (11)$$

In this way, the distribution of $\hat{P}(f|e)$ is sharper and more focused in the context of a sentence pair.

We'll use the aforementioned two generative models as our baselines. The sub models are generalized and extended as feature functions in our proposed log-linear model for phrase-pair extraction in Section 5.

5 A Log-Linear Model

The phrase level fertility model (3.1), distortion model(3.2), lexicon model(3.3) and the bracketing model in 4.2 are all real-valued and bounded ($\in [0, 1]$). We define a log-linear model to combine these sub-models in Eqn. 12:

$$Pr(X|\mathbf{e}, \mathbf{f}) = \frac{exp(\sum_{m=1}^{M} \lambda_m \phi_m(X, \mathbf{e}, \mathbf{f}))}{\sum_{\{X'\}} exp(\sum_{m=1}^{M} \lambda_m \phi_m(X', \mathbf{e}, \mathbf{f}))} \quad (12)$$

where $\phi_m(X, \mathbf{e}, \mathbf{f})$ is a feature function corresponding to the *log probabilities* (i.e. raw scores) from the models listed above. The parameters are the feature functions' weights $\{\lambda_m\}$.

5.1 Feature Extensions with Brackets

We define three base feature functions *E2FFScoreIn*: $P(l + 1|e_i^{i+k})$; *E2FIBMScoreIN*: $P(f_j^{j+l}|e_i^{i+k})$; and *E2FIBMBracket*: $Pr(X|\mathbf{e}, \mathbf{f})$ as refereed in Section 4.

We then extend the base feature functions by considering the remaining part of the sentence pair excluding the block. This means, the region exclude block A in Figure 3. The motivation is if the block is of high quality, the remaining part should also be explained well by the model. Therefore, we add the following three extended feature functions:

- *E2FFScoreOut*: $P(J-l-1|e_{i'\notin[i,i+k]})$ which estimates how well the remaining English words $e_{i'\notin[i,i+k]}$ can generate the remaining sentence length of $(J-l-1)$. This model can be computed similarly via dynamic programming as in 3.

- *E2FIBMScoreOut*: Generating the remaining French words in the sentence pair:

$$P(f_{j'\notin[j,j+l]}|e_{i'\notin[i,i+k]}) = \prod_{j'\notin[j,j+l]} \sum_{i'\notin[i,i+k]} P(f_{j'}|e_{i'})P(e_{i'}|e_{i'\notin[i,i+k]}).$$

  This estimates how well the translational equivalence are kept in accordance with the philosophy of the phrase extraction from a parallel sentence pair.

- *AlignmentLinks*: Averaged word alignment links per source word. We count how many alignment links within the block and normalize this number by the length of the source phrase.

5.2 Feature Extensions via Symmetrization

As introduced in Eqn. 1, so far all our models' parameters are using one direction noisy-channel model. In practice, we train both directions of IBM Model-4 — source-to-target and target-to-source to further extend our base feature functions. In this way, we obtain the lexicon models $P(f|e)$ and $P(e|f)$, the fertility models $P(\phi|e)$ and $P(\phi|f)$ to compute the feature functions defined in Section 5.1. Therefore, we have additional five more feature functions of *F2EFScoreIn*, *F2EFScoreOut*, *F2EIBMScoreIN*, *F2EIBMScoreOut* and *F2EIBMBracket* defined accordingly as in Section 5.1. Therefore, we have in total 11 real-valued feature functions for bilingual phrase-pair extraction. Except the feature function of AlignmentLinks, the other 10 feature functions are all bounded in the range of $[0, 1]$.

5.3 Learning and Inference

Using direct maximum entropy model for statistical machine translation was explored in (Papineni et al., 1998). To learn the log-linear model in Eqn. 12, a maximum bleu score optimizer implemented in (Koehn, 2004) is modified with a sampling of N-Best list phrase pairs generated by an initial assignment of weights. To optimize the weights, we view each extracted phrase-pair as a hypothesis block and the reference blocks are extracted from the human word-aligned sentence pairs as described in Section 3.2. We compute word-level F-measure for each extracted block according to all the reference blocks, which contain the same extracted source phrase. Therefore, the data point for optimization is M raw scores [2] of feature functions together with a performance indicator of word-level F-measure. Finally, a modified optimizer similar to (Och and Ney, 2002) is utilized to obtain the optimized weights for the proposed feature functions.

The inference is similar to the one in Section 4.3: a hill-climbing with a performance measure to score the phrase pairs (f_j^{j+l}, e_i^{i+k}) according to the log-linear model as in Eqn 13:

$$\hat{X} = \arg\max_{\{X\}} \sum_{m=1}^{M} \lambda_m \phi_m(X, \mathbf{e}, \mathbf{f}), \qquad (13)$$

where $\phi_m(X, \mathbf{e}, \mathbf{f})$ are log probabilities computed using the models from Section 3 and their extensions in Section 5.1 and 5.2.

6 Experimental Results

We evaluate our proposed phrase extraction models under the conditions of TIDES'03 Chinese-English statistical machine translation Small-Data track. A small $10K$ LDC bilingual dictionary is allowed to be used and the entries in the dictionary are used as additional phrase pairs. Table 1 summarizes the data statistics.

		English	Chinese
Train	Sent. Pairs	4172	
	Words	133598	105331
	Voc Size	8359	7984
Test	Sent. Pairs	919	
	Words	-	26232
	Voc Size	-	4947

Table 1: Training and Test data statistics

Using GIZA++(Och and Ney, 2003), we trained the IBM-Model-4 in both directions for the fertility tables, lexicons and word alignments. We then refine the word alignment by growing the intersections from two directions with new unaligned word pairs which occur in the union (Koehn et al., 2003). We report NIST and *Bleu* (Papineni et al., 2002) scores as the translation performance measures using a decoder in (Vogel et al., 2003). The trigram language model is trained using Gigaword Xinhua news part.

6.1 Baseline Generative Models

The two generative models Eqn. 8 and Eqn. 10 give strong baselines. In the local search of phrase pairs in Eqn. 8 and 10, the *Top-N* scored target phrase candidates for each source phrase within the sentence pair are collected for decoding. There is no significant difference observed between the two generative models. Figure 4 shows the performance of Model-2 over Top-N configurations, in which the Top-7 gives the best performance. However, Top-4 configuration already gives performance close to the optimal and we can avoid extracting too many noisy phrase-pairs which significantly slow down the decoding process. In the experiments so forth, we'll use up to Top-4 candidates for phrase-pair extraction.

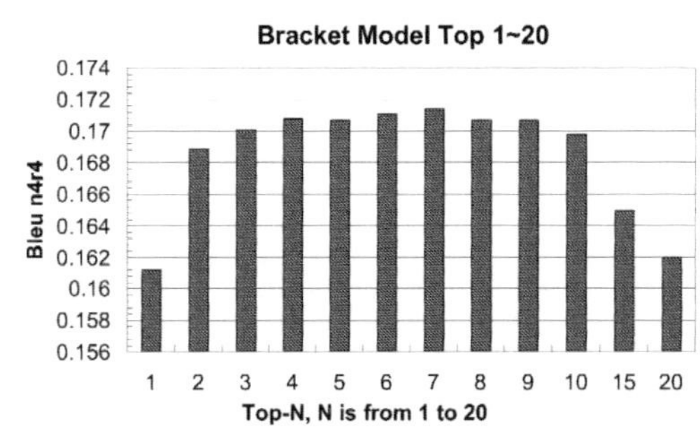

Figure 4: Baseline of Generative Model-2: Bracketing Models

Table 2 summarizes the baselines from the two generative models. The best baseline model is Model-1 using the Top-2 configuration for phrase-pair extraction.

6.2 Pair-wise Correlations among Features

The pair-wise correlations among the 11 (M=11) real-valued feature functions are investigated. The $M \times M$ correlation matrix is obtained by

[2]The log probabilities from sub-models

	Mode-1		Model-2	
Top-N	Nist	Bleu	Nist	Bleu
Top-1	6.4976	0.1597	6.3618	0.1611
Top-2	6.6749	**0.1726**	6.5385	0.1688
Top-3	6.5934	0.1687	6.5364	0.1700
Top-4	6.5752	0.1701	6.5243	0.1707

Table 2: Baselines of two generative models

computing the pairwise linear correlation coefficient between the feature functions using the phrase-pairs extracted from Model-2. The feature functions which are highly correlated are regrouped close to each other via standard K-means. The result is shown in Figure 5 and the clusters are shown in Table 3.

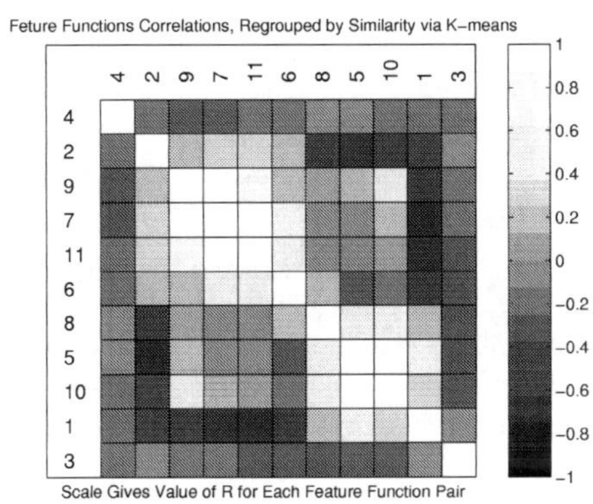

Figure 5: Pair-wise correlations among 11 Feature Functions.

Feature Func.	FID	Feature Func.	FID
E2FFScoreIn	2	E2FIBMBracket	9
E2FIBMScoreIN	7	AlignmentLinks	11
F2EIBMScoreOut	6		
F2EFScoreIn	1	*E2FIBMScoreOut*	8
F2EIBMScoreIN	5	F2EIBMBracket	10
E2FFScoreOut	4		
F2EFScoreOut	3		

Table 3: Clustered Feature Functions with *FID*

The more correlated the two feature functions are, the more overlapping information the two share with. In Figure 5, intuitively, features of FID $2, 9, 7, 11, 6$ are grouped together with aspects using the noisy channel model in English-to-Chinese direction and FID of $8, 5, 10, 1$ are clustered together related to the Chinese-to-English direction. The feature functions for the outer brackets like F2EIBMScoreOut (FID 6) and E2FIBMScoreOut (FID 8) are somewhat misplaced and the the fertility models for outside parts F2EFScoreOut and E2FFScoreOut are singled out in the clustering process. These evidences illustrate that feature functions from the outer part of the block have little overlap with the feature functions from the inner part of the block. Two directions of the noisy channel model are weakly correlated. All these observations confirm our intuitions.

6.3 Log-Linear Model

We hold 627 sentence pairs with one reference each from the 2001 Dry-Run test as development dataset, which were word-aligned by bilingual speakers. From the word alignment, we can extract the gold-standard blocks (phrase pairs). On the same held-out 627 sentence pairs, we run our baseline models with up to Top-20 target phrase candidates for each source phrase to collect the raw scores from all feature functions and we compute word-level F-measure for each extracted block.

Datasets	Size
Word alignment Links	14769
Gold Blocks	30803
Hypothesis Blocks	297,829

Table 4: Development Dataset Statistics

The final optimized weights learnt are (0.0480, 0.0660, 0.0048, 0.0032, 0.1376, 0.1332, 0.1662, 0.1113, 0.2495, 0.4621, 0.0753), in the order of the FIDs assigned in Table 3. Table 5 summarizes the log-linear model's performances at different configurations. The best Bleu score for the log-linear model is 0.1834, an improvement over the best generative models' performance of 0.1726.

The log-linear model based on maximum entropy principle has several advantages over the generative models. It introduces less data fragmentation, requiring fewer independence assumptions and exploiting a principled technique for automatic feature weighting. However, a drawback of our approach is we have to simu-

Model Settings		Nist	Bleu
Log-Linear Model	Top1	6.8069	0.1790
	Top2	6.9517	0.1811
	Top3	**6.9620**	**0.1834**
	Top4	6.8632	0.1790

Table 5: Log-Linear Model with M=11 Feature Functions for Phrase-Pair Extraction.

late the phrase-pair extraction performance measure from the hand-aligned data set to compute the word-level F-measure. This potentially introduces some errors before the optimizations.

7 Conclusions and Discussions

We presented a set of informative feature functions for bilingual phrase-pair extractions. A log-linear model is proposed to combine these feature functions and improvements are demonstrated in Chinese-English TIDES'03 small data track evaluations. The log-linear model is a promising framework which has the advantage of leveraging the overlapping features and it has flexibilities of exploiting more informative feature functions. However, the optimization took long to converge and run random restarts were needed to avoid local optima. Different optimization criteria, efficient algorithms and better feature functions can potentially bring more improvements.

Acknowledgements

We thank Jaime Carbonell and Chiori Hori for their valuable comments and Philipp Koehn for his help with the Pharaoh software package; in particular, the optimization toolkit.

References

P.F. Brown, Stephen A. Della Pietra, Vincent. J. Della Pietra, and Robert L. Mercer. 1993. The mathematics of statistical machine translation: Parameter estimation. In *Computational Linguistics*, volume 19(2), pages 263–331.

Heidi J. Fox. 2002. Phrasal cohesion and statistical machine translation. In *Proc. of the Conference on Empirical Methods in Natural Language Processing*, pages 304–311, Philadelphia, PA, July 6-7.

Philipp Koehn, Franz Josef Och, and Daniel Marcu. 2003. Statistical phrase-based machine translation. In *Proc. of HLT-NAACL 2003*, pages 48–54, Edmonton, Canada, May-June.

Philip Koehn. 2004. Pharaoh: a beam search decoder for phrase-based smt. In *Proceedings of the Conference of the Association for Machine Translation in the Americans (AMTA)*.

Franz J. Och and Hermann Ney. 2002. Discriminative training and maximum entropy models for statistical machine translation. In *Proceedings of the 40th Annual Meeting of ACL*, pages 440–447.

Franz J. Och and Hermann Ney. 2003. A systematic comparison of various statistical alignment models. In *Computational Linguistics*, volume 29, pages 19–51.

Franz J. Och and Hermann Ney. 2004. The alignment template approach to statistical machine translation. In *Computational Linguistics*, volume 30, pages 417–449.

Kishore Papineni, Salim Roukos, and Todd Ward. 1998. Maximum likelihood and discriminative training of direct translation models. In *Proceedings of the 1998 IEEE International Conference on Acoustics, Speech & Signal Processing*, volume 1, pages 189–192, Seattle, May.

Kishore Papineni, Salim Roukos, Todd Ward, and Wei-Jing Zhu. 2002. Bleu: a method for automatic evaluation of machine translation. In *Proc. of the 40th Annual Conf. of the Association for Computational Linguistics (ACL 02)*, pages 311–318, Philadelphia, PA, July.

Christoph Tillmann. 2003. A projection extension algorithm for statistical machine translation. In *Proc. of the Conference on Empirical Methods in Natural Language Processing*.

Stephan Vogel, Ying Zhang, Fei Huang, Alicia Tribble, Ashish Venogupal, Bing Zhao, and Alex Waibel. 2003. The cmu statistical machine translation system. In *Proc. of MT SUMMIT IX*, pages 257–264, New Orleans, LA, September.

Dekai Wu. 1997. Stochastic inversion transduction grammars and bilingual parsing of parallel corpora. In *Computational Linguistics*, volume 23(3), pages 377–403.

R. Zens and H. Ney. 2004. Improvements in phrase-based statistical machine translation. In *Proceedings of the Human Language Technology Conference (HLT-NAACL)s*, pages 257–264, Boston, MA, May.

Bing Zhao and Stephan Vogel. 2005. A generalized alignment-free phrase extraction. In *Proceedings of the ACL Workshop on Building and Using Parallel Texts*, pages 141–144, Ann Arbor, Michigan, June. Association for Computational Linguistics.

Integrating Collocation Features in Chinese Word Sense Disambiguation

Wanyin Li
Department of Computing
The Hong Kong Polytechnic University
Hong Hom, Kowloon, HK
cswyli@comp.polyu.edu.hk

Qin Lu
Department of Computing
The Hong Kong Polytechnic University
Hong Hom, Kowloon, HK
csqinlu@comp.polyu.edu.hk

Wenjie Li
Department of Computing
The Hong Kong Polytechnic University
Hong Hom, Kowloon, HK
cswjli@comp.polyu.edu.hk

Abstract

The selection of features is critical in providing discriminative information for classifiers in Word Sense Disambiguation (WSD). Uninformative features will degrade the performance of classifiers. Based on the strong evidence that an ambiguous word expresses a unique sense in a given collocation, this paper reports our experiments on automatic WSD using collocation as local features based on the corpus extracted from People's Daily News (PDN) as well as the standard SENSEVAL-3 data set. Using the Naïve Bayes classifier as our core algorithm, we have implemented a classifier using a feature set combining both local collocation features and topical features. The average precision on the PDN corpus has 3.2% improvement compared to 81.5% of the baseline system where collocation features are not considered. For the SENSEVAL-3 data, we have reached the precision rate of 37.6% by integrating collocation features into contextual features, to achieve 37% improvement over 26.7% of precision in the baseline system. Our experiments have shown that collocation features can be used to reduce the size of human tagged corpus.

1 Introduction

WSD tries to resolve lexical ambiguity which refers to the fact that a word may have multiple meanings such as the word "walk" in "Walk or Bike to school" and "BBC Education Walk Through Time", or the Chinese word "地方" in "地方政府"("local government") and "他也有对的地方"("He is also partly right"). WSD tries to automatically assign an appropriate sense to an occurrence of a word in a given context.

Various approaches have been proposed to deal with the word sense disambiguation problem including rule-based approaches, knowledge or dictionary based approaches, corpus-based approaches, and hybrid approaches. Among these approaches, the supervised corpus-based approach had been applied and discussed by many researches ([2-8]). According to [1], the corpus-based supervised machine learning methods are the most successful approaches to WSD where contextual features have been used mainly to distinguish ambiguous words in these methods. However, word occurrences in the context are too diverse to capture the right pattern, which means that the dimension of contextual words will be very large when all words in the training samples are used for WSD [14]. Certain uninformative features will weaken the discriminative power of a classifier resulting in a lower precision rate. To narrow down the context, we propose to use collocations as contextual information as defined in Section 3.1.2. It is generally understood that the sense of an ambiguous word is unique in a given collocation [19]. For example, "包袱" means "burden" but not "baggage" when it appears in the collocation "思想包袱" (" burden of thought").

In this paper, we apply a classifier to combine the local features of collocations which contain the target word with other contextual features to discriminate the ambiguous words. The intuition is that when the target context captures a collocation, the influence of other dimensions of contextual words can be reduced or even ignored. For example, in the expression “恐怖分子焚毁了基因室” (“terrorists burned down the gene laboratory”), the influence of contextual word “基因” (“gene”) should be reduced to work on the target word “分子” because “恐怖分子” is a collocation whereas “分子” and “基因” are not collocations even though they do co-occur. Our intention is not to generally replace contextual information by collocation only. Rather, we would like to use collocation as an additional feature in WSD. We still make use of other contextual features because of the following reasons. Firstly, contextual information is proven to be effective for WSD in the previous research works. Secondly, collocations may be independent on the training corpus and a sentence in consideration may not contain any collocation. Thirdly, to fix the tie case such as “…恐怖分子基因测试…” (“terrorists’ gene checking”), “分子” means “human” when presented in the collocation “恐怖分子”, but “particle” in the collocation “分子基因”. The primary purpose of using collocation in WSD is to improve precision rate without any sacrifices in recall rate. We also want to investigate whether the use of collocation as an additional feature can reduce the size of hand tagged sense corpus.

The rest of this paper is organized as follows. Section 2 summarizes the existing Word Sense Disambiguation techniques based on annotated corpora. Section 3 describes the classifier and the features in our proposed WSD approach. Section 4 describes the experiments and the analysis of our results. Section 5 is the conclusion.

2 Related Work

Automating word sense disambiguation tasks based on annotated corpora have been proposed. Examples of supervised learning methods for WSD appear in [2-4], [7-8]. The learning algorithms applied including: decision tree, decision-list [15], neural networks [7], naïve Bayesian learning ([5],[11]) and maximum entropy [10]. Among these leaning methods, the most important issue is what features will be used to construct the classifier. It is common in WSD to use contextual information that can be found in the neighborhood of the ambiguous word in training data ([6], [16-18]). It is generally true that when words are used in the same sense, they have similar context and co-occurrence information [13]. It is also generally true that the nearby context words of an ambiguous word give more effective patterns and features values than those far from it [12]. The existing methods consider features selection for context representation including both local and topic features where local features refer to the information pertained only to the given context and topical features are statistically obtained from a training corpus. Most of the recent works for English corpus including [7] and [8], which combine both local and topical information in order to improve their performance. An interesting study on feature selection for Chinese [10] has considered topical features as well as local collocational, syntactic, and semantic features using the maximum entropy model. In Dang’s [10] work, collocational features refer to the local PoS information and bi-gram co-occurrences of words within 2 positions of the ambiguous word. A useful result from this work based on (about one million words) the tagged People’s Daily News shows that adding more features from richer levels of linguistic information such as PoS tagging yielded no significant improvement (less than 1%) over using only the bi-gram co-occurrences information. Another similar study for Chinese [11] is based on the Naive Bayes classifier model which has taken into consideration PoS with position information and bi-gram templates in the local context. The system has a reported 60.40% in both precision and recall based on the SENSEVAL-3 Chinese training data. Even though in both approaches, statistically significant bi-gram co-occurrence information is used, they are not necessarily true collocations. For example, in the express “掌握/和/监视/本州/各地/新纳粹/分子/的/活动/情况”, the bi-grams in their system are (掌握, 和), (和, 监视), (监视, 本州), (本州, 各地), (各地, 新纳粹), (新纳粹, 的), (的, 活动), (活动, 情况). Some bi-grams such as (活动, 情况) may have higher frequency but may introduce noise when considering it as features in disambiguating the sense “human|人” and “symbol|符号” like in the example case of “水分子活动情况”. In our system, we do not rely on co-occurrence information. Instead, we utilize true collocation information (新纳粹, 分子) which fall in the window size of (-5, +5) as features and the sense of "human|人" can be decided clearly using this features. The collocation information is a pre-prepared collocation list obtained from a collocation extraction system and verified with syntactic and semantic methods ([21], [24]).

Yarowsky [9] used the one sense per collocation property as an essential ingredient for an unsupervised Word-Sense Disambiguation algorithm to perform bootstrapping algorithm on a more general high-recall disambiguation. A few recent research works have begun to pay attention to collocation features on WSD. Domminic [19] used three different methods called bilingual method, collocation method and UMLS (Unified Medical Language System) relation based method to disambiguate unsupervised English and German medical documents. As expected, the collocation method achieved a good precision around 79% in English and 82% in German but a very low recall which is 3% in English and 1% in German. The low recall is due to the nature of UMLS where many collocations would almost never occur in natural text. To avoid this problem, we combine the contextual features in the target context with the pre-prepared collocations list to build our classifier.

3 The Classifier With Topical Contextual and Local Collocation Features

3.1 The Feature Set

As stated early, an important issue is what features will be used to construct the classifier in WSD. Early researches have proven that using lexical statistical information, such as bi-gram co-occurrences was sufficient to produce close to the best results [10] for Chinese WSD. Instead of including bi-gram features as part of discrimination features, in our system, we consider both topical contextual features as well as local collocation features. These features are extracted form the 60MB human sense-tagged People's Daily News with segmentation information.

3.1.1 Topical Contextual Features

Niu [11] proved in his experiments that Naïve Bayes classifier achieved best disambiguation accuracy with small topical context window size (< 10 words). We follow their method and set the contextual window size as 10 in our system. Each of the Chinese words except the stop words inside the window range will be considered as one topical feature. Their frequencies are calculated over the entire corpus with respect to each sense of an ambiguous word w. The sense definitions are obtained from HowNet.

3.1.2 Local Collocation Features

We chose collocations as the local features. A collocation is a recurrent and conventional fixed expression of words which holds syntactic and semantic relations [21]. Collocations can be classified as fully fixed collocations, fixed collocations, strong collocations and loose collocations. Fixed collocations means the appearance of one word implies the co-occurrence of another one such as "历史<u>包袱</u>" ("burden of history"), while strong collocations allows very limited substitution of the components, for example, "<u>地方</u>院校" ("local college"), or " <u>地方</u>大学" ("local university"). The sense of ambiguous words can be uniquely determined in these two types of collocations, therefore are the collocations applied in our system. The sources of the collocations will be explained in Section 4.1.

In both Niu [11] and Dang's [10] work, topical features as well as the so called collocational features were used. However, as discussed in Section 2, they both used bi-gram co-occurrences as the additional local features. However, bi-gram co-occurrences only indicate statistical significance which may not actually satisfy the conceptual definition of collocations. Thus instead of using co-occurrences of bi-grams, we take the true bi-gram collocations extracted from our system and use this data to compare with bi-gram co-occurrences to test the usefulness of collocation for WSD. The local features in our system make use of the collocations using the template (w_i, w) within a window size of ten (where $i = \pm 5$). For example, "政府部门/ 和/ 地方/ 政府/ 认为" ("Government departments and local government commanded that") fits the bi-gram collocation template (w, w_1) with the value of (地方, 政府). During the training and the testing processes, the counting of frequency value of the collocation feature will be increased by 1 if a collocation containing the ambiguous word occurs in a sentence. To have a good analysis on collocation features, we have also developed an algorithm using lonely adjacent bi-gram as locals features(named Sys-

adjacent bi-gram as locals features(named System A) and another using collocation as local features(named System B).

3.2 The Collocation Classifier

We consider all the features in the features set $\boldsymbol{F} = F_t \cup F_l = \{f_1, f_2, \ \ldots \ , f_m\}$ as independent, where F_t stands for the topical contextual features set, and F_l stands for the local collocation features set. For an ambiguous word w with n senses, let $\boldsymbol{S_w} = \{w_{s1}, w_{s2}, \ \ldots \ , w_{sn}\}$ be the sense set. For the contextual features, we directly apply the Naïve Bayes algorithm using Add-Lambda Smoothing to handle unknown words:

$$score_1(w_{si}) = \log p(w_{si}) + \sum_{f_j \in F_t} \log p(f_j \mid w_{si})$$

(1)

For each sense w_{si} of an ambiguous word w:

$$p(w_{si}) = \frac{freq(w_{si})}{freq(w)} \qquad (2)$$

For each contextual feature f_j respects to each sense w_{si} of w:

$$p(f_j \mid w_{si}) = \frac{freq(f_j, w_{si})}{\sum_{f_t \in F_t} freq(f_t, w_{si})} \qquad (3)$$

To integrate the local collocation feature $f_j \in F_l$ with respect to each sense w_{si} of w, we use the follows formula:

$$score(w_{si}) = score_1(w_{si}) + \alpha \bullet score_2(w_{si}) \quad (4)$$

where α is tuned from experiments (Section 4.5), score$_1$(w_{si}) refers the score of the topical contextual features based on formula (1) and score$_2$(w_{si}) refers the score of collocation features with respect to the sense w_{sj} of w defined below.

$$score_2(w_{si}) = \sum_{f_j \in F_l} \delta(f_j \mid w_{sj}) \qquad (5)$$

where $\delta(f_j \mid w_{sj}) = 1$ for $f_j \in F_l$ if the collocation occurs in the local context. Otherwise this term is set as 0.

Finally, we choose the right w_{sk} so that

$$s = \arg\max_{s_k} score(w_{sk}) \qquad (6)$$

4 Experimental Results

We have designed a set of experiments to compare the classifier with and without the collocation features. In system ***A***, the classifier is built with local bi-gram features and topical contextual features. The classifier in system ***B*** is constructed from combining the local collocation features with topical features.

4.1 Preparation the Data Set

We have selected 20 ambiguous words from nouns and verbs with the sense number as 4 in average. The sense definition is taken from HowNet [22]. To show the effect of the algorithm, we try to choose words with high degree of ambiguity, high frequency of use [23], and high frequency of constructing collocations. The selection of these 20 words is not completely random although within each criterion class we do try to pick word randomly.

Based on the 20 words, we extracted 28,000 sentences from the 60 MB People's Daily News with segmentation information as our training/test set which is then manually sense-tagged. The collocation list is constructed from a combination of a digital collocation dictionary, a return result from a collocation automatic extraction system [21], and a hand collection from the People's Daily News. As we stated early, the sense of ambiguous words in the fixed collocations and strong collocations can be decided uniquely although they are not unique in loose collocations. For example, the ambiguous word "面目" in the collocation "崭新的面目" may have both the sense of "appearance|外观" or "reputation|名声". Therefore, when labeling the sense of collocations, we filter out the ones which cannot uniquely determine the sense of ambiguous words inside. However, this does not mean that loose collocations have no contribution in WSD classification. We simply reduce its weight when combining it with the contextual features compared with the fixed and strong collocations. The sense and collocation distribution over the 20 words on the training examples can be found in **Table 1**.

Table 1. Sense and Collocation Distribution of the 20 target words in the training corpus

Am. W	T#	S1 co#	S2 co#	S3 co#	S4 co#	S5 co#	S6 co#

保管	31	1 1	30 10	NA			
保险	499	479 324	18 0	0	0	NA	
纪念	944	908 129	1 1	17 10	18 0	0	NA
程序	409	3 2	389 171	17 0	NA		
包袱	110	3 0	101 36	6 9	NA		
结晶	41	3 0	37 6	1 0	NA		
关系	4885	26 0	34 0	72 0	4492 1356	261 1	NA
精神	3508	7 0	48 4	3194 1448	259 194	NA	
接触	348	312 117	22 11	14 4	NA		
活动	4438	3983 721	33 10	123 37	153 123	102 23	44 5
报告	1987	1712 723	274 10	NA			
攻击	83	36 14	47 4	00	NA		
程度	995	168 108	827 513	NA			
面目	31	11 3	20 11	NA			
基本	2725	227 1772	498 49	102 424	1898 201	NA	
把握	592	1 0	208 63	367 124	16 1	NA	
贷款	1155	756 571	399 135	NA			
决定	2792	691 98	1765 113	336 29	0	NA	
地方	2460	82 63	36 11	1231 474	877 103	NA	
意思	125	11 0	64 0	15 3	32 4	3 0	NA

T#: total number of sentences contain the ambiguous word
s_1- s_6: sense no; co#: number of collocations in each sense

4.2 The Effect of Collocation Features

We recorded 6 trials with average precision over six-fold validation for each word. Their average precision for the six trials in the system A, and B can be found in **Table 2** and **Table 3**. From **Table 3**, regarding to precision, there are 16 words have improved and 4 words remained the same in the system B. The results from the both system confirmed that collocation features do improve the precision. Note that 4 words have the same precision in the two systems, which fall into two cases. In the first case, it can be seen that these words already have very high precision in the system A (over 93%) which means that one sense dominates all other senses. In this case, the additional collation information is not necessary. In fact, when we checked the intermediate outputs, the score of the candidate senses of the ambiguous words contained in the collocations get improved. Even though, it would not change the result. Secondly, no collocation appeared in the sentences which are tagged incorrectly in the system A. This is confirmed when we check the error files. For example, the word "关系" with the sense as "亲疏" ("closeness") appeared in 4492 examples over the total 4885 examples (91.9%). In the mean time, 99% of collocation in its collocation list has the same sense of "亲疏" ("closeness"). Only one collocation "关系户" has the sense of "势力" ("power"). Therefore, the collocation features improved the score of sense "亲疏" which is already the highest one based on the contextual features.

As can be seen from **Table 3**, the collocation features work well for the sparse data. For example, the word "保管" in the training corpus has only one example with the sense "人" ("human"), the other 30 examples all have the sense "管理" ("management"). Under this situation, the topical contextual features failed to identify the right sense for the only appearance of the sense "人" ("human") in the training instance "有相应的粮食检验、保管专业人员…". However, it can be correctly identified in the system B because the appearance of the collocation "保管专业人员".

To well show the effect of collocations on the accuracy of classifier for the task of WSD, we also tested both systems on SENSEVAL-3 data set, and the result is recorded in the **Table 4**. From the difference in the relative improvement of both data sets, we can see that collocation features work well when the statistical model is not sufficiently built up such as from a small corpus like SENSEVAL-3. Actually, in this case, the training examples appear in the corpus only once or twice so that the parameters for such sparse training examples may not be accurate to forecast the test examples, which convinces us that collocation features are effective on handling sparse training data even for unknown words. **Fig. 1** shows the precision comparison in the system A, and B on SENVESAL-3.

Table 2. Average Precision (5/6 training, 1/6 test) of system A on People's Daily News

Amb. W	T1	T2	T3	T4	T5	T6	Ave. Prec.
保管	1.00	1.00	1.00	1.00	1.00	.83	.972
保险	.90	.97	1.00	1.00	.97	.98	.972
纪念	.97	.96	.96	.92	.98	.96	.958

程序	.94	.94	.97	.92	.97	.97	.951
包袱	1.00	1.00	.77	.94	.88	1.00	.932
结晶	.83	1.00	1.00	1.00	.83	.90	.927
关系	.93	.95	.91	.92	.92	.92	.925
精神	.93	.94	.89	.91	.89	.90	.91
接触	.94	.93	.86	.93	.89	.87	.903
活动	.83	.94	.89	.90	.88	.94	.897
报告	.86	.88	.92	.84	.82	.87	.865
攻击	.92	.84	.92	.76	.84	.72	.833
程度	.84	.83	.88	.82	.88	.71	.827
面目	.80	.60	.80	.20	1.00	1.00	.733
基本	.68	.72	.67	.77	.70	.68	.703
地方	.51	.67	.47	.60	.68	.59	.586
决定	.70	.63	.66	.64	.64	.64	.652
把握	.57	.74	.55	.64	.72	.67	.648
贷款	.65	.58	.66	.64	.54	.47	.58
意思	.55	.50	.45	.45	.45	.64	.507
Total Average Precision					0.815		

Table 3. Average Precision (5/6 training, 1/6 test) of system B on People's Daily News

Amb. W	T1	T2	T3	T4	T5	T6	Ave. Prec.
保管	1.00	1.00	1.00	1.00	1.00	1.00	1.00
保险	.90	.97	1.00	1.00	.97	.98	.970
纪念	.96	.98	.97	.96	.98	.96	.968
程序	.94	.94	.97	.94	.97	.98	.957
包袱	1.00	1.00	.77	.94	.88	1.00	.931
结晶	.83	1.00	1.00	1.00	.83	.90	.927
关系	.93	.95	.91	.92	.92	.92	.925
精神	.92	.95	.92	.92	.91	.91	.922
接触	.94	.94	.86	.93	.91	.87	.908
活动	.80	.95	.89	.93	.89	.94	.902
报告	.87	.88	.92	.84	.83	.91	.875
攻击	.84	1.00	.92	.76	.84	.77	.855
程度	.88	.86	.89	.84	.90	.74	.852
面目	1.00	.80	.80	.20	1.00	1.00	.800
基本	.69	.72	.68	.79	.75	.72	.725
把握	.69	.76	.73	.74	.82	.79	.755
贷款	.58	.59	.70	.67	.64	.59	.628
决定	.68	.67	.66	.63	.65	.63	.653
地方	.65	.68	.71	.61	.70	.69	.673
意思	.60	.55	.54	.54	.54	.64	.568
Total Average Precision					0.840		

Table 4. Average Precision of System A & B on SENSEVAL-3 Data Set

Amb. Word	Total S	Ave. Prec. in Sys A	Ave. Prec. in Sys B
日子	48	.207	.290
材料	20	.742	.742
走	49	.165	.325
坐	25	.325	.325
活动	36	.260	.373
研究	30	.167	.267
没有	30	.192	.392
分子	36	.635	.635
路	57	.238	.275
地方	36	.327	.385
把握	31	.100	.322
钱	40	.358	.442
起来	40	.308	.308
包	76	.110	.123
穿	28	.308	.475
突出	30	.500	.667
少	42	.165	.260
老	57	.037	.422
冲击	28	.833	.103
Total Precision	Ave.	.276	.376

Fig. 1. The precision comparison in system A, and B based on SENSEVAL-3

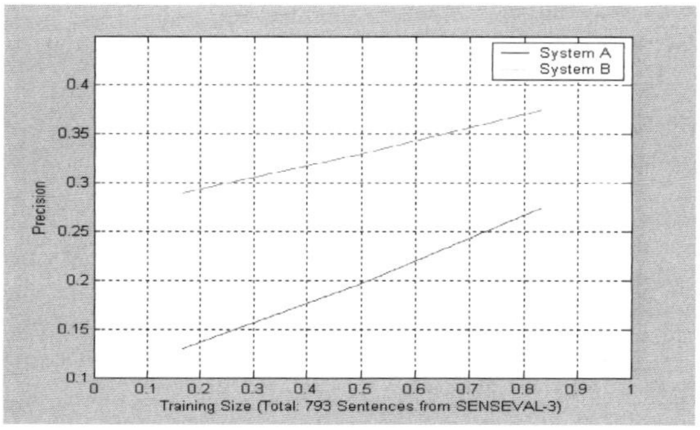

4.3 The Effect of Collocations on the Size of Training Corpus Needed

Hwee [21] stated that a large-scale, human sense-tagged corpus is critical for a supervised learning approach to achieve broad coverage and high accuracy WSD. He conducted a thorough study on the effect of training examples on the accuracy of supervised corpus based WSD. As the result showed, WSD accuracy continues to climb as the number of training examples increases. Similarly, we have tested the system A, and B with the different size of training corpus based on the PDN corpus we prepared. Our experiment results shown in **Fig 2** follow the same fact. The purpose we did the testing is that we hope to disclose the effect of collocations on the size of training corpus needed. From **Fig 2**, we can see by using the collocation features, the precision of the system B has increased slower along with the growth of training examples than the precision of the system A. The result is reasonable because with collocation feature, the statistical contextual information over the entire corpus becomes side effect. Actually, as can be seen from **Fig. 2**, after using collocation features in the system B, even we use 1/6 corpus as training, the precision is still higher than we use 5/6 train corpus in the system A.

Fig. 2. The precision variation respect to the size of training corpus in system A, and B based on PDN corpus

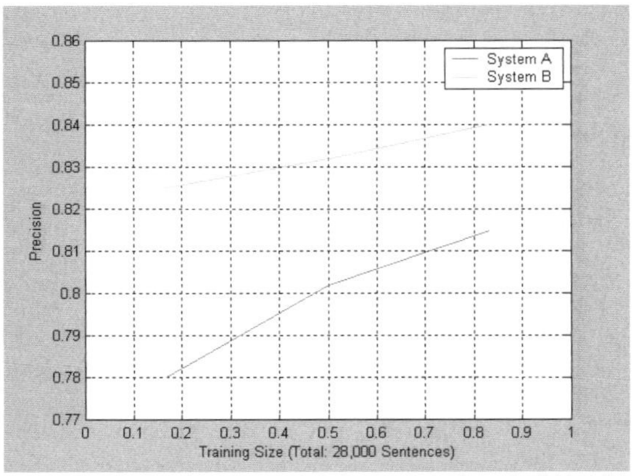

4.4 Investigation of Sense Distribution on the Effect of Collocation Features

To investigate the sense distribution on the effect of collocation features, we selected the ambiguous words with the number of sense varied from 2 to 6. In each level of the sense number, the words are selected randomly. **Table 5** shows the effect of sense distribution on the effect of collocation features. From the table, we can see that the collocation features work well when the sense distribution is even for a particular ambiguous word under which case the classifier may get confused.

Table 5. The Effect of Sense Distribution on the Effect of collocation Features

Amb. word	Prec. Wihtout coll	Prec. With coll	Sense #	Sense Distri.
保管	.972	1	2	97% *
保险	.97	.97	4	96% *
纪念	.957	.968	5	96% *
程序	.951	.957	3	95% *
包袱	.931	.931	3	92% *
结晶	.927	.927	3	90% *
关系	.925	.925	5	92% *
精神	.915	.922	4	91% *
接触	.903	.908	3	90% *
活动	.902	.902	6	90% *
报告	.865	.875	2	86% o
攻击	.833	.855	3	^
程度	.823	.852	2	83% o
面目	.733	.8	2	^
基本	.706	.725	4	^
把握	.65	.653	4	^
贷款	.618	.755	4	^
决定	.582	.628	2	^
地方	.563	.673	4	^
意思	.507	.568	5	^

*: over 90% samples fall in one dominate sense
^: Even distribution over all senses
o: 83% to 86% samples fall in one dominate sense

4.5 The Test of α

We have conducted a set of experiments based on both the PDN corpus and SENSEVLA-3 data to set the best value of α for the formula (4) described in Section 3.2. The best start value of α is tested based on the precision rate which is shown in **Fig. 3**. It is shown from the experiment that α takes the start value of 0.5 for both corpuses.

Fig. 3. The best value of α vs the precision rate

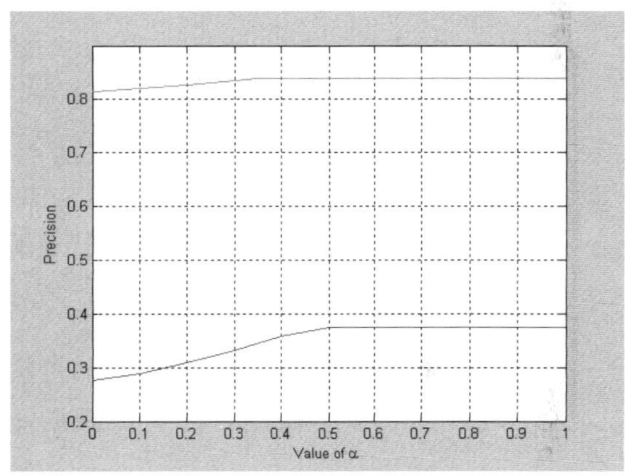

5 Conclusion and the Future Work

This paper reports a corpus-based Word Sense Disambiguation approach for Chinese word using local collocation features and topical contextual features. Compared with the base-line systems in which a Naïve Bayes classifier is constructed by combining the contextual features with the bi-gram features, the new system achieves 3% precision improvement in average in Peoples' Daily News corpus and 10% improvement in SENSEVAL-3 data set. Actually, it works very well when disambiguating the sense with sparse distribution over the entire corpus under which the statistic calculation prone to identify it incorrectly. In the same time, because disambiguating using collocation features does not need statistical calculation, it makes contribution to reduce the size of human tagged corpus needed which is critical and time consuming in corpus based approach.

Because different types of collocations may play different roles in classifying the sense of an ambiguous word, we hope to extend this work by integrating collocations with different weight based on their types in the future, which may need a pre-processing job to categorize the collocations automatically.

6 Acknowledgements

We would like to present our thanks to the IR Laboratory in HIT University of China for sharing their sense number definition automatically extracted from HowNet with us.

References

1. Hwee Tou Ng, Bin Wang, Yee Seng Chan. Exploiting Parallel Texts for Word Sense Disambiguation. ACL-03 (2003)
2. Black E.: An experiment in computational discrimination of English word senses. IBM Journal of Research and Development, v.32, n.2, (1988) 185-194
3. Gale, W. A., Church, K. W. and Yarowsky, D.: A method for disambiguating word senses in a large corpus. Computers and the Humanities, v.26, (1993) 415-439
4. Leacock, C., Towell, G. and Voorhees, E. M.: Corpus-based statistical sense resolution. In Proceedings of the ARPA Human Languages Technology Workshop (1993)
5. Leacock, C., Chodorow, M., & Miller G. A..Using Corpus Statistics and WordNet Relations for Sense Identification. Computational Linguistics, 24:1, (1998) 147–165
6. Schütze, H.: Automatic word sense discrimination. Computational Linguistics, v.24, n.1, (1998) 97-124
7. Towell, G. and Voorhees, E. M.: Disambiguating highly ambiguous words. Computational Linguistics, v.24, n.1, (1998) 125-146
8. Yarowsky, D.: Decision lists for lexical ambiguity resolution: Application to accent restoration in Spanish and French. In Proceedings of the Annual Meeting of the Association for Computational Linguistics, (1994) 88-95
9. Yarowsky, D.: Unsupervised word sense disambiguation rivaling supervised methods. In Proceedings of the Annual Meeting of the Association for Computational Linguistics, (1995)189-196
10. Dang, H. T., Chia, C. Y., Palmer M., & Chiou, F.D., Simple Features for Chinese Word Sense Disambiguation. In Proc. of COLING (2002)
11. Zheng-Yu Niu, Dong-Hong Ji, Chew Lim Tan, Optimizing Feature Set for Chinese Word Sense Disambiguation. To appear in Proceedings of the 3rd International Workshop on the Evaluation of Systems for the Semantic Analysis of Text (SENSEVAL-3). Barcelona, Spain (2004)
12. Chen, Jen Nan and Jason S. Chang, A Concept-based Adaptive Approach to Word SenseDisambiguation, Proceedings of 36th Annual Meeting of the Association for Computational Linguistics and 17th International Conference on Computational linguistics. COLING/ACL-98 (1998) 237-243
13. Rigau, G., J. Atserias and E. Agirre, Combining Unsupervised Lexical Knowledge Methods for Word Sense Disambiguation, Proceedings of joint 35th Annual Meeting of the Association for Computational Linguistics and 8th Conference of the European Chapter of the Association for Computational Linguistics (ACL/EACL'97), Madrid, Spain (1997)
14. Jong-Hoon Oh, and Key-Sun Choi, C02-1098.: Word Sense Disambiguation using Static and Dynamic Sense Vectors. COLING (2002)
15. Yarowsky, D., Hierarchical Decision Lists for Word Sense Disambiguation. Computers and the Humanities, 34(1-2), (2000) 179–186
16. Agirre, E. and G. Rigau (1996) Word Sense Disambiguation using Conceptual Density, Proceedings of 16th International Conference on Computational Linguistics. Copenhagen, Denmark, COLING (1996)
17. Escudero, G., L. Màrquez and G. Rigau, Boosting Applied to Word Sense Disambiguation. Proceedings of the 11th European Conference on Machine Learning (ECML 2000) Barcelona, Spain. 2000. Lecture Notes in Artificial Intelligence 1810. R. L. de Mántaras and E. Plaza (Eds.). Springer Verlag (2000)
18. Gruber, T. R., Subject-Dependent Co-occurrence and Word Sense Disambiguation. Proceedings of 29th Annual Meeting of the Association for Computational Linguistics (1991)
19. Dominic Widdows, Stanley Peters, Scott Cederberg, Chiu-Ki Chan, Diana Steffen, Paul Buitelaar, Unsupervised Monolingual and Bilingual Word-Sense Disambiguation of Medical Documents using UMLS. Appeared in Natural Language Processing in Biomedicine,. ACL 2003 Workshop, Sapporo, Japan (2003) 9–16
20. Hwee Tou Ng., Getting serious about word sense disambiguation. In Proceedings of the ACL SIGLEX Workshop on Tagging Text with Lexical Semantics:Why, What, and How? (1997) 1–7
21. Ruifeng Xu , Qin Lu, and Yin Li, An automatic Chinese Collocation Extraction Algorithm Based On Lexical Statistics. In Proceedings of the NLPKE Workshop (2003)
22. D. Dong and Q. Dong, HowNet. http://www.keenage.com, (1991)
23. Chih-Hao Tsai, http://technology.chtsai.org/wordlist/, (1995-2004)
24. Q. Lu, Y. Li, and R. F. Xu, Improving Xtract for Chinese Collocation Extraction. Proceedings of IEEE International Conference on Natural Language Processing and Knowledge Engineering, Beijing (2003)

NIL Is Not Nothing: Recognition of Chinese Network Informal Language Expressions

Yunqing Xia, Kam-Fai Wong, Wei Gao
Department of Systems Engineering and Engineering Management
The Chinese University of Hong Kong, Shatin, Hong Kong
{yqxia, kfwong, wgao}@se.cuhk.edu.hk

Abstract

Informal language is actively used in network-mediated communication, e.g. chat room, BBS, email and text message. We refer the anomalous terms used in such context as network informal language (NIL) expressions. For example, "偶(ou3)" is used to replace "我(wo3)" in Chinese ICQ. Without unconventional resource, knowledge and techniques, the existing natural language processing approaches exhibit less effectiveness in dealing with NIL text. We propose to study NIL expressions with a NIL corpus and investigate techniques in processing NIL expressions. Two methods for Chinese NIL expression recognition are designed in NILER system. The experimental results show that pattern matching method produces higher precision and support vector machines method higher F-1 measure. These results are encouraging and justify our future research effort in NIL processing.

1 Introduction

The rapid global proliferation of Internet applications has been showing no deceleration since the new millennium. For example, in commerce more and more physical customer services/call centers are replaced by Internet solutions, e.g. via MSN, ICQ, etc. Network informal language (NIL) is actively used in these applications. Following this trend, we forecast that NIL would become a key language for human communication via network.

Today NIL expressions are ubiquitous. They appear, for example, in chat rooms, BBS, email, text message, etc. There is growing importance in understanding NIL expressions from both technology and humanity research points of view. For instance, comprehension of customer-operator dialogues in the aforesaid commercial application would facilitate effective Customer Relationship Management (CRM).

Recently, sociologists showed many interests in studying impact of network-mediated communication on language evolution from psychological and cognitive perspectives (Danet, 2002; McElhearn, 2000; Nishimura, 2003). Researchers claim that languages have never been changing as fast as today since inception of the Internet; and the language for Internet communication, i.e. NIL, gets more concise and effective than formal language.

Processing NIL text requires unconventional linguistic knowledge and techniques. Unfortunately, developed to handle formal language text, the existing natural language processing (NLP) approaches exhibit less effectiveness in dealing with NIL text. For example, we use ICTCLAS (Zhang et al., 2003) tool to process sentence "他细八细要开会啊? (Is he going to attend a meeting?)". The word segmentation result is "他|细|八|细|要|开会|啊|? ". In this sentence , "细八细 (xi4 ba1 xi4)" is a NIL expression which means 'is he ….?' in this case. It can be concluded that without identifying the expression, further Chinese text processing techniques are not able to produce reasonable result.

This problem leads to our recent research in "*NIL is Not Nothing*" project, which aims to produce techniques for NIL processing, thus avails understanding of change patterns and behaviors in language (particularly in Internet language) evolution. The latter could make us more adaptive to the dynamic language environment in the cyber world.

Recently some linguistic works have been carried out on NIL for English. A shared dictionary has been compiled and made available online. It contains 308 English NIL expressions including English abbreviations, acronyms and emoticons. Similar efforts for Chinese are rare. This is because Chinese language has not been widely used on the Internet until ten years ago. Moreover, Chinese NIL expression involves processing of Chinese Pinyin and dialects, which results in higher complexity in Chinese NIL processing.

In "*NIL is Not Nothing*" project, we develop a comprehensive Chinese NIL dictionary. This is a difficult task because resource of NIL text is rather restricted. We download a collection of BBS text from an Internet BBS system and construct a NIL corpus by annotating NIL expressions in this collection by hand. An empirical study is conducted on the NIL expressions with the NIL corpus and a knowledge mining tool is designed to construct the NIL dictionary and generate statistical NIL features automatically. With these knowledge and resources, the NIL processing system, i.e. NILER, is developed to extract NIL expressions from NIL text by employing state-of-the-art information extraction techniques.

The remaining sections of this paper are organized as follow. In Section 2, we observe formation of NIL expressions. In Section 3 we present the related works. In Section 4, we describe NIL corpus and the knowledge engineering component in NIL dictionary construction and NIL features generation. In Section 5 we present the methods for NIL expression recognition. We outline the experiments, discussions and error analysis in Section 6, and finally Section 7 concludes the paper.

2 The Ways NIL Expressions Are Typically Formed

NIL expressions were first introduced for expediting writing or computer input, especially for online chat where the input speed is crucial to prompt and effective communication. For example, it is rather annoying to input full Chinese sentences in text-based chatting environment, e.g. over the mobile phone. Thus abbreviations and acronyms are then created by forming words in capital with the first letters of a series of either English words or Chinese Pinyin.

Chinese Pinyin is a popular approach to Chinese character input. Some Pinyin input methods incorporate lexical intelligence to support word or phrase input. This improves input rate greatly. However, Pinyin input is not error free. Firstly, options are usually prompted to user and selection errors result in homophone, e.g. "斑竹 (ban1 zu2)" and "版主 (ban1 zhu3)". Secondly, input with incorrect Pinyin or dialect produces wrong Chinese words with similar pronunciation, e.g. "稀饭 (xi1 fan4)" and "喜欢 (xi3 huan1)". Nonetheless, prompt communication spares little time to user to correct such a mistake. The same mistake in text is constantly repeated, and the wrong word thus becomes accepted by the chat community. This, in fact, is one common way that a new Chinese NIL expression is created.

We collect a large number of "sentences" (strictly speaking, not all of them are sentences) from a Chinese BBS system and identify NIL expressions by hand. An empirical study on NIL expressions in this collection shows that NIL expressions can be classified into four classes as follow based on their origins.

1) Abbreviation (A). Many Chinese NIL expressions are derived from abbreviation of Chinese Pinyin. For example, "PF" equals to "佩服 (pei4 fu2)" which means "admire".
2) Foreign expression (F). Popular Informal expressions from foreign languages such as English are adopted, e.g. "ASAP" is used for "as soon as possible".
3) Homophone (H). A NIL expression is sometimes generated by borrowing a word with similar sound (i.e. similar Pinyin). For example "稀饭" equals "喜欢" which means "like". "稀饭" and "喜欢" hold homophony in a Chinese dialect.
4) Transliteration (T) is a transcription from one alphabet to another and a letter-for-letter or sound-for-letter spelling is applied to represent a word in another language. For example, "拜拜 (bai4 bai4)" is transliteration of "bye-bye".

A thorough observation, in turn, reveals that, based on the ways NIL expressions are formed and/or their part of speech (POS) attributes, we observe a NIL expression usually takes one of the forms presented in Table 1 and Table 2.

The above empirical study is essential to NIL lexicography and feature definition.

Table 1: NIL expression forms based on word formation.

Word Formation	# of NIL Expressions	Examples
Chinese Word or Phrase	33	"稀饭" represents "喜欢" and means "like".
Sequence of English Capitals	341	"PF" represents "佩服" and means "admire".
Number	8	"94 (jiu3 si4)" represents "就是 (jiu4 shi4)" and means "exactly be".
Mixture of the Above Forms	30	"8 错 (ba1 cuo4)" represents "不错 (bu3 cuo4)" and means "not bad".
Emoticons	239	":-(" represents a sad emotion.

Table 2: NIL expression forms based on POS attribute.

POS Attribute	# of NIL Expressions	Examples
Number	1	"W" represents "万 (wan4)" and means "ten thousand".
Pronoun	9	"偶" represents "我" and means "I".
Noun	29	"LG" represents "老公 (lao3 gong1)" and means "husband".
Adjective	250	"FB" represents "腐败 (fu3 bai4)" and means "corrupt".
Verb	34	"葱白 (cong1 bai2)" represents "崇拜 (chong3 bai4)" and means "adore".
Adverb	10	"粉 (fen3)" represents "很 (hen3)" and means "very".
Exclamation	9	"捏 (nie0)" represents "呢 (ne0)" and equals a descriptive exclamation.
Phrase	309	"AFK" represents "Away From Keyboard".

3 Related Works

NIL expression recognition, in particular, can be considered as a subtask of information extraction (IE). Named entity recognition (NER) happens to hold similar objective with NIL expression recognition, i.e. to extract meaningful text segments from unstructured text according to certain predefined criteria.

NER is a key technology for NLP applications such as IE and question & answering. It typically aims to recognize names for person, organization, location, and expressions of number, time and currency. The objective is achieved by employing either handcrafted knowledge or supervised learning techniques. The latter is currently dominating in NER amongst which the most popular methods are decision tree (Sekine et al., 1998; Pailouras et al., 2000), Hidden Markov Model (Zhang et al., 2003; Zhao, 2004), maximum entropy (Chieu and Ng, 2002; Bender et al., 2003), and support vector machines (Isozaki and Kazawa, 2002; Takeuchi and Collier, 2002; Mayfield, 2003).

From the linguistic perspective, NIL expressions are rather different from named entities in nature. Firstly, named entity is typically noun or noun phrase (NP), but NIL expression can be any kind, e.g. number "94" in NIL represents "就是" which is a verb meaning "exactly be". Secondly, named entities often have well-defined meanings in text and are tractable from a standard dictionary; but NIL expressions are either unknown to the dictionary or ambiguous. For example, "稀饭" appears in conventional dictionary with the meaning of Chinese porridge, but in NIL text it represents "喜欢" which surprisingly represents "like". The issue that concerns us is that these expressions like "稀饭" may also appear in NIL text with their formal meaning. This leads to ambiguity and makes it more difficult in NIL processing.

Another notable work is the project of "*Normalization of Non-standard Words*" (Sproat et al., 2001) which aims to detect and normalize the "*Non-Standard Words* (NSW)" such as digit sequence; capital word or letter sequence; mixed case word; abbreviation; Roman numeral; URL and e-mail address. In our work, we consider most types of the NSW in English except URL and email address. Moreover, we consider Chinese NIL expressions that contain same characters as the normal words. For example, "稀饭" and "葱白" both appear in common dictionaries, but they carry anomalous meanings in NIL text. Ambiguity arises and basically brings NIL expressions recognition beyond the scope of NSW detection.

According to the above observations, we propose to employ the existing IE techniques to handle NIL expressions. Our goal is to develop a NIL expression recognition system to facilitate network-mediated communication. For this purpose, we first construct the required NIL knowledge resources, namely, a NIL dictionary and n-gram statistical features.

4 Knowledge Engineering

Recognition of NIL expressions relies on unconventional linguistic knowledge such as NIL dictionary and NIL features. We construct a NIL corpus and develop a knowledge engineering component to obtain these knowledge by running a knowledge mining tool on the NIL corpus. The knowledge mining tool is a text processing program that extracts NIL expressions and their attributes and contextual information, i.e. n-grams, from the NIL corpus. Workflow for this component is presented in Figure 1.

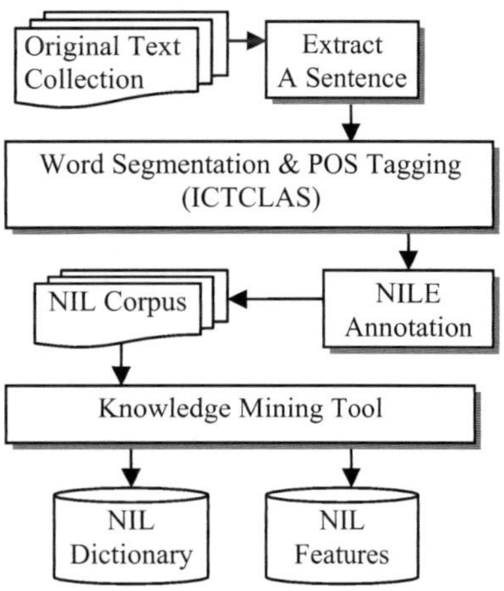

Figure 1: Workflow for NIL knowledge engineering component. NILE refers to NIL expression, which is identified and annotated by human annotator.

4.1 NIL Corpus

The NIL corpus is a collection of network informal sentences which provides training data for NIL dictionary and statistical NIL features. The NIL corpus is constructed by annotating a collection of NIL text manually.

Obtaining real chat text is difficult because of the privacy restriction. Fortunately, we find BBS text within "大嘴区 (da4 zui3 qu1)" zone in YESKY system (http://bbs.yesky.com/bbs/) reflects remarkable colloquial characteristics and contains a vast amount of NIL expressions. We download BBS text posted from December 2004 and February 2005 in this zone. Sentences with NIL expressions are selected by human annotators, and NIL expressions are manually identified and annotated with their attributes. We finally collected 22,432 sentences including 451,193 words and 22,648 NIL expressions.

The NIL expressions are marked up with SGML. The typical example, i.e. "他细八细要开会啊？" in Section 1, is annotated as follows.

他<*NILEX string*="细八细" *class*="H" *normal*="是不是" *pinyin*="xi4 ba1 xi4" *segments*="细|八|细" *pos*="VERB" *posseg*="ADJ|NUM|ADJ">细八细 </*NILEX*>要开会啊？

where *NILEX* is the SGML tag to label a NIL expression, which entails NIL linguistic attributes including *class, normal, pinyin, segments, pos,* and *posseg* (see Section 4.2). *H* is a value of *class* (see Section 2). Value *VERB* demotes verb, ADJ adjective, NUM number and *AUX* auxiliary.

4.2 NIL Dictionary

The NIL dictionary is a structured databank that contains NIL expression entries. Each entity in turn entails nine attributes described as follow.

1. *ID*: an unique identification number for the NIL expression, e.g. 915800;
2. *string*: string of the NIL expression, e.g. "细八细";
3. *class*: class of the NIL expression (see Section 2), e.g. "H" for homophony;
4. *pinyin*: Chinese Pinyin for the NIL expression, e.g. "xi4 ba1 xi4";
5. *normal*: corresponding normal text for the NIL expression, e.g. "是不是";
6. *segments*: word segments of the NIL expression, e.g. "细|八|细";
7. *pos*: POS tag associated with the expression, e.g. "VERB" denoting a verb;
8. *posseg*: a POS tag list for the word segments, e.g. "VERB|AUX|VERB";
9. *frequency*: number of occurrences of the NIL expression.

We run the knowledge mining tool to extract all annotated NIL expressions together with their attributes from the NIL corpus. The NIL expressions are then each assigned an ID number and inserted into an indexed data file, i.e. the NIL dictionary. Current NIL dictionary contains 651 NIL entries.

4.3 NIL Feature Set

The NIL features are required by support vector machines method in NIL expression recognition. We define two types of statistical features for NIL expressions, i.e. Chinese word n-grams and POS tag n-grams. Bigger *n* leads to more contextual information, but results in higher computational complexity. To compromise, we generate n-grams with n = 1, 2, 3, 4. For example, "你们/细八细" is a bi-gram for "细八细" in terms of word segmentation, and its POS tag bi-gram is "PRONOUN/ VERB".

We run the knowledge mining tool on the NIL corpus to produce all n-grams for Chinese words and their POS tags in which NIL expression appears. 8379 features were generated including 7416 word-based n-grams and 963 POS tag-based n-grams. These statistical NIL features are linked to the corresponding NIL dictionary entries by their global NIL expression IDs.

Besides, we consider some morphological features including being/containing a number, some English capitals or Chinese characters. These features can be extracted by parsing string of the NIL expressions.

5 NILER System

5.1 Architecture

We develop NILER system to recognize NIL expressions in NIL text and convert them to normal language text. The latter functionality is discussed in other literatures. Architecture of NILER system is presented in Figure 2.

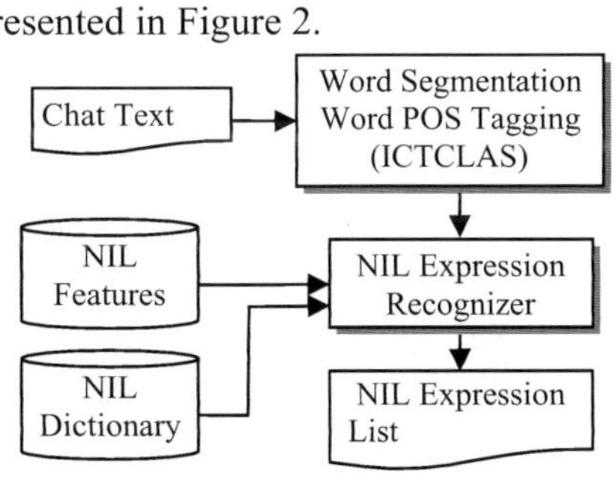

Figure 2: Architecture of NILER system.

The input chat text is first segmented and POS tagged with ICTCLAS tool. Because ICTCLAS is not able to identify NIL expressions, some expressions are broken into several segments. NIL expression recognizer processes the segments and POS tags and identifies the NIL expressions.

5.2 NIL Expression Recognizer

We implement two methods in NIL expression recognition, i.e. pattern matching and support vector machines.

5.2.1 Method I: Pattern Matching

Pattern matching (PM) is a traditional method in information extraction systems. It uses a handcrafted rule set and dictionary for this purpose. Because it's simple, fast and independent of corpus, this method is widely used in IE tasks.

By applying NIL dictionary, candidates of NIL expressions are first extracted from the input text with longest matching. As ambiguity occurs constantly, 24 patterns are produced and employed to disambiguate. We first extract those word and POS tag n-grams from the NIL corpus and create patterns by generalizing them manually. An illustrative pattern is presented as follows.

$$[< v\_any >]\ 8 < not(v\_unit) > [< v\_any >] \Rightarrow \text{不}$$

where v_any and v_unit are variables denoting any word and any unit word respectively; $not(\bullet)$ is the negation operator. The illustrative pattern determines "8" to be a NIL expression if it is succeeded by a unit word. With this pattern, "8" within sentence "他工作了 8 个小时。 (He has been working for eight hours.)" is not recognized as a NIL expression.

5.2.2 Method II: Support Vector Machines

Support vector machines (SVM) method produces high performance in many classification tasks (Joachims, 1998; Kudo and Matsumoto, 2001). As SVM can handle large numbers of features efficiently, we employ SVM classification method to NIL expression recognition.

Suppose we have a set of training data for a two-class classification problem $\{(x_1,y_1), (x_2, y_2),...,(x_N, y_N)\}$, where $x_i \in R^D (i = 1,2,...N)$ is a feature vector of the i-th order sample in the training set and $y_i \in \{+1,-1\}$ is the label for the sample. The goal of SVM is to find a decision function that accurately predicts y for unseen x. A non-linear SVM classifier gives a decision function $f(x) = sign(g(x))$ for an input vector x, where

$$g(x) = \sum_{i=1}^{l} \varpi_i K(x, z_i) + b$$

The $z_i s$ are so-called support vectors, and represents the training samples. ϖ_i and b are parameters for SVM motel. l is number of training samples. $K(x,z)$ is a kernel function that implicitly maps vector x into a higher dimensional space. A typical kernel is defined as dot products, i.e. $K(x,z)=k(x \bullet z)$.

Based on the training process, the SVM algorithm constructs the support vectors and parameters. When text is input for classification, it is first converted into feature vector x. The SVM method then classifies the vector x by determining sign of $g(x)$, in which $f(x)=1$ means that word x is positive and otherwise if $f(x)=-1$. The SVM algorithm was later extended in $SVM^{multiclass}$ to predict multivariate outputs (Joachims, 1998).

In NIL expression recognition, we consider NIL corpus as training set and the annotated NIL expressions as samples. NIL expression recognition is achieved with the five-class SVM classification task, in which four classes are those defined in Section 2 and reflected by *class* attribute within NIL annotation scheme. The fifth class is *NOCLASS*, which means the input text is not any NIL expression class.

6 Experiments

6.1 Experiment Description

We conduct experiments to evaluate the two methods in performing the task of NIL expression recognition. In training phase we use NIL corpus to construct NIL dictionary and pattern set for PM method, and generate statistical NIL features, support vectors and parameters for SVM methods. To observe how performance is influenced by the volume of training data, we create five NIL corpora, i.e. C#1~C#5, with five numbers of NIL sentences, i.e. 10,000, 13,000, 16,000, 19,000 and 22,432, by randomly selecting sentence from NIL corpus described in Section 4.1.

To generate test set, we download 5,690 sentences from YESKY system which cover BBS text in March 2005. We identify and annotate NIL expressions within these sentences manually and consider the annotation results as gold standard.

We first train the system with the five corpora to produce five versions of NIL dictionary, pattern set, statistical NIL feature set and SVM model. We then run the two methods with each version of the above knowledge over the test set to produce recognition results automatically. We compare these results against the gold stand and present experimental results with criteria including precision, recall and F1-measure.

6.2 Experimental Results

We present experimental results of the two methods on the five corpora in Table 3.

Table 3: Experimental results for the two methods on the five corpora. PRE denotes precision, REC denotes recall, and F1 denotes F1-Measure.

Corpus	PM			SVM		
	PRE	REC	F1	PRE	REC	F1
C#1	0.742	0.547	0.630	0.683	0.703	0.693
C#2	0.815	0.634	0.713	0.761	0.768	0.764
C#3	0.873	0.709	0.783	0.812	0.824	0.818
C#4	0.904	0.759	0.825	0.847	0.851	0.849
C#5	0.915	0.793	0.850	0.867	0.875	0.871

6.3 Discussion I: The Two Methods

To compare performance of the two methods, we present the experimental results with smoothed curves for precision, recall and F1-Mesure in Figure 3, Figure 4 and Figure 5 respectively.

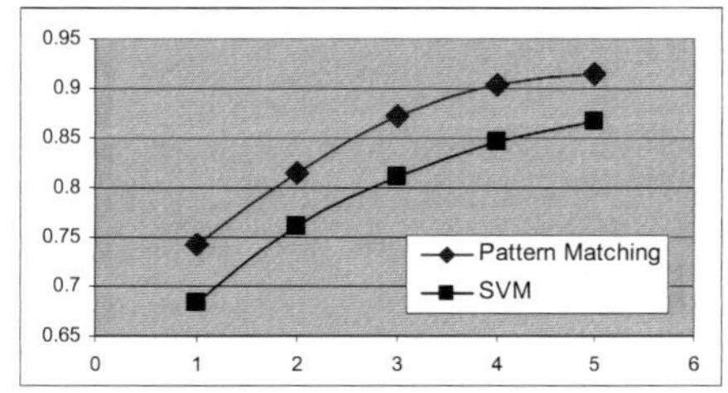

Figure 3: Smoothed precision curves over the five corpora.

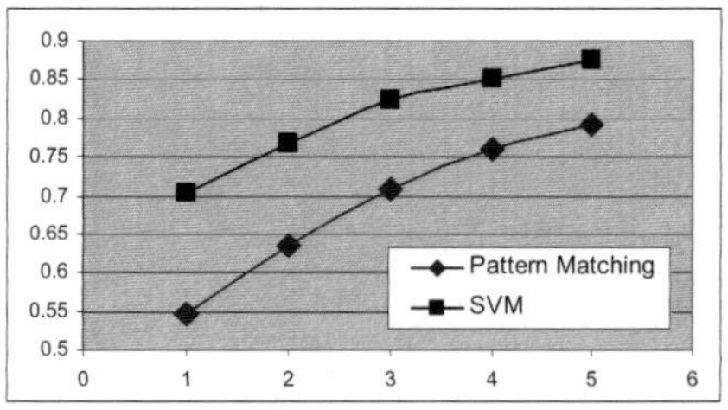

Figure 4: Smoothed recall curves over the five corpora.

Figure 3 reveals that PM method produces higher precision, i.e. 91.5%, and SVM produces higher recall, i.e. 79.3%, and higher F1-Measure, i.e. 87.1%, with corpus C#5. It can be inferred that PM method is self-restrained. In other words, if a NIL expression is identified with this method, it is very likely that the decision is right. However, the weakness is that more NIL expressions are neglected. On the other hand, SVM method outperforms PM method regarding overall capability, i.e. F1-Measure, according to Figure 5.

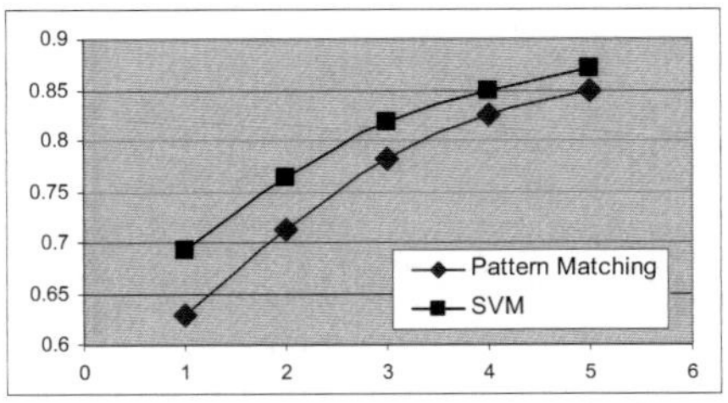

Figure 5: Smoothed F1-Measure curves over the five corpora.

We argue that each method holds strength and weakness. Different methods should be adopted to cater to different application demands. For example, in CRM text processing, we might favor precision. So PM method may be the better choice. On the other hand, to perform the task of chat room security monitoring, recall is more important. Then SVM method becomes the better option. We claim that there exists an optimized approach which combines the two methods and yields higher precision and better robustness at the same time.

6.4 Discussion II: How Volume Influences Performance

To observe how training corpus influences performance in the two methods regarding volume, we present experimental results with smoothed quality curves for the two method in Figure 6 and Figure 7 respectively.

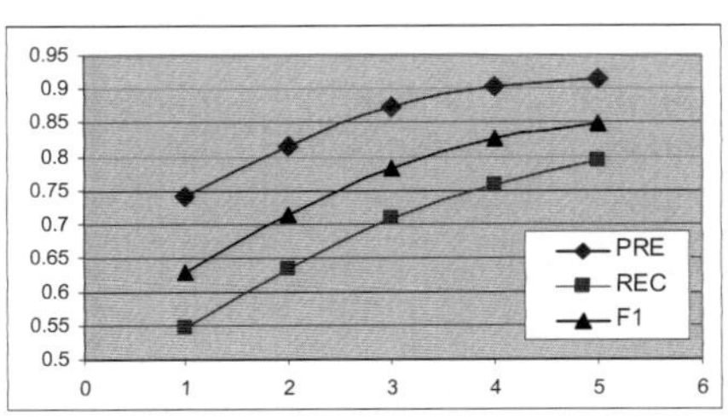

Figure 6: Smoothed quality curves for PM method over the five corpora.

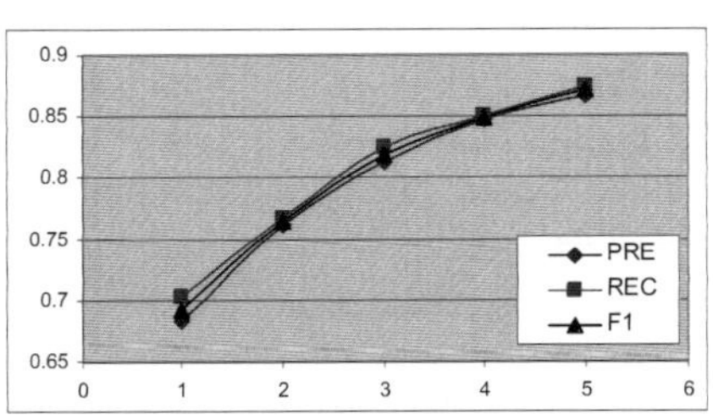

Figure 7: Smoothed quality curves for SVM method over the five corpora.

The smoothed quality curves in Figure 6 and Figure 7 reveal the tendency that bigger volume of training data leads to better processing quality. Meanwhile, the improvement tends to decrease along with increasing of volume. It thus predicts that there exists a corpus with a certain volume that produces the best quality according to the tendency. Although current corpus is not big enough to prove the optimal volume, the tendency revealed by the curves is obvious.

6.5 Error Analysis

We present two examples to analyze errors occur within our experiments.

Err.1 Ambiguous NIL Expression
Example 1:
[Sentence]: 我还是 8 米白
[Meaning]: I still don't understand.
[NIL expression found(Y/N)?]: Y
[Normal language text]: 我还是不明白

Error in Example 1 is caused by failure in identifying "米白 (mi3 bai2)". Because "米 (mi3)" succeeds "8(ba1)" in the word segments, i.e. "我|还是|8|米|白", and it can be used as a unit word, PM method therefore refuses to identify "8(ba)" as a NIL expression according to the pattern described in Section 5.2.1. In fact, "米白" is an unseen NIL expression. SVM method successfully recognizes "米白" to be "米有(mi3 you3)", thus recognizes "8". In our experiments 56 errors in PM method suffer the same failure, while SVM method identifies 48 of them. This demonstrates that PM method is self-restrained and SVM method is relatively scalable in processing NIL text.

Err.2 Unseen NIL expression
Example 2:
[Sentence]: 刚刚从 4U 回来
[Meaning]: Just came back from 4U.
[NIL expression found (Y/N)?] : N

Actually, there is no NIL expression in example 2. But because of a same 1-gram with "4D", i.e. "4", SVM outputs "4U" as a NIL expression. In fact, it is the name for a mobile dealer. There are 78 same errors in SVM method in our experiments, which reveals that SVM method is sometimes over-predicting. In other words, some NIL expressions are recognized with SVM method by mistake, which results in lower precision.

7 Conclusions and Future Works

Network informal language processing is a new NLP research application, which seeks to recognize and normalize NIL expressions automatically in a robust and adaptive manner. This research is crucial to improve capability of NLP techniques in dealing with NIL text. With empirical study on Chinese network informal text and NIL expressions, we propose two NIL expression recognition methods, i.e. pattern matching and support vector machines. The experimental results show that PM method produces higher precision, i.e. 91.5%, and SVM method higher F-1 measure, i.e. 87.1%. These results are encouraging and justify our future research effort in NIL processing.

Research presented in this paper is preliminary but significant. We address future works as follow. Firstly, NIL corpus constructed in our work is fundamental. Not only will difficulty in seeking for text resource be overcome, but a large quantity of manpower will be allocated to this laborious and significant work. Secondly, new NIL expressions will appear constantly with booming of network-mediated communication. A powerful NIL expression recognizer will be designed to improve adaptivity of the recognition methods and handle the unseen NIL expressions effectively. Finally, we state that research in this paper targets in special at NIL expressions in China mainland. Due to cultural/geographical variance, NIL expressions in Hong Kong and Taiwan could be different. Further research will be conducted to adapt our methods to other NIL communities.

References

Bender, O., Och, F. J. and Ney, H. 2003. *Maximum Entropy Models for Named Entity Recognition,* CoNLL-2003, pp. 148-151.

Chieu, H. L. and Ng, H. T. 2002. *Named Entity Recognition: A Maximum Entropy Approach Using Global Information*. COLING-02, pp. 190-196.

Danet, B. 2002. *The Language of Email*, European Union Summer School, University of Rome.

Isozaki, H. and Kazawa, H. 2002. *Efficient Support Vector Classifiers for Named Entity Recognition*, COLING-02, pp. 390-396..

Joachims, T. 1998. *Text categorization with Support Vector Machines: Learning with many relevant features*. ECML'98, pp. 137-142.

Kudo, T. and Matsumoto, Y. 2001. *Chunking with Support Vector Machines*. NAACL 2001, pp.192-199.

Mayfield, J. 2003. Paul McNamee; Christine Piatko, *Named Entity Recognition using Hundreds of Thousands of Features*, CoNLL-2003, pp. 184-187.

McElhearn, K. 2000. *Writing Conversation - An Analysis of Speech Events in E-mail Mailing Lists*, http://www.mcelhearn.com/cmc.html, Revue Française de Linguistique Appliquée, volume V-1.

Nishimura, Y. 2003. *Linguistic Innovations and Interactional Features of Casual Online Communication in Japanese*, JCMC 9 (1).

Pailouras, G., Karkaletsis, V. and Spyropoulos, C. D. 2000. *Learning Decision Trees for Named-Entity Recognition and Classification*. Workshop on Machine Learning for Information Extraction, ECAI(2000).

Sekine, S., Grishman, R. and Shinnou, H. 1998. *A Decision Tree Method for Finding and Classifying Names in Japanese Texts*, WVLC 98.

Snitt, E. N. 2000. *The Use of Language on the Internet*, http://www.eng.umu.se/vw2000/Emma/linguistics1.htm.

Sproat, R., Black, A., Chen, S., Kumar, S., Ostendorf, M. and Richards, M. 2001. *Normalization of Non-standard Words*. Computer Speech and Languages, 15(3):287- 333.

Takeuchi, K. and Collier, N. 2002. *Use of Support Vector Machines in Extended Named Entity Recognition*. CoNLL-2002, pp. 119-125.

Zhang, Z., Yu, H., Xiong, D. and Liu, Q. 2003. *HMM-based Chinese Lexical Analyzer ICTCLAS*. In the 2nd SIGHAN workshop affiliated with ACL'03, pp. 184-187.

Zhao, S. 2004. *Named Entity Recognition in Biomedical Texts Using an HMM model*, COLING-04 workshop on Natural Language Processing in Biomedicine and its Applications.

The Robustness of Domain Lexico-Taxonomy: Expanding Domain Lexicon with CiLin

Chu-Ren Huang
Institute of Linguistics,
Academia Sinica, Taipei
churen@sinica.edu.tw

Xiang-Bing Li
Institute of Information Science,
Academia Sinica, Taipei
dreamer@hp.iis.sinica.edu.tw

Jia-Fei Hong
Institute of Linguistics,
Academia Sinica, Taipei
jiafei@gate.sinica.edu.tw

Abstract.

This paper deals with the robust expansion of Domain Lexico-Taxonomy (DLT). DLT is a domain taxonomy enriched with domain lexica. DLT was proposed as an infrastructure for crossing domain barriers (Huang et al. 2004). The DLT proposal is based on the observation that domain lexica contain entries that are also part of a general lexicon. Hence, when entries of a general lexicon are marked with their associated domain attributes, this information can have two important applications. First, the DLT will serve as seeds for domain lexica. Second, the DLT offers the most reliable evidence for deciding the domain of a new text since these lexical clues belong to the general lexicon and do occur reliably in all texts. Hence general lexicon lemmas are extracted to populate domain lexica, which are situated in domain taxonomy. Based on this previous work, we show in this paper that the original DLT can be further expanded when a new language resource is introduced. We applied CiLin, a Chinese thesaurus, and added more than 1000 new entries for DLT and show with evaluation that the DLT approach is robust since the size and number of domain lexica increased effectively.

1. Introduction

Domain-based language processing has an inherent research dilemma when the construction of domain lexicons is involved. The standard approach of building domain lexicon from domain corpora requires a very high threshold of existing domain resources and knowledge. Since only well-documented domains can provide enough quality corpora, it is likely these fields already have good manually constructed domain lexica. Hence this approach is can only deal with domains where only marginal benefit can be achieved, while it cannot deal with domains where it can make most contribution since there is not enough resources to work with.

It was observed that the type of domain language processing that has the widest application and best potentials are cross-domain and multi-domain in nature. For instance, a typical web-search is a search for specific domain information from the www as an archive of mixed and heterogeneous domains. The contribution will be immediate and salient to be able to acquire resources and information for a new domain that is not well documented yet.

A new approach towards domain language processing by constructing an infrastructure for multi-domain language processing called the Domain Lexico-Taxonomy (DLT) was proposed in Huang et al. (2004). In the DLT approach, domain lexica are semi-automatically acquired to populate domain taxonomy. This lexically populated domain taxonomy serves two purposes: as the basis of stylo-statistical prediction of the domain of a new text, and as the core seed of complete domain lexica. For the first purpose, the DLT approach relies crucially on the ability to effectively identify words that are good indicators of specific domains. For the second purpose, the DLT needs to be robust enough to allow incremental expansion when new content resources are integrated. In this study, we integrate CiLin, a Chinese thesaurus, to show that the DLT architecture is indeed robust.

2. Related Work

Typical studies on domain lexica focuses on assigning texts to specific classes, hence they use a limited taxonomy augmented with a small set of features (e.g. Avancini et al. 2003, Sebastiani 2002, and Yand and Pederson 1997). However, specialized lemmas cannot be useful in multi-domain processing. To achieve domain versatility in processing, it is necessary to identify lemmas with wider distributions and yet is associated with particular domain(s). We follow the DLT architecture (Huang et al. 2004), which was shown to be effective in predicting the domain of documents extracted from the web. We aim to elaborate that framework by proposing a domain lexica can be incrementally expanded with knowledge from a new resource.

3. Domain Taxonomy

A domain taxonomy containing 549 nodes was manually constructed. The main sources of domain classification are from Chinese Library Classification system, Encyclopedia Britannica and the Global View English-Chinese dictionary. Two important criteria were chosen: that the taxonomy is bilingual and that it is maintained locally. First, the bilingual taxonomy is essential for future cross-lingual processing but also allows us to access relevant resources in both languages. Second, since our emphasis was not on the correctness of a dogmatic taxonomy but on the flexibility that allows monotonic extensions, it is essential to be able to monitor any changes in the taxonomy.

There are four layers in the constructed domain taxonomy. Fourteen (14) domains are in the upper layer, including Humanities, Social Science, Formal Science, Natural Science, Medical Science, Engineering Science, Agriculture and Industry, Fine Arts, Recreation, Proper Name, Genre/Strata, Etymology, Country Name, Country People. The Second layer has 147 domains. The third layer has 279 domains. Lastly the fourth layer has only 109 domains since not all branches need to be expanded at this level. In sum, there are 549 possible domain tags when the hierarchy is ignored. The domain taxonomy is available online at the Sinica BOW website (http://BOW.sinica.edu.tw/, Huang and Chang 2004).

4. Detection of Domain Lexicon in DLT

The challenge in integrating heterogeneous language resources for domain information is that conceptual classification varies from one resource to another and hence cannot be directly harvested. We propose to utilize the inheritance relations of these resources, instead of their hierarchy. In other words, lexical (and hence conceptual) identity is established first, following by expanding this matching with logical inheritance but without branching out on the conceptual hierarchy.

DLT establish the correspondences between the taxonomic nodes of domains and the linguistic resources of sub-lexica. Note that a lexical knowledgebase, in a Wordnet fashion, also contains hierarchical relations. The domain taxonomy can be enriched by taking the hierarchical information internal to the lexica. If these resources directly encodes the 'is-a' relation by hyponymy, we assume that both the node (lexicons) and their hyponym node (lexicons) belong to that domain. Using the simple supposition, we can observe the domain knowledge with various resources, and strengthens the domain lexica for domain taxonomy. The process of populating DLT is shown in Fig. 1.

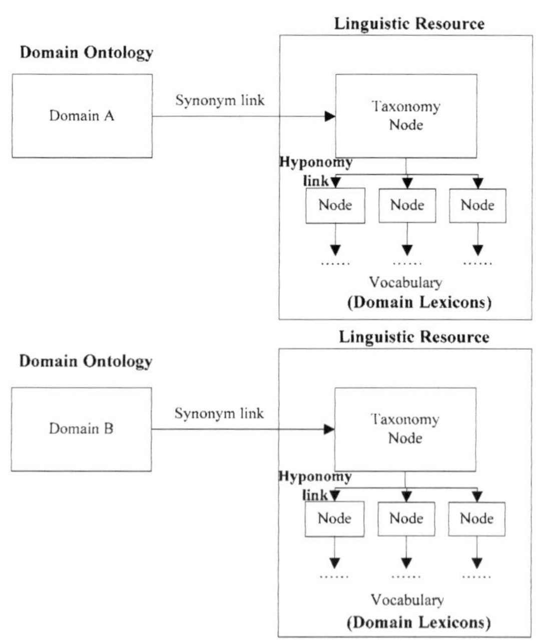

Figure. 1. Populating DLT from Linguistic Resource

5. Experiment

5.1. The Original Study with Bilingual WordNet

The original DLT work was based on bilingual Wordnet (Huang et al. 2004). This is because of the Wordnet lexical knowledgebase is highly enriched with lexical semantic relation information. In addition, the bilingual Wordnet adds an unparallel dimension of knowledge coverage. The bilingual Wordnet used is Sinica BOW (The Academia Sinica Bilingual Ontological WordNet, Huang and Chang (2004)). Sinica BOW is bilingual lexical knowledgebase connecting WordNet and SUMO and mapping both between English and Chinese. The study reported in Huang et al. (2004) also contains a small domain identification experiment to show the application of DLT.

5.1.1 Description of WordNet and Sinica BOW

WordNet is inspired by current psycholinguistic and computational theories of human lexical memory (Fellbaum (1998), Miller et al. (1993)). English nouns, verbs, adjectives, and adverbs are organized into synonym sets, each representing one underlying lexicalized concept. Different semantic relations link the synonym sets (synsets). The version of WordNet that Sinica BOW implemented is version 1.6, with nearly 100,000 synsets.

In Sinica BOW, ach English synset was given up to 3 most appropriate Chinese translation equivalents. And in cases where the translation pairs are not synonyms, their semantic relations are marked (Huang et al. 2003). The bilingual WordNet is further linked to the SUMO ontology. We use the semantic relations in bilingual resource to expand and predict domain classification when it cannot be judged directly from a lexical lemma.

5.1.2 Experiment and Result with WordNet

463 of the 549 nodes in the domain taxonomy were successfully mapped to a WordNet synset through an identical lemma. 452 or 463 mappings were manually confirmed to be correct, a precision score of over 97%. These domains were expanded to cover a total of 11,918 synsets corresponding to 15,160 Chinese lemmas. Note that both English and Chinese correspondences are used since our resources (WordNet and domain taxonomy) are both bilingual.

Due mostly to hyponymy expansion, each lemma is mapped to 1.38 domains in average. While each lemma is assigned to no more than 8 domains, with the majority (6,464) assigned to only one. These mapped lemmas populate a set of domain lexica. The number of entries in these domain lexica ranges from 1 to 3762. The average size of these domain lexica is 32.8 lemmas. Only 41 domains lexical contain 33 or more lemmas. Since we cannot know the effective of the lexicon of a domain a priori, we take those whose size are above average as the effective domain lexica.

These domain lexica and their sizes are shown in Table 1.

5.1.3 Evaluation: precision of domain lexica

It is impossible to formally evaluate the recall rate of this domain lexica study since we do not know the total number of entries to be recalled. However, it is possible to evaluate the precision rate of the constructed domain lexica. First, the precision of all recalled lemmas is tested. Among the mapped lemmas, 8696 (out of 15,160) lemmas are assigned to multiple domains, while 6,464 are assigned to single domain. The single domain mappings were spot-checked to be correct. On the other hand, the precision of all 8,696 multi-domain lemmas are carefully evaluated. Among these lemmas, only 4.81% (418) proves to be wrong; and an overwhelming majority of 95.19% turns out to be correct (8278).

Second, a more meaningful test is to evaluate how well the domain lexica are defined. Five effective domain lexica with over 100 entries were randomly chosen for evaluation: Insect (515 entries), Natural Science (262 entries), Sports (180 entries), Dance (124 entries) and Religious Music (48 entries).

The manually checked precision of these domain lexica is listed below the Table 2:

Domain	Domain	Domain	Domain
Vertebrates 脊椎動物 3676	Food 食品 2968	Bird 鳥類 1059	Fish 魚類 729
Language 語言 699	Recreation 休閒娛樂 548	Insect 昆蟲 515	Natural Science 自然科學 262
Country 國家 250	contest 競賽 207	music 音樂 192	Indian 印地安 188
Sports 運動 180	commerce 商業 144	Business 生意 144	Dance 舞蹈 124
Heraldic design 紋章設計 120	Medical Science 醫療科學 85	Medicine 醫學 76	Pathological medicine 病理醫學 76
Clinical medicine 臨床醫學 76	Mathematics 數學 69	Humanities 人文學科 64	Social Science 社會科學 62
physics 物理學 56	Religion 宗教 52	Religious Music 宗教音樂 48	Plastic art 造形藝術 45
Pure mathematics 純數學 44	Anthropology 人類學 42	Earth science 地球科學 39	drawing 素描 39
Norse Mythology 北歐神話 39	Philosophy 哲學 37	Telecommunication 電信通訊 35	theater 戲劇 34
Fine Arts 藝術 33			

Table 1. Domain lexica containing 33 or more lemmas

Domain Label	# of entries	Precision (%)
Insect	515	99.03
Natural Science	262	69.85
Sports	180	86.11
Dance	124	100.00
Religious Music	48	93.75

Table 2. Size and Precision of selected domain lexica

Table 2 shows an overall precision of over 95%, while no other lexica has precision lower than 86%, natural science is lowest at just below 70%. This is because "Natural Science" is a higher level domain and hence open to more noises in the detection process. This study clearly showed that the WordNet helped to effectively build core domain lexica.

We take the domain "Dance" as an example to explain the process. First, we map "Dance" to the Wordnet synset—"dance", and we look for the hyponym synsets. Table3 will be shown the expanding lexica of one of hyponym synsets. These lexical entries are associated with domain "Dance" and populate the domain lexicon.

Level	synset
1	social_dancing
2	folk_dancing, folk_dance
3	country-dance, country_dancing,
4	square_dance, square_dancing
5	quadrille

Table 3. The expanding hyponym synsets of "dance"

5.2 For CiLin

5.2.1 Description of CiLin

CiLin, a short name for Tongyici CiLin, is a Chinese thesaurus published in 1984 (Mei et al. 1984). The terms in CiLin are organized in a conceptual hierarchy, with near-synonym terms forming a set. There are five levels in the taxonomy structure of CiLin. The CiLin terms between Level1 to Level4 are taxonomy categories. Level1 is the upper class, and it includes 12 categories, like as people, object, time and space, abstract etc. Level2 has 106 categories. Level3 has 3,948 categories. Level4 has 4,014 categories. There are 64,157 terms in Level5 since all branches need to be expanded at this level. These terms are classified to 12,193 sets by the meaning. The average number of terms in each set is 5.34. Fig. 2 shows the structure of CiLin.

Figure. 2. The structure of CiLin

5.2.2. Experiment and Result with CiLin

First, we map the 549 domains to CiLin's taxonomy. Unlike the previous study, only Chinese terms were available on CiLin. The result is given in Table 4.

	# of entries	# of domains	entries/domains
Level 1	146	1	146
Level 2	1,587	3	529
Level 4	1,222	32	38.19

Table 4. Number of expanding entries and mapping domains

Manual checking showed that mappings to Level 1 and Level 2 are both imprecise and small in number. Hence we take Level 4 as the lexical anchor for enriching domain lexica. 1,222 lexical items are expanded from 32 domains, and these domain lexica and their sizes are shown in Table 5.

Domain	Domain
Insect(昆蟲) -- 146	Sewing(縫紉) -- 25
Country(國家) -- 128	Movie(電影) -- 25
Theater(戲劇) -- 116	Game(遊戲) -- 25
Painting(繪畫) -- 88	Photography(攝影) -- 21
Capital(資本) -- 54	Payment(支付) -- 20
Cookery(烹飪) -- 52	Printing(印刷) -- 20
Dance(舞蹈) -- 52	Literature(文學) -- 18
Law(法律) -- 50	Investment(投資) -- 14
Education(教育) -- 47	Swimming(游泳) -- 12
Martial_art(武術) -- 45	Broadcasting(廣播) -- 11
Religion(宗教) -- 39	Ranching_and_animal_husbandry(畜牧) -- 10
Architecture(建築) -- 38	Textile_industry 紡織 10
Carving(雕刻) -- 37	Boating(划船) -- 8
Language(語言) -- 37	Trade(貿易) -- 7

Table 5. Domain lexica

When all mappings are evaluated, 873(71.44%) of them are correct, and 349 (28.56%) incorrect. Five effective domain lexica are evaluated, as shown below in Table 6:

Domain Label	# of entries	Precision (%)
Insect	146	58.9
Country	128	55.47
Theater	116	80.17
Painting	88	80.68
Dance	52	80.77

Table 6. Size and Precision of selected domain lexica

Compared with the work reported in (Huang et al. 2004), both the number of lemma (1,222 vs. 15,160) and precision (71.44% vs. nearly 95%) are lower. This result is expected since CiLin has a simple taxonomy without the rich lexical information of a Wordnet. The crucial fact shown, however, is that DLT can be incrementally enhanced with the new mappings. Of the 873 correct domain lexica entries, 79.5% (694) are new entries that were not identified previously. Even more impressive is the effectiveness of increase in lexica sizes for applicable domains, as shown below in Table 7.

domain	WN/old	CiLin/new	increase	domain	WN/old	CiLin/new	increase
戲劇	34	80	0.7018	文學	12	15	0.5556
昆蟲	515	65	0.1121	印刷	22	15	0.4054
繪畫	17	61	0.7821	縫紉	28	14	0.3333
國家	250	44	0.1497	音樂	192	12	0.0588
舞蹈	124	34	0.2152	支付	20	11	0.3548
武術	7	33	0.8250	攝影	23	10	0.3030
資本	26	33	0.5593	游泳	15	9	0.3750
烹飪	14	32	0.6957	投資	5	8	0.6154
建築	2	29	0.9355	紡織	9	7	0.4375
雕刻	2	27	0.9310	廣播	2	7	0.7778
法律	22	24	0.5217	畜牧	0	5	1.0000
教育	26	23	0.4694	遊戲	16	5	0.2381
語言	699	22	0.0305	划船	27	4	0.1290
宗教	52	21	0.2877	貿易	4	4	0.5000
計算	55	19	0.2568	料理	6	2	0.2500
電影	21	17	0.4474	鍛造	1	2	0.6667

Table 7. Increase in Domain Lexicon Size after CiLin Integration

Table 7 shows that, even though adding CiLin only helped 32 domain lexica, 14 of them have their lexicon size more than doubled. One of them, ranching and animal husbandry is a new domain lexicon where no mapping was possible with WordNet. In other words, adding the CiLin resource substantially enhanced effective domain coverage of DLT.

6. Conclusion

In this paper, test the robustness of the DLT architecture. We show both the coverage and the sizes of the domain lexica on DLT can be effectively expanded by integrating a new language resource. The robustness is convincing given that the coverage and quality of the new resource is actually not as good as the original reference resources. In other words, we showed the open architecture of DLT facilitates integration of new domain information without imposing any high threshold on the format and quality of new resources. We also verify partial results of previous work since 205 lemma mappings were repeated. For future work, we plan to continue to populate DLT, as well as to explore other possibilities for putting DLT to actual applications.

References

Chu-Ren Huang, Elanna I. J. Tseng, Dylan B. S. Tsai, Brian Murphy. Cross-lingual Portability of Semantic relations: Bootstrapping Chinese WordNet with English WordNet Relations. Languages and Linguistics. 4.3. (2003)509-532

Chu-Ren, Huang and Ru-Yng Chang. Sinica BOW (Bilingual Ontological Wordnet): Integration of Bilingual WordNet and SUMO". Presented at the 4th International Conference on Language Resources and Evaluation (LREC2004). Lisbon. Portugal. 26-28 May (2004)

Chu-Ren Huang, Xiang-Bing Li, Jia-Fei Hong. "Domain Lexico-Taxonomy:An Approach Towards Multi-domain Language Processing", Asian Symposium on Natural Language Processing to Overcome Language Barriers, The First International Joint Conference on Natural Language Processing (IJCNLP-04). Sanya City, Hainan Island, China. 22-24 March (2004)

F. Sebastiani., "Machine learning in automated text categorization". ACM Computing Surveys, 34(1) (2002)1-47

Fellbaum C.. WordNet: An Electronic Lexical Database. Cambridge: MIT Press (1998)

G. A. Miller, R. Beckwith, C. Fellbaum, D. Gross and K. Miller. "Introduction to WordNet: An On-line Lexical Database," In Proceedings of the fifteenth International Joint Conference on

Artificial Intelligence. Chambéry, France. 28 August- 3 September (1993)

Henri Avancini, Alberto Lavelli, Bernardo Magnini, Fabrizio Sebastiani, Roberto Zanoli. Expanding Domain-Specific Lexicons by Term Categorization. Proceedings of the 2003 ACM symposium on Applied computing. Melbourne, Florida, USA. 9-12 March (2003)

Jia-ju Mei, Yi-Ming Zheng, Yun- Qi Gao and Hung-Xiang Yin. TongYiCi CiLin. Shanghai: the COMMERCIAL Press (1984)

Y. Yang and J. O. Pedersen. A comparative study on feature selection in text categorization. In D. H. Fisher, editor, Proceedings of ICML-97, 14th International Conference on Machine Learning, pages 412 420. San Francisco: Morgan Kaufmann (1997)

Some Studies on Chinese Domain Knowledge Dictionary and Its Application to Text Classification

Jingbo Zhu
Natural Language Processing Lab
Institute of Computer Software & Theory
Northeastern University, Shenyang
zhujingbo@mail.neu.edu.cn

Wenliang Chen
Natural Language Processing Lab
Institute of Computer Software & Theory
Northeastern University, Shenyang
Chenwl@mail.neu.edu.cn

Abstract

In this paper, we study some issues on Chinese domain knowledge dictionary and its application to text classification task. First a domain knowledge hierarchy description framework and our Chinese domain knowledge dictionary named NEUKD are introduced. Second, to alleviate the cost of construction of domain knowledge dictionary by hand, we use a boostrapping-based algorithm to learn new domain associated terms from a large amount of unlabeled data. Third, we propose two models (BOTW and BOF) which use domain knowledge as textual features for text categorization. But due to limitation of size of domain knowledge dictionary, we further study machine learning technique to solve the problem, and propose a BOL model which could be considered as the extended version of BOF model. Naïve Bayes classifier based on BOW model is used as baseline system in the comparison experiments. Experimental results show that domain knowledge is very useful for text categorization, and BOL model performs better than other three models, including BOW, BOTW and BOF models.

1 Introduction

It is natural for people to know the topic of the document when they see some specific words in the document. For example, when we read a news, if title of the news includes a word "姚明 (Yao Ming)", as we know, "姚明(Yao Ming)" is a famous China basketball athlete in US NBA game, so we could recognize the topic of the document is about "篮球，体育 (Basketball, Sports)" with our domain knowledge. In this paper, we call the specific word "姚明(Yao Ming)" as a *Domain Associated Term* (DAT). A DAT is a word or a phrase (compound words) that enable humans to recognize intuitively a topic of text with their domain knowledge. In fact, domain knowledge is a kind of commonsense knowledge. We think that domain knowledge is very useful for text understanding tasks, such as text classification, document summarization, and information retrieval.

In previous literatures, some researchers used knowledge bases for text understanding tasks(Scott et al., 1998), such as WordNet for English and HowNet for Chinese. We know that WordNet and HowNet are lexical and semantic knowledge resources. Other researchers tried to use commonsense knowledge such as field-associated terms for text understanding tasks(M. Fuketa et al., 2000, Sangkon Lee and Masami Shishibori, 2002). But the problem of limitation of size of such knowledge base is still a key bottleneck for using domain knowledge dictionary for text understanding tasks, and how to solve it is an ongoing research focus.

In the following content, we try to give answers to four questions: 1)What is our Chinese domain knowledge dictionary NEUKD? 2)How to learn DATs from a large amount of unlabelled data? 3)How to use the Chinese domain knowledge dictionary NEUKD for text classification? 4)Due to the problem of limitation of size of domain knowledge dictionary, how to solve the problem and improve performance of text classification using domain knowledge dictionary?

2 Domain Knowledge Dictionary

We first introduce briefly domain knowledge hierarchy description framework (DKF) which includes three levels: *Domain Level* (DL), *Domain Feature Level* (DFL) and *Domain Associated Term Level* (DATL). The DL is the top level which defines many domains, such as "体育(Sports)", "军事(Military Affairs)". The DFL is the second level which defines many domain features. A domain defined in the DL has a lot of domain features defined in the DFL. For example, domain "军事(Military Affairs)" has many domain features, such as "军队(Army Feature)", "武器(Weapon Feature)" and "战争(War Feature)". The DATL is the third level which defines many domain associated terms. Many domain associated terms could indicate a same domain feature defined in the DFL. For example, some domain associated terms, such as some domain associated terms, such as "中东战争(Mid-East War)", "伊拉克战争(Iraq War)" and "阿富汗战争(Afghanistan War)", indicate domain feature "战争(War)".

Since 1996 we employed a semi-automatic machine learning technique to acquire domain knowledge from a large amount of labeled and unlabeled corpus, and built a general-purpose domain knowledge dictionary named NEUKD according to the domain knowledge hierarchy description framework(Zhu Jingbo et al., 2002). Items defined in the NEUKD include domain associated term, domain feature and domain. Currently 40 domains, 982 domain features and more than 610,000 domain associated terms are defined in the NEUKD. Some instances of NEUKD are given in Table 1. Because the size of NEUKD is limited, so in following content we will study machine learning techniques to solve the problem of using NEUKD for text classification task.

Domain Associated Terms	Domain Features	Domain
姚明 (Yao Ming)	篮球，运动员 (Basketball, Athlete)	体育 (Sports)
三峡工程 (The Sanxia project)	水利工程 (Irrigation Project)	水利 (Irrigation Works)
赛季 (Match Season)	比赛 (Match)	体育 (Sports)
阿森纳队 (Arsenal Team)	足球 (Football)	体育 (Sports)
中国工商银行 (Industrial and commercial bank of China)	银行 (Bank)	金融 (Finance)

Table 1. Some instances defined in the NEUKD

3 Bootstrapping-based DAT Learning Algorithm

To extend domain knowledge dictionary, in this paper, we will use a *feature learning algorithm based on bootstrapping* (FLB)(Zhu Jingbo et al., 2004) to learning new DATs. In the FLB learning procedure, some seed words are given in advance. In fact, seed words are some important DATs. For example, ten seed words of domain "金融(finance)" are 股票(stock), 金融(finance), 贷款(loan), 证券(stock), 财经(finance and economics), 银行(bank), 税收(tax), 外汇(foreign exchange), 投资(investment) and 股市(stock market).

The FLB learning procedure is described as follows:

- **Initialization**: Use a small number of seed words initialize DAT set
- **Iterate Bootstrapping**:
  - **Candidate DAT Learner**: Learn some new DATs as candidate DATs from unlabeled data.
  - **Evaluation**: Score all candidate DATs, and select top-n best DATs as new seed words, and add them into DAT set.

In the beginning of algorithm, all words except stopwords in the unlabeled corpus could be considered as candidate DATs. In fact, we can regard bootstrapping as iterative clustering. In the evaluation step of FLB algorithm, RlogF metric method(Ellen Riloff, Rosie Jones, 1999) is used as evaluation function which assigns a score to a word(candidate DAT). The score of a word is computed as:

$$M(w_i) = Log_2 F(w_i, X) \times R_i \qquad (1)$$

Where $F(w_i,X)$ is the frequency of co-occurrence of word w_i and X (set of seed words) in the same sentence, $F(w_i)$ is the frequency of w_i in the corpus, and $R_i=F(w_i,X)/F(w_i)$. The RlogF metric tries to strike a balance between reliability and frequency: R is high when the word is highly correlated with set of seed words, and F is high when the word and X highly co-occur in the same sentence.

In the experiments, we use the corpus from 1996-1998 People's Daily as unlabeled data which has about 50 million words. For domain "金融(finance)", we select ten seed words shown in above example, the bootstrapping-based DAT learning algorithm obtains 65% precision performance within top-1000 new learned DATs according to human judgment.

4 Domain Knowledge based Text Classification

In this paper, naïve Bayes(NB) model (McCallum and K.Nigam, 1998) is used to build text classifier. We want to study how to use our Chinese domain knowledge dictionary NEUKD to improve text categorization.

4.1 BOW Model

The most commonly used document representation is the so called vector space model(G.Salton and M.J.McGill, 1983). In the vector space model, documents are represented by vectors of terms (textual features, e.g. words, phases, etc.). Conventional bag-of-words model (BOW) uses common words as textual features. In the comparison experiments, we use the BOW model as baseline NB system.

4.2 BOTW Model

As above mentioned, more than 610000 domain associated terms (DATs) are defined in the NEUKD, such as "姚明(Yao Ming) ", "三峡工程(The Sanxia project)", and "中国工商银行(Industrial and commercial bank of China)" shown in table 1. We use domain associated terms and common words as textual features, called BOTW models (short for bag-of-terms and words model). For example, in the previous examples, the DAT "三峡工程(The Sanxia project, Sanxia is a LOCATION name of China)" can be used as a textual feature in BOTW model. But in BOW model(baseline system) we consider two common words "三峡(The Sanxia)" and "工程(project)" as two different textual features.

4.3 BOF Model

Similar to BOTW model, we use domain features as textual features in the NB classifier, called BOF model (short for bag-of-features model). In BOF model, we first transform all DATs into domain features according to definitions in the NEUKD, and group DATs with same domain features as a cluster, called ***Topic Cluster***. For Examples, Topic Cluster "体育(sports)" includes some DATs, such as "赛季(match season)", "阿森纳队(Arsenal)", "奥运会(Olympic Games)", "乒乓球(Table Tennis)", "姚明(Yao Ming)". In BOF model, we use topic clusters as textual features for text categorization. Also the classification computation procedure of BOF model is same as of BOW model.

4.4 BOL Model

To solve the problem of the limitation of NEUKD, in this paper, we propose a machine learning technique to improve BOF model. The basic ideas are that we wish to learn new DATs from pre-classified documents, and group them into the predefined topic clusters which are formed and used as textual features in BOF model discussed in section 4.3. Then these new topic clusters could be used as textual features for text categorization. We call the new model as BOL model(short for bag-of-learned features model) which could be consider as an extended version of BOF model.

First we group all DATs originally defined in NEUKD into a lot of topic clusters as described in BOF model, which are used as seeds in following learning procedure. Then we group other words (not be defined in NEUKD) into these topic clusters. The Learning algorithm is described as following:

- **Preprocessing**: Text segmentation, extracting candidate words, and sort the candidate words by CHI method. As above mentioned, all candidate words except stopwords which are not defined in NEUKD will be grouped into topic clusters in this process.

- **Initialization**: These words, which are defined in NEUKD, are first added to corresponding topic clusters according to their associated domain features, respectively.
- **Iteration**: Loop until all candidate words have been put into topic clusters:
  - Measure similarity of a candidate word and each topic cluster, respectively.
  - Put the candidate word into the most similar topic cluster(Note that a word can only be grouped into one cluster).

The important issue of above procedures is how to measure the similarity between a word and a topic cluster. Chen Wenliang *et. al.*(2004) proposed a measure for word clustering algorithm used in text classification. So in this paper, we use Chen's measure to measure the similarity between a word and a topic cluster in above learning algorithm. The similarity of a word w_t and a topic cluster f_j is defined as

$$S = \lambda(w_t)(\xi(w_t, w_t \vee f_j) + \xi(f_j, w_t \vee f_j))$$

$$\lambda(w_t) = \frac{N(w_t) + N(f_j)}{\sum_{i=1}^{|L|} N(f_i) + |W|} \tag{2}$$

Where

$$\xi(w_t, w_t \vee f_j) = \frac{P(w_t)}{P(w_t) + P(f_j)} \times D(P(C \mid w_t) \,\|\, P(C \mid w_t \vee f_j))$$

$$\xi(f_j, w_t \vee f_j) = \frac{P(f_j)}{P(w_t) + P(f_j)} \times D(P(C \mid f_j) \,\|\, P(C \mid w_t \vee f_j))$$

Where we define the distribution $P(C|w_t)$ as the random variable over classes C, and its distribution given a particular word w_t. $N(f_i)$ denote the number of words in the topic cluster f_i, W is the list of candidate words.

To describe how to estimate distribution $P(C|f)$, we first assume that in the beginning of learning procedure, only a word w_1 is included in topic cluster f_1, we could say that $P(C|f_1) = P(C|w_1)$. When a new word w_2 is added into topic cluster f_1, we could get a new topic cluster f_2. How to estimate the new distribution $P(C|f_2)$ is key step, where $f_2=w_2 \vee f_1$. We could use the following formula (3) to estimate distribution $P(C|f_2) =P(C|w_2 \vee f_1)$. Similarly, we could know if the new word w_n is added into topic cluster f_{n-1} to form a new topic cluster f_n, we also could estimate $P(C|f_n)=P(C|w_n \vee f_{n-1})$ following this way, and so on.

$$\begin{aligned} P(C \mid f_2) &= P(C \mid w_2 \vee f_1) \\ &= \frac{P(w_2)}{P(w_2) + P(f_1)} P(C \mid w_2) \\ &+ \frac{P(f_1)}{P(w_2) + P(f_1)} P(C \mid f_1) \end{aligned} \tag{3}$$

We turn back the question about how to measure the difference between two probability distributions. Kullback-Leibler divergence is used to do this. The KL divergence between two class distributions induced by w_t and w_s is written as

$$\begin{aligned} & D(P(C \mid w_t) \,\|\, P(C \mid w_s)) = \\ & -\sum_{j=1}^{|C|} P(c_j \mid w_t) \log\left(\frac{P(c_j \mid w_t)}{P(c_j \mid w_s)}\right) \end{aligned} \tag{4}$$

In preprocessing step, the CHI statistic measures the lack of independence of feature t and category c.

$$\chi 2(\mathrm{t,c}) = \frac{\mathrm{N(AD-BC)^2}}{\mathrm{(A+C)(B+D)(A+B)(C+D)}}$$

Where t refers to a feature and c refers to a category, A is the number of times t and c co-occur, B is the number of times t occurs without c, C is the number of times c occurs without t, D is the number of times neither c nor t co-occur, and N is the total number of documents.

5 Experimental Results

In this paper, we use naïve Bayes for classifying documents. Here we only describe multinomial naïve Bayes briefly since full details have been presented in the paper(McCallum and K.Nigam, 1998). The basic idea in naïve Bayes approaches is to use the joint probabilities of words and categories to estimate the probabilities of categories when a document is given. Given a document *d* for classification, we calculate the probabilities of each category *c* as follows:

$$\begin{aligned} P(c \mid d) &= \frac{P(c)P(d \mid c)}{P(d)} \\ &\propto P(c) \prod_{i=1}^{|T|} \frac{P(t_i \mid c)^{N(t_i|d)}}{N(t_i \mid d)!} \end{aligned}$$

Where $N(t_i|d)$ is the frequency of word t_i in document *d*, T is the vocabulary and |T| is the size of T, t_i is the ith word in the vocabulary, and $P(t_i|c)$ thus represents the probability that a randomly drawn word from a randomly drawn document in category *c* will be the word t_i.

In the experiments, we use NEU_TC data set(Chen Wenliang et. al. 2004) to evaluate the performance of baseline NB classifier and our classifiers. The NEU_TC data set contains Chinese web pages collected from web sites. The pages are divided into 37 classes according to "Chinese Library Categorization"(CLCEB, 1999). It consists of 14,459 documents. We do not use tag information of pages. We use the toolkit CipSegSDK(Yao Tianshun *et. al.* 2002) for word segmentation. We removed all words that had less than two occurrences. The resulting vocabulary has about 60000 words.

In the experiments, we use 5-fold cross validation where we randomly and uniformly split each class into 5 folds and we take four folds for training and one fold for testing. In the cross-validated experiments we report on the average performance. For evaluating the effectiveness of category assignments by classifiers to documents, we use the conventional recall, precision and F1 measures. Recall is defined to be the ratio of correct assignments by the system divided by the total number of correct assignments. Precision is the ratio of correct assignments by the system divided by the total number of the system's assignments. The F1 measure combines recall (r) and precision (p) with an equal weight in the following form:

$$F_1(r,p) = \frac{2rp}{r+p}$$

In fact, these scores can be computed for the binary decisions on each individual category first and then be averaged over categories. The way is called macro-averaging method. For evaluating performance average across class, we use the former way called micro averaging method in this paper which balances recall and precision in a way that gives them equal weight. The micro-averaged F1 measure has been widely used in cross-method comparisons.

To evaluate the performance of these four models based on NB classifier, we construct four systems in the experiments, including BOW, BOTW, BOF and BOL classifier. CHI measure is used to feature selection in all text classifiers.

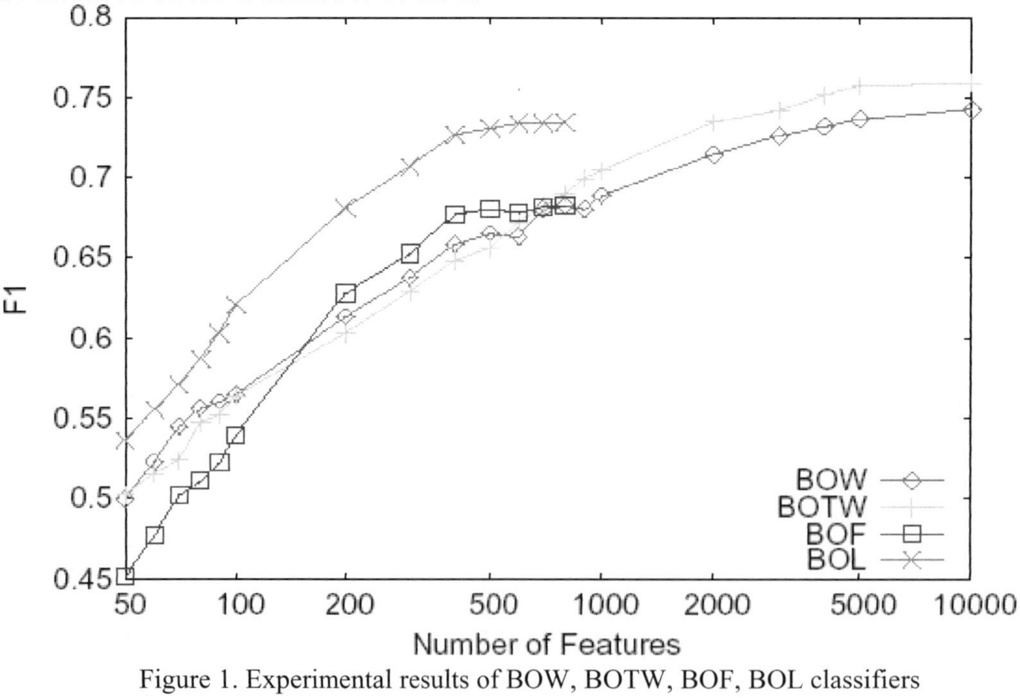

Figure 1. Experimental results of BOW, BOTW, BOF, BOL classifiers

In figure 1, we could find that BOTW classifier always performs better than BOW classifier when the number of features is larger than about 500. From comparative experimental results of BOTW and BOW classifiers, we think that domain associated items are a richer and more precise representation of meaning than common words. Because the total number of domain features in NEUKD is only 982, in figure 1 we find the maximum number of features (domain features) for BOF and BOL classifier is less than 1000. When the number of features is between 200 and 1000, BOF classifier performs better than BOW and BOTW classifiers. It is also obvious that BOL classifier always performs better than other three classifiers when the number of features is less than 1000. As above mentioned, in BOL model, we use a machine learning technique to solve the problem of limitation of size of NEUKD, and group rest 65.01% words into predefined topic clusters as textual features in BOL model. So the classifier based on BOL model can yield better performance than BOF model.

6 Conclusions and Future Work

In this paper, we first introduce our Chinese domain knowledge dictionary NEUKD. To alleviate the cost of construction of domain knowledge dictionary by hand, we propose a boostrapping-based algorithm to learn new domain associated terms from a large amount of unlabeled data. This paper studies how to improve text categorization by using domain knowledge dictionary. To do it, we propose two models using domain knowledge as textual features. The first one is BOTW model which uses domain associated terms and common words as textual features. The other one is BOF model which uses domain features as textual features. But due to limitation of size of domain knowledge dictionary, many useful words are lost in the training procedure. We study and use a machine learning technique to solve the problem to improve knowledge-based text categorization, and propose a BOL model which could be considered as the extension version of BOF model. Comparison experimental results of those four models (BOW, BOTW, BOF and BOL) show that domain knowledge is very useful for improving text categorization. In fact, a lot of knowledge-based NLP application systems have to face the problem of limitation of size of knowledge bases. Like our work discussed in this paper, we think that using machine learning techniques is a good way to solve such problem. In the future work, we will study how to apply the domain knowledge to improve other text understanding tasks, such as information retrieval, information extraction, topic detection and tracking (TDT).

Acknowledgements

This research was supported in part by the National Natural Science Foundation of China & Microsoft Research Asia (No. 60203019), the Key Project of Chinese Ministry of Education (No. 104065), and the National Natural Science Foundation of China (No. 60473140).

References

Chen Wenliang, Chang Xingzhi, Wang Huizhen, Zhu Jingbo, and Yao Tianshun. 2004. Automatic Word Clustering for Text Categorization Using Global Information. *First Asia Information Retrieval Symposium (AIRS 2004)*, LNCS, Beijing, pp.1-6

CLCEB. 1999. China Library Categorization Editorial Board. China Library Categorization (The 4th ed.) (In Chinese), Beijing, *Beijing Library Press.*

Ellen Riloff, Rosie Jones. 1999. Learning Dictionaries for Information Extraction by Multi-Level Bootstrapping, *Proceedings of the Sixteenth National Conference on Artificial Intelligence.*

G.Salton and M.J.McGill, 1983. An introduction to modern information retrieval, *McGraw-Hill.*

McCallum and K.Nigam. 1998. A Comparison of Event Models for naïve Bayes Text Classification, *In AAAI-98 Workshop on Learning for Text Categorization.*

M. Fuketa, S.Lee, T.Tsuji, M.Okada and J. Aoe. 2000. A document classification method by using field associated words. *International Journal of Information Sciences.* 126(1-4), p57-70

Sangkon Lee, Masami Shishibori. 2002. Passage segmentation based on topic matter, *International journal of computer processing of oriental languages*, 15(3), p305-339.

Scott, Sam, Stan Matwin. 1998. Text classification using WordNet hypernyms. *Proceedings of the COLING/ACL Workshop on Usage of WordNet in Natural Language Processing Systems*, Montreal.

Yao Tianshun, Zhu Jingbo, Zhang li, and Yang Ying, 2002. Natural Language Processing- research on making computers understand human languages, *Tsinghua University Press*, (In Chinese).

Zhu Jingbo and Yao Tianshun. 2002. FIFA-based Text Classification, *Journal of Chinese Information Processing*, V16, No3.(In Chinese)

Zhu Jingbo, Chen Wenliang, and Yao Tianshun. 2004. Using Seed Words to Learn to Categorize Chinese Text. *Advances in Natural Language Processing: 4th International Conference (EsTAL 2004)*, pp.464-473

Resolving Pronominal References in Chinese with the Hobbs Algorithm

Susan P. Converse
CIS, University of Pennsylvania
spc@seas.upenn.edu

Abstract

This study addresses pronominal anaphora resolution, including zero pronouns, in Chinese. A syntactic, rule-based pronoun resolution algorithm, the "Hobbs algorithm" was run on "gold standard" hand parses from the Penn Chinese Treebank. While first proposed for English, the algorithm counts for its success on two characteristics that Chinese and English have in common. Both languages are SVO, and both are fixed word order languages. No changes were made to adapt the algorithm to Chinese. The accuracy of the algorithm on overt, third-person pronouns at the matrix level was 77.6%, and the accuracy for resolving matrix-level zero pronouns was 73.3%. In contrast, the accuracy of the algorithm on pronouns that appeared in subordinate constructions was only 43.3%, providing support for Miltsakaki's two-mechanism proposal for resolving inter- *vs.* intra-sentential anaphors.

1 Introduction

The goal of this study is pronoun resolution, including null/zero pronouns, in Chinese. There has been extensive research for many years into computational approaches to automatic anaphora resolution in English, and increasingly in other languages as well (Mitkov, 1999; Mitkov, 2002). Yet although there have been countless linguistic studies in Chinese on anaphora and zero anaphora (for example, (Huang, 1984; Huang, 1994; Yang et al., 1999) just to illustrate the range), the published computational work to date is limited to just a few studies (Chen, 1992; Yeh and Chen, 2001; Yeh and Chen, 2005).

In 1978 Jerry Hobbs proposed an algorithm for the resolution of pronominal coreference in English (Hobbs, 1978). The performance of this algorithm has frequently been used as a baseline reference for computational methods in English. The most basic version of the Hobbs algorithm is subject biased, relying on a basic strategy of left-to-right, breadth-first searches, subject to a few structural constraints.

Chinese, like English, is an SVO language. Chinese has also been regarded as a topic-comment language. From either viewpoint, it is worth examining how well the left-to-right, SVO-biased process of the Hobbs algorithm works for Chinese, perhaps so it could be used as a baseline against which to measure other automated approaches to Chinese anaphora resolution.

While Chinese and English are both SVO languages, they differ in another important parameter: Chinese is a pro-drop language, while standard English is not. Thus it will be of particular interest to see how well the Hobbs algorithm performs when proposing antecedents for zero pronouns.

The Hobbs algorithm operates on parsed sentences. In order to evaluate its performance on zero pronouns as well as overt ones, it would be useful to have text that already has the locations of the zero pronouns marked. Because the Penn Chinese Treebank has overt strings to denote the positions of dropped arguments, test sentences were selected from that corpus.

2 The Corpus and Annotations

The source texts for this study are taken from the first 100K of the CTB 5.0 release of the Penn Chinese Treebank (CTB). The CTB consists of Xinhua news articles that have been segmented, part-of-speech tagged, and bracketed with syntactic labels and functional tags (Xue et al., 2004)[1]. In the corpus, zero pronouns are denoted using the string "***pro***". An example is given in Figure 1.

In order to provide an answer key or "gold standard" against which to test automatic anaphora resolution methods, we are annotating the CTB to indicate the pronominal coreference relations. All third-person pronouns (including 其 (his, hers, its, theirs) and 之 (he/she/it/they)), reflexives, demonstratives, and ***pro*** are being annotated.

Only those coreference relations that are between these anaphors and *nominal* entities are being co-indexed, however. That is, only *NPs* that denote the same entity as the entity referred to by the anaphor are being co-indexed. Since not every instance of one of these anaphors necessarily refers to a nominal entity, non-coreferring anaphors are being tagged with labels that categorize them roughly by type.

The categories are: **DD** (discourse deictic) for anaphors that refer to propositions or events in the text; **EXT** (existential) for ***pro*** in existential contexts analogous to the English "there is/are"; **INFR** (inferrable) to be put on an anaphor that refers to a specific nominal entity when that entity does not have an overt NP denoting it in the text; **AMB** (ambiguous) when the interpretation of an anaphor is ambiguous between two (or more) referents; and **ARB** (arbitrary) for anaphors that don't fall into the other categories[2].

Complex NPs abound in the CTB and present a choice for the placement of the indices and category labels. The decision was made to put the index for a complex NP referent on the entire complex NP rather than on just the head of the phrase

```
(IP
  (ADVP (AD 同时))
  (PU ，)
  (IP(IP(NP#2-SBJ (NP (NP (DP (DT 全))
                          (NP (NN 国)))
                      (NP (NN 城镇)
                          (NN 公房)))
                  (NP (NN 月)
                      (NN 租金)))
        (VP (VE 有)(AS 了)
            (NP-OBJ (CP (WHNP-1 (-NONE- *OP*))
                        (IP (NP-SBJ (-NONE- *T*-1))
                            (VP (ADVP (AD 较))
                                (VP (VA 大)))))
                    (NP (NN 提高)))))
    (PU ，)
    (IP(NP#2-SBJ (-NONE- *pro*))
       (VP(NP-LOC (QP (CLP (M 部分)))
                  (NP (NN 地区)))
          (VP(VRD (VV 提高)(VV 到))
             (IP-OBJ
               (NP-SBJ (-NONE- *PRO*))
               (VP(VV 占)
                  (LCP-OBJ
                    (QP(DNP(NP(NP(NP(QP (CD 双))
                                    (NP (NN 职工)))
                                 (NP (NN 家庭)))
                              (NP (NN 收入)))
                           (DEG 的))
                       (QP (CD 百分之十)))
                    (LC 左右))))))))
  (PU 。))
```

At the same time, there has been a comparatively large increase in **the entire country's monthly rent for public housing in cities and townships**$_2$, with **that**$_2$ in a portion of the regions increasing to account for about 10% of the income of dual income families.

Figure 1: Sample of the annotation and example of annotating high.

[1] **http://www.cis.upenn.edu/~ chinese**

[2] Linguists beware: this is far more general than the arbitrary in "arbitrary PRO"

(that is, to annotate "high" in the NP tree). Figure 1 has such a case. The annotation **#2** is placed on the parent **NP-SBJ** level, rather than at the level of the head (NP (NN 月)(NN 租金)) (monthly rent).

The reasoning for this choice was that the full NP unambiguously distinguishes between different nominal entities whose NPs have identical head nouns. Head nouns of complex NPs can always be algorithmically obtained.

3 The Hobbs Algorithm

The "Hobbs Algorithm" was outlined in a paper by Jerry Hobbs in 1978 (Hobbs, 1978). The algorithm is shown in the Appendix. While the algorithm is naive in that the steps proceed merely according to the structure of the parse tree, there are two meta-level points to consider in the execution of the steps. First, the algorithm counts on number and gender agreement. Second, in his paper, Hobbs proposes applying "simple selectional constraints" to the antecedents that the algorithm proposes, and illustrates their use in the sentence he uses to explain the operation of the algorithm:

> "The castle in Camelot remained the residence of the king until 536 when he moved *it* to London."

When trying to resolve the pronoun "it" in this sentence, the algorithm would first propose "536" as the antecedent. But dates cannot move, so on selectional grounds it is ruled out. The algorithm continues and next proposes "the castle" as the antecedent. But castles cannot move any more than dates can, so selectional restrictions rule that choice out as well. Finally, "the residence" is proposed, and does not fail the selectional constraints (although one might find that these "simple" constraints require a fair amount of encoded world knowledge).

In the paper, Hobbs reported the results of testing the algorithm on the pronouns "he", "she", "it"[3], and "they", 300 instances in total (100 consecutive pronouns each from three different genres). He found that the algorithm alone worked in 88.3% of the cases, and that the algorithm plus selectional restrictions resolved 91.7% of the cases correctly. But of the 300 examples, only 132 actually had more than one "plausible" antecedent nearby. When he tested the algorithm on just those 132 cases, 96 were resolved by the "naive" algorithm alone, a success rate of 72.7%. When selectional restrictions were added the algorithm correctly resolved 12 more, to give 81.8%.

The Hobbs algorithm was implemented to execute on the CTB. The S label in the CTB is IP, so the two "markable" nodes from the point of view of the algorithm are IP and NP. There were two types of NPs that were excluded, however, NP-TMP and NP-ADV.

No selectional constraints were applied in this experiment. In addition, no gender or number agreement features were used.

While the written versions of Chinese third-person pronouns do have number and gender, and demonstratives have number, there is no morphology on verbs to match. Nor, without extra-syntactic lexical features, are there gender markings on nouns or proper names (the titles in this corpus as a rule do not include gender-specific honorifics).

There is a plural "suffix" (们) on some nouns denoting human groups, and one can sometimes glean number information from determiner phrases modifying head nouns, but no extra coding was done here to do so.

Zero pronouns, of course, provide no clues about gender or number, nor do 其 (his, hers, its, theirs) or 之 (he/she/it/they).

Structurally, there are many sentences in the CTB that consist of just a sequence of parallel independent clauses, separated by commas or semicolons. These multi-clause sentences were treated as single sentences from the point of view of the algorithm.

The implementation of the algorithm is one that has a core of code that can run on either the Penn Treebank (Marcus et al., 1993) or on the Chinese Treebank. The only differences between the two executables are in the tables for the part-of-speech tags and the syntactic phrase labels (e.g., PN *vs.* PRN for pronouns and IP *vs.* S for clauses), and in separate NP head-finding routines (not used in the current study).

Despite the SVO similarity between Chinese and English, we were interested to see if there

[3] excluding "it" in time or weather constructions, as well as pleonastic and discourse deictic "it"

might be differences in the success of the algorithm due to structural differences between the languages that might require adapting its steps to Chinese. The most obvious place to look was in the placement of modifiers relative to the head noun in an NP. Although unplanned, it turned out that the policy of annotating complex NPs at the parent level rather than at the head noun level actually made this a moot point because of the top-down nature of the tree traversal. That is, because the algorithm proposes an NP that contains both the modifier and the head, differences between English and Chinese in head-modifier word order does not matter.

Another place in which the head-modifier ordering might come into play is in Step 6 of the algorithm. This is still under investigation, since the step did not "fire" in the set of files used here, and only proposed an antecedent once when the algorithm was run on the whole CTB.

4 The Data

As mentioned, in addition to the third person pronouns that Hobbs tested, the algorithm here was run on reflexives, possessives, demonstrative pronouns, and the zero pronoun.

A sample of 95 files, containing a total of 850 sentences (including headlines, but excluding bylines, and excluding the (End) "sentence" at the end of most articles) was used for this experiment.

In all there were 479 anaphors in the 95 files. The distribution of the anaphors for these files is shown in Table 1.

Of the anaphors in the gold standard, 331 (69.1%) were co-indexed with antecedents, while 117 (24.4%) did not corefer with entities denoted by NPs and were categorized. The remaining 6.5%, 31 anaphors (two overt and 29 ***pro***), were marked ambiguous.

Of the anaphors that were co-indexed, just over half (53.2%, 176 pronouns) were overt. In contrast, only 24.8% of the categorized pronouns were overt, and these were usually demonstratives labeled **#DD**.

5 Results

The performance of the Hobbs algorithm on these data varied considerably depending on the syntactic position of the anaphor, and less so on whether the anaphor was overt or not.

Performance was analyzed separately for pronouns that appeared as matrix subjects (M), pronouns that appeared as subjects of parallel, independent clauses in multi-clause sentences (M2), and pronouns that were found in any kind of subordinate construction (S).

The counts for all anaphors are listed in Table 2 and the counts for third-person pronouns only in Table 3. The scores for third-person pronouns only are given in Table 4 and for all coindexed anaphors in Table 5[4].

As shown in Table 4, the accuracy for matrix-level, third-person pronouns was 77.6%, while for all pronouns at the matrix level (Table 5) the algorithm achieved a respectable 76.3% accuracy, considering the fact that not only zero pronouns, but reflexives, possessives, and demonstratives are included.

This contrasts with 43.2% correct for third-person pronouns in subordinate constructions and 43.3% correct for all subordinate-level pronouns.

The accuracy for matrix level (M) and independent clause level (M2) combined was 75.7% for third-person pronouns, and 71.6% for all pronouns.

When results are not broken down by the syntactic position of the anaphor, the performance is less impressive, with just 63.2% accuracy for just third-person pronouns and only 53.2% correct for all anaphors at all syntactic levels.

The zero anaphors alone showed the same pattern, with 73.3% correct at the matrix level and 66.7% correct for matrix and matrix2 levels combined (Table 6), but just 42.5% accuracy at the subordinate level.

6 Discussion

The difference in performance of the algorithm by syntactic level clearly suggests that a one-method-fits-all approach (at least in the case of a rule-based method) to anaphora resolution will not succeed, and that further analysis of anaphors at the non-matrix level is in order.

[4]Of the 31 anaphors marked **AMB**, in only eight cases (25.8%) did the algorithm pick an antecedent that was one of the choices given by the annotators. All eight were ***pro***.

Table 1: Distribution of all anaphors

	Indexed		AMB		Cat, no AMB		Total	
	count	%	count	%	count	%	counts	%
overt	176	53.2%	2	6.5%	29	24.8%	207	43.2%
pro	155	46.8%	29	93.5%	88	75.2%	272	56.8%
	331	69.1%	31	6.5%	117	24.4%	479	

Table 2: Counts by syntactic level for all anaphors

	Correct			Wrong			Cat(incl AMB)			
	M	M2	S	M	M2	S	M	M2	S	**Total**
overt	47	8	45	14	5	57	10	2	19	207
pro	11	17	48	4	10	65	15	21	81	272
	58	25	93	18	15	122	25	23	100	479

These data are consistent with the observations made by Miltsakaki in her 2002 paper (Miltsakaki, 2002). Taking a main clause and all its dependent clauses as a unit, she found that there were different mechanisms needed to account for (1) topic continuity from unit to unit (inter-sentential), and (2) focusing preferences within a unit (intra-sentential). Topic continuity was best modeled structurally but the semantics and pragmatics of verbs and connectives were prominent within a unit.

Since inter-sentential anaphoric links relate to topic continuity, structural rules work best for resolution at the matrix level, while anaphors in subordinate clauses are subject to the semantic/pragmatic constraints of the predicates and connectives.

In our results the anaphors that are subjects of matrix clauses tend to resolve inter-sententially (that is, Step 4 of the algorithm is the resolving condition), while the anaphors in subordinate constructions are more likely to have intra-sentential antecedents. That the strictly structural version of the Hobbs algorithm used here performed better for matrix-level anaphors and did not do well at all on anaphors in subordinate constructions agrees with Miltsakaki's findings.

In our data the "unit" is not always a single main clause with its dependent clauses, however. In the M2 case, the unit is a sentence containing parallel main clauses, each of which may have its own dependent clauses. An examination of

Table 3: Counts by syntactic level for third-person pronouns

	Correct			Wrong			
	M	M2	S	M	M2	S	**Tot.**
he	38	4	13	8	1	12	76
he-they	1	1	2	3	2	3	12
she	1	-	-	-	-	-	1
she-they	-	-	-	-	-	-	0
it	4	3	4	2	1	8	22
it-they	1	-	-	-	-	2	3
	45	8	19	13	4	25	114

the errors made for these M2 cases might show that an improvement of performance for these anaphors could be obtained by treating the independent clauses as separate sentences.

7 Future Work

As mentioned in Section 3 above, in addition to some limited information that can be obtained from just the parses to check for number agreement, a logical next step is to implement some selectional constraints. For example, the semantic categories in the Rocling dictionary could be used in combination with selectional restrictions on verb arguments. Simple features such as animacy or concreteness could prevent some incorrect choices by the algorithm.

We also plan to investigate the operation of Step 6 with respect to the original intent of the

Table 4: Performance by syntactic level: third-person pronouns

	Correct	Wrong	Total
matrix (M)	45	13	58
	77.6%	22.4%	
matrix2 (M2)	8	4	12
	66.7%	33.3%	
subord. (S)	19	25	44
	43.2%	56.8%	
All 3 levels	72	42	114
	63.2%	36.8%	
M + M2	75.7%	24.3%	

Table 5: Performance by syntactic level: coindexed overt and ***pro***

	Correct	Wrong	Total
matrix (M)	58	18	86
	76.3%	23.7%	
matrix2 (M2)	25	15	40
	62.5%	37.5%	
subord. (S)	93	122	215
	43.3%	56.7%	
All 3 levels	176	155	331
	53.2%	46.8%	
M + M2	71.6%	28.4%	

Table 6: Performance by syntactic level: ***pro*** alone

	Correct	Wrong	Total
matrix (M)	11	4	15
	73.3%	26.7%	
matrix2 (M2)	17	10	27
	63.0%	37.0%	
subord. (S)	48	65	113
	42.5%	57.5%	
All 3 levels	76	79	155
	49.0%	51.0%	
M + M2	66.7%	33.3%	

rule, the bracketing conventions used in the CTB, and the difference in the headedness of NPs between Chinese and English.

As discussed in Section 6, the performance of this rule-based algorithm on subordinate-level anaphors confirmed Miltsakaki's observations about the need for different models for inter- *vs.* intra-sentential anaphora resolution. We therefore plan to investigate alternative strategies for the resolution of subordinate-level anaphors.

8 Appendix

Naive Hobbs Algorithm
This algorithm traverses the surface parse tree, searching for a noun phrase *of the correct gender and number* using the following traversal order:

```
1) begin at NP node immediately dominating
   the pronoun

2) go up the tree to the first NP or S
   node encountered
       call this node X
       call the path to reach X "p"

3) traverse all branches below node X
    to the left of path p,
    in left-to-right,breadth-first manner

   propose as the antecedent any NP node
     that is encountered that has an NP or
     an S node between it and X

4) if node X is the highest S node in
   the sentence
      traverse the parse trees of previous
         sentences in order of recency
         (the most recent first), from
         left-to-right, breadth-first
         and
      propose as antecedent the first NP
         encountered

   else goto step (5)

5) from node X go up the tree to the
   first NP or S node encountered
      call this new node 'X', and
      call the path traversed to reach
         it from the original X 'p'

6) if X is an NP node AND
   if the path p to X did not pass through
      the N-bar node that X immediately
      dominates,
      propose X as the antecedent

7) traverse all branches below node X
   to the *left* of path p,
   left-to-right, breadth-first
```

```
   propose any NP node encountered as
     the antecedent

8) if X is an S node
     traverse all branches of node X
         to the *right* of path p,'
         left-to-right, breadth-first,
       but do not go below any NP or S
         encountered

   propose any NP node encountered as
     the antecedent

9) goto step 4
```

References

Hsin-Hsi Chen. 1992. The transfer of anaphors in translation. *Literary and Linguistic Computing*, 7(4):231–238.

Jerry Hobbs. 1978. Resolving pronoun references. *Lingua*, 44:311–338.

C.-T. James Huang. 1984. On the distribution and reference of empty pronouns. *Linguistic Inquiry*, 5(4):531–574.

Yan Huang. 1994. *The Syntax and Pragmatics of Anaphora. A study with special reference to Chinese*. Cambridge University Press, Cambridge.

Mitchell P. Marcus, Beatrice Santorini, and Mary Ann Marcinkiewicz. 1993. Building a large annotated corpus of English: The Penn Treebank. *Computational Linguistics*, 19(2):313–330.

Eleni Miltsakaki. 2002. Toward an aposynthesis of topic continuity and intrasentential anaphora. *Computational Linguistics*, 28(3):319–355.

Ruslan Mitkov, editor. 1999. *Machine Translation: Special Issue on Anaphora Resolution in Machine Translation*, volume 14. numbers 3-4.

Ruslan Mitkov. 2002. *Anaphora Resolution*. Longman, London.

Nianwen Xue, Fei Xia, Fu-Dong Chiou, and Martha Palmer. 2004. The Penn Chinese Treebank: Phrase structure annotation of a large corpus. *Natural Language Engineering*, 10(4):1–30. **http://www.cis.upenn.edu/˜ chinese/**.

Chin Lung Yang, Peter C. Gordon, and Randall Hendrick. 1999. Comprehension of referring expressions in Chinese. *Language and Cognitive Processes*, 14(5/6):715–742.

Ching-Long Yeh and Yi-Chun Chen. 2001. An empirical study of zero anaphora resolution in Chinese based on centering model. In *Proceedings of ROCLING*.

Ching-Long Yeh and Yi-Chun Chen. 2005. Zero anaphora resolution in Chinese with shallow parsing. *Journal of Chinese Language and Computing*, to appear.

The Second International Chinese Word Segmentation Bakeoff

Thomas Emerson
Basis Technology Corp.
150 CambridgePark Drive
Cambridge, MA 02140
tree@basistech.com

Abstract

The second international Chinese word segmentation bakeoff was held in the summer of 2005 to evaluate the current state of the art in word segmentation. Twenty three groups submitted 130 result sets over two tracks and four different corpora. We found that the technology has improved over the intervening two years, though the out-of-vocabulary problem is still or paramount importance.

1 Introduction

Chinese is written without inter-word spaces, so finding word-boundaries is an essential first step in many natural language processing applications including mono- and cross-lingual information retrieval and text-to-speech systems. This word segmentation problem has been active area of research in computational linguistics for almost two decades and is a topic of active research around the world. As the very notion of "word-hood" in Chinese is hotly debated, so the determination of the correct division of a Chinese sentence into "words" can be very complex.

In 2003 SIGHAN, the Special Interest Group for Chinese Language Processing of the Association for Computational Linguistics (ACL) conducted the first International Chinese Word Segmentation Bakeoff (Sproat and Emerson, 2003). That competition was the first conducted outside of China and has become the benchmark with which researchers evaluate their segmentation systems. During the winter of 2004 it was decided to hold a second evaluation to determine how the latest research has affected segmentation technology.

2 Details of the Contest

2.1 The Corpora

Four corpora were used in the evaluation, two each using Simplified and Traditional Chinese characters.[1] The Simplified Chinese corpora were provided by Beijing University and Microsoft Research Beijing. The Traditional Chinese corpora were provided by Academia Sinica in Taiwan and the City University of Hong Kong. Each provider supplied separate training and truth data sets. Details on each corpus are provided in Table 1.

With one exception, all of the corpora were provided in a single character encoding. We decided to provide all of the data in both Unicode (UTF-8 encoding) and the standard encoding used in each locale. This would allow systems that use one or the other encoding to chose appropriately while ensuring consistent transcoding across all sites. This conversion was problematic in two cases:

1. The Academia Sinica corpus, provided in Unicode (UTF-16), contained characters found in Big Five Plus that are not found in Microsoft's CP950 or standard Big Five. It also contained compatibility characters that led to transcoding errors when converting from Unicode to Big Five Plus. A detailed description of these issues can be found on the Bakeoff 2005

[1] A fifth (Simplified Chinese) corpus was provided by the University of Pennsylvania, but for numerous technical reasons it was not used in the evaluation. However, it has been made available (both training and truth data) on the SIGHAN website along with the other corpora.

Corpus	Abbrev.	Encodings	Training Size (Words/Types)	Test Size (Words/Types)
Academia Sinica (Taipei)	AS	Big Five Plus, Unicode	5.45M / 141K	122K / 19K
Beijing University	PK	CP936, Unicode	1.1M / 55K	104K / 13K
City University of Hong Kong	CityU	Big Five/HKSCS, Unicode	1.46M / 69K	41K / 9K
Microsoft Research (Beijing)	MSR	CP936, Unicode	2.37M / 88K	107K / 13K

Table 1. Corpus Information

pages on the SIGHAN website. The data also included 11 instances of an invalid character that could not be converted to Big Five Plus.

2. The City University of Hong Kong data was initially supplied in Big Five/ HKSCS. We initially converted this to Unicode but found that there were characters appearing in Unicode Ideograph Extension B, which many systems are unable to handle. City University was gracious enough to provide Unicode versions for their files with all characters in the Unicode BMP. Specific details can be found on the Bakeoff 2005 pages of the SIGHAN website.

The truth data was provided in segmented and unsegmented form by all of the providers except Academia Sinica, who only provided the segmented truth files. These were converted to unsegmented form using a simple Perl script. Unfortunately this script also removed spaces separating non-Chinese (i.e., English) tokens. We had no expectation of correct segmentation on non-Chinese text, so the spaces were manually removed between non-Chinese text in the truth data prior to scoring.

The Academia Sinica data separated tokens in both the training and truth data using a full-width space instead of one or more half-width (i.e., ASCII) spaces. The scoring script was modified to ignore the type of space used so that teams would not be penalized during scoring for using a different separator.

The segmentation standard used by each provider were made available to the participants, though late in the training period. These standards are either extremely terse (MSR), verbose but in Chinese only (PKU, AS), or are verbose and moderately bilingual. The PKU corpus uses a standard derived from GB 13715, the Chinese government standard for text segmentation in computer applications. Similarly AS uses a Taiwanese national standard for segmentation in computer applications. The CityU data was segmented using the LIVAC corpus standard, and the MSR data to Microsoft's internal standard. The standards are available on the bakeoff web site.

The PKU data was edited by the organizers to remove a numeric identifier from the start of each line. Unless otherwise noted in this paper no changes beyond transcoding were made to the data furnished by contributors.

2.2 Rules and Procedures

The bakeoff was run almost identically to the first described in Sproat and Emerson (2003): the detailed instructions provided to the participants are available on the bakeoff website at `http://www.sighan.org/bakeoff2005/` . Groups (or "sites" as they were also called) interested in participating in the competition registered on the SIGHAN website. Only the primary researcher for each group was asked to register. Registration was opened on June 1,

ID	Site	Contact	Country	AS	PKU	CityU	MSR
2	ICL, Beijing University	Wuguang SHI	ZH				◇
3	Xiamen	Xiaodong SHI	ZH	◆◇	◆◇	◆◇	◆◇
4	ITNLP Lab, Harbin Institute of Technology	Wei JIANG	ZH	◆◇	◆◇	◆◇	◆◇
5	France Telecom R&D Beijing	Heng LI	ZH	◆◇	◆◇	◆◇	◆◇
6	Information Retrieval Lab, Harbin Institute of Technology	Huipeng ZHANG	ZH		◆◇		
7	Dept. of Linguistics, The University of Hong Kong	Guohong FU	HK	◆◇	◆◇	◆◇	◆◇
8	Computer Science Dept., Xiamen University	Hua-lin Zeng	ZH		◆◇		◆◇
9	Dept. of Linguistics, The Ohio State University	Xiaofei LU	US		◆		
12	Dept. of Computer Science, The University of Sheffield	Yaoyong LI	GB	◆◇	◆◇	◆◇	◆◇
13	Nanjing University	Jiajun CHEN	ZH		◆◇		◆◇
14	Stanford NL Group	Huihsin TSENG	US	◆	◆	◆	◆
15	Nara Institute of Science and Technology	Masayuki ASAHARA	JP	◆	◆	◆	◆
16	Academia Sinica	Yu-Fang TSAI	TW		◇	◇	
19	National University of Singapore	Hwee Tou NG	SG	◇	◇	◇	◇
21	Kookmin University	Seung-Shik KANG	KO		◆	◆	◆
23	US Dept. of Defense	Thomas Keenan	US		◇		◇
24	Dept. of Information Management, Tung Nan Institute of Technology	Jia-Lin TSAI	TW				◆
26	ICL, Peking University	Huiming DUAN	ZH				◆◇
27	Yahoo! Inc.	Aitao CHEN	US	◆◇	◆◇	◆◇	◆◇
29	The Chinese University of Hong Kong	Tak Pang LAU	HK		◆	◆	◆
31	City University of Hong Kong	Ka Po CHOW	HK	◇	◇		
33	City University of Hong Kong	Chun Yu KIT	HK	◆	◆		◆
34	Institute of Computing Technology, Chinese Academy of Sciences	ShuangLong LI	ZH		◆◇		◆◇

Table 2. Participating Groups (◆ = closed test, ◇ = open test)

2005 and allowed to continue through the time the training data was made available on July 11. When a site registered they selected which corpus or corpora there were interested in using, and whether they would take part in the open or closed tracks (described below.) On July 11 the training data was made available on the Bakeoff website for downloading: the same data was used regardless of the tracks the sites registered for. The web site did not allow a participant to

Corpus	Word Count	R	P	F	OOV	Roov	Riv
AS	122,610	0.909	0.857	0.882	0.043	0.004	0.950
CityU	40936	0.882	0.790	0.833	0.074	0.000	0.952
MSR	106,873	0.955	0.912	0.933	0.026	0.000	0.981
PKU	104,372	0.904	0.836	0.869	0.058	0.059	0.956

Table 3: Baseline scores generated via maximal matching using only words from the training data

Corpus	Word Count	R	P	F	OOV	Roov	Riv
AS	122,610	0.979	0.985	0.982	0.043	0.996	0.978
CityU	40,936	0.988	0.991	0.989	0.074	0.997	0.988
MSR	106,873	0.991	0.992	0.991	0.026	0.998	0.990
PKU	104,372	0.985	0.988	0.987	0.058	0.994	0.985

Table 4: Topline scores generated via maximal matching using only words from the testing data

add a corpus to the set they initially selected, though at least one asked us via email to add one and this was done manually. Groups were given until July 27 to train their systems, when the testing data was released on the web site. They then had two days to process the test corpora and return them to the organizer via email on Jul 29 for scoring. Each participant's results were posted to their section of the web site on August 6, and the summary results for all participants were made available to all groups on August 12.

Two tracks were available for each corpus, open and closed:

- In the open tests participants could use any external data in addition to the training corpus to train their system. This included, but was not limited to, external lexica, character set knowledge, part-of-speech information, etc. Sites participating in an open test were required to describe this external data in their system description.

- In closed tests, participants were only allowed to use information found in the training data. Absolutely no other data or information could be used beyond that in the training document. This included knowledge of character sets, punctuation characters, etc. These seemingly artificial restrictions (when compared to "real world" systems) were formulated to study exactly how far one can get without supplemental information.

Other obvious restrictions applied: groups could not participate using corpora that they or their organization provided or that they had used before or otherwise seen.

Sites were allowed submit multiple runs within a track, allowing them to compare various approaches.

Scoring was done automatically using a combination of Perl and shell scripts. Participants were asked to submit their data using very strict naming conventions to facilitate this: in only a couple of instances were these not followed and human intervention was required. After the scoring was done the script would mail the detailed results to the participant. The scripts used for scoring can be downloaded from the

Participant	Run ID	Word Count	R	C_r	P	C_p	F	OOV	R_{oov}	R_{iv}
15	b	122610	0.952	±0.00122	0.951	±0.00123	0.952	0.043	0.696	0.963
15	a	122610	0.955	±0.00118	0.939	±0.00137	0.947	0.043	0.606	0.971
14		122610	0.95	±0.00124	0.943	±0.00132	0.947	0.043	0.718	0.960
27		122610	0.955	±0.00118	0.934	±0.00142	0.945	0.043	0.468	0.978
12		122610	0.946	±0.00129	0.942	±0.00134	0.944	0.043	0.648	0.959
7		122610	0.947	±0.00128	0.934	±0.00142	0.94	0.043	0.523	0.966
15	c	122610	0.944	±0.00131	0.934	±0.00142	0.939	0.043	0.445	0.967
33		122610	0.944	±0.00131	0.902	±0.00170	0.923	0.043	0.234	0.976
5		122610	0.948	±0.00127	0.900	±0.00171	0.923	0.043	0.158	0.983
4		122610	0.943	±0.00132	0.895	±0.00175	0.918	0.043	0.137	0.979
3		122610	0.877	±0.00188	0.796	±0.00230	*0.835*	0.043	0.128	0.911

Table 5. Academia Sinica — Closed (italics indicate performance below baseline)

Participant	Run ID	Word Count	R	C_r	P	C_p	F	OOV	R_{oov}	R_{iv}
19		122610	0.962	±0.00109	0.95	±0.00124	0.956	0.043	0.684	0.975
27		122610	0.958	±0.00115	0.938	±0.00138	0.948	0.043	0.506	0.978
12		122610	0.949	±0.00126	0.947	±0.00128	0.948	0.043	0.686	0.961
7		122610	0.955	±0.00118	0.938	±0.00138	0.946	0.043	0.579	0.972
31		122610	0.943	±0.00132	0.931	±0.00145	0.937	0.043	0.531	0.962
4		122610	0.952	±0.00122	0.92	±0.00155	0.936	0.043	0.354	0.979
5		122610	0.952	±0.00122	0.919	±0.00156	0.935	0.043	0.311	0.981
3		122610	0.004	±0.00036	0.004	±0.00036	*0.004*	0.043	0.085	0

Table 6. Academia Sinica — Open (italics indicate performance below baseline)

Bakeoff 2005 web site. It was provided to the participants to aid in the their data analysis. As noted above, some of the training/truth data used a full-width space to separate tokens: the scoring script was modified to ignore the differences between full-width and half-width spaces. This is the *only* case where the half-width/full-width distinction was ignored: a system that converted tokens from full-width to half-width was penalized by the script.

2.3 Participating Sites

Thirty-six sites representing 10 countries initially signed up for the bakeoff. The People's Republic of China had the greatest number with 17, followed by the United States (6), Hong Kong (5), Taiwan (3), six others with one each. Of these, 23 submitted results for scoring and subsequently submitted a paper for these proceedings. A summary of participating groups and the tracks for which they submitted results can be found in Table 2 on the preceding page. All together 130 runs were submitted for scoring.

3 Results

In order to provide hypothetical best and worst case results (i.e., we expect systems to do no worse than the base-line and to generally underperform the top-line), we used a simple left-to-right maximal matching algorithm implemented in Perl to generate "top-line" and "base-line"

Participant	Run ID	Word Count	R	Cr	P	Cp	F	OOV	Roov	Riv
14		40936	0.941	±0.00233	0.946	±0.00223	0.943	0.074	0.698	0.961
15	a	40936	0.942	±0.00231	0.941	±0.00233	0.942	0.074	0.629	0.967
15	b	40936	0.937	±0.00240	0.946	±0.00223	0.941	0.074	0.736	0.953
27		40936	0.949	±0.00217	0.931	±0.00251	0.94	0.074	0.561	0.98
7		40936	0.944	±0.00227	0.933	±0.00247	0.939	0.074	0.626	0.969
12		40936	0.931	±0.00251	0.941	±0.00233	0.936	0.074	0.657	0.953
29	d	40936	0.937	±0.00240	0.922	±0.00265	0.929	0.074	0.698	0.956
15	c	40936	0.915	±0.00276	0.94	±0.00235	0.928	0.074	0.598	0.94
29	a	40936	0.938	±0.00238	0.915	±0.00276	0.927	0.074	0.658	0.961
29	b	40936	0.936	±0.00242	0.913	±0.00279	0.925	0.074	0.656	0.959
21		40936	0.917	±0.00273	0.925	±0.00260	0.921	0.074	0.539	0.948
29	c	40936	0.925	±0.00260	0.896	±0.00302	0.91	0.074	0.639	0.948
4		40936	0.934	±0.00245	0.865	±0.00338	0.898	0.074	0.248	0.989
5		40936	0.932	±0.00249	0.862	±0.00341	0.895	0.074	0.215	0.989
3		40936	0.814	±0.00385	0.711	±0.00448	*0.759*	0.074	0.227	0.86

Table 7: City University of Hong Kong — Closed (italics indicate performance below baseline)

Participant	Run ID	Word Count	R	Cr	P	Cp	F	OOV	Roov	Riv
19		40936	0.967	±0.00177	0.956	±0.00203	0.962	0.074	0.806	0.98
16		40936	0.958	±0.00198	0.95	±0.00215	0.954	0.074	0.775	0.973
27		40936	0.952	±0.00211	0.937	±0.00240	0.945	0.074	0.608	0.98
7		40936	0.944	±0.00227	0.938	±0.00238	0.941	0.074	0.667	0.966
12		40936	0.933	±0.00247	0.94	±0.00235	0.936	0.074	0.653	0.955
4		40936	0.946	±0.00223	0.898	±0.00299	0.922	0.074	0.417	0.989
5		40936	0.94	±0.00235	0.901	±0.00295	0.92	0.074	0.41	0.982
3		40936	0.014	±0.00116	0.013	±0.00112	*0.013*	0.074	0.029	0.012

Table 8: City University of Hong Kong — Open (italics indicate performance below baseline)

numbers. This was done by generating word lists based only on the vocabulary in each truth (top-line) and training (bottom-line) corpus and segmenting the respective test corpora. These results are presented in Tables 3 and 4.

All of the results comprise the following data: test *recall* (R), test *precision* (P), balanced *F score* (where $F = 2PR/(P + R)$), the *out-of-vocabulary* (OOV) rate on the test corpus, the *recall on OOV* words (R_{oov}), and the *recall on in-vocabulary words* (R_{iv}). We use the usual definition of out-of-vocabulary words as the set of words occurring in the test corpus that are not in the training corpus.

As in the previous evaluation, to test the confidence level that two trials are significantly different from each other we used the Central Limit Theorem for Bernoulli trials (Grinstead and Snell, 1997), assuming that the recall rates from the various trials represents the probability that a word will be successfully identified, and that a binomial distribution is appropriate for the experiment. We calculated these values at the 95% confidence interval with the formula $\pm 2 \sqrt{(p}$

Participant	Run ID	Word Count	R	Cr	P	Cp	F	OOV	Roov	Riv
14		106873	0.962	±0.00117	0.966	±0.00111	0.964	0.026	0.717	0.968
7		106873	0.962	±0.00117	0.962	±0.00117	0.962	0.026	0.592	0.972
27	a	106873	0.969	±0.00106	0.952	±0.00131	0.960	0.026	0.379	0.985
27	b	106873	0.968	±0.00108	0.953	±0.00129	0.960	0.026	0.381	0.984
4		106873	0.973	±0.00099	0.945	±0.00139	0.959	0.026	0.323	0.991
15	b	106873	0.952	±0.00131	0.964	±0.00114	0.958	0.026	0.718	0.958
5		106873	0.974	±0.00097	0.940	±0.00145	0.957	0.026	0.21	0.995
13		106873	0.959	±0.00121	0.956	±0.00125	0.957	0.026	0.496	0.972
12		106873	0.952	±0.00131	0.960	±0.00120	0.956	0.026	0.673	0.96
24	6	106873	0.958	±0.00123	0.952	±0.00131	0.955	0.026	0.503	0.97
24	7	106873	0.958	±0.00123	0.952	±0.00131	0.955	0.026	0.504	0.97
24	4	106873	0.958	±0.00123	0.949	±0.00135	0.954	0.026	0.465	0.972
24	5	106873	0.958	±0.00123	0.951	±0.00132	0.954	0.026	0.493	0.971
24	3	106873	0.968	±0.00108	0.938	±0.00148	0.953	0.026	0.205	0.989
33		106873	0.965	±0.00112	0.935	±0.00151	0.950	0.026	0.189	0.986
15	a	106873	0.955	±0.00127	0.942	±0.00143	0.949	0.026	0.378	0.971
21		106873	0.945	±0.00139	0.949	±0.00135	0.947	0.026	0.576	0.955
24	0	106873	0.956	±0.00125	0.938	±0.00148	0.947	0.026	0.327	0.973
34		106873	0.948	±0.00136	0.942	±0.00143	0.945	0.026	0.664	0.955
24	2	106873	0.964	±0.00114	0.924	±0.00162	0.944	0.026	0.025	0.989
15	c	106873	0.964	±0.00114	0.923	±0.00163	0.943	0.026	0.025	0.99
24	1	106873	0.963	±0.00115	0.924	±0.00162	0.943	0.026	0.025	0.989
29	a	106873	0.946	±0.00138	0.933	±0.00153	0.939	0.026	0.587	0.956
29	b	106873	0.941	±0.00144	0.932	±0.00154	0.937	0.026	0.624	0.95
8	b	106873	0.957	±0.00124	0.917	±0.00169	0.936	0.026	0.025	0.982
8	c	106873	0.955	±0.00127	0.915	±0.00171	0.935	0.026	0.025	0.98
26		106873	0.937	±0.00149	0.928	±0.00158	*0.932*	0.026	0.457	0.95
3		106873	0.908	±0.00177	0.927	±0.00159	*0.917*	0.026	0.247	0.926
8	a	106873	0.898	±0.00185	0.896	±0.00187	*0.897*	0.026	0.327	0.914

Table 9: Microsoft Research — Closed (italics indicate performance below baseline)

$(1 - p)/n)$ where n is the number of words. This value appears in subsequent tables under the column c_r. We also calculate the confidence that the a character string segmented as a word is actually a word by treating p as the precision rates of each system. This is referred to as c_p in the result tables. Two systems are then considered to be statistically different (at a 95% confidence level) if one of their c_r or c_p are different. Tables 5–12 contain the results for each corpus and track (groups are referenced by their ID as found in Table 2) ordered by F score.

Participant	Run ID	Word Count	R	Cr	P	Cp	F	OOV	Roov	Riv
4		106873	0.98	±0.00086	0.965	±0.00112	0.972	0.026	0.59	0.99
19		106873	0.969	±0.00106	0.968	±0.00108	0.968	0.026	0.736	0.975
7		106873	0.969	±0.00106	0.966	±0.00111	0.967	0.026	0.612	0.979
27	b	106873	0.971	±0.00103	0.961	±0.00118	0.966	0.026	0.512	0.983
5		106873	0.975	±0.00096	0.957	±0.00124	0.966	0.026	0.453	0.989
13		106873	0.959	±0.00121	0.971	±0.00103	0.965	0.026	0.785	0.964
27	a	106873	0.97	±0.00104	0.957	±0.00124	0.963	0.026	0.466	0.984
12		106873	0.95	±0.00133	0.958	±0.00123	0.954	0.026	0.648	0.958
26		106873	0.925	±0.00161	0.936	±0.00150	*0.930*	0.026	0.617	0.933
8	a	106873	0.94	±0.00145	0.917	±0.00169	*0.928*	0.026	0.239	0.959
34		106873	0.916	±0.00170	0.933	±0.00153	*0.924*	0.026	0.705	0.922
8	c	106873	0.928	±0.00158	0.913	±0.00172	*0.920*	0.026	0.355	0.944
8	b	106873	0.923	±0.00163	0.914	±0.00172	*0.918*	0.026	0.354	0.938
2		106873	0.913	±0.00172	0.915	±0.00171	*0.914*	0.026	0.725	0.918
3		106873	0.921	±0.00165	0.897	±0.00186	*0.909*	0.026	0.562	0.93
8	d	106873	0.92	±0.00166	0.889	±0.00192	*0.904*	0.026	0.332	0.936
8	e	106873	0.9	±0.00184	0.861	±0.00212	*0.880*	0.026	0.309	0.916
27	c	106873	0.865	±0.00209	0.844	±0.00222	*0.855*	0.026	0.391	0.878
23		106873	0.788	±0.00250	0.818	±0.00236	*0.803*	0.026	0.37	0.8

Table 10: Microsoft Research — Open (italics indicate performance below baseline)

4 Discussion

Across all of the corpora the best performing system, in terms of F score, achieved a 0.972, with an average of 0.918 and median of 0.941. As one would expect the best F score on the open tests was higher than the best on the closed tests, 0.972 vs. 0.964, both on the MSR corpus. This result follows from the fact that systems taking part on the open test can utilize more information than those on the closed. Also interesting to compare are the OOV recall rates between the Open and Closed tracks. The best OOV recall in the open evaluation was 0.872 compared to just 0.813 on the closed track. These data indicate that OOV handling is still the Achilles heel of segmentation systems, even when the OOV rates are relatively small. These OOV recall scores are better than those observed in the first bakeoff in 2003, with similar OOV values, which suggests that advances in unknown word recognition have occurred. Nevertheless OOV is still the most significant problem in segmentation systems.

The best score on any track in the 2003 bakeoff was F=0.961, while the best for this evaluation was F=0.972, followed by 17 other scores above 0.961. This shows a general trend to a decrease in error rates, from 3.9% to 2.8%! These scores are still far below the theoretical 0.99 level reflected in the topline and the higher numbers often reflected in the literature. It is plain that one can construct a test set that any given system will achieve very high measures of precision and recall on, but these numbers must viewed with caution as they may not scale to other applications or other problem sets.

Three participants that used the scoring script in their system evaluation observed different behavior from that of the organizers in the

Participant	Run ID	Word Count	R	Cr	P	Cp	F	OOV	Roov	Riv
27		104372	0.953	±0.00131	0.946	±0.00140	0.95	0.058	0.636	0.972
14		104372	0.946	±0.00140	0.954	±0.00130	0.95	0.058	0.787	0.956
6	a	104372	0.952	±0.00132	0.945	±0.00141	0.949	0.058	0.673	0.969
6	b	104372	0.952	±0.00132	0.943	±0.00144	0.947	0.058	0.673	0.969
13		104372	0.941	±0.00146	0.95	±0.00135	0.946	0.058	0.813	0.949
7		104372	0.943	±0.00144	0.944	±0.00142	0.944	0.058	0.656	0.961
15	b	104372	0.93	±0.00158	0.951	±0.00134	0.941	0.058	0.76	0.941
4		104372	0.954	±0.00130	0.927	±0.00161	0.941	0.058	0.518	0.981
34		104372	0.938	±0.00149	0.942	±0.00145	0.94	0.058	0.767	0.948
15	a	104372	0.93	±0.00158	0.938	±0.00149	0.934	0.058	0.521	0.955
5		104372	0.95	±0.00135	0.919	±0.00169	0.934	0.058	0.449	0.98
9		104372	0.922	±0.00166	0.934	±0.00154	0.928	0.058	0.728	0.934
12		104372	0.919	±0.00169	0.935	±0.00153	0.927	0.058	0.593	0.939
15	c	104372	0.904	±0.00182	0.93	±0.00158	0.917	0.058	0.325	0.94
29	a	104372	0.926	±0.00162	0.908	±0.00179	0.917	0.058	0.535	0.95
29	c	104372	0.918	±0.00170	0.915	±0.00173	0.917	0.058	0.621	0.936
33		104372	0.929	±0.00159	0.904	±0.00182	0.916	0.058	0.252	0.971
21		104372	0.9	±0.00186	0.925	±0.00163	0.912	0.058	0.389	0.931
29	b	104372	0.917	±0.00171	0.903	±0.00183	0.91	0.058	0.6	0.937
8	a	104372	0.906	±0.00181	0.886	±0.00197	0.896	0.058	0.29	0.943
8	c	104372	0.907	±0.00180	0.843	±0.00225	0.874	0.058	0.082	0.958
8	b	104372	0.906	±0.00181	0.842	±0.00226	0.873	0.058	0.081	0.956
3		104372	0.843	±0.00225	0.737	±0.00273	*0.786*	0.058	0.153	0.885

Table 11: Peking University — Closed (italics indicate performance below baseline)

generation of the recall numbers, thereby affecting the F score. We were unable to replicate the behavior observed by the participant, nor could we determine a common set of software versions that might lead to the problem. We verified our computed scores on two different operating systems and two different hardware architectures. In each case the difference was in the participants favor (i.e., resulted in an increased F score) though the impact was minimal. If there is an error in the scripts then it affects all data sets identically, so we are confident in the scores as reported here. Nevertheless, we hope that further investigation will uncover the cause of the discrepancy so that it can be rectified in the future.

4.1 Future Directions

This second bakeoff was an unqualified success, both in the number of systems represented and in the demonstrable improvement in segmentation technology since 2003. However, there are still open questions that future evaluations can attempt to answer, including: how well a system trained on one genre performs when faced with text from a different register. This will stress OOV handling in the extreme. Consider a situation where a system trained on PRC newswire

Participant	Run ID	Word Count	R	Cr	P	Cp	F	OOV	Roov	Riv
19		104372	0.968	±0.00109	0.969	±0.00107	0.969	0.058	0.838	0.976
4		104372	0.968	±0.00109	0.966	±0.00112	0.967	0.058	0.826	0.977
13		104372	0.964	±0.00115	0.97	±0.00106	0.967	0.058	0.864	0.97
27	a	104372	0.964	±0.00115	0.966	±0.00112	0.965	0.058	0.841	0.971
6	a	104372	0.961	±0.00120	0.969	±0.00107	0.965	0.058	0.872	0.966
6	b	104372	0.961	±0.00120	0.966	±0.00112	0.963	0.058	0.869	0.966
7		104372	0.959	±0.00123	0.965	±0.00114	0.962	0.058	0.853	0.966
5		104372	0.964	±0.00115	0.96	±0.00121	0.962	0.058	0.788	0.974
3		104372	0.959	±0.00123	0.954	±0.00130	0.957	0.058	0.776	0.97
34		104372	0.944	±0.00142	0.961	±0.00120	0.952	0.058	0.869	0.948
16		104372	0.945	±0.00141	0.956	±0.00127	0.951	0.058	0.79	0.955
31		104372	0.952	±0.00132	0.951	±0.00134	0.951	0.058	0.784	0.962
8	a	104372	0.943	±0.00144	0.944	±0.00142	0.943	0.058	0.737	0.955
12		104372	0.932	±0.00156	0.944	±0.00142	0.938	0.058	0.755	0.943
8	b	104372	0.886	±0.00197	0.919	±0.00169	0.902	0.058	0.561	0.905
27	b	104372	0.877	±0.00203	0.904	±0.00182	0.89	0.058	0.72	0.886
23		104372	0.781	±0.00256	0.846	±0.00223	*0.813*	0.058	0.628	0.791

Table 12: Peking University — Open (italics indicate performance below baseline)

text is given the Chinese translation of the Arabic *al Jazeera* newspaper. A more detailed evaluation of different techniques for dealing with certain constructs is also in order, finding the right balance of learned and heuristic knowledge is paramount. Tied to the accuracy performance of such hybrid systems is the runtime speed: the trade-off between accuracy and throughput is vitally important as more and more data becomes computerized. The overall effects of the various segmentation standards on the comparison of disparate systems has yet to be studied. In particular, a categorization of the differences in standards and the prevalence of the features reflected would be a worth while study. Xia (2000) compares the Penn Chinese Treebank's standard with those used in Taiwan and China, and concludes that, "most disagreements among these three guidelines do not make much difference in bracketing or sentence interpretation." This is probably not so transparent when evaluating segmentation accuracy, however.

No segmentation study has yet to examine the handling of short strings where there is little surrounding context, as in search engine queries. Future evaluations should be designed to focus on these and other specific areas of interest.

Acknowledgments

This bakeoff could not have taken place without the following institutions who provided training and testing data:

- Institute of Linguistics, Academia Sinica, Taipei, Taiwan
- Institute for Computational Linguistics, Beijing University, Beijing, China
- Language Information Sciences Research Centre, City University of Hong Kong, Hong Kong SAR
- Microsoft Research Asia, Beijing, China

I would like to thank Gina Lavow and Chu-Ren Huang for their organization of the fourth SIGHAN workshop of which this bakeoff is part, and John O'Neil for his comments on an earlier draft of this paper. Finally I would also like to thank the participants for their interest and hard work in making this bakeoff a success.

References

Charles M. Grinstead and J. Laurie Snell. 1997. *Introduction to Probability.* American Mathematical Society, Providence, RI, 2nd Edition.

Richard Sproat and Thomas Emerson. 2003. *The First International Chinese Word Segmentation Bakeoff.* In Proceedings of the Second SIGHAN Workshop on Chinese Language Processing, July 11–12, 2003, Sapporo, Japan.

Fei Xia. 2000. *The Segmentation Guidelines for the Penn Chinese Treebank (3.0).*

Combination of Machine Learning Methods for Optimum Chinese Word Segmentation

Masayuki Asahara **Kenta Fukuoka** **Ai Azuma**
Chooi-Ling Goh **Yotaro Watanabe** **Yuji Matsumoto**
Nara Institute of Science and Technology, Japan
E-mail: `cje@is.naist.jp`

Takashi Tsuzuki
Matsushita Electric
Industrial Co., Ltd.

Abstract

This article presents our recent work for participation in the Second International Chinese Word Segmentation Bakeoff. Our system performs two procedures: Out-of-vocabulary extraction and word segmentation. We compose three out-of-vocabulary extraction modules: Character-based tagging with different classifiers – maximum entropy, support vector machines, and conditional random fields. We also compose three word segmentation modules – character-based tagging by maximum entropy classifier, maximum entropy markov model, and conditional random fields. All modules are based on previously proposed methods. We submitted three systems which are different combination of the modules.

1 Overview

We compose three systems: *Models a*, *b* and *c* for the closed test tracks on all four data sets.

For *Models a* and *c*, three out-of-vocabulary (OOV) word extraction modules are composed: 1. Maximum Entropy (MaxEnt) classifier-based tagging; 2. Maximum Entropy Markov Model (MEMM)-based word segmenter with Conditional Random Fields (CRF)-based chunking; 3. MEMM-based word segmenter with Support Vector Machines (SVM)-based chunking. Two lists of OOV word candidates are constructed either by voting or merging the three OOV word extraction modules. Finally, a CRFs-based word segmenter produces the final results using either of the voted list (*Model a*) or the merged list (*Model c*).

Most of the classifiers use surrounding words and characters as the contextual features. Since word and character features may cause data sparse problem, we utilize a hard clustering algorithm (K-means) to define word classes and character classes in order to overcome the data sparse problem. The word classes are used as the hidden states in MEMM and CRF-based word segmenters. The character classes are used as the features in character-based tagging, character-based chunking and word segmentation.

Model b is our previous method proposed in (Goh et al., 2004b): First, a MaxEnt classifier is used to perform character-based tagging to identify OOV words in the test data. In-vocabulary (IV) word list together with the extracted OOV word candidates is used in Maximum Matching algorithm. Overlapping ambiguity is denoted by the different outputs from Forward and Backward Maximum Matching algorithm. Finally, character-based tagging by MaxEnt classifier resolves the ambiguity.

Section 2 describes *Models a* and *c*. Section 3 describes *Model b*. Section 4 discusses the differences among the three models.

2 Models a and c

Models a and *c* use several modules. First, a hard clustering algorithm is used to define word classes and character classes. Second, three OOV extraction modules are trained with the training data. These modules, then, extract the OOV words in the test data. Third, the OOV word candidates produced by the three OOV extraction modules are refined by voting (*Model a*) or merging (*Model c*) them. The final word list is composed by appending the OOV word candidates to the IV word list. Finally, a CRF-based word segmenter analyzes the sentence based on the new word list.

2.1 Clustering for word/character classes

We perform hard clustering for all words and characters in the training data. K-means algorithm is utilized. We use R 2.2.1 (`http://www.r-project.org/`) to perform k-means clustering.

Since the word types are too large, we cannot run k-means clustering on the whole data. Therefore, we divide the word types into 4 groups randomly. K-means clustering is performed for each group. Words in each group are divided into 5 disjoint classes, producing 20 classes in total. Preceding and succeeding words in the top 2000 rank are used as the features for the clustering. We define the set of the OOV words as the 21st class. We also define two other classes for the begin-of-sentence (BOS) and end-of-sentence (EOS). So, we define 23 classes in total.

20 classes are defined for characters. K-means clustering is performed for all characters in the training data. Preceding and succeeding characters and BIES position tags are used as features for the clustering: "B" stands for 'the first character of a word'; "I" stands for 'an intermediate character of a word'; "E" stands for 'the last character of a word'; "S" stands for 'the single character word'. Characters only in the test data are not assigned with any character class.

2.2 Three OOV extraction modules

In *Models a* and *c*, we use three OOV extraction modules.

First and second OOV extraction modules use the output of a Maximam Entropy Markov Model (MEMM)-based word segmenter (McCallum et al., 2000) (Uchimoto et al., 2001). Word list is composed by the words appeared in 80% of the training data. The words occured only in the remaining 20% of the training data are regarded as OOV words. All word candidates in a sentence are extracted to form a trellis. Each word is assigned with a word class. The word classes are used as the hidden states in the trellis. In encoding, MaxEnt estimates state transition probabilities based on the preceding word class (state) and observed features such as the first character, last character, first character class, last character class of the current word. In decoding, a simple Viterbi algorithm is used.

The output of the MEMM-based word segmenter is splitted character by character. Next, character-based chunking is performed to extract OOV words. We use two chunkers: based on SVM (Kudo and Matsumoto, 2001) and CRF (Lafferty et al., 2001). The chunker annotates BIO position tags: "B" stands for 'the first character of an OOV word'; "I" stands for 'other characters in an OOV word'; "O" stands for 'a character outside an OOV word'.

The features used in the two chunkers are the characters, the character classes and the information of other characters in five-character window size. The word sequence output by the MEMM-based word segmenter is converted into character sequence with BIES position tags and the word classes. The position tags with the word classes are also introduced as the features.

The third one is a variation of the OOV module in section 3 which is character-based tagging by MaxEnt classifier. The difference is that we newly introduce character classes in section 2.1 as the features.

In summary, we introduce three OOV word extraction modules: "MEMM+SVM", "MEMM+CRF" and "MaxEnt classifier".

2.3 Voting/Merging the OOV words

The word list for the final word segmenter are composed by voting or merging. Voting means the OOV words which are extracted by two or more OOV word extraction modules. Merging means the OOV words which are extracted by any of the OOV word extraction modules. The model with the former (voting) OOV word list is used in *Model a*, and the model with the latter (merging) OOV word list is used in *Model c*.

2.4 CRF-based word segmenter

Final word segmentation is carried out by a CRF-based word segmenter (Kudo and Matsumoto, 2004) (Peng and McCallum, 2004). The word trellis is composed by the similar method with MEMM-based word segmenter. Though state transition probabilities are estimated in the case of MaxEnt framework, the probabilities are normalized in the whole sentence in CRF-based method. CRF-based word segmenter is robust to length-bias problem (Kudo and Matsumoto, 2004) by the global normalization. We will discuss the length-bias problem in section 4.

2.5 Note on MSR data

Unfortunately, we could not complete *Models a* and *c* for the MSR data due to time constraints. Therefore, we submitted the following 2 fragmented models: *Model a* for MSR data is MEMM-based word segmenter with OOV word list by voting; *Model c* for MSR data is CRF-based word segmenter with no OOV word candidate.

3 Model b

Model b uses a different approach. First, we extract the OOV words using a MaxEnt classifier with only the character as the features. We did not use the character classes as the features. Each character is assigned with BIES position tags. Word segmentation by character-based tagging is firstly introduced by (Xue and Converse, 2002). In encoding, we extract characters within five-character window size for each character position in the training data as the features for the classifier. In decoding, the BIES position tag is deterministically annotated character by character in the test data. The words that appear only in the test data are treated as OOV word candidates.

We can obtain quite high unknown word recall with this model but the precision is a bit low. However, the following segmentation model will try to eliminate some false unknown words. In the next step, we append OOV word candidates into the IV word list extracted from the training data. The segmentation model is similar to the OOV extraction method, except that the features include the output from the Maximum Matching (MaxMatch) algorithm. The algorithm runs in both forward (FMaxMatch) and backward (BMaxMatch) directions using the final word list as the references. The outputs of FMaxMatch and BMaxMatch are also assigned with BIES tags. The differences between the FMaxMatch and BMaxMatch outputs indicate the positions where the overlapping ambiguities occur. The final word segmentation is carried out by MaxEnt classifier again.

Note, both procedures in *Model b* use whole training data in the training phase. The dictionary used in the MaxMatch algorithm is extracted from the training data only during the training phase. So, the training of segmentation model does not explicitly consider OOV words. We did not use the word and character classes as features in *Model b* unlike in the case of *Models a* and *c*. The details of the model can be found in (Goh et al., 2004b). The difference is that we do not provide character types here because it is forbidden in this round. Besides, we also did not prune the OOV words because this step involve the intervention of human knowledge.

4 Discussions and Conclusions

Table 1 summarizes the results of the three models. The proposed systems employ purely corpus-based statistical/machine learning method. Now, we discuss what we observe in the three models. We remark two problems in word segmentation: OOV word problem and length-bias problem.

OOV word problem is that simple word-based Markov Model family cannot analyze the words not included in the word list. One of the solutions is character-based tagging (Xue and Converse, 2002) (Goh et al., 2004a). The simple character-based tagging (*Model b*) achieved high R_{OOV} but the precision is low. We tried to refine OOV extraction by voting and merging (*Model a* and *c*). However, the R_{OOV} of *Models a* and *c* are not as good as that of *Model b*. Figure 1 shows type-precision and type-recall of each OOV extraction modules. While voting helps to make the precision higher, voting deteriorates the recall. Defining some hand written rules to prune false OOV words will help to improve the IV word segmentation (Goh et al., 2004b), because the precision of OOV word extraction becomes higher. Other types of OOV word extraction methods should be introduced. For example, (Uchimoto et al., 2001) embeded OOV models in MEMM-based word segmenter (with POS tagging). Less than six-character substrings are extracted as the OOV word candidates in the word trellis. (Peng and McCallum, 2004) proposed OOV word extraction methods based on CRF-based word segmenter. Their CRF-based word segmenter can compute a confidence in each segment. The high confident segments that are not in the IV word list are regarded as OOV word candidates. (Nakagawa, 2004) proposed integration of word and OOV word position tag in a trellis. These three OOV extraction method are different from our methods – character-based tagging. Future work will include implementation of these different sorts of OOV word extraction modules.

Length bias problem means the tendency that the locally normalized Markov Model family prefers longer words. Since choosing the longer words reduces the number of words in a sentence, the state-transitions are reduced. The less the state-transitions, the larger the likelihood of the whole sentence. Actually, the length-bias reflects the real distribution in the corpus. Still, the length-bias problem is nonnegligible to achieve high accuracy due to small exceptional cases. We used CRF-based word segmenter which relaxes the problem (Kudo and Matsumoto, 2004). Actually, the CRF-based word segmenter achieved high R_{IV}.

We could not complete *Model a* and *c* for MSR. After the deadline, we managed to complete *Model a* (CRF + Voted Unk.) and *c* (CRF + Merged Unk.) The result of *Model a* was precesion 0.976, recall 0.966, F-measure 0.971, OOV recall 0.570 and IV recall 0.988. The result of *Model c* was precesion 0.969, recall 0.963, F-measure 0.966, OOV recall 0.571 and IV recall 0.974. While the results are quite good, unfortunately, we could not submit the outputs in time.

While our results for the three data sets (AS, CITYU, MSR) are fairly good, the result for the PKU data is not as good. There is no correlation between scores and OOV word rates. We investigate unseen character distributions in the data set. There is no correlation between scores and unseen character distributions.

We expected *Model c* (merging) to achieve higher recall for OOV words than *Model a* (voting). However, the result was opposite. The noises in OOV word candidates should have deteriorated the F-value of overall word segmentation. One reason might be that our CRF-based segmenter could not encode the occurence of OOV words. We defined the 21st word class for OOV words. However, the training data for CRF-based segmenter did not contain the 21st class. We should include the 21st class in the training data

Table 1: Our Three Models and Results: F-value/R_{OOV}/R_{IV} (Rank of F-value)

	AS	CITYU	MSR	PKU
Model a	CRF + Voted Unk. 0.947/0.606/0.971 (2/11)	CRF + Voted Unk. 0.942/0.629/0.967 (2/15)	MEMM + Voted Unk. 0.949/0.378/0.971 (16/29)	CRF + Voted Unk. 0.934/0.521/0.955 (10/23)
Model b	Char.-based tagging 0.952/0.696/0.963 (1/11)	Char.-based tagging 0.941/0.736/0.953 (3/15)	Char.-based tagging 0.958/0.718/0.958 (6/29)	Char.-based tagging 0.941/0.760/0.941 (7/23)
Model c	CRF + Merged Unk. 0.939/0.445/0.967 (7/11)	CRF + Merged Unk. 0.928/0.598/0.940 (8/15)	CRF + No Unk. 0.943/0.025/0.990 (21/29)	CRF + Merged Unk. 0.917/0.325/0.940 (14/23)

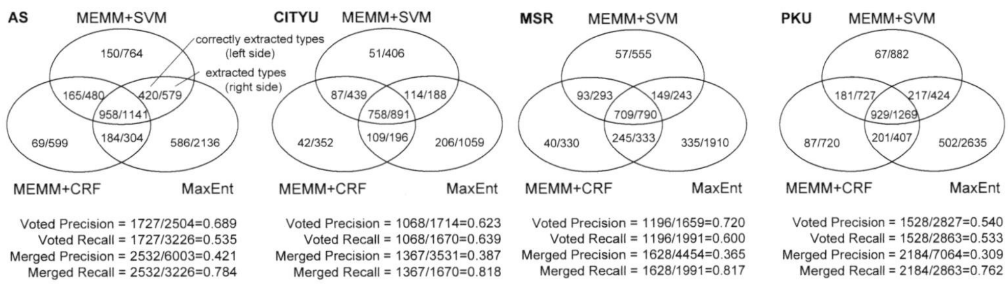

Figure 1: OOV Extraction Precision and Recall by Type

by regarding some words as pseudo OOV words.

We also found a bug in the CRF-based OOV word extration module. The accuracy of the module might be slightly better than the reported results. However, the effect of the bug on overall F-value might be limited, since the module was only part of the OOV extraction module combination – voting and merging.

Acknowledgement

We would like to express our appreciation to Dr. Taku Kudo who developed SVM-based chunker and gave us several fruitful comments.

References

Chooi-Ling Goh, Masayuki Asahara, and Yuji Matsumoto. 2004a. Chinese Word Segmentation by Classification of Characters. In *Proc. of Third SIGHAN Workshop*, pages 57–64.

Chooi-Ling Goh, Masayuki Asahara, and Yuji Matsumoto. 2004b. Pruning False Unknown Words to Improve Chinese Word Segmentation. In *Proc. of PACLIC-18*, pages 139–149.

Taku Kudo and Yuji Matsumoto. 2001. Chunking with Support Vector Machines. In *Proc. of NAACL-2001*, pages 192–199.

Taku Kudo and Yuji Matsumoto. 2004. Applying Conditional Random Fields to Japanese Morphological Analysis. In *Proc. of EMNLP-2004*, pages 230–237.

John Lafferty, Andrew McCallum, and Fernando Pereira. 2001. Conditional Random Fields: Probabilistic Models for Segmenting and Labeling Sequence Data. In *Proc. of ICML-2001*, pages 282–289.

Andrew McCallum, Dayne Freitag, and Fernando Pereira. 2000. Maximum Entropy Markov Models for Information Extraction and Segmentation. In *Proc. of ICML-2000*, pages 591–598.

Tetsuji Nakagawa. 2004. Chinese and Japanese Word Segmentation Using Word-Level and Character-Level Information. In *Proc. of COLING-2004*, pages 466–472.

Fuchun Peng and Andrew McCallum. 2004. Chinese Segmentation and New Word Detection using Conditional Random Fields. In *Proc. of COLING-2004*, pages 562–568.

Kiyotaka Uchimoto, Satoshi Sekine, and Hitoshi Isahara. 2001. The Unknown Word Problem: a Morphological Analysis of Japanese Using Maximum Entropy Aided by a Dictionary. In *Proc. of EMNLP-2001*, pages 91–99.

Nianwen Xue and Susan P. Converse. 2002. Combining Classifiers for Chinese Word Segmentation. In *Proc. of First SIGHAN Workshop*, pages 63–70.

Unigram Language Model for Chinese Word Segmentation

Aitao Chen	Yiping Zhou	Anne Zhang	Gordon Sun
Yahoo! Inc.	Yahoo! Inc.	Yahoo! Inc.	Yahoo! Inc.
701 First Avenue	701 First Avenue	701 First Avenue	701 First Avenue
Sunnyvale, CA 94089	Sunnyvale, CA 94089	Sunnyvale, CA 94089	Sunnyvale, CA 94089
aitao@yahoo-inc.com	zhouy@yahoo-inc.com	annezhangya@yahoo.com	gzsun@yahoo-inc.com

Abstract

This paper describes a Chinese word segmentation system based on unigram language model for resolving segmentation ambiguities. The system is augmented with a set of pre-processors and post-processors to extract new words in the input texts.

1 Introduction

The Yahoo team participated in all four closed tasks and all four open tasks at the second international Chinese word segmentation bakeoff.

2 System Description

The underlying algorithm in our word segmentation system is the unigram language model in which words in a sentence are assumed to occur independently. For an input sentence, we examine all possible ways to segment the new sentence with respect to the segmentation dictionary, and choose the segmentation of the highest probability, which is estimated based on the unigram model.

Our system also has a few preprocessors and postprocessors. The main preprocessors include recognizers for extracting names of people, places and organizations, and recognizer for numeric expressions. The proper name recognizers are built based on the maximum entropy model, and the numeric expression recognizer is built as a finite state automaton. The conditional maximum entropy model in our implementation is based on the one described in Section 2.5 in (Ratnaparkhi, 1998), and features are the same as those described in (Xue and Shen, 2003).

One of the post-processing steps is to combine single characters in the initial segmentation if each character in a sequence of characters occurs in a word much more frequently than as a word on its own. The other post-processing procedure checks the segmentation of a text fragment in the input text against the segmentation in the training data. If the segmentation produced by our system is different from the one in the training data, we will use the segmentation in the training data as the final segmentation. More details on the segmentation algorithm and the preprocessors and postprocessors can be found in (Chen, 2003).

Our system processes a sentence independently. For an input sentence, the preprocessors are applied to the input sentence to extract numeric expressions and proper names. The extracted numeric expressions and proper names are added to the segmentation dictionary, if they are not already in the dictionary. Then the input sentence is segmented into words. Finally the post-processing procedures are applied to the initial segmentation to produce the final segmentation. Our system processes texts encoded in UTF-8; and it is used in all 8 tasks.

3 Results

Table 1 presents the results of the 10 official runs we submitted in all 8 tasks.

Run id	R	P	F	R-oov	R-in
as-closed	0.955	0.934	0.947	0.468	0.978
as-open	0.958	0.938	0.948	0.506	0.978

cityu-closed	0.949	0.931	0.940	0.561	0.980
cityu-open	0.952	0.937	0.945	0.608	0.980
pku-closed	0.953	0.946	0.950	0.636	0.972
pku-open-a	0.964	0.966	0.965	0.841	0.971
msr-closed-a	0.969	0.952	0.960	0.379	0.985
msr-closed-b	0.968	0.953	0.960	0.381	0.984
msr-open-a	0.970	0.957	0.963	0.466	0.984
msr-open-b	0.971	0.961	0.966	0.512	0.983

Table 1: Summary of Yahoo official results.

The first element in the run id is the corpus name, *as* referring to the Academia Sinica corpus, *cityu* the City University of Hong Kong corpus, *pk*u the Peking University Corpus, and *msr* the Microsoft Research corpus. The second element in the run id is the type of task, *closed* or *open*. The second column shows the recall, the third column the precision, and the fourth column F-score. The last two columns present the recall of the out-of-vocabulary words and the recall of the words in the training data, respectively.

3.1 Closed Tasks

For the AS closed task run *as-closed*, we manually identified about 15 thousands person names and about 4 thousands place names from the AS training corpus. We then built a person name recognizer and a place name recognizer from the AS training data. All the name recognizers we built are based on the maximum entropy model. We also built a rule-based numeric expression recognizer implemented as a finite state automaton.

The segmentation dictionary consists of the words in the training data with occurrence frequency compiled from the training data. For each character, the probability that a character occurs in a word is also computed from the training data only.

Each line of texts in the testing data set is processed independently. From an input line, first the person name recognizer and place name recognizer are used to extract person and place names; the numeric expression recognizer is used to extract numeric expressions. The extracted new proper names and new numeric expressions are added to the segmentation dictionary with a constant occurrence frequency of 0.5 before the input text is segmented. After the segmentation, a sequence of single characters is combined into a single unit if each of the characters in the sequence occurs much more frequently in a word than as a word on its own. The threshold of a character occurring in a word is set to 0.80. Also the quad-grams down to unigrams in the segmentation are checked against the training data. When a text fragment is segmented in a different way by our system than in the training data, we use the segmentation of the text fragment in the training data as the final output.

The runs *cityu-closed* and *pku-closed* are produced in the same way. We first manually identified the person names and place names in the training data, and then built name recognizers from the training data. The name recognizers and numeric expression recognizer are used first to extract proper names and numeric expressions before segmentation. The post-processing is also the same.

Two runs, named *msr-closed-a* and *msr-closed-b*, respectively, are submitted using the Microsoft Research corpus for the closed task. Unlike in the other three corpora, the numeric expressions are much more versatile, and therefore, more difficult to write regular expressions to identify them. We manually identified the numeric expressions, person names, place names, and organization names in the training data, and then built maximum entropy model-based recognizers for extracting numeric expressions and names of people, place, and organizations. Also the organization names in this corpus are not segmented into words like in the other three corpora. The organization name recognizer is word-based while the other three recognizers are character-based. The only difference between these two runs is that the run *msr-closed-b* includes an organization name recognizer while the other run *msr-closed-a* does not.

3.2 Open Tasks

For the AS open task, we used a user dictionary and a person name recognizer and a place name recognizer, both trained on the combined AS corpus and the CITYU corpus. However, the base dictionary and word frequency counts are compiled from only the AS corpus. For the open run, we used the annotated AS corpus we acquired from Academia Sinica. Also the phrase segmentation table is built from the AS training data only. The AS open run *as-open* was produced with the new person and place name recognizers and with the user dictionary. The performance of the open run is almost the same as that of the close run.

The training data used in the CITYU open task is the same as in the closed task. We built a person name recognizer and a place name recognizer from the combined AS and CITYU corpora. In training a recognizer, we only kept the sentences that contain at least one person or place name. The run *cityu-open* was produced with new person name and place name recognizers trained on the combined corpora but *without* user dictionary. The base dictionary and frequency counts are from the CITYU training data. We prepared a user dictionary for the CITYU open run but forgot to turn on this feature in the configuration file. We repeated the CITYU open run *cityu-open* with user dictionary. The recall is 0.959; precision is 0.953; and F-score is 0.956.

For the PKU open task run *pku-open-a*, we trained our segmenter from the word-segmented People's Daily corpus covering the period of January 1 through June 30, 1998. Our base dictionary with word frequency counts, character counts, and phrase segmentation table are built from this larger training corpus of about 7 million words. The words in this corpus are annotated with part-of-speech categories. Both the names of people and the names of places are uniquely tagged in this corpus. We created a training set for person name recognizer by combining the sentences in the People's Daily corpus that contain at least one person name with the sentences in the MSR training corpus that contain at least one person name. The person names in the MSR corpus were manually identified. From the combined training data for person names, we built a person name recognizer based on the maximum entropy model. The place name recognizer was built in the same way. The PKU open run *pku-open-a* was produced using the segmenter trained on the 6-month People's Daily corpus with the new person and place name recognizer trained on the People's Daily corpus and the MSR corpus. A user dictionary of about 100 thousand entries, most being proper names, was used in the PKU open run.

The training data used for the MSR open runs is the same MSR training corpus. Our base dictionary, together with word frequency counts, and phrase segmentation table are built from the MSR training data only. The numeric expression recognizer is the same as the one used in the closed task. The person name recognizer and place name recognizer are the same as those used in the PKU open task. We built an organization name recognizer from the People's Daily corpus where organization names are marked. For example, the text fragment "[上海/ns 社科院/j]nt" is marked by a pair of brackets and tagged with "nt" in the annotated People's Daily corpus. We extracted all the sentences containing at least one organization name and built a word-based recognizer. The feature templates are the same as in person name or place name recognizer. We submitted two MSR open task runs, named *msr-open-a* and *msr-open-b*, respectively. The only difference between these two runs is that the first run *msr-open-a* did not include an organization name recognizer, while the run *msr-open-b* used the organization name recognizer built on the annotated People's Daily corpus. Both runs were produced with a user dictionary, the new person name recognizer and new place name recognizer. The increase of F-score from 0.963 to 0.966 is due to the organization name recognizer. While the organization name recognizer correctly identified many organization names, it also generated many false positives. So the positive impact was offset by the false positives.

At about 12 hours before the due time, we learned that multiple submissions for the same task are acceptable. A colleague of ours submitted one PKU open run with the run id 'b' and one MSR open run with the run id 'c' in the bakeoff official results using a different word segmentation system without being tuning for the bakeoff. These two open runs are not discussed in this paper.

4 Discussions

The differences between our closed task runs and open task runs are rather small for both the AS corpus and the CITYU corpus. Our CITYU open run would be substantially better had we used our user dictionary. The open task run using the PKU corpus is much better than the closed task run. We performed a number of additional evaluations in both the PKU closed task and the PKU open task. Table 2 below presents the evaluation results with different features activated in our system. The PKU training corpus was used in all the experiments presented in Table 2.

Run	Features	R	P	F
1	base-dict	0.9386	0.9095	0.9238
2	1+num-expr	0.9411	0.9161	0.9285
3	2+person+place	0.9440	0.9249	0.9343
4	3+single-char	0.9404	0.9420	0.9412
5	4+consistency-checking	0.9529	0.9464	0.9496

Table 2: Results with different features applied in PKU closed task.

Table 3 presents the results with different features applied in the PKU open task. The 6-month annotated People's Daily corpus was used in all the experiments shown in Table 3.

Run	Features	R	P	F
1	base-dict	0.9523	0.9503	0.9513
2	1+user-dict	0.9534	0.9565	0.9549
3	2+num-expr	0.9547	0.9605	0.9576
4	3+person+place	0.9562	0.9647	0.9604
5	4+single-char	0.9487	0.9650	0.9568
6	5+consistency-checking	0.9637	0.9664	0.9650

Table 3: Results with different features applied in PKU open task.

In the features column, *base-dict* refers to the base dictionary built from the training data only; *user-dict* the additional user dictionary; *num-expr* the numeric expression recognizer implemented as a finite state automaton; *person* the person name recognizer; *place* the place name recognizer; *single-char* combining a sequence of single characters when each one of them occurs in words much more frequently than as a word on its own; and lastly *consistency-checking* checking segmentations against the training texts and choosing the segmentation in the training texts if the segmentation of a text fragment produced by our system is different from the one in the training data. The tables show the results with more and more features included. Each run in the both tables includes one or two new features over the previous run. The last run numbered 5 in Table 2 is our official PKU closed run labeled *pku-closed* in Table 1; and the last run numbered 6 in Table 3 is our official PKU open run labeled *pku-open-a* in Table 1.

The F-score for our closed PKU task run is 0.950 with all available features, while using the larger People's Daily corpus as training data and its dictionary alone, the F-score is 0.9513. So a larger training data contributed significantly to the increase in performance in our PKU open task run. The user dictionary, the numeric expression recognizer, the person name recognizer, and the place name recognizer all contributed to the better performance of our PKU closed run and open run. Selectively combining sequence of single characters appreciably improved the precision while marginally decreased the recall in the PKU closed run. However, in the open task run, combining single characters did not result in better performance, probably because the new words recovered by combining single characters are already in our user dictionary for the open run. Finally consistency checking substantially improved the performance for both the closed run and the open run.

5 Conclusion

We presented a word segmentation system that uses unigram language model to select the most probable segmentation among all possible candidates for an input text. The system is augmented with proper name recognizers, numeric expression recognizers, and post-processing modules to extract new words. Overall the recognizers and the post-processing modules substantially improved the baseline performance. The larger training data set used in the PKU open task also significantly increased the performance of our PKU open run. The additional user dictionary is another major contributor to our better performance in the open tasks over the closed tasks.

References

Aitao Chen. 2003. *Chinese Word Segmentation Using Minimal Linguistic Knowledge*. In: Proceedings of the Second SIGHAN Workshop on Chinese Language Processing.

Nianwen Xue and Libin Shen. 2003. *Chinese Word Segmentation as LMR Tagging*. In: Proceedings of the Second SIGHAN Workshop on Chinese Language Processing.

Adwait Ratnaparkhi. 1998. *Maximum Entropy Models for Natural Language Ambiguity Resolution*. Dissertation in Computer and Information Science, University of Pennsylvania.

Report to BMM-based Chinese Word Segmentor with Context-based Unknown Word Identifier for the Second International Chinese Word Segmentation Bakeoff

Jia-Lin Tsai
Tung Nan Institute of Technology, Department of Information Management
Taipei 222, Taiwan, R.O.C.
tsaijl@mail.tnit.edu.tw

Abstract

This paper describes a Chinese word segmentor (CWS) based on backward maximum matching (BMM) technique for the 2nd Chinese Word Segmentation Bakeoff in the Microsoft Research (MSR) closed testing track. Our CWS comprises of a context-based Chinese unknown word identifier (UWI). All the context-based knowledge for the UWI is fully automatically generated by the MSR training corpus. According to the scored results of the MSR closed testing track and our analysis, it shows that our BMM-based CWS with the context-based UWI is a simple and effective system to achieve high Chinese word segmentation performance of more than 95.5% F-measure.

1 Introduction

In the research fields of Chinese natural language processing (NLP), a high-performance Chinese word segmentor (CWS) is a useful preprocessing stage to produce an intermediate result for later processes, such as search engines, text mining and speech recognition, etc. The bottleneck of developing a high-performance CWS is to comprise of a high-performance Chinese UWI (Lin et al. 1993; Tsai et al. 2003). It is because Chinese is written without any separation between words and meanwhile more than 50% words of the Chinese texts in web corpus are out-of-vocabulary (Tsai et al. 2003).

Conventionally, there are four approaches to develop a CWS: (1) **Dictionary-based** approach (Cheng et al. 1999), especial forward and backward maximum matching (Wong and Chan, 1996); (2) **Linguistic** approach based on syntax-semantic knowledge (Chen et al. 2002); (3) **Statistical** approach based on statistical language model (SLM) (Sproat and Shih, 1990; Teahan et al. 2000; Gao et al. 2003); and (4) **Hybrid** approach trying to combine the benefits of dictionary-based, linguistic and statistical approaches (Tsai et al. 2003; Ma and Chen, 2003). In practice, statistical approaches are most widely used because their effective and reasonable performance. For a CWS, there are two types of word segmentation ambiguities while there are no unknown words in them: (1) **Overlap ambiguity** (OA), take a character string ABC as an example. If its segmentation can be either AB/C or A/BC depending on different context, the ABC is called an overlap ambiguity string (OAS), such as "將軍(a general)/用(use)" and "將(to get)/軍用(for military use)" (the symbol "/" indicates a word boundary); (2) **Combination ambiguity** (CA), take a character string AB as an example. If its segmentation can be either A/B or AB depending on different context, the AB is called a combination ambiguity string (CAS), such as "才(just)/能(can)" and "才能(ability)." Meantime, there are two types of error segmentation caused by unknown word problem: (1) **Lack of unknown word** (LUW), it means the error segmentation occurred by lack of an unknown word in the system dictionary, such as "瓦/西/里斯"; (2) **Error identified word** (EIW), it means the error segmentation occurred by an error identified unknown words, such as "切合

点." To sum up, for a CWS in most case the UWI is a pre-processing stage to detect unknown words for the optimization of LUW-EIW tradeoff, and then to disambiguate those auto-detected OAS and CAS problems from the segmentation results.

The goal of this paper is to illustrate and report the effectiveness and the scored results of our BMM-based CWS for the second International Chinese Word Segmentation Bakeoff in the MSR closed (MSR_C) track. For this Bakeoff, our CWS is mainly addressed on optimizing the LUW-EIW tradeoff.

The remainder of this paper is arranged as follows. In Section 2, we present the details of our BMM-based CWS comprised of a context-based UWI. In Section 3, we present the scored results of the CWS in the MSR_C track and give our analysis. Finally, in Section 4, we give our conclusions and suggest some future research directions.

2 Development of BMM-based CWS

As per (Tsai et al. 2004), the Chinese word segmentation performance of BMM technique is about 1% greater than that of FMM technique. Thus, we adopt BMM technique as base to develop our CWS. The descriptions of symbols used in our CWS are given as below:

<BOS>: begin of sentence;
<EOS>: end of sentence;
<BOW>: begin of word;
<EOW>: end of word;
/: word boundary;
+: inner word boundaries of the segmentation of a system word segmented by BMM technique with the system dictionary exclusive of this system word;

SWS (stop word string): for a system word (such as "的(of)"), if the ratio (non-SWS probability) of total frequency of the other system words including it (such as "美的(beautiful)") and its character string frequency is less than or equal to 1%, it is a SWS;

SWBS (stop word bigram string): for a word bigram (such as "才(just)/能(can)"), if the ratio (non-SWBS probability) of its character string (such as "才能(ability)" frequency and its character string frequency is less than or equal to 1%, it is a SWBS;

BMM-ASM (BMM ambiguity string mapping table: the BMM-ASM table lists all the pairs of correct SS (given in training corpus) and the error BMM SS (generated by BMM with the training system dictionary). Take the Chinese sentence "效果真好" as an example. As per its MSR-standard segmentation "效果(effect)/真(really)/好(good)" and its BMM segmentation "效(follow)/果真(indeed)/好(good)," the pair "效果/真"-"效/果真" is a BMM-ASM;

TCT (triple context template): a TCT comprised of three items from left to right are: the left word, the segmented system word and the right word, where the system word is not a mono-syllabic Chinese word. Take the Chinese sentence "效果/真/好" as an example. The two generated TCT are:
"<BOS>/效+1-char-word/真"
"<BOS>/1-char-word+果/真"; and

WCT (word context template): a WCT comprised of three items from left to right are: "<BOW>", the segmented system word and "<EOW>", where the system word is not a mono-syllabic word. Take the system word "喇嘛寺(lamasery)" as an example. Its two WCT are:
"<BOW>/喇嘛+1-char-word/<EOW>"
"<BOW>/2-char-word+寺/<EOW>."

The algorithm of our BMM-based CWS comprised of a context-based UWI is as below:

Step 1. Generate BMM segmentation for the input Chinese sentence with system dictionary, firstly. The system dictionary comprised of all word types found in the training corpus. Then, use BMM-ASM table to revise the matched BMM ambiguity string.

Step 2. Use UWI to identify unknown words from the segmentation of Step 1 by the TCT knowledge, firstly. For the matched TCT, the characters between the left word and the right word will be combined as an UWI-identified word. If the UWI-identified word includes a SWS or a SWBS, it will be not an UWI-identified word. Then, use the system dictionary of Step 1 inclusive of the UWI-identified words of this step to repeat Step 1 process.

Step 3. Add tags "<BOW>" and "<EOW>" at

the left-side and right-side of the continue 1-char character segmentations of Step 2, firstly. Then, use UWI to identify unknown words by the WCT knowledge. If the number of characters between "<BOW>" and "EOW>" is same with that of the matched WCT, these 1-char characters will be combined as an UWI-identified word. If the UWI-identified word includes a SWS or a SWBS, it will be not an UWI-identified word. Finally, use the system dictionary of Step 2 inclusive of those UWI-identified words of this step to repeat Step 1 process.

Step 4. Use UWI to combine a word bigram into a word by the following two conditions: (1) if the non-SWS probability of the right first character of the left-side word is greater or equal to 99% and (2) if the non-SWS probability of the left first character of the right-side word is greater or equal to 99%. Take the word bigram "２００/２" as an example. Since the non-SWS probability of the right first character "０" of the left-side word "２００" is 99.95%, "２００２" is identified as an UWI-identified word. If the UWI-identified word includes a SWS or a SWBS, it will be not an UWI-identified word. Finally, use the system dictionary of Step 3 inclusive of those UWI-identified words of this step to repeat the Step 1 process.

Step 5. Repeat the Step 2 process.

Step 6. Repeat the Step 3 process.

Step 7. Repeat the Step 4 process.

Step 8. Stop.

In the above algorithm, Steps 2, 3 and 4 repeated at Steps 5, 6 and 7, respectively, are designed to show the recursive effect of our CWS.

3 The Scored Results and Analysis

In the 2nd Chinese Word Segmentation Bakeoff, there are four training corpus: AS (Academia Sinica) and CU (City University of Hong Kong) are traditional Chinese corpus, PU (Peking University) and Microsoft Research (MSR) are simplified Chinese corpus. Meanwhile, there are two testing tracks of this bakeoff: closed and open. We attend MSR_C track. The non-SWS and the non-SWBS probabilities of our CWS for this bakeoff are all set to 1%. And, the segmentation results of each step of our CWS are collected and scored, respectively.

3.1 The Scored Results

Table 1 shows the details of MSR training and testing corpus. Note that, in Table 1, the details of MSR testing corpus were computed by us according to the MSR gold testing corpus. From Table 1, it indicates that the MSR testing track seems to be a 25-folds experiment design.

Table 1. The details of MSR_C corpus

	Training	Testing
Sentences	86,924	3,985
Word types	88,119	12,924
Words	2,368,391	109,002
Character types	5,167	2,839
Characters	4,050,469	184,356

Table 2 shows the scored results of our CWS in MSR_C track. The performance of "Step 1(P)" in Table 2 was computed by us and the others were from the scored results. It shows a very high performance of 99.1% F-measure can be achieved while the BMM-based CWS by using a system dictionary comprised of word types found in the MSR training and testing corpus at Step 1 ("P" means "Perfect").

Table 2. The performance of each step of our CWS in the MSR-C track (OOV is 0.026)

Step	R	P	F	R_{OOV}	R_{IV}
1(P)	0.993	0.989	0.991	-	-
1	0.963	0.924	0.943	0.025	0.989
2	0.964	0.924	0.944	0.025	0.989
3	0.968	0.938	0.953	0.205	0.989
4	0.958	0.949	0.954	0.465	0.972
5	0.958	0.951	0.954	0.493	0.971
6	0.958	0.952	0.955	0.503	0.970
7	0.958	0.952	0.955	0.504	0.970

3.2 The Analysis

Table 3 (see next page) shows the differences of F-measure and R_{OOV} between each near-by step of our CWS. From Table 3, it indicates that the most contribution for increasing the overall performance (F-measure) of our CWS is at Step 3, which uses WCT knowledge.

Table 4 (see next page) shows the distributions of four segmentation error types (OAS, CAS, LUW and EIW) for each step of our CWS. From Table 4, it shows that our context-based UWI with the knowledge of TCT and WCT can effectively to optimize the LUW-EIW tradeoff. Moreover, from Table 4, it also shows that the knowledge of SWS, SWBS and BMM-ASM can effectively to resolve the CAS errors.

Table 3. The differences of F-measure and R_{OOV} between near-by steps of our CWS

Step	F	F(d)	R_{OOV}	R_{OOV}(d)
1	0.943	-	0.025	-
2	0.944	0.001	0.025	0
3	0.953	0.011	0.205	0.18
4	0.954	0.001	0.465	0.26
5	0.954	0	0.493	0.028
6	0.955	0.001	0.503	0.01
7	0.955	0	0.504	0.001

Table 4. The number of OAS (types), CAS (types), LUW (types) and EIW (types) for each step of our CWS

	OAS	CAS	LUW	EIW
1	210(194)	233(80)	2702(1930)	157(96)
2	184(173)	233(80)	2698(1927)	157(96)
3	185(174)	232(80)	2169(1473)	187(126)
4	250(226)	226(77)	1373(1090)	946(609)
5	250(226)	226(77)	1283(1018)	991(658)
6	251(227)	224(77)	1255(1001)	1005(669)
7	262(216)	224(76)	1260(1005)	1007(668)

4 Conclusions and Future Directions

In this paper, we have applied a BMM-based CWS comprised of a context-based UWI to the Chinese word segmentation and obtained a high performance of 95.5% F-measure in the MSR closed track. To sum up the results of this study, we have following conclusions and future directions:

(1) Since the F-measure of Step 1 of our CWS is 94.3%, it indicates that the BMM with BMM-ASM knowledge is a simple but probably effective technique as a good base in developing a high performance CWS;

(2) Since 82% of segmentation errors of our CWS caused by LUW problem, this result supports that a high performance CWS is relied on a high performance Chinese UWI.

(3) For a CWS, there are two critical and probably independent tasks: the optimization of LUW-EIW tradeoff and the detection and disambiguation of OAS and CAS error segmentation. We believe the former task is more critical than the later one.

(4) We will continue to expand our CWS with other linguistic knowledge (such as part-of-speech information and morphology) and BTM model (Tsai 2005) to improve our BMM-based CWS for attending the third International Chinese Word Segmentation Bakeoff in both closed and open testing tracks.

References

Chen, Keh-Jiann and Wei-Yun, Ma. 2002. Unknown Word Extraction for Chinese Documents, *Proceedings of 19th COLING 2002*, Taipei, 169-175.

Cheng, Kowk-Shing, Gilbert H. Yong and Kam-Fai Wong.. 1999. A study on word-based and integral-bit Chinese text compression algorithms. *JASIS*, 50(3): 218-228.

Gao, Jianfeng, Mu Li and Chang-Ning uang. 2003. Improved Source-Channel Models for Chinese Word Segmentation. *Proceedings of the 41st Annual Meeting of the Association for Computational Linguistics*, 272-279.

Lin, Ming-Yu, Tung-Hui Chiang and Keh-Yi Su. 1993. A preliminary study on unknown word problem in Chinese word segmentation. ROCLING 6, 119-141.

Ma, Wei-Yun and Keh-Jiann Chen, 2003, "Introduction to CKIP Chinese Word Segmentation System for the First International Chinese Word Segmentation Bakeoff", *Proceedings of ACL, Second SIGHAN Workshop on Chinese Language Processing*, pp168-171.

Sproat, R. and C., Shih. 1990. A Statistical Method for Finding Word Boundaries in Chinese Text. Computer proceeding of Chinese and Oriental Language, 4(4):336 349.

Teahan, W. J., Yingying Wen, Rodger McNad and Ian Witten. 2000. A compression-based algorithm for Chinese word segmentation. *Computational Linguistics*, 26(3): 375-393.

Tsai, Jia-Lin, C.L., Sung and W.L., Hsu. 2003. Chinese Word Auto-Confirmation Agent, *Proceedings of ROCLING XV*, Taiwan, 175-192.

Tsai, Jia-Lin, G., Hsieh and W.L., Hsu. 2004. Auto-Generation of NVEF knowledge in Chinese, *Computational Linguistics and Chinese Language Processing*, 9(1):41-64.

Tsai, Jia-Lin. 2005. A Study of Applying BTM Model on the Chinese Chunk Bracketing. *Proceedings of IJCNLP, 6th International Workshop on Linguistically Interpreted Corpora*, Jeju Island.

Wong, Pak-Kwong and Chorkin ChanWong. 1996. Chinese Word Segmentation. based on Maximum Matching and Word Binding Force. *Proceedings of the 16th International conference on Computational linguistic,* 1:200-203.

An Example-Based Chinese Word Segmentation System for CWSB-2

Chunyu Kit **Xiaoyue Liu**
Department of Chinese, Translation and Linguistics
City University of Hong Kong
Tat Chee Ave., Kowloon, Hong Kong
{ctckit, xyliu0}@cityu.edu.hk

Abstract

This paper reports the example-based segmentation system for our participation in the second Chinese Word Segmentation Bakeoff (CWSB-2), presenting its basic ideas, technical details and evaluation. It is a preliminary implementation. CWSB-2 valuation shows that it performs very well in identifying known words. Its unknown word detection module also illustrates great potential. However, proper facilities for identifying time expressions, numbers and other types of unknown words are needed for improvement.

1 Introduction

Word segmentation is to identify lexical items, especially individual word forms, in a text. It involves two fundamental tasks, both aiming at minimizing segmentation errors: one is to infer out-of-vocabulary (OOV) words, also known as unknown (or unseen) word detection, and the other to identify in-vocabulary (IV) words, with an emphasis on disambiguation. OOV words and ambiguities are the two major causes to segmentation errors.

Accordingly, word segmentation approaches can be divided into the categories summarized in Table 1 in terms of the resources in use to tackle these two causes. The closed and open tracks in CWSB correspond, respectively, to the last two categories, both involving inferring OOV words beyond disambiguating IV words. Word discovery and OOV word detection pursue a similar target, i.e., inferring new words. The continuum connecting them is the size of the lexicon in use: the former assumes few words known and the latter an existing lexicon to some scale. Inferring new words is an essential task in word segmentation, for a complete lexicon is rarely a realistic assumption in practice.

Category	Resource in use		Major Task	
	Lexicon	Tr. Corpus	OOV	Disamb.
WD[a]	-	(-)[b]	+	
WS/CL[c]	+	-	-	+
WS/IL[d]	+	-	+	+
WS/TC[e]	(+)[f]	+	+	+
WS/TC+L[g]	+	+	+	+

[a]Word discovery, or unsupervised lexical acquisition
[b]Input data is used for unsupervised training
[c]Word segmentation with a complete lexicon
[d]Word segmentation with an incomplete lexicon
[e]Word segmentation with a pre-segmented training corpus
[f]It can be extracted from the given training corpus.
[g]Word segmentation with a pre-segmented training corpus and an extra lexicon

Table 1: Categories of segmentation approach

This paper presents our segmentation system for participation in CWSB-2. It takes an example-based approach to recognize IV words and follows description length gain (DLG) to infer OOV words in terms of their text compression effect. Sections 2 and 3 below introduce the example-based and DLG-based segmentation respectively. Section 4 presents a strategy to combine their strength and Section 5 reports our system's performance in CWSB-2. Following error analysis in Section 6, Section 7 concludes the paper.

2 Example-based segmentation

How to utilize as much information as possible from the training corpus to adapt a segmentation system towards a segmentation standard has been a critical issue. Kit et al. (2002) and Kit et al. (2003) attempt to integrate case-based learning with statistical models (e.g., n-gram) by extracting transformation rules from the training corpus for disambiguation via error correction; Gao et al. (2004) adopt a similar strategy for adaptive segmentation, with transformation templates (instead of case-based rules) to modify word boundaries (instead of individual words).

The basic idea of example-based segmentation is very simple: existing pre-segmented strings in training corpus provide reliable examples for segmenting similar strings in input texts. In contrast to dictionary checking for locating *possible* words in an input sentence to facilitate later segmentation operations, pre-segmented examples give *exact* segmentation to copy.

The example-based segmentation can be implemented in the following steps.

1. Find all exemplar pre-segmented fragments, with regards to a training corpus, and all possible words, with regards to a lexicon, from each character in an input sentence;
2. Identify the optimal sequence, among all possibilities, of the above items over the sentence following some optimization criterion.

If adopting the minimal number of fragments or words in a sequence as optimization criterion, we have a maximal matching approach to word segmentation. However, it differs remarkably from the previous maximal matching approaches: it matches pre-segmented fragments, instead of dictionary words, against an input sentence. It can be carried out by a best-first strategy: repeatedly select the next longest example or word until the entire sentence is properly covered. Unfortunately, the best-first approach does not guarantee to give the best answer. For CWSB-2, we implemented a program following the Viterbi algorithm to perform a complete search in terms of the number of fragments, and then words, in a sequence.

However, a serious problem with this example-based approach is the *sparse data* problem. Long exemplar fragments are more reliable but small in number, whereas short ones are large in number but less reliable. In the case of no exemplar fragment available for an input sentence, this approach draws back to the maximal match segmentation with a dictionary. How to incorporate statistical inference into example-based segmentation to infer more reliable optimal segmentation beyond string matching remains a critical issue for us to tackle.

3 DLG-based segmentation

DLG is formulated in Kit and Wilks (1999) and Kit (2000) as an empirical measure for the compression effect of extracting a substring from a given corpus as a lexical item. DLG optimization is applied to detect OOV words for our participation in CWSB-2. It works as follows in two steps.

1. Calculate the DLG for all known words and all new word candidate (i.e., substrings with frequency $\geq$ 2, preferably, in the test corpus), based on frequency information in the training and the test corpora;
2. Find the optimal sequence of such items over an input sentence with the greatest sum of DLG.

Step 2 above in our system re-implements only the first round of DLG-based lexical learning in Kit (2000). It is implemented by the same algorithm as the one for example-based segmentation, with DLG as optimization criterion. Evaluation results show that this learning-via-compression approach discovers many OOV words successfully, in particular, person names.

4 Integration

The example-based segmentation is good at identifying IV words but incapable of recognizing any new words. In contrast, the DLG-based segmentation performs slightly worse but has potential to detect new words. It is expected that the strength of the two could be combined together for performance enhancement.

However, because of inadequate time we had to take a shortcut in order to catch the CWSB-2 deadline: DLG segmentation is only applied to recognize new words among the sequences of mono-character items in the example-based segmentation output.

Track	P	R	F	OOV	R_{OOV}	R_{IV}
AS_c	.944	.902	.923	.043	.234	.976
PKU_c	.929	.904	.916	.058	.252	.971
MSR_c	.965	.935	.950	.026	.189	.986

Table 2: System performance in CWSB-2

5 Performance

Our group took part in three closed tracks in CWSB-2, namely, AS_c, PKU_c and MSR_c, with a preliminary implementation of the example-based word segmentation presented above. Our system's performance in terms of CWSB-2's official scores is presented in Table 2. Its R_{OOV} scores look undesirable, showing that applying the first round of DLG-based segmentation to sequences of mono-character items is inadequate for the OOV word discovery task. Nevertheless, its R_{IV} scores are, in general, quite close to the top systems in CWSB-2, although it does not have a disambiguation module to polish its maximal matching output.

However, this is not to say that the DLG-based segmentation deserves no credit in unknown word detection. It does recognize many OOV words, as shown in Table 3. The low R_{OOV} rate has to do with our system's incapability in handling time expressions, numbers, and foreign words.

6 Error analysis

Most errors made by our system are due to the following causes: (1) no knowledge, overt or implicit, in use for recognizing time expressions, numbers and foreign words, as restricted by CWSB-2 rules, (2) a premature module for OOV word detection, (3) no further disambiguation besides example application, and (4) significant inconsistency in the training and test data.

The inconsistency exists not only between the training and test corpora for each track but, more surprisingly, also within individual training corpora. Some suspected cases are illustrated in Tables 4, 5 and 6. They are observed to be in a large number in the CWSB-2 corpora. Scoring with a golden standard involving so many of them appears to be problematic, for it penalizes the systems for handling such cases right and rewards the others for producing "correct" answers. What

AS_c: 小森(106) 左詩雅(45) 馮禮(31) 霍金(29) 瑪雅(21) 丹紐(20) 張庭(18) 英特爾(17) 黑盤鮑(16) 沈時華(15) 證期會(13) 厲莉(12) 黃銘坤(11) 卡門(11) 佛指舍利(11) 陳慶浩(10) 璩女(9) 范曉萱(8) 郭女(8) 邱太三(7) 網站(7) 狄亞尼(7) 張惠妹(6) 米田真澄(6) 鄭優(5) 丁克華(5) 經發會(5) 蘇盈貴(5) 陳秀玲(5) 八美圖(5) 房貸(5) 蔡信弘(5) 郭玉鈴(4) 地型(4) 御膳(4) 白藜蘆醇(4) 羅麗泰(3) 張玨(3) 米仓涼子(3) 陳兆伸(2) 羅勒(2) 幼發拉底河(2) 溥傑(2) ······

PKU_c: 罢免(38) 世清(23) 任免(21) 拉姆斯菲尔德(20) 哈苏(19) 海合会(17) 军级(16) 加纳(15) 水心村(12) 网友(11) 小阜村(10) 宋双(10) 吐逊江(9) 申奥(9) 库福尔(8) 金税(8) 亚布力(8) 金门(7) 三阳镇(7) 教主(6) 罢免书(6) 法轮功(6) 香客(6) 普京(6) 福清市(5) 柯尔克孜(5) 华能(5) 罗林斯(5) 松诺斯(5) 洋务(5) 马祖(5) 甲午(5) 哈斯达(4) 奥申委(4) 高唐县(4) 文津(4) 门市部(4) 妈祖(4) 刁民(4) 闭会(4) 商机(4) 临武县(4) 湄洲岛(4) 圈套(4) 法塔赫(3) 流星雨(3) 堆龙德庆县(3) 阿族(3) 哥德堡(3) 信众(3) 钱柜(3) 衡水(3) 内坦亚(3) 双丰村(3) ······

MSR_c: 博古(26) 玲英(19) 游景玉(19) 任尧森(17) 秦机(15) 亚仿(14) 进占(14) 刘积仁(13) 东宝(13) ｉｎｔｅｒｎｅｔ(12) 猴王(12) 双保(11) 张肇群(10) 抚州(10) 南丁格尔(10) 彭珮云(10) 海塘(10) 王常力(9) 穆守家(9) 大关村(8) 赞皇(8) 张钧(8) 嶂石岩(7) 三老四严(7) 局域网(7) 透支(6) 秦家山(6) 东软(6) 后金(6) 八旗(6) 弄堂(5) 黎秀芳(5) 提灌(5) 大关(5) 王丙乾(5) 棉铃虫(5) 百亿次(4) 西文(4) 米夫(4) 陆冰(4) 郑守仁(4) 秦邦宪(4) 关小瑛(3) 二进制(3) 顺延(3) 李朋朋(3) 瞿秋白(3) 黄华平(3) 汪赛进(3) 汪延(3) 何元亮(3) 陆佑楣(3) 阜平县(3) 中信所(3) 导流(3) 徐殿龙(3) 重男轻女(2) ······

Table 3: Illustration of new words successfully detected, with frequency in parentheses

is even more worth noting is that (1) an inconsistent case involves more than one word, and (2) the difference between a correct and an erroneous judgment of a word is 1, in a sense, but the difference between one system that loses it for doing right and another that earns it by doing wrong is surely greater.

7 Conclusions

In the above sections we have reported the example-based word segmentation system for our participation in CWSB-2, including its basic ideas, technical details and evaluation results. It has illustrated an excellent performance in IV word identification and nice potential in OOV word discovery. However, its weakness in handling time expressions, numbers and other types of unknown words has hindered it from performing better. We are expecting to implement a full-fledged version of the system for improvement.

Acknowledgements

The work described in this paper was supported by the RGC of HKSAR, China, through the CERG grant 9040861. We wish to thank Alex Fang and Robert Neather for their help.

Training & Answer	f_T/f_A	Golden Standard	f_T/f_A
繁殖 場	4/8	繁殖場	0/0
老 歌	28/7	老歌	0/0
準備 率	5/7	準備率	0/0
小 火車	11/6	小火車	0/0
本 文	186/5	本文	0/0
第三 者	41/4	第三者	0/0
新 一 代	29/4	新一代	0/0
稱 之 為	129/4	稱之為	0/0
夠 不 夠	23/3	夠不夠	0/0
短 時間	47/3	短時間	0/0
中正 機場	33/2	中正機場	0/0
台北 市長	32/2	台北市長	0/0
民意 代表	85/2	民意代表	0/0
清醒過來	10/2	清醒 過來	0/0
統治 者	62/2	統治者	0/0
新 生命	23/2	新生命	0/0
也就是說	192/1	也 就是 說	0/0
不景氣	149/1	不 景氣	0/0
中央 政府	66/1	中央政府	0/0
挑戰性	31/1	挑戰 性	0/0
看 電影	80/1	看電影	0/0
研究 者	68/1	研究者	0/0
面 無 表情	13/1	面無表情	0/0
曾文 水庫	13/1	曾文水庫	0/0
無 意識	20/1	無意識	0/0
無 話 不 談	6/1	無話不談	0/0
另 一 面	29/1	另一面	0/0
紅透 半 邊 天	4/1	紅透半邊天	0/0
民間團體	24/7	民間 團體	25/0
女性主義	17/3	女性 主義	53/0
是 不 是	1201/2	是不是	2/0

Table 4: Some inconsistent cases in AS corpus

Training & Answer	f_T/f_A	Golden Standard	f_T/f_A
乡政府	14/26	乡 政府	0/0
区政府	6/1	区 政府	0/0
镇政府	5/21	镇 政府	0/0
世纪之交	24/19	世纪 之 交	0/0
改 为	23/18	改为	0/0
生产总值	66/15	生产 总值	0/0
个人所得税	10/9	个人 所得税	0/0
无党派人士	10/5	无 党派 人士	0/0
新年伊始	45/5	新年 伊始	0/0
组成部分	42/5	组成 部分	0/0
固定资产	27/4	固定 资产	0/0
世界各地	21/4	世界 各地	0/0
乡镇企业	126/4	乡镇 企业	0/0
至关重要	20/4	至关 重要	0/0
综合国力	15/4	综合 国力	0/0
总参谋长	25/4	总 参谋长	0/0
经济社会	25/3	经济 社会	0/0
劳动生产率	13/3	劳动 生产率	0/0
去年底	32/3	去年 底	0/0
世界纪录	30/3	世界 纪录	0/0
无党派	11/3	无 党派	0/0
议事日程	15/3	议事 日程	0/0
中小企业	22/3	中小 企业	0/0
不同 于	11/2	不 同于	0/0
此事	25/2	此 事	0/0
火树银花不夜天	3/1	火树银花 不 夜 天	0/0
雨夹雪	13/1	雨 夹 雪	0/0
县政府	24/5	县 政府	1/0
意味着	49/4	意味 着	1/0
很多	112/3	很 多	14/0
发达国家	48/1	发达 国家	1/0

Table 5: Some inconsistent cases in PKU corpus

Training & Answer	f_T/f_A	Golden Standard	f_T/f_A
营业 部	12/7	营业部	0/0
高性能	16/6	高 性能	0/0
“ 八五	29/5	“八五	0/0
大型 企业集团	6/3	大型企业 集团	0/0
径流 量	3/3	径 流量	0/0
海信电器	1/2	海信 电器	0/0
投资银行$^?$	4/2	投资 银行	0/0
一 版	10/2	一版	0/0
浙东	3/2	浙 东	0/0
２０００ 多 人	7/1	２０００多人	0/0
采访团	2/1	采访 团	0/0
产油国 家	1/1	产 油 国家	0/0
第一、二、三$^?$	4/1	第一 、 二 、 三	0/0
葛洲坝大江	1/1	葛洲坝 大江	0/0
国际互联网 络	1/1	国际 互联网络	0/0
计算机 应用软件	1/1	计算机应用 软件	0/0
家 门口$^?$	10/1	家门 口	0/0
两点$^?$	16/1	两 点	0/0
吕梁$^?$	4/1	吕 梁	0/0
一口气$^?$	16/1	一 口 气	0/0
中国人民	122/1	中国 人民	0/0
中外合资 经营	3/1	中外 合资经营	0/0

Table 6: Some inconsistent cases in MSR corpus

References

E. Brill. 1993. *A Corpus-Based Approach to Language Learning*. PhD thesis, University of Pennsylvania, Philadelphia.

J. Gao, A. Wu, M. Li, C. Huang, H. Li, X. Xia and H. Qin. 2004. Adaptive Chinese word segmentation. In *ACL-04*. Barcelona, July 21-26.

C. Kit and Y. Wilks. 1999. Unsupervised learning of word boundary with description length gain. In M. Osborne and E. T. K. Sang (eds.), *CoNLL-99*, pp.1-6. Bergen, Norway, June 12.

C. Kit 2000. *Unsupervised Lexical Learning as Inductive Inference*. PhD thesis, University of Sheffield.

C. Kit, H. Pan and H. Chen. 2002. Learning case-based knowledge for disambiguating Chinese word segmentation: A preliminary study. *SIGHAN-1*, pp.33－39. Taipei, Sept. 1, 2002.

C. Kit, Z. Xu and J. J. Webster. 2003. Integrating n-gram model and case-based learning for Chinese word segmentation. In Q. Ma and F. Xia (eds.), *SIGHAN-2*, pp.160-163. Sapporo, 11 July, 2003.

D. Palmer. A trainable rule-based algorithm for word segmentation. In *ACL-97*, pp.321-328. Madrid.

Chinese Word Segmentation in FTRD Beijing

Heng LI
France Telecom R&D Beijing
heng.li@francetelecom.com

Yuan DONG
France Telecom R&D Beijing
yuan.dong@francetelecom.com

Xinnian MAO
France Telecom R&D Beijing
xinnian.mao@francetelecom.com

Haila WANG
France Telecom R&D Beijing
haila.wang@francetelecom.com

Wu LIU
Beijing University of Posts and Telecommunications
wu.liu@francetelecom.com.cn

Abstract

This paper presents a word segmentation system in France Telecom R&D Beijing, which uses a unified approach to word breaking and OOV identification. The output can be customized to meet different segmentation standards through the application of an ordered list of transformation. The system participated in all the tracks of the segmentation bakeoff -- PK-open, PK-closed, AS-open, AS-closed, HK-open, HK-closed, MSR-open and MSR-closed -- and achieved the state-of-the-art performance in MSR-open, MSR-close and PK-open tracks. Analysis of the results shows that each component of the system contributed to the scores.

1 Introduction

The development of the Chinese word segmentation system presented in this bakeoff began in Feb. this year, and will last for one year with the support of the ILAB Beijing initial project within France Telecom R&D.

Although the project last only half year by now, the main components of the system has been implemented, including code identification and conversion, basic segmentation, factoid detection, morphological analysis, name entity identification, segmentation standards adaptor, except the components of code identification and conversion and segmentation standards adaptors, other components are integrated in a statistical framework of n-gram language model.

2 System Description

2.1 Code identification and conversion

For processing both Simplified and Traditional Chinese text from a variety of locales, including Mainland China, Hong Kong and Taiwan, we choose UTF-8 as internal character representation within the system. The ability to transparently handle Chinese text from any Chinese locale greatly simplifies the logic of the segmentation system.

2.2 N-gram language model

In our system, Chinese words can be categorized into one of the following types: lexicon words, morphological words, factoids, name entities. These types of words are processed in different ways in our system, and are incorporated into a unified statistical framework of the trigram language model.

2.2.1 Basic segmentation

Each input sentence is first segmented into individual characters. These characters and the character strings are then looked up in a lexicon. For the efficient search, the lexicon is represented by a TRIE compressed in a double-array data structure. Given a character string, all its prefix strings that form lexicon words can be retrieved efficiently by browsing the TRIE whose root represents its first character.

2.2.2 Factoid detection

There are twenty four kinds of factoid words, such as time, date, money, etc. All the factoid words are represented as regular expressions, and compiled into a compressed DFA with the row-index algorithm.

2.2.3 Morphological analysis

As (Wu 2003) discussed in the paper, it is those morphologically derived words (MDWs hereafter) that are most controversial and most likely to be treated differently in different standards and different systems. In our system, there are six main categories of morphological processes, affixation, directional verb, resultative verb, splitting verb, reduplication and merging, and we employ a chart parsing algorithm augmented with word lattices structure which incorporates the morphological rules especially designed for Chinese languages with restrictive CFG.

2.2.4 Name entity identification

Our NE identification concentrates on three types of NEs, namely, personal names (PERs), location names (LOCs) and organization names (ORGs). For Chinese person names, we only consider PN candidates that begin with a family name stored in the family name list and follow a given name which is of one or two characters long. For transliterations of foreign person names, a PN candidate would be generated if it contains only characters stored in a transliterated character list. For location names and organizations names, we only use the LN list and ON list to generate the candidates.

2.3 Segmentation standards adaptor

In this bakeoff, there are four segmentation standards and slightly different from ours. Standard adaptation is conducted with the application of an ordered list of transformations on the output of our segmentation system. The method we use is Transformation-Based Learning, and the transformation templates are lexicalized templates. In our system, we designed 14 lexicalized templates.

2.4 Speed

As we optimized our lexicon and decoding process, the speed of segmentation is very fast. On a single 2.80 GHz, 1G bytes memory, Xeon machine, the system is able to process about 0.73 Mega bytes per second.

The speed may vary according to the sentence lengths: given texts of the same size, those containing longer sentences will take more time. The number reported here is an average of the time taken to process the test sets of the eight tracks we participated in.

3 Evaluation

3.1 Open tracks

In the open tracks, we used four lexicons of 210,319 entries, 165,103 entries, 174,268 entries, 165,655 entries respectively on AS-open, HK-open, MSR-open, PK-open tracks, which include the entries of 2,430 MDWs, 12,487 PNs, 22,907 LNs and 29,032 ONs, 10,414 four-character idioms, plus the word lists generated from the training data provided by the bakeoff. We use the training data provided by the bakeoff for training our trigram word-based language model. We also used a family name list (which contains 399 entries in our system), and a 1,021-entry transliterated name character list.

3.2 Closed tracks

In the close tracks, the lexicon we use could only be generated from the training data provided by the bakeoff. We could only use the training data provided by the bakeoff for training our word-based language model. Also, since the training data we used is only from the bakeoff, there does not exist any different standards, standards adaptor component is not necessarily needed.

3.3 Result analysis

Our system is designed so that components such as the factoid detection and NE identification can be switched on or off, so that we can investigate the relative contribution of each component to the overall word segmentation performance. The results are summarized in the table 1. For comparison, we also include in the table (Row 1) the results of using FMM. Row 2 shows the baseline results of our system, where only the lexicon is used. Each cell in the table has six fields. From the top, there are respectively Precision, Recall, F-measure, OOV Recall, IV Recall and Speed (Mega bytes/second). We don't list the speed in Row 6 since it decreases a factor of 10 to 60 because of application of thousands of TBL rules.

	PK_o	PK_c	MSR_o	MSR_c	AS_o	AS_c	HK_o	HK_c
1. FMM	0.857	0.841	0.921	0.917	0.871	0.864	0.842	0.838
	0.925	0.906	0.968	0.957	0.925	0.911	0.928	0.908
	0.891	0.872	0.945	0.936	0.898	0.887	0.885	0.872
	0.143	0.069	0.107	0.025	0.097	0.014	0.175	0.162
	0.947	0.957	0.971	0.982	0.947	0.952	0.961	0.968
	2.435	2.570	2.951	3.090	2.813	2.937	2.748	2.850
2. Baseline	0.869	0.855	0.931	0.926	0.891	0.877	0.863	0.851
	0.941	0.928	0.973	0.969	0.943	0.942	0.930	0.929
	0.905	0.890	0.952	0.947	0.917	0.908	0.897	0.888
	0.235	0.069	0.275	0.025	0.132	0.014	0.194	0.162
	0.960	0.987	0.987	0.995	0.982	0.984	0.985	0.990
	0.967	1.017	0.879	0.923	0.703	0.728	0.921	0.956
3. 2+FT	0.946	0.919	0.950	0.940	0.903	0.900	0.873	0.862
	0.951	0.950	0.973	0.973	0.945	0.947	0.932	0.932
	0.948	0.934	0.961	0.956	0.924	0.923	0.902	0.895
	0.748	0.448	0.396	0.205	0.180	0.156	0.292	0.215
	0.963	0.980	0.990	0.944	0.979	0.983	0.983	0.989
	0.819	0.879	0.779	0.787	0.631	0.635	0.821	0.830
4. 3+MA	0.946	0.919	0.950	0.940	0.903	0.900	0.873	0.862
	0.951	0.950	0.973	0.973	0.945	0.947	0.932	0.932
	0.948	0.934	0.961	0.956	0.924	0.923	0.902	0.895
	0.748	0.448	0.371	0.205	0.181	0.156	0.295	0.215
	0.963	0.980	0.989	0.944	0.979	0.983	0.983	0.989
	0.807	0.879	0.753	0.787	0.626	0.635	0.815	0.830
5. 4+NE	0.951	0.919	0.956	0.940	0.920	0.900	0.900	0.862
	0.957	0.950	0.973	0.973	0.949	0.947	0.938	0.932
	0.954	0.934	0.965	0.956	0.934	0.923	0.918	0.895
	0.788	0.448	0.454	0.205	0.330	0.156	0.411	0.215
	0.967	0.980	0.956	0.944	0.977	0.983	0.980	0.989
	0.679	0.879	0.716	0.787	0.604	0.635	0.748	0.830
6. 5+adaptation	0.960	0.919	0.957	0.940	0.919	0.900	0.901	0.862
	0.964	0.950	0.975	0.974	0.952	0.948	0.940	0.932
	0.962	0.934	0.966	0.957	0.935	0.923	0.920	0.895
	0.788	0.449	0.453	0.210	0.311	0.158	0.410	0.215
	0.974	0.980	0.989	0.995	0.981	0.983	0.982	0.989

Table 1. Our system results on all the tracks.

From Table 1 we can find that, in rows 1 and 2, the dictionary-based methods already achieve quite good recall, but the precisions are not very good because they cannot correctly identify unknown words that are not in the lexicon such as factoids and name entities. We also find that even using the same lexicon, our approach that is based on the N-gram language models outperforms the greedy approach because the use of context model resolves more ambiguities in segmentation. As shown in Rows 3 to 5, when components are switched on in turn, the overall word segmentation performance increases consistently. The morphological analysis has no contribution to the overall performance in Row 4. The main reason is that the number of MDWs used in our system is very small (only 2,430) and there may exist very small MDWs in the test sets. The similar cases occur on NE identification in the close tracks in Row 5 since we would not do NE identification at all in the close tracks. We also notice that the contribution of NE identification is very little in the open tracks, which shows that the performance of NE identification is not very good in our system, and explains why our OOV recall is not very high compared with other participants in the bakeoff. This is one area of our future work to improve. The results of standards adaptation on four bakeoff test sets are shown in Row 6. It turns out that performance except IV recall improves slightly across the board in all four test sets. The main reason is that the training data and lexicon we used are mainly from the four providers in the bakeoff, there does not exist any different segmentation standards.

4 Conclusions

The evaluation results show that the closed tests is not very good compared with other participants, the one main reason is that the word-based language model we used is not competitive compared with other algorithms in the closed tracks. One area of our future work is to apply other machine learning algorithm, like Maximum Entropy (ME), Support Vector Machine (SVM), Conditional Random Field (CRF), etc.

Acknowledgements

The work reported here was a team effort. We thank Wu Liu, Haitao Zeng, Nan He for their help in the experimentation and evaluation of the system.

References

Andi Wu. 2003. Customizable segmentation of morphologically derived words in Chinese. *International Journal of Computational Linguistics and Chinese Language Processing,* 8(1): 1-27.

Aoe, J. 1989. An Efficient Digital Search Algorithm by Using a Double-Array Structure. *IEEE Transactions on Software Engineering,* Vol. 15, 9: 1066-1077.

George Anton Kiraz. 1999. Compressed Storage of Sparse Finite-State Transducers. *4th International Workshop on Automata Implementation*, Pages: 109-121.

Jian Sun, Ming Zhou and Jianfeng Gao. 2003. Chinese named entity identification using class-based language model. *International Journal of Computational Linguistics and Chinese Language Processing,* 8(1).

Jianfeng Gao, Mu Li, Andi Wu and Chang-Ning Huang. 2004a. Chinese word segmentation: a pragmatic approach. Microsoft Research Technical Report, MSR-TR-2004-123.

Julia Hockenmaier, Chris Brew. 1998. Error driven segmentation of Chinese. *Communications of COLIPS,* 8(1): 69-84.

Xinnian Mao, Heng Li, Yuan Dong, Haila Wang. 2005. Chinese Morphological Analyzer. *IEEE NLP-KE 2005*, submitted.

Perceptron Learning for Chinese Word Segmentation

Yaoyong Li[†], **Chuanjiang Miao**[‡], **Kalina Bontcheva**[†], **Hamish Cunningham**[†]
[†]Department of Computer Science, The University of Sheffield, Sheffield, S1 4DP, UK
{yaoyong,kalina,hamish}@dcs.shef.ac.uk
[‡]Institute of Chinese Information Processing, Beijing Normal University, Beijing, 100875, China
miaochj@bnu.edu.cn

Abstract

We explored a simple, fast and effective learning algorithm, the uneven margins Perceptron, for Chinese word segmentation. We adopted the character-based classification framework and transformed the task into several binary classification problems. We participated the close and open tests for all the four corpora. For the open test we only used the utf-8 code knowledge for discrimination among Latin characters, Arabic numbers and all other characters. Our system performed well on the as, cityu and msr corpora but was clearly worse than the best result on the pku corpus.

1 Introduction

We participated in the closed and open tests for all the four corpora, referred to as, cityu, msr and pku, respectively. We adopted the character-based methodology for Chinese word segmentation, that processed text character by character. We explored a simple and effective learning algorithm, the Perceptron with Uneven Margins (PAUM) for Chinese word segmentation task.

For the open task, we only used the minimal external information – the utf-8 code knowledge to distinguish Latin characters and Arabic numbers from other characters, justified by the fact that the English text requires no segmentation since they has been segmented already, and another fact that any Arabic number in one particular context should have the same segmentation.

2 Character Based Chinese Word Segmentation

We adopted the character based methodology for Chinese word segmentation, in which every character in a sentence was checked one by one to see if it was a word on its own or it was beginning, middle, or end character of a multi-character word. In contrast, another commonly used strategy, the word based methodology segments a Chinese sentence into the words in a pre-defined word list possibly with probability information about each word, according to some maximum probability criteria (see e.g. Chen (2003)). The performance of word based segmentation is dependent upon the quality of word list used, while the character based method does not need any word list – it segments a sentence only based on the characters in the sentence.

Using character based methodology, we transform the word segmentation problem into four binary classification problems, corresponding to single-character word, the beginning, middle and end character of multi-character word, respectively. For each of the four classes a classifier was learnt from training set using the one vs. all others paradigm, in which every character in the training data belonging to the class considered was regarded as positive example and all other characters were negative examples.

After learning, we applied the four classifiers to each character in test text and assigned the character the class which classifier had the maximal output among the four. This kind of strategy has been widely used in the applications of machine learning to named entity recognition and has also been used in Chinese word segmentation (Xue and Shen, 2003). Finally a word delimiter (often a blank space, depending on particular corpus) was added to the right of one character if it was not the last character of a sentence and it was predicted as end character of word or as a single character word.

3 Learning Algorithm

Perceptron is a simple and effective learning algorithm. For a binary classification problem, it checks the training examples one by one by predicting their labels. If the prediction is correct, the example is passed; otherwise, the example is used to correct the model. The algorithm stops when the model classifies all training examples correctly. The margin Perceptron not only classifies every training example correctly but also outputs for every training example a value (before thresholding) larger than a predefined parameter (margin). The margin Perceptron has better generalisation capability than the standard Perceptron. Li et al. (2002) proposed the Perceptron algorithm with uneven margins (PAUM) by introducing two margin parameters τ_+ and τ_- into the update rules for the positive and negative examples, respectively. Two margin parameters allow the PAUM to handle imbalanced datasets better than both the standard Perceptron and the margin Perceptron. PAUM has been successfully used for document classification and information extraction (Li et al., 2005).

We used the PAUM algorithm to train a classifier for each of four classes for Chinese word segmentation. For one test example, the output of the Perceptron classifier before thresholding was used for comparison among the four classifiers. The important parameters of the learning algorithm are the uneven margins parameters τ_+ and τ_-. In all our experiments $\tau_+ = 20$ and $\tau_- = 1$ were used.

Table 1 presents the results for each of the four classification problems, obtained from 4-fold cross-validation on training set. Not surprisingly, the classification for middle character of multi-character word was much harder than other three classification problems, since middle character of Chinese word is less characteristic than beginning or end character or single-character word. On the other hand, improvement on the classification for middle character, while keeping the performances of other classification, would improve the overall performance of segmentation.

Table 1: Results for each of the four classifiers: F1 (%) averaged over 4-fold cross-validation on training sets of the four corpora. C1, C2 and C3 refer to the classifier for beginning, middle and end character of multi-character word, respectively, and C4 refers to the classifier for single character word.

	C1	C2	C3	C4
as	95.64	90.07	95.47	95.27
cityu	96.64	90.06	96.43	95.14
msr	96.36	89.79	96.00	94.99
pku	96.09	89.99	96.18	94.12

Support vector machines (SVM) is a popular learning algorithm, which has been successfully applied to many classification problems in natural language processing. Similar to the PAUM, SVM is a maximal margin algorithm. Table 2 presents a comparison of performances and computation times between the PAUM and the SVM with linear kernel[1] on three subsets of cityu corpora with different sizes. The performance of SVM was better than the PAUM. However, the larger the training data was, the closer the performance of PAUM to that of SVM. On the other hand, SVM took much longer computation time than PAUM. As a matter of fact, we have run the SVM with linear kernel on the whole cityu training corpus using 4-fold cross-validation for one month and it has not finished yet. In contrast, PAUM just took about one hour to run the same experiment.

4 Features for Each Character

In our system every character was regarded as one instance for classification. The features for one character were the character form itself and the character forms of the two preceding and the two following characters of the current one. In other word, the features for one character c_0 were the character forms from a context win-

[1] The SVM^{light} package version 5.0, available from http://svmlight.joachims.org/, was used to learn the SVM classifiers in our experiments.

Table 2: Comparison of the Perceptron with SVM for Chinese word segmentation: averaged F1 (%) over the 4-fold cross-validation on three subsets of cityu corpus and the computation time (in second) for each experiment. The three subsets have 100, 1000 and 5000 sentences, respectively.

	100	1000	5000
PAUM	73.55	78.00	88.08
	4s	14s	92s
SVM	75.50	79.15	88.78
	227s	3977s	49353s

dow centering at c_0 and containing five characters $\{c_{-2}, c_{-1}, c_0, c_1, c_2\}$ in a sentence. Our experiments on training data showed that co-occurrences of characters in the context window were helpful. Taking account of all co-occurrences of characters in context window is equivalent to using a quadratic kernel in Perceptron, while not using any co-occurrence amounts to a linear kernel. Actually we can only use part of co-occurrences as features, which can be regarded as some kind of semi-quadratic kernel.

Table 3 compares the three types of kernel for Perceptron, where for the semi-quadratic kernel we used the co-occurrences of characters in context window as those used in (Xue and Shen, 2003), namely $\{c_{-2}c_{-1}, c_{-1}c_0, c_0c_1, c_1c_2, c_{-1}c_1\}$. It was shown that the quadratic kernel gave much better results than linear kernel and the semi-quadratic kernel was slightly better than fully quadratic kernel. Semi-quadratic kernel also led to less feature and less computation time than fully quadratic kernel. Therefore, this kind of semi-quadratic kernel was used in our submissions.

Table 3: Comparisons between different kernels for Perceptron: F1 (%) averaged over 4-fold cross-validation on three training sets.

	linear	quadratic	semi-quadratic
cityu	81.30	94.78	95.13
msr	79.80	94.78	94.93
pku	82.33	94.80	95.05

Actually it has been noted that quadratic kernel for Perceptron, as well as for SVM, performed better than linear kernel for information extraction and other NLP tasks (see e.g. Carreras et al. (2003)). However, quadratic kernel was usually implemented in dual form for Perceptron and it took very long time for training. We implemented the quadratic kernel for Perceptron in primal form by encoding the linear and quadratic features into feature vector explicitly. Actually our implementation performed even slightly better than the Perceptron with quadratic kernel as we used only part of quadratic features, and it was still as efficient as the Perceptron with linear kernel.

5 Open Test

While closed test required the participants only to use the information presented in training material, open test allowed to use any external information or resources besides the training data. In our submissions for the open test we just used the minimal external information, namely the utf-8 code knowledge for identifying a piece of English text or an Arabic number. and What we did by using this kind of knowledge was to pre-process the text by replacing each piece of English text with a symbol "E" and replacing every Arabic number with another symbol "N". This kind of pre-processing resulted in a smaller training data and less computation time and yet slightly better performance on training data, as shown in Table 4 which compares the results of collapsing the English text only and collapsing both the English text and Arabic number with those for closed test. Table 4 also presents the 95% confidence intervals for the F-measures.

6 Results on Test Data

Table 5 presents our official results on test corpora for both close and open tests. First, comparing with the results in Table 4, the results on test set are significantly different from the result using 4-fold cross validation on training set for all the four corpora. The test result was better than the results on training set for the msr corpus but was worse for other three corpora, especially for the pku corpora. We suspected that this may be caused by difference between training and test data, which needs further investigation.

Table 4: Comparisons between the results for close and open tests: averaged F1 (%) and the 95% confidence interval on the 4-fold cross-validation on the training sets of four corpora and the computation time (in hour) for each experiment. "English" means only collapsing English texts and "E & N" means collapsing both English texts and Arabic numbers.

	close test	English	E & N
as	95.53±0.46	95.65±0.47	95.78±0.46
	8.88h	7.66h	7.07h
cityu	95.13 ±1.49	95.25 ±1.48	95.25 ±1.48
	1.03h	0.86h	0.82h
msr	94.92 ±0.36	94.98 ±0.40	95.00 ±0.39
	2.62h	1.69h	1.62h
pku	95.05 ±0.43	95.08 ±0.36	95.15 ±0.46
	0.70h	0.63h	0.60h

Secondly, the test results for close and open tests are close to each other on other three corpora except the pku corpora, for which the result for open test is clearly better than that for close test. This was mainly because of different encoding of Arabic number in training and test sets of the pku corpus. Since Arabic number was encoded in three bytes in training set but was encoded in one byte in test set for the pku corpora, for close test the trained model for Arabic number was not applicable to the Arabic numbers in test set. However, for open test, as we replaced Arabic number with one symbol in both training and test sets, the different encoding of Arabic number in training and test sets could not cause any problem at all, which led to better result. On the other hand, our pre-processing with respect to the English text and Arabic numbers seemed have slightly effect on the F-measure for other three corpora.

Finally, comparing with the results of closed test from other participants, our F1 figures were no more than 0.008 lower than the best ones on the as, cityu and msr corpora, but was 0.023 lower than the best one on the pku corpus.

7 Conclusion

We applied the uneven margins Perceptron to Chinese word segmentation. The learning algorithm is simple, fast and effective. The results obtained are encouraging.

Table 5: The official results on test set: F-measure (%) for close and open tests, respectively.

	as	cityu	msr	pku
close	94.4	93.6	95.6	92.7
open	94.8	93.6	95.4	93.8

The performance of Perceptron was close to that of the SVM on Chinese word segmentation for large training data. On the other hand, the Perceptron took much less computation time than SVM. We implemented the Perceptron with semi-quadratic kernel in primal form. Our implementation was both effective and efficient.

Our system performed well for the three of four corpora, as, cityu and msr corpora. But it was significantly worse than the best result on the pku corpora, which needs further investigation.

Acknowledgements

This work is supported by the EU-funded SEKT project (http://www.sekt-project.org).

References

X. Carreras, L. Màrquez, and L. Padró. 2003. Learning a perceptron-based named entity chunker via online recognition feedback. In *Proceedings of CoNLL-2003*, pages 156–159. Edmonton, Canada.

A. Chen. 2003. Chinese Word Segmentation Using Minimal Linguistic Knowledge. In *Proceedings of the 2nd SIGHAN Workshop on Chinese Language Processing*.

Y. Li, H. Zaragoza, R. Herbrich, J. Shawe-Taylor, and J. Kandola. 2002. The Perceptron Algorithm with Uneven Margins. In *Proceedings of the 9th International Conference on Machine Learning (ICML-2002)*, pages 379–386.

Y. Li, K. Bontcheva, and H. Cunningham. 2005. Using Uneven Margins SVM and Perceptron for Information Extraction. In *Proceedings of Ninth Conference on Computational Natural Language Learning (CoNLL-2005)*.

N. Xue and L. Shen. 2003. Chinese Word Segmentation as LMR Tagging. In *Proceedings of the 2nd SIGHAN Workshop on Chinese Language Processing*.

Data-driven Language Independent Word Segmentation Using Character-Level Information

Dong-Hee Lim, Seung-Shik Kang
School of Computer Science, Kookmin Univerity
861-1 Chongnung-dong, Songbuk-gu, Seoul 136-702, Korea
{nlp, sskang}@cs.kookmin.ac.kr

Abstract

This paper presents a data-driven language independent word segmentation system that has been trained for Chinese corpus at the second Chinese word segmentation bakeoff. The system consists of a base segmentation algorithm and the refining procedures for the undecided character sequences. It does not use any lexicon and the base segmentation is simply done by character bigram and HMM-model is applied for the remaining character sequences. As a final step, high-frequency character trigram modifies the error-prone parts of the text.

1 Introduction

We participated in the closed track of the second Chinese word segmentation bakeoff for the training corpus of HK (City University of Hong Kong, PK (Beijing University), and MS (Microsoft Research). Our system is independent of the corpus or the language that we also registered for AS (Academia Sinica) track, but failed to generate a result because of the code set problem. AS uses two-byte space characters instead of a blank(0x20), and more 0x0A is used in AS that is regarded as EOF in Windows environment.

The result of our system is not a top-level system when compared to other systems. However, our approach is quite acceptable because the data-driven methods can contribute to improving the accuracy of other word segmentation systems because we did not performed a tuning the system to fix the frequently repeating error patterns.

This work was supported by the Korea Science and Engineering Foundation(KOSEF) through Advaned Information Technology Research Center(AITrc).

2 Bigram and trigram data

We extracted a character bigram data from the training corpus. In the previous studies, Shim(1996) and Kang(2001) constructed space generation probability for each adjacent two characters XY. They are inside probability "X_Y", left-side probability "_XY", and right-side probability "XY_".[2] That is, they ignored 'space information'. In our bigram data, inside and outside space information is extracted from the training corpus, together with the character pairs. We call it 'extended bigram data' and it has eight types of frequency data. For example, XY consists of the frequencies of "0X0Y0", "0X0Y1", "0X1Y0", "0X1Y1", "1X0Y0", "1X0Y1", "1X1Y0", and "1X1Y1".[3] From the frequencies of the extended bigram data, we compute the space generation probability of $P_{t=000}(C_iC_{i+1})$ and left/right/inside probabilities are also computed from the extended bigram data.

$$P_{t=000}(C_iC_{i+1}) = F_{t=000}(C_iC_{i+1}) \,/\, \sum_{t=000}^{t=111} Ft(CiCi+1)$$

Extended bigram data is more sophisticated than the basic bigram data that the accuracy is better than that of the basic bigram data.

3 Segmentation algorithm

3.1 Base Algorithm

The base segmentation algorithm is a HMM model together with the space-insertion probability. HMM model chooses the

[2] Lee(2002) used bigram and trigram data for HMM model which requires a more memory space.

[3] '0' is a non-space tag and '1' is a space tag.

segmentation with the higheset probability. Given a sentence of n characters, $S = c_1c_2...c_n$, has a segmentation of m words, then segmentation probability is estimated as P(T,S) = P($t_{1,n}$, $c_{1,n}$) $\approx \prod_{i=0}^{i=n} p(t_i \mid c_{i-1}c_i, t_{i-2}t_{i-1})$. Our starting point of the word segmentation was the high precision ratio for the Korean language. We first tried to simply applying the extended bigram data with an appropriate threshold. However, it is supposed that there is a limitation of this approach because of the low recall ratio. It caused an adoption of HMM model together with the extended bigram data. Table 1 shows the results of HMM with extended bigram data.

Table 1. Results of HMM with extended bigram

Testing data	Recall	Precision	F-measure
HK	0.924	0.921	0.923
PK	0.902	0.919	0.910
MS	0.942	0.939	0.940

3.2 Postprocessing by trigram data

Extended bigram data in Section 2 consists of 2 adjacent characters and 3 space information (2C3S). In contrast, we may extract trigram data that is constructed by 3 characters and 2 space information(3C2S). This 3C2S trigram data has a form of "X0Y0Z", "X0Y1Z", "X1Y0Z", and "X1Y1Z". That is 3 character sequence XYZ has 4 frequency data. We supposed that "there are frequent 3-character sequences that are biased to one of the spacing pattern".

We verified this supposition by improving the accuracy of the word segmentation result. Table 2 shows the final result of the postprocessing. Postprocessing by trigram data got an increase of both recall and precision. When compared to the base segmentation results of Table 1, F-measures are increased by 0.3%, 0.4%, and 0.8%, respectively.

As an improvement of the system performance, character trigram data has been extracted from the training corpus.

Table 2. Final segmentation results[4]

Testing data	Recall	Precision	F-measure
HK	0.926	0.925	0.926
PK	0.904	0.925	0.914
MS	0.947	0.949	0.948

4 Pure data-driven method without using HMM

Only after submitting the results for bakeoff 2005, we noticed that the accuracy of HMM model is low. It is not clear what the problem is and there is a possibility of the implementation error. So, we looked for a pure data-driven method without using HMM model. The first step in the base segmentation is to apply extended bigram with no space information. In this step, only the spaces with high confidence are fixed and others are marked as 'undecided'.[5] In the second step, extended bigram with space information is applied. Two more postprocessing modules are added for refinements. One of them is to adopt the word-length feature by using the fact that average length of Chinese word is 1.6 characters. The other is to construct 'error dictionary' for the training data. Error dictionary is constructed by running training data and comparing the differences. The context information of error dictionary is four characters (left two and right two characters). The new approach got a better result than that of the final result of bakeoff 2005 as shown in Table 3.

Table 3. Pure data-driven method without HMM

Testng data	Recall	Precision	F-measure
HK	0.933	0.921	0.927
PK	0.912	0.929	0.920
MS	0.952	0.953	0.952

[4] The final results in Table 2 are a bit higher than the bakeoff 2005 results. F-measures of bakeoff 2005 results are 0.921, 0.912, and 0.947, respectively. The reason was not identified. Table 1 and Table 2 are computed by the evaluation program 'score.txt' in the website of SIGHAN bakeoff 2005.

[5] If space generation probability is higher than 0.7, space is inserted. With less than 0.3, space is not inserted, and 'undecided' mark for the range 0.3~0.7,

5 Conclusion

We presented our word segmentation method for the closed track of bakeoff 2005. Our approach is data-driven and language independent. That is, our method is purely statistical method that no language dependent features are applied for tuning or improving the accuracy. Word segmentation system for bakeoff 2005 applied HMM model together with extended bigram and trigram data. The results show that word segmentation problem can be solved with no lexicons or language-dependent resources.

One of the good point of our approach is that data-driven language independent approach is quite acceptable for the word segmentation problem. We also expect that our data-driven method would be a good solution for the enhancement of word segmentation systems as a postprocessing module.

References

Chen, A., Chinese Word Segmentation Using Minimal Linguistic Knowledge, SIGHAN 2003, pp.148-151, 2003.

Gao, J., M. Li, and C.N. Huang, Improved Source-Channel Models for Chinese Word Segmentation, ACL 2003.

Kang, S. S. and C. W. Woo, Automatic Segmentation of Words using Syllable Bigram Statistics, Proceedings of NLPRS'2001, pp.729-732, 2001.

Lee D. G, S. Z. Lee, and H. C. Rim, H. S. Lim, Automatic Word Spacing Using Hidden Markov Model for Refining Korean Text Corpora, Proc. of the 3rd Workshop on Asian Language Resources and International Standardization, pp.51-57, 2002.

Maosong, S., S. Dayang, and B. K. Tsou, Chinese Word Segmentation without Using Lexicon and Hand-crafted Training Data, Proceedings of the 17th International Conference on Computational Linguistics (Coling'98), pp.1265-1271, 1998.

Asahara, M., C. L. Go, X. Wang, and Y. Matsumoto, Combining Segmenter and Chunker for Chinese Word Segmentation, Proceedings of the 2nd SIGHAN Workshop on Chinese Language Processing, pp144-147, 2003.

Nakagawa, T., Chinese and Japanese Word Segmentation Using Word-Level and Character-Level Information, COLING'04., pp.466-472, 2004.

Ng, H.T. and J.K. Low, Chinese Part-of-Speech Tagging: One-at-a-Time or All-at-Once? Word-Based or Character-Based, EMNLP'04.

Shim, K. S., Automated Word-Segmentation for Korean using Mutual Information of Syllables, Journal of KISS: Software and Applications, pp.991-1000, 1996.

Sproat, R. and T. Emerson, The First International Chinese Word Segmentation Bakeoff, SIGHAN 2003.

A Maximum Entropy Approach to Chinese Word Segmentation

Jin Kiat Low [1] and **Hwee Tou Ng** [1,2] and **Wenyuan Guo** [2]
1. Department of Computer Science, National University of Singapore,
3 Science Drive 2, Singapore 117543
2. Singapore-MIT Alliance, E4-04-10, 4 Engineering Drive 3, Singapore 117576
{lowjinki, nght, guowy}@comp.nus.edu.sg

Abstract

We participated in the Second International Chinese Word Segmentation Bakeoff. Specifically, we evaluated our Chinese word segmenter in the open track, on all four corpora, namely Academia Sinica (AS), City University of Hong Kong (CITYU), Microsoft Research (MSR), and Peking University (PKU). Based on a maximum entropy approach, our word segmenter achieved the highest F measure for AS, CITYU, and PKU, and the second highest for MSR. We found that the use of an external dictionary and additional training corpora of different segmentation standards helped to further improve segmentation accuracy.

1 Chinese Word Segmenter

The Chinese word segmenter we built is similar to the maximum entropy word segmenter we employed in our previous work (Ng and Low, 2004). Our word segmenter uses a maximum entropy framework (Ratnaparkhi, 1998; Xue and Shen, 2003) and is trained on manually segmented sentences. It classifies each Chinese character given the features derived from its surrounding context. Each Chinese character can be assigned one of four possible boundary tags: s for a character that occurs as a single-character word, b for a character that begins a multi-character (i.e., two or more characters) word, e for a character that ends a multi-character word, and m for a character that is neither the first nor last in a multi-character word. Our implementation used the opennlp maximum entropy package v2.1.0 from sourceforge.[1]

1.1 Basic Features

The basic features of our word segmenter are similar to our previous work (Ng and Low, 2004):

(a) $C_n(n = -2, -1, 0, 1, 2)$
(b) $C_nC_{n+1}(n = -2, -1, 0, 1)$
(c) $C_{-1}C_1$
(d) $Pu(C_0)$
(e) $T(C_{-2})T(C_{-1})T(C_0)T(C_1)T(C_2)$

In the above feature templates, C refers to a Chinese character. Templates (a) – (c) refer to a context of five characters (the current character and two characters to its left and right). C_0 denotes the current character, $C_n(C_{-n}$) denotes the character n positions to the right (left) of the current character. For example, given the character sequence "新华社北京", when considering the character C_0 "社", C_{-2} denotes "新", C_1C_2 denotes "北京", etc. The punctuation feature, $Pu(C_0)$, checks whether C_0 is a punctuation symbol (such as "?", "–", ","). For the type feature (e), four type classes are defined: numbers represent class 1, dates ("日", "月", "年", the Chinese characters for "day", "month", "year", respectively) represent class 2, English letters represent class 3, and other characters represent class 4. For example, when considering the character "年" in the character sequence "九零年代R", the feature $T(C_{-2}) \ldots T(C_2) = 11243$

[1] http://maxent.sourceforge.net/

will be set to 1 ("九" is the Chinese character for "9" and "零" is the Chinese character for "0").

Besides these basic features, we also made use of character normalization. We note that characters like punctuation symbols and Arabic digits have different character codes in the ASCII, GB, and BIG5 encoding standard, although they mean the same thing. For example, comma "," is represented as the hexadecimal value `0x2c` in ASCII, but as the hexadecimal value `0xa3ac` in GB. In our segmenter, these different character codes are normalized and replaced by the corresponding character code in ASCII. Also, all Arabic digits are replaced by the ASCII digit "0" to denote any digit. Incorporating character normalization enables our segmenter to be more robust against the use of different encodings to represent the same character.

For all the experiments that we conducted, training was done with a feature cutoff of 2 and 100 iterations, except for the AS corpus which had a feature cutoff of 3.

A major difficulty faced by a Chinese word segmenter is the presence of out-of-vocabulary (OOV) words. Segmenting a text with many OOV words tends to result in lower accuracy. We address the problem of OOV words in two ways: using an external dictionary containing a list of predefined words, and using additional training corpora which are not segmented according to the same segmentation standard.

1.2 External Dictionary

If a sequence of characters in a sentence matches a word in an existing dictionary, it may be a clue that the sequence of characters should be segmented as one word. We used an online dictionary from Peking University downloadable from the Internet[2], consisting of about 108,000 words of length one to four characters. If there is some sequence of neighboring characters around C_0 in the sentence that matches a word in this dictionary, then we greedily choose the longest such matching word W in the dictionary. Let t_0 be the boundary tag of C_0 in W, L the number of characters in W, and $C_1(C_{-1})$ be the character immediately following (preceding) C_0 in the sentence. We then add the following features derived from the dictionary:

(f) Lt_0
(g) $C_n t_0 (n = -1, 0, 1)$

For example, consider the sentence "新华社北京...". When processing the current character C_0 "华", we will attempt to match the following candidate sequences "华", "新华", "华社", "新华社", "华社北", "新华社北", and "华社北京" against existing words in our dictionary. Suppose both "华社" and "新华社" are found in the dictionary. Then the longest matching word W chosen is "新华社", t_0 is m, L is 3, C_{-1} is "新", and C_1 is "社".

1.3 Additional Training Corpora

The presence of different standards in Chinese word segmentation limits the amount of training corpora available for the community, due to different organizations preparing training corpora in their own standards. Indeed, if one uniform segmentation standard were adopted, more training data would have been available, and the OOV problem could be significantly reduced.

We observed that although different segmentation standards exist, the differences are limited, and many words are still segmented in the same way across two different segmentation standards. As such, in our work, we attempt to incorporate corpora from other segmentation standards as additional training data, to help reduce the OOV problem.

Specifically, the steps taken are:

1. Perform training with maximum entropy modeling using the original training corpus D_0 annotated in a given segmentation standard.

2. Use the trained word segmenter to segment another corpus D annotated in a different segmentation standard.

3. Suppose a Chinese character C in D is assigned a boundary tag t by the word segmenter with probability p. If t is identical to the boundary tag of C in the gold-standard

[2]http://ccl.pku.edu.cn/doubtfire/Course/Chinese%20Information%20Processing/Source_Code/Chapter_8/Lexicon_full_2000.zip

annotated corpus D, and p is less than some threshold θ, then C (with its surrounding context in D) is used as additional training data.

4. Add all such characters C as additional training data to the original training corpus D_0, and train a new word segmenter using the enlarged training data.

5. Evaluate the accuracy of the new word segmenter on the same test data annotated in the original segmentation standard of D_0.

For the current bakeoff, when training a word segmenter on a particular training corpus, the additional training corpora are all the three corpora in the other segmentation standards. For example, when training a word segmenter for the AS corpus, the additional training corpora are CITYU, MSR, and PKU. The necessary character encoding conversion between GB and BIG5 is performed, and the probability threshold θ is set to 0.8. We found from our experiments that setting θ to a higher value did not further improve segmentation accuracy, but would instead increase the training set size and incur longer training time.

2 Testing

During testing, the probability of a boundary tag sequence assignment $t_1 \ldots t_n$ given a character sequence $C_1 \ldots C_n$ is determined by using the maximum entropy classifier to compute the probability that a boundary tag t_i is assigned to each individual character C_i. If we were to just assign each character the boundary tag with the highest probability, it is possible that the classifier produces a sequence of invalid tags (e.g., m followed by s). To eliminate such possibilities, we implemented a dynamic programming algorithm which considers only valid boundary tag sequences given an input character sequence. At each character position i, the algorithm considers each last word candidate ending at position i and consisting of K characters in length ($K = 1, \ldots, 20$ in our experiments). To determine the boundary tag assignment to the last word W with K characters, the first character of W is assigned boundary tag b, the last character of W is assigned tag e, and the intervening characters are assigned tag m. (If W is a single-character word, then the single character is assigned tag s). In this way, the dynamic programming algorithm only considers valid tag sequences.

After word segmentation is done by the maximum entropy classifier, a post-processing step is applied to correct inconsistently segmented words made up of 3 or more characters. A word W is defined to be inconsistently segmented if the concatenation of 2 to 6 consecutive words elsewhere in the segmented output document matches W. In the post-processing step, the segmentation of the characters of these consecutive words is changed so that they are segmented as a single word. To illustrate, if the concatenation of 2 consecutive words "香格" and "里拉" in the segmented output document matches another word "香格里拉", then the 2 consecutive words "香格" and "里拉" will be re-segmented as a single word "香格里拉".

Corpus	R	P	F	R_{OOV}	R_{IV}
AS	0.962	0.950	0.956	0.684	0.975
CITYU	0.967	0.956	0.962	0.806	0.980
MSR	0.969	0.968	0.968	0.736	0.975
PKU	0.968	0.969	0.969	0.838	0.976

Table 1: Our official SIGHAN bakeoff results

3 Evaluation Results

We evaluated our Chinese word segmenter in the open track, on all 4 corpora, namely Academia Sinica (AS), City University of Hong Kong (CITYU), Microsoft Research (MSR), and Peking University (PKU). Table 1 shows our official SIGHAN bakeoff results. The columns R, P, and F show the recall, precision, and F measure, respectively. The columns R_{OOV} and R_{IV} show the recall on out-of-vocabulary words and in-vocabulary words, respectively. Our Chinese word segmenter which participated in the bakeoff was trained with the basic features (Section 1.1), and made use of the external dictionary (Section 1.2) and additional training corpora (Section 1.3). Our word segmenter achieved the highest F measure for AS, CITYU, and PKU, and the second highest for MSR.

After the release of the official bakeoff results,

Corpus	V1	V2	V3	V4
AS	0.953	0.955	0.956	0.956
CITYU	0.950	0.960	0.961	0.962
MSR	0.960	0.968	0.963	0.968
PKU	0.948	0.965	0.956	0.969

Table 2: Word segmentation accuracy (F measure) of different versions of our word segmenter

we ran a series of experiments to determine the contribution of each component of our word segmenter, using the official scorer and test sets with gold-standard segmentations. Version V1 used only the basic features (Section 1.1); Version V2 used the basic features and additional features derived from our external dictionary (Section 1.2); Version V3 used the basic features but with additional training corpora (Section 1.3); and Version V4 is our official submitted version combining basic features, external dictionary, and additional training corpora. Table 2 shows the word segmentation accuracy (F measure) of the different versions of our word segmenter, when tested on the official test sets of the four corpora. The results indicate that the use of external dictionary increases segmentation accuracy. Similarly, the use of additional training corpora of different segmentation standards also increases segmentation accuracy.

4 Conclusion

Using a maximum entropy approach, our Chinese word segmenter achieves state-of-the-art accuracy, when evaluated on all four corpora in the open track of the Second International Chinese Word Segmentation Bakeoff. The use of an external dictionary and additional training corpora of different segmentation standards helps to further improve segmentation accuracy.

Acknowledgements

This research is partially supported by a research grant R252-000-125-112 from National University of Singapore Academic Research Fund, as well as the Singapore-MIT Alliance.

References

Hwee Tou Ng and Jin Kiat Low. 2004. Chinese part-of-speech tagging: One-at-a-time or all-at-once? word-based or character-based? In *Proceedings of the 2004 Conference on Empirical Methods in Natural Language Processing (EMNLP 2004)*, pages 277–284.

Adwait Ratnaparkhi. 1998. *Maximum Entropy Models for Natural Language Ambiguity Resolution.* Ph.D. thesis, University of Pennsylvania.

Nianwen Xue and Libin Shen. 2003. Chinese word segmentation as LMR tagging. In *Proceedings of the Second SIGHAN Workshop on Chinese Language Processing*, pages 176–179.

Description of the HKU Chinese Word Segmentation System for Sighan Bakeoff 2005

Guohong Fu
Department of Linguistics
The University of Hong Kong
Pokfulam Road, Hong Kong
ghfu@hkucc.hku.hk

Kang-Kwong Luke
Department of Linguistics
The University of Hong Kong
Pokfulam Road, Hong Kong
kkluke@hkusua.hku.hk

Percy Ping-Wai WONG
Department of Linguistics
The University of Hong Kong
Pokfulam Road, Hong Kong
wongpw@hkusua.hku.hk

Abstract

In this paper, we describe in brief our system for the Second International Chinese Word Segmentation Bakeoff sponsored by the ACL-SIGHAN. We participated in all tracks at the bakeoff. The evaluation results show our system can achieve an F measure of 0.940-0.967 for different testing corpora.

1 Introduction

Word segmentation is very important for Chinese text processing, which is aiming at recognizing the implicit word boundaries in plain Chinese text. Over the past decades, great progress has been made with Chinese word segmentation technology. However, two difficulties still face us while developing a practical segmentation system for large open applications, i.e. the resolution of ambiguous segmentation and the identification of unknown or out-of-vocabulary (OOV) words.

In order to resolve the above two problems, we developed a purely statistical Chinese word segmentation system using a two-stage strategy. We participated in eight tracks at the Second International Chinese Word Segmentation Bakeoff sponsored by the ACL-SIGHAN, and tested our system on different testing corpora. The scored results show that our system is effective for most of ambiguous segmentation and unknown words in Chinese text. In this paper, we make a summary of this work and give some analysis on the results.

The rest of this paper is organized as follows: First in Section 2, we describe in brief a two-stage strategy for Chinese word segmentation. Then in Section 3, we give details about the settings or configuration of our system for different testing tracks, particularly the training data and the dictionaries used in our system. Finally, we report the results of our system at this bakeoff in Section 4, and give our conclusions on this work in Section 5.

2 Overview of the System

In practice, our system works in two major steps as follows:

The first step is a process of known word segmentation, which aims to segment an input sequence of Chinese characters into a sequence of known words that are listed in the system dictionary. In our current system, we apply a known word bigram model to perform this task (Fu and Luke, 2003; Fu and Luke, 2004; Fu and Luke, 2005).

Actually, known word segmentation is a process of disambiguation. Given a Chinese character string $C = c_1 c_2 \cdots c_n$, there are usually multiple possible segmentations of known words $W = w_1 w_2 \cdots w_m$ according to the system dictionary. The task of known word segmentation is to find a proper segmentation $\hat{W} = w_1 w_2 \cdots w_m$ that maximizes the probability $\prod_{i=1}^{m} P(w_i \mid w_{i-1})$, i.e.

$$\hat{W} = \arg\max_{W} P(W \mid C) \approx \arg\max_{W} \prod_{i=1}^{m} P(w_i \mid w_{i-1}) \quad (1)$$

The second step is actually a tagging task on the sequence of known words acquired in the first step, which intends to detect unknown words or out-of-vocabulary (OOV) words in the input. In this process, each known word yielded in the first step will be further assigned a proper tag that indicates whether the known word is an independent segmented word by itself or a beginning/middle/ending component of an OOV word (Fu and Luke, 2004). In order to improve our system, part-of-speech information is also introduced in some tracks such as the PKU open test and the AS open test. Furthermore, a lexicalized HMM tagger is developed to perform this task (Fu and Luke, 2004).

Given a sequence of known words $W = w_1 w_2 \cdots w_n$, the lexicalized HMM tagger attempt to find an appropriate sequence of tags $\hat{T} = t_1 t_2 \cdots t_n$ that maximizes the conditional probability $P(T \mid W)$, namely

$$\hat{T} = \arg\max_{T} P(T \mid W) \approx \arg\max_{T} \prod_{i=1}^{n} P(w_i \mid w_{i-1}, t_i) P(t_i \mid w_{i-1}, t_{i-1}) \tag{2}$$

3 Settings for Different Tracks

Table 1. Training corpora for different tracks

Table 1 presents the corpora used to train our system for different tracks. In the Academia Sinica (AS) open test and the Peking University (PKU) open test, our system is trained respectively using the *Sinica Corpus* (3.0) and *the PFR Corpus*. In all other tests, including all closed tests, City University of Hong Kong (CityU) open test and Microsoft Research (MSR) open test, we trained our system using the relevant training corpora provided for the bakeoff.

Track	Training Corpus	Word counts
AS-O	*The Sinica Corpus 3.0*	5,692,150
AS-C	AS corpus for Bakeoff 2005	5,449,698
CityU-O	CityU corpus for Bakeoff 2005	1,455,629
CityU-C	CityU corpus for Bakeoff 2005	1,455,629
MSR-O	MSR corpus for Bakeoff 2005	2,368,391
MSR-C	MSR corpus for Bakeoff 2005	2,368,391
PKU-O	*The PFR Corpus*	7,286,960
PKU-C	PKU corpus for Bakeoff 2005	1,109,947

Table 2 shows all the dictionaries used in our system for different tracks.

In the closed test, the system dictionaries are derived automatically from the relevant training corpora for this bakeoff by using the following three criteria: (1) Each character in the training corpus is taken as an independent entry and collected into the relevant system dictionary. (2) A standard Chinese word in the training corpus will enter to the relevant dictionary if it has four or less Chinese characters within it, and at the same time, its counts of occurrence in the corpus is observed to be larger than a threshold. In our current system, the threshold is set to 10 for the AS closed test and 5 for other closed tests. (3) For non-standard Chinese words such as numeral expressions, English words and punctuations, if they consist of multiple characters, they will be not included in the system dictionary.

As for the open test, some other dictionaries are applied. As can be seen from Table 2, *the CKIP Lexicon and Chinese Grammar* is used in both AS and CityU open test, and the *Grammatical Knowledge-base of Contemporary Chinese* developed by the Peking University is utilized in both PKU and MSR open test.

Track	System dictionary	# of entries
AS-O	*The CKIP Lexicon and Chinese Grammar*	84K
AS-C	Automatically extracted from AS corpus for Bakeoff 2005	30K
CityU-O	*The CKIP Lexicon and Chinese Grammar* (without part-of-speech)	84K
CityU-C	Automatically extracted from CityU corpus for Bakeoff 2005	22K
MSR-O	*The Grammatical Knowledge-base of Contemporary Chinese* (without part-of-speech)	65K
MSR-C	Automatically extracted from MSR corpus for Bakeoff 2005	17K
PKU-O	*The Grammatical Knowledge-base of Contemporary Chinese*	65K
PKU-C	Automatically extracted from PKU corpus for Bakeoff 2005	17K

Table 2. System dictionaries for different tracks

It should be noted that part-of-speech information is also utilized in the AS open test and the PKU open test, because part-of-speech information proved to be informative in identifying OOV words in Chinese text (Fu and Luke, 2004). Therefore, the training corpora for the two tests are tagged with part-of-speech, and entries in the relevant dictionaries are defined with their potential part-of-speech categories.

4 The Scored Results

In Bakeoff 2005, six measures are employed to score the performance of a word segmentation system, namely recall (*R*), precision (*P*), the evenly-weighted F-measure (*F*), out-of-vocabulary (OOV) rate for the test corpus, recall with respect to OOV words (R_{OOV}) or in-vocabulary words (R_{iv}).

In order to achieve a consistent evaluation of our system in both the closed test and the open test, OOV is defined in this paper as the set of words in the test corpus but not occurring in both the training corpus and the system dictionary. Furthermore, the additional two rates, i.e. OOV-C and OOV-D are used to denote the out-of-vocabulary rate with respect to the training corpus and the out-of-vocabulary rate with respect to the system dictionary, respectively. At the same time, the precision with regard to in-vocabulary words (P_{iv}) and OOV words (P_{OOV}) are also computed in this paper to give a more complete evalution of our system in unknown word identification.

Track	OOV-C	OOV-D	OOV
AS-O	0.043	0.096	0.039
AS-C	0.043	0.096	0.043
CityU-O	0.074	0.140	0.049
CityU-C	0.074	0.127	0.074
MSR-O	0.026	0.076	0.023
MSR-C	0.026	0.087	0.026
PKU-O	0.038	0.070	0.033
PKU-C	0.058	0.091	0.058

Table 3. OOV rates for different tracks

Track	F	R	P	R_{iv}	P_{iv}	R_{OOV}	P_{OOV}
AS-O	0.946	0.955	0.938	0.972	0.947	0.532	0.660
AS-C	0.940	0.947	0.934	0.966	0.949	0.523	0.566
CityU-O	0.941	0.944	0.938	0.962	0.956	0.592	0.599
CityU-C	0.939	0.944	0.933	0.969	0.952	0.626	0.677
MSR-O	0.967	0.969	0.966	0.978	0.977	0.586	0.537
MSR-C	0.962	0.962	0.962	0.972	0.977	0.592	0.499
PKU-O	0.962	0.959	0.965	0.963	0.970	0.835	0.816
PKU-C	0.944	0.943	0.944	0.961	0.958	0.656	0.700

Table 4. Scores for different tracks

The OOV rates and scores of our system are summarized respectively in Table 3 and Table 4. The results show that our system can achieve a F-measure of 0.940-0.967 for different testing corpora while the relevant OOV rates are from 0.023 to 0.074.

Although our system has achieved a promising performance, there is still much to be done to improve it. Firstly, our system is purely statistics-based, it cannot yield correct segmentations for all non-standard words (NSWs) such as numeral expressions and English strings in Chinese text. Secondly, known word segmentation and unknown word identification are taken as two independent stages in our system. This strategy is obviously simple and more easily applicable (Fu and Luke, 2003). Although the known word bigram model can partly resolve this problem, it is not always effective for some complicated strings that contains a mixture of ambiguities and unknown words, such as "31 日夜" and the fragment "中行长葛" in the sentence "中行长葛支行注重健身".

5 Conclusions

This paper presents a two-stage statistical word segmentation system for Chinese. We participated in all testing tracks at the second Sighan bakeoff. The scored results show that our system can achieve a F-measure of 0.940-0.967 as a whole for different corpora. This indicates that the proposed system is effective for most ambiguous segmentations and unknown words in Chinese test. For future work, we hope to improve our system by incorporating some pattern rules to handle complicated ambiguous fragments and non-standard words in Chinese text.

References

Guohong Fu, and Kang-Kwong Luke. 2003. A two-stage statistical word segmentation system for Chinese. In: *Proceedings of the 2nd SIGHAN Workshop on Chinese Language Processing*, Sapporo, Japan, 156-159.

Guohong Fu, and Kang-Kwong Luke. 2004. Chinese unknown word identification as known word tagging. In: *Proceedings of the Third IEEE International Conference on Machine Learning and Cybernetics (ICMLC 2004)*, Shanghai, China, 2612-2617.

Guohong Fu, and Kang-Kwong Luke. 2005. Chinese unknown word identification using class-based LM. *Lecture Notes in Computer Science (IJCNLP 2004)*, 3248: 704-713.

A Conditional Random Field Word Segmenter for Sighan Bakeoff 2005

Huihsin Tseng
Dept. of Linguistics
University of Colorado
Boulder, CO 80302
tseng@colorado.edu

Pichuan Chang, Galen Andrew, Daniel Jurafsky, Christopher Manning
Stanford Natural Language Processing Group
Stanford University
Stanford, CA 94309
{pichuan, pupochik, jurafsky, manning}@stanford.edu

Abstract

We present a Chinese word segmentation system submitted to the closed track of Sighan bakeoff 2005. Our segmenter was built using a conditional random field sequence model that provides a framework to use a large number of linguistic features such as character identity, morphological and character reduplication features. Because our morphological features were extracted from the training corpora automatically, our system was not biased toward any particular variety of Mandarin. Thus, our system does not overfit the variety of Mandarin most familiar to the system's designers. Our final system achieved a F-score of 0.947 (AS), 0.943 (HK), 0.950 (PK) and 0.964 (MSR).

1 Introduction

The 2005 Sighan Bakeoff included four different corpora, Academia Sinica (AS), City University of Hong Kong (HK), Peking University (PK), and Microsoft Research Asia (MSR), each of which has its own definition of a word.

In the 2003 Sighan Bakeoff (Sproat & Emerson 2003), no single model performed well on all corpora included in the task. Rather, systems tended to do well on corpora largely drawn from a set of similar Mandarin varieties to the one they were originally developed for. Across corpora, variation is seen in both the lexicons and also in the word segmentation standards. We concluded that, for future systems, generalization across such different Mandarin varieties is crucial. To this end, we proposed a new model using character identity, morphological and character reduplication features in a conditional random field modeling framework.

2 Algorithm

Our system builds on research into conditional random field (CRF), a statistical sequence modeling framework first introduced by Lafferty et al. (2001). Work by Peng et al. (2004) first used this framework for Chinese word segmentation by treating it as a binary decision task, such that each character is labeled either as the beginning of a word or the continuation of one. Gaussian priors were used to prevent overfitting and a quasi-Newton method was used for parameter optimization.

The probability assigned to a label sequence for a particular sequence of characters by a CRF is given by the equation below:

$$P_{\lambda}(Y \mid X) = \frac{1}{Z(X)} \exp\left(\sum_{c \in C} \sum_{k} \lambda_k f_k \;(Y_c, X, c) \right)$$

Y is the label sequence for the sentence, X is the sequence of unsegmented characters, Z(X) is a normalization term, f_k is a feature function, and c indexes into characters in the sequence being labeled.

A CRF allows us to utilize a large number of n-gram features and different state sequence based features and also provides an intuitive framework for the use of morphological features.

3 Feature engineering

3.1 Features

The linguistic features used in our model fall into three categories: character identity *n*-grams, morphological and character reduplication features.

For each state, the character identity features (Ng & Low 2004, Xue & Shen 2003, Goh et al. 2003) are represented using feature functions that key off of the identity of the character in the current, proceeding and subsequent positions. Specifically, we used four types of unigram feature functions, designated as C_0 (current character), C_1 (next character), C_{-1} (previous character), C_{-2} (the character two characters back). Furthermore, four types of bi-gram features were used, and are notationally designated here as conjunctions of the previously specified unigram features, C_0C_1, $C_{-1}C_0$, $C_{-1}C1$, $C_{-2}C_{-1}$, and C_2C_0.

Given that unknown words are normally more than one character long, when representing the morphological features as feature functions, such feature functions keyed off the morphological information extracted from both the proceeding state and the current state. Our morphological features are based upon the intuition regarding unknown word features given in Gao et al. (2004). Specifically, their idea was to use productive affixes and characters that only occurred independently to predict boundaries of unknown words. To construct a table containing affixes of unknown words, rather than using threshold-filtered affix tables in a separate unknown word model as was done in Gao et al. (2004), we first extracted rare words from a corpus and then collected the first and last characters to construct the prefix and suffix tables. For the table of individual character words, we collected an individual character word table for each corpus of the characters that always occurred alone as a separate word in the given corpus. We also collected a list of bi-grams from each training corpus to distinguish known strings from unknown. Adopting all the features together in a model and using the automatically generated morphological tables prevented our system from manually overfitting the Mandarin varieties we are most familiar with.

The tables are used in the following ways:

1) C_{-1}+C_0 unknown word feature functions were created for each specific pair of characters in the bi-gram tables. Such feature functions are active if the characters in the respective states match the corresponding feature function's characters. These feature functions are designed to distinguish known strings from unknown.

2) C_{-1}, C_0, and C_1 individual character feature functions were created for each character in the individual character word table, and are likewise active if the respective character matches the feature function's character.

3) C_{-1} prefix feature functions are defined over characters in the prefix table, and fire if the character in the proceeding state matches the feature function's character.

4) C_0 suffix feature functions are defined over suffix table characters, and fire if the character in the current state matches the feature function's character.

Additionally, we also use reduplication feature functions that are active based on the repetition of a given character. We used two such feature functions, one that fires if the previous and the current character, C_{-1} and C_0, are identical and one that does so if the subsequent and the previous characters, C_{-1} and C_1, are identical.

Most features appeared in the first-order templates with a few of character identity features in the both zero-order and first-order templates. We also did normalization of punctuations due to the fact that Mandarin has a huge variety of punctuations.

Table 1 shows the number of data features and lambda weights in each corpus.

Table 1 The number of features in each corpus

	# of data features	*# of lambda weights*
AS	2,558,840	8,076,916
HK	2,308,067	7,481,164
PK	1,659,654	5,377,146
MSR	3,634,585	12,468,890

3.2 Experiments

3.2.1 Results on Sighan bakeoff 2003

Experiments done while developing this system showed that its performance was significantly better than that of Peng et al. (2004).

As seen in Table 2, our system's F-score was 0.863 on CTB (Chinese Treebank from University of Pennsylvania) versus 0.849 F on Peng et al. (2004). We do not at present have a good understanding of which aspects of our system give it superior performance.

Table 2 Comparisons of Peng et al. (2004) and our F-score on the closed track in Sighan bakeoff 2003

Sighan Bakeoff 2003	***Our F-score***	***F-score Peng et al. (2004)***
CTB	0.863	0.849
AS	0.970	0.956
HK	0.947	0.928
PK	0.953	0.941

3.2.2 Results on Sighan bakeoff 2005

Our final system achieved a F-score of 0.947 (AS), 0.943 (HK), 0.950 (PK) and 0.964 (MSR). This shows that our system successfully generalized and achieved state of the art performance on all four corpora.

Table 3 Performance of the features cumulatively, starting with the *n*-gram.

F-score	***AS***	***HK***	***PK***	***MSR***
***n*-gram**	0.943	0.946	0.950	0.961
***n*-gram (PU fixed)**		0.953		
+Unk&redupl	0.947	0.943	0.950	0.964
+Unk&redupl (PU fixed)		0.952		

Table 3 lists our results on the four corpora. We give our results using just character identity based features; character identity features plus unknown words and reduplication features. Our unknown word features only helped on AS and MSR. Both of these corpora have words that have more characters than HK and PK. This indicates that our unknown word features were more useful for corpora with segmentation standards that tend to result in longer words.

In the HK corpus, when we added in unknown word features, our performance dropped. However, we found that the testing data uses different punctuation than the training set. Our system could not distinguish new word characters from new punctuation, since having a complete punctuation list is considered external knowledge for closed track systems. If the new punctuation were not unknown to us, our performance on HK data would have gone up to 0.952 F and the unknown word features would have not hurt the system too much.

Table 4 present recalls (R), precisions (P), f-scores (F) and recalls on both unknown (R_{oov}) and known words (R_{iv}).

Table 4 Detailed performances of each corpus

	R	***P***	***F***	R_{oov}	R_{iv}
AS	0.950	0.943	0.947	0.718	0.960
HK	0.941	0.946	0.943	0.698	0.961
HK (PU-fix)	0.952	0.952	0.952	0.791	0.965
PK	0.946	0.954	0.950	0.787	0.956
MSR	0.962	0.966	0.964	0.717	0.968

3.3 Error analysis

Our system performed reasonably well on morphologically complex new words, such as 電纜線 (CABLE in AS) and 殺人案 (MURDER CASE in PK), where 線 (LINE) and 案 (CASE) are suffixes. However, it over-generalized to words with frequent suffixes such as 灼人 (it should be 灼 人 "to burn someone" in PK) and 过头 (it should be 回 过 头 "to look backward" in PK). For the corpora that considered 4 character idioms as a word, our system combined most of new idioms together. This differs greatly from the results that one would likely obtain with a more traditional MaxMatch based technique, as such an algorithm would segment novel idioms.

One short coming of our system is that it is not robust enough to distinguish the difference between ordinal numbers and numbers with measure nouns. For example, 三年 (3rd year) and 三年 (three years) are not distinguishable to our system. In order to avoid this problem, it might require having more syntactic knowledge than was implicitly given in the training data.

Finally, some errors are due to inconsistencies in the gold segmentation of non-*hanzi* character. For example, "Pentium4" is a word, but "PC133" is two words. Sometimes, −8℃ is a word, but sometimes it is segmented into two words.

4 Conclusion

Our system used a conditional random field sequence model in conjunction with character identity features, morphological features and character reduplication features. We extracted our morphological information automatically to prevent overfitting Mandarin from particular Mandarin-speaking area. Our final system achieved a F-score of 0.947 (AS), 0.943 (HK), 0.950 (PK) and 0.964 (MSR).

5 Acknowledgment

Thanks to Kristina Toutanova for her generous help and to Jenny Rose Finkel who developed such a great conditional random field package. This work was funded by the Advanced Research and Development Activity's Advanced Question Answering for Intelligence Program, National Science Foundation award IIS-0325646 and a Stanford Graduate Fellowship.

References

Lafferty, John, A. McCallum, and F. Pereira. 2001. Conditional Random Field: Probabilistic Models for Segmenting and Labeling Sequence Data. In *ICML* 18.

Gao, Jianfeng Andi Wu, Mu Li, Chang-Ning Huang, Hongqiao Li, Xinsong Xia and Haowei Qin. 2004. Adaptive Chinese word segmentation. In *ACL-2004*.

Goh, Chooi-Ling, Masayuki Asahara, Yuji Matsumoto. 2003. Chinese unknown word identification using character-based tagging and chunking. In ACL 2003 Interactive Poster/Demo Sessions.

Ng, Hwee Tou and Jin Kiat Low. 2004. Chinese Part-of-Speech Tagging: One-at-a-Time or All-at-Once? Word-Based or Character-Based? In *EMNLP* 9.

Peng, Fuchun, Fangfang Feng and Andrew McCallum. 2004. Chinese segmentation and new word detection using conditional random fields. In *COLING 2004*.

Sproat, Richard and Tom Emerson. 2003. The first international Chinese word segmentation bakeoff. In *SIGHAN 2*.

Xue, Nianwen and Libin Shen. 2003. Chinese Word Segmentation as LMR Tagging. In *SIGHAN 2*.

Chinese Word Segmentation with Multiple Postprocessors in HIT-IRLab

Huipeng Zhang Ting Liu Jinshan Ma Xiantao Liao
Information Retrieval Lab, Harbin Institute of Technology, Harbin, 150001 CHINA
{zhp,tliu,mjs,taozi}@ir.hit.edu.cn

Abstract

This paper presents the results of the system IRLAS[1] from HIT-IRLab in the Second International Chinese Word Segmentation Bakeoff. IRLAS consists of several basic components and multiple postprocessors. The basic components include basic segmentation, factoid recognition, and named entity recognition. These components maintain a segment graph together. The postprocessors include merging of adjoining words, morphologically derived word recognition, and new word identification. These postprocessors do some modifications on the best word sequence which is selected from the segment graph. Our system participated in the open and closed tracks of PK corpus and ranked #4 and #3 respectively. Our scores were very close to the highest level. It proves that our system has reached the current state of the art.

1 Introduction

IRLAS participated in both the open and closed tracks of PK corpus. The sections below descript in detail the components of our system and the tracks we participated in.

The structure of this paper is as follows. Section 2 presents the system description. Section 3 describes in detail the tracks we participated in. Section 4 gives some experiments and discussions. Section 5 enumerates some external factors that affect our performance. Section 6 gives our conclusion.

2 System Description

2.1 Basic Segmentation

When a line is input into the system, it is first split into sentences separated by period. The reason to split a line into sentences is that in named entity recognition, the processing of several shorter sentences can reach a higher named entity recall rate than that of a long sentence. The reason to split the line only by period is for the simplicity for programming, and the sentences separated by period are short enough to process.

Then every sentence is segmented into single atoms. For example, a sentence like "HIT-IRLab 参加了第二届 SIGHAN 分词评测。" will be segmented as "HIT-IRLab/参/加/了/第/二/届/SIGHAN/分/词/评/测/。".

After atom segmentation, a segment graph is created. The number of nodes in the graph is the number of atoms plus 1, and every atom corresponds to an arc in the graph.

Then all the words in the dictionary[2] that appear in the sentence will be added to the segment graph. The graph contains various information such as the bigram possibility of every word. Figure 1 shows the segment graph of the above sentence after basic segmentation.

2.2 Factoid Recognition

After basic segmentation, a graph with all the atoms and all the words in the dictionary is set up. On this basis, we find out all the factoids

[1] IRLAS is the abbreviation for "Information Retrieval Lab Lexical Analysis System".

[2] The dictionary is trained with training corpus.

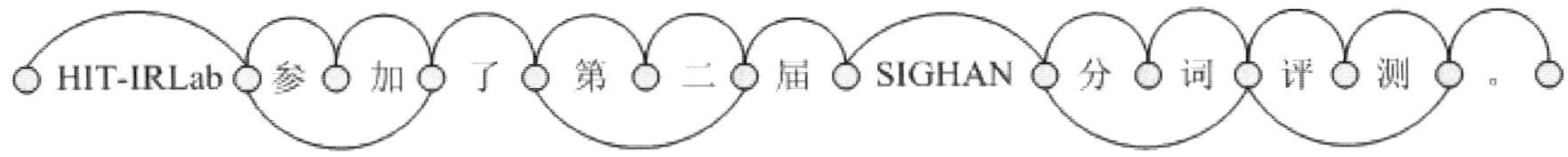

Figure 1: The segment graph
Note: the probability of each word is not shown in the graph.

such as numbers, times and e-mails with a set of rules. Then, we also add all these factoids to the segment graph.

2.3 Named Entity Recognition

Then we will recognize the named entities such as persons and locations. First, we select N[3] best paths from the segment graph with Dijkstra algorithm. Then for every path of the N+1 paths[4] (N best paths and the atom path), we perform a process of Roles Tagging with HMM model (Zhang et al. 2003). The process of it is much like that of Part of Speech Tagging. Then with the best role sequence of every path, we can find out all the named entities and add them to the segment graph as usual. Take the sentence "张会鹏是个好学生。" for example. After basic segmentation and factoid recognition, the N+1 paths are as follows:

张/会/鹏/是/个/好/学生/。
张/会/鹏/是/个/好/学/生/。

Then for each path, the process of Roles Tagging is performed and the following role sequences are generated:

X/S/W/N/O/O/O/O[5]
X/S/W/N/O/O/O/O/O

From these role sequences, we can find out that "XSW" is a 3-character Chinese name. So the word "张会鹏" is recognized as a person name and be added to the segment graph.

[3] N is a constant which is 8 in our system.
[4] It may be smaller than N+1 if the sentence is short enough; exactly, N+1 is the upper bound of the path number.
[5] X, S, W, N and O are all roles for person name recognition, X is surname, S is the first character of given name, W is the second character of given name, N is the word following a person name, and O is other remote context. We defined 17 roles for person name recognition and 10 roles for location name recognition.

2.4 Merging of Adjoining Words

After the steps above, the segment graph is completed and a best word sequence is generated with Dijkstra algorithm. This merging operation and all the following operations are done to the best word sequence.

There are many inconsistencies in the PK corpus. For example, in PK training corpus, the word "就是" sometimes is considered as one word, but sometimes is considered as two separate words as "就 是". The inconsistencies lower the system's performance to some extent.

To solve this problem, we first train from the training corpus the probability of a word to be one word and the probability to be two separate words. Then we perform a process of merging: if two adjoining words in the best word sequence are more likely to be one word, then we just merge them together.

2.5 Morphologically Derived Word Recognition

To deal with the words with the postfix like "性", "者", "率" and so on, we perform the process to merge the preceding word and the postfix into one word. We train a list of postfixes from the training corpus. Then we scan the best word sequence, if there is a single character word that appears in the postfix list, we merge the preceding word and this postfix into one word. For example, a best word sequence like "长跑 者 身 披 彩带" will be converted to "长跑者 身 披 彩带" after this operation.

2.6 New Word Identification

As for the words that are not in the dictionary and cannot be identified with the steps above, we perform a process of New Word Identification (NWI). We train from the training corpus the probability of a word to be independent and the probability to be a special part of another word. In our system, we only consider the words that have one or two characters. Then we scan the best word sequence, if the product of the probabilities of two adjoining words exceed a threshold, then we merge the two words into one word.

Take the word "甘薯" for example. It is segmented as "甘 薯" after all the above steps since this word is not in the dictionary. We find that the word "甘" has a probability of 0.83 to be the first character of a two character word, and the word "薯" has a probability of 0.94 to be the last character of a two character word. The product of them is 0.78 which is larger than 0.65, which is the threshold in our system. So the word "甘薯" is recognized as a single word.

3 Tracks

3.1 Closed Track

As for the PK closed track, we first extract all the common words and tokens from the training corpus and set up a dictionary of 55,335 entries. Then we extract every kind of named entity respectively. With these named entities, we train parameters for Roles Tagging. We also train all the other parameters mentioned in Section 2 with the training corpus.

3.2 Open Track

The PK open track is similar to closed one. In open track, we use all the 6 months corpus of *People's Daily* and set up a dictionary of 107,749 entries. Additionally, we find 101 new words from the Web and add them to the dictionary. We train the parameters of named entity recognition with a person list and a location list in our laboratory. The training of other parameters is the same with closed track.

4 Experiments and Discussions

We do several experiments on PK test corpus to see the contribution of each postprocessor. We cut off one postprocessor at a time from the complete system and record its F-score. The evaluation results are shown in Table 1. In the table, MDW represents Morphologically Derived Word Recognition, and NWI represents New Word Identification.

	PK open	PK closed
Complete System	96.5%	94.9%
Without Merging	96.3%	94.7%
Without MDW	96.6%	94.4%
Without NWI	96.5%	94.9%

Table 1: Evaluation results of IRLAS with each postprocessor cut off at a time

From Table 1, we can come to some interesting facts:

! The Merging of Adjoining Words has good effect on both open and closed tracks. So we can conclude that this module can solve the problem of inconsistent training corpus to some extent.

! Morphologically Derived Word Recognition does some harm in open track, but it has a very good effect in closed track. Maybe it is because that in open track, we can make a comparatively larger dictionary since we can use any resource we have. So most MDWs[6] are in the dictionary and the MDWs that are not in the dictionary are mostly difficult to recognize. So it does more harm than good in many cases. But in closed track, we have a small dictionary and many common MDWs are not in the dictionary. So it does much more good in closed track.

! New Word Identification is minimal in both open and closed tracks. Maybe it is because that the above steps have recognized the most OOV words and it is hard to recognize any more new words.

5 External Factors That Affect Our Performance

The difference on the definition of words is the main factor that affects our performance. In many cases such as "异彩纷呈", "极大", "世纪颂" are all considered as one word in our system but not so in the PK gold standard corpus. Another factor is the inconsistencies in training corpus, although this problem has been solved to some extent with the module of merging. But

[6] It refers to Morphologically Derived Words.

because the inconsistencies also exist in test corpus and there are some instances that a word is more likely to be a single word in training corpus but more likely to be separated into two words in test corpus. For example, the word "紧跟" is more likely to be a single word in training corpus but is more likely to be separated into two words in test corpus. There is another factor that affects MDW, many postfixes in our system are not considered as postfixes in PK gold standard corpus. For example, the word "太空港" is recognized as a MDW in our system since "港" is a postfix, however, it is segmented into two separate words as "太空 港" in PK gold standard corpus.

6 Conclusion

Through the second SIGHAN bakeoff, we find the segmentation model and the algorithm in our system is effective and the multiple postprocessors we use can also enhance the performance of our system. At the same time, we also find some problems of us. It also has potential for us to improve our system. Take MDW for example, we can make use of more features such as the POS and the length of the preceding word to enhance the recall and precision rate. The bakeoff points out the direction for us to improve our system.

References

Huaping Zhang, Qun Liu, Hongkui Yu, Xueqi Cheng, Shuo Bai, *Chinese Named Entity Recognition Using Role Model*. International Journal of Computational Linguistics and Chinese Language Processing, 2003, Vol.8(2)

Andi Wu, Zixin Jiang, 2000. *Statistically-Enhanced New Word Identification in a Rule-Based Chinese System*. In Proceedings of the Second Chinese Language Processing Workshop, pp. 46-51, HKUST, Hong Kong.

Huaping Zhang, Hongkui Yu, Deyi Xiong, Qun Liu, *HHMM-based Chinese Lexical Analyzer ICTCLAS*. In Proceedings of the Second SIGHAN Workshop on Chinese Language Processing, July 11-12, 2003, Sapporo, Japan.

Aitao Chen, *Chinese Word Segmentation Using Minimal Linguistics Knowledge*. In Proceedings of the Second SIGHAN Workshop on Chinese Language Processing, July 11-12, 2003, Sapporo, Japan.

Andi Wu, *Chinese Word Segmentation in MSR-NLP*. In Proceedings of the Second SIGHAN Workshop on Chinese Language Processing, July 11-12, 2003, Sapporo, Japan.

Maximal Match Chinese Segmentation Augmented by Resources Generated from a Very Large Dictionary for Post-Processing

Ka-Po Chow **Andy C. Chin** **Wing Fu Tsoi**
Language Information Sciences Research Centre
City University of Hong Kong
Tat Chee Avenue, Kowloon, Hong Kong
{kapo.chow,cochin,rlwftsoi}@cityu.edu.hk

Abstract

We used a production segmentation system, which draws heavily on a large dictionary derived from processing a large amount (over 150 million Chinese characters) of synchronous textual data gathered from various Chinese speech communities, including Beijing, Hong Kong, Taipei, and others. We run this system in two tracks in the Second International Chinese Word Segmentation Bakeoff, with Backward Maximal Matching (right-to-left) as the primary mechanism. We also explored the use of a number of supplementary features offered by the large dictionary in post-processing, in an attempt to resolve ambiguities and detect unknown words. While the results might not have reached their fullest potential, they nevertheless reinforced the importance and usefulness of a large dictionary as a basis for segmentation, and the implication of following a uniform standard on the segmentation performance on data from various sources.

1 Introduction

Our team has participated in two tracks of the ACL SIGHAN-sponsored Second International Chinese Word Segmentation Bakeoff, namely Academia Sinica open (ASo) and Peking University open (PKo). The production segmentation system we used draws heavily on a large dictionary derived from processing a very large amount of synchronous textual data. In Section 2, our segmentation flow for the current Bakeoff will be described, and in Section 3, the results will be evaluated and analysed. Errors will be analysed and implications discussed in Section 4, followed by a conclusion in Section 5.

2 Segmentation Framework

The major resource of our segmentation system is a large dictionary. In the following, we describe the main segmentation mechanism based on maximal matching, and other supplementary features for post-processing attempted in the current Bakeoff.

2.1 Dictionary-based Segmentation

The primary mechanism of segmentation makes use of a large dictionary derived from processing a large amount (over 150 million Chinese characters) of synchronous textual data, mostly printed news, gathered from various Chinese speech communities, including Beijing, Hong Kong, Taipei, and others, following a uniform segmentation standard. The dictionary has now grown to a size of over 800,000 word types, with frequencies of each entry being tracked closely. For this Bakeoff, additional items from the respective training data were also included in the existing dictionary for segmentation. Thus unsegmented texts will first go through a process of Backward Maximal Matching (BMM) segmentation equipped with the combined dictionary.

2.2 Supplementary Features

2.2.1 Rule Development

According to specific divergence of the segmentation standard of each test corpus from our production standard, a set of general adaptation rules were applied to transform the texts to achieve "standard complacency" as much as possible. The adaptation rules vary in nature, depending on how intense the segmentation standard differences are between each test corpus and our own. Hence some rules are based on linguistic structures while others are based on particular treatment of elements like numerals and units.

These adaptation rules are coupled with a set of heuristic segmentation disambiguation rules derived from our long-term and extensive processing of text data. Such rules are based on BMM, and amount to around 20,000 at the time of writing. Each rule has gone through careful consideration before putting to real production use, to ensure that they produce correct results in most cases without overgeneralisation.

2.2.2 Statistical BMM/FMM Comparison and Replacement

After texts were segmented by BMM, the forward counterpart (Forward Maximal Matching, FMM) was also done for comparison, as the discrepancies between the two segmented texts often indicate potential ambiguities. Statistical information such as the frequency distributions of the segmented units in question were obtained from our large dictionary. By comparing the independent joint likelihood of the two combinations, segmented units with exceptionally low frequency are likely to be disregarded, allowing us to choose the correct segmentation. For example, in the test data, the phrase 開設有 is segmented as 開/設有 by the backward approach, whereas 開設/有 will be obtained if segmented forwardly. The latter segmented alternative, 開設/有, is more likely to appear in the text.

2.2.3 Unknown Word Detection

One of the most challenging issues in Chinese word segmentation is the treatment of unknown words which can be further divided into two categories: new words (NWs) and named entities (NEs). In our treatment of unknown words, a slight distinction was made between Chinese NEs and other NWs including foreign names. The detection processes are similar but statistical data were gathered from different portions of our textual data. When a sequence of single characters is hit, windows of two and three characters (only nominal morphemes were considered) were extracted to form "potential NE/NW candidates". The likelihood of these characters being monosyllabic words (i.e. out-word) and that of being part of multi-syllabic words (i.e. in-word) were compared to make the best guess whether they should be combined or segmented.

For NE detection, the in-word statistics was based on all the multi-syllabic named entities in the Taipei portion from our dictionary and the out-word statistics on the rest of it. The in-word frequency of a given character is thus the number of times the character appears within a multi-syllabic named entity. The in-word probability is the in-word frequency divided by the total number of times the character appears in all our textual data. The independent joint in-word and out-word probabilities were computed and compared for each candidate, which would be combined as a word if the in-word probability is greater than the out-word probability and the first character in the candidate is within a list of Chinese surnames, again collected from all textual data.

For NW detection, the in-word statistics was based on all the multi-syllabic words in our dictionary. For every newly combined word, neighbouring prefixes and suffixes (according to those provided in the segmentation standard) were also detected and combined, if any. A list of foreign names and all the characters appearing in them was also extracted from our dictionary. When a new word is detected, its neighbouring words would be scanned and would be combined if they are within this foreign name list, thus enabling the identification of names like 芬妮亞當.

3 Results and Analysis

The results of the different stages of segmentation are shown in Table 1 and Table 2.

In both test corpora, the primary dictionary-based segmentation alone has achieved a significant percentage (over 95% in recall and over 90% in precision). This exemplifies that the rich vocabulary we have offers a useful resource for language engineering, and provides a solid platform for further enhancement.

Post-processing with supplementary features from the dictionary shows consistent incremental improvement in segmentation. The scores (F-measure) due to FMM and BMM with heuristic rules demonstrate a relatively substantial gap at the very beginning, largely because of the heuristic rules developed and accumulated through the precise and systematic processing of our sizable textual data.

Operation	R	P	F	R_{OOV}	R_{IV}
FMM only	0.953	0.903	0.927	0.658	0.966
BMM, plus heuristic rules	0.960	0.915	0.937	0.661	0.974
Comparison and replacement	0.964	0.921	0.942	0.663	0.978
Unknown word detection	0.966	0.931	0.948	0.715	0.977
Official results*	0.943	0.931	0.937	0.531	0.962

Table 1: Results for ASo using combined dictionary

Operation	R	P	F	R_{OOV}	R_{IV}
FMM only	0.957	0.928	0.942	0.842	0.964
BMM, plus heuristic rules	0.967	0.947	0.957	0.849	0.974
Comparison and replacement	0.969	0.951	0.960	0.851	0.977
Official results*	0.952	0.951	0.951	0.784	0.962

Table 2: Results for PKo using combined dictionary

The performance of unknown word detection can be seen from the leap in R_{OOV} after the operation. It increases remarkably from 0.663 to 0.715, offsetting the fall in R_{IV}, which drops by 0.001 and this may be due to the concatenation of some monosyllabic morphemes which are supposed to be independent words.

The results of the comparison between FMM and BMM are summarized in Table 3 and Table 4. A noticeable drawback of such comparison is that some phrases will be mis-segmented in either direction. For example, the phrase 絲毫不覺得 will be segmented backwardly into 絲/毫不/覺得 but 絲毫/不覺/得 forwardly. The correct segmentation, 絲毫/不/覺得, cannot be attained in both cases. Hence as an experiment, for any combination of five characters which are segmented into 1/2/2 pattern by BMM and 2/2/1 pattern by FMM, the 2/1/2 pattern will be also tested against the overall probabilities. For the former example, 絲毫/不/覺得 will override the other two.

Table 3 shows that the number of correct replacements from FMM is 399 in the AS test corpus, combining the gain from the reshuffling of 5-character strings, the total is 408. Since the default choice is the BMM segmented texts, the sum 408 is the total gain from this BMM/FMM comparison, while 77 correct segmented texts have been mis-replaced, the gain/loss ratio is 5.30. This means that our system only loses 1 correct segmentation in exchange of gaining 5.3 correct ones.

Likewise in the case of the PK test corpus in Table 4, the gain/loss ratio is 4.67. The ratio is smaller than that for the AS test corpus. It is thus evident that the comparison and replacement by means of BMM and FMM offers a substantial achievement in the accuracy of the segmentation process.

	BMM	FMM	Re-shuffle	Total
Correct Replacement	1124	399	9	1532
Incorrect Replacement	281	267	0	548
Mis-replaced Correct Segmentation	77	78	/	155

Table 3: Analysis of BMM/FMM comparison for ASo

	BMM	FMM	Re-shuffle	Total
Correct Replacement	1097	254	3	1354
Incorrect Replacement	131	117	2	250
Mis-replaced Correct Segmentation	55	33	/	88

Table 4: Analysis of BMM/FMM comparison for PKo

We are aware that the performance of replacement may be improved by using probabilities of *n*-grams, conditional probabilities involving the boundary words, and perhaps by considering all possibilities of segmentations for the same string of texts, as in some other segmentation systems. On the semantic level, the overall message of a paragraph can be examined as well by gathering statistics of collocating words. The ordering of applying these algorithms, however, should be important, and how they interplay with one another will be an arena to explore.

Although we have not incorporated such enhancement measures into our system in this exercise, the dictionary can nevertheless support such extension with the necessary statistical data. All previous results are based on the first-stage of segmentation with a large dictionary. Since

* The reported figures differ from those computed on our platform, probably due to system differences. The official scorer program is publicly available and described in (Sproat and Emerson, 2003).

we had processed texts from different Chinese speech communities including Beijing, Hong Kong, Taipei, and others, the dictionary used for segmentation also consists of all words appearing in any of these communities. In order to investigate the effect of locality on the dictionary used in segmentation, two independent dictionaries have been generated from the Beijing portion and Taipei portion, and all the above stages were repeated for the two test corpora, with results shown below in Table 5 and Table 6.

Operation	R	P	F	R_{OOV}	R_{IV}
FMM only	0.942	0.891	0.916	0.602	0.957
BMM, plus heuristic rules	0.948	0.901	0.924	0.603	0.964
Comparison and replacement	0.951	0.907	0.929	0.605	0.967

Table 5: Results for ASo using Taipei dictionary

Operation	R	P	F	R_{OOV}	R_{IV}
FMM only	0.954	0.923	0.938	0.800	0.963
BMM, plus heuristic rules	0.969	0.941	0.955	0.814	0.978
Comparison and replacement	0.971	0.946	0.958	0.815	0.981

Table 6: Results for PKo using Beijing dictionary

The results show that dictionaries derived from specific communities alone yield slightly smaller F-measures than that derived from all places together. The largest difference lies in R_{OOV} where it is 0.605 and 0.663 for ASo and 0.815 and 0.851 for PKo, confirming the significance of adopting a large and all-rounded dictionary in word segmentation.

4 Error Analysis

We have examined the discrepancies between the gold standard files and our resultant segmented files, and it is found that the segmentation errors can be basically classified into several categories.

The errors due to standard divergence have the most impact. For example, 性/取向 is considered the correct segmentation in the AS test corpus while 性取向 is one word in our large dictionary.

Inconsistencies within the same corpus (both training and test corpora) also give rise to performance fluctuations. There are cases where the same phrase is segmented differently. For example, in the AS training corpus, both 藝術/工作/者 and 藝術/工作者 are found. Similar cases are also found in the test corpus, e.g. 性/工作/者 vs. 性/工作者.

Another factor that affects the segmentation performance over the PK corpus is encoding conversion. Our production system is based primarily on materials which are in BIG5 encoding, specifically traditional Chinese characters in the BIG5 encoding space. Since the given test data are in simplified Chinese characters, a process of encoding conversion to BIG5 is in place. Such a conversion is a one-to-many mapping and thus some original words will be distorted, influencing segmentation correctness.

5 Conclusion

We have reported our results on two open tracks of the Second International Chinese Word Segmentation Bakeoff, based on a production segmentation system, which draws heavily on a large and unique dictionary. The dictionary is derived from processing a very large amount of synchronous textual data gathered from various Chinese speech communities, based on a uniform segmentation standard. It is shown that the primary dictionary-based BMM segmentation alone contribute the most in our segmentation system, with over 95% in recall and over 90% in precision, attributable to the large size of the dictionary, although our uniform segmentation standard may not have realized its full potential given the test corpora with different and changing standards. We also explored supplementary features offered by the large dictionary in post-processing, and results incrementally improve. Hence our large dictionary derived from our uniform treatment of synchronous data provides a useful resource and provides a good platform for further extension in various aspects of language engineering.

References

Richard Sproat and Tom Emerson. 2003. *The First International Chinese Word Segmentation Bakeoff.* In proceedings of the Second SIGHAN Workshop on Chinese Language Processing, July 11-12, 2003, Sapporo, Japan.

Chinese Word Segmentation based on Mixing Model

Wei Jiang **Jian Zhao** **Yi Guan** **Zhiming Xu**
ITNLP, Harbin Institute of Technology, Heilongjiang Province, 150001 China
jiangwei@insun.hit.edu.cn

Abstract

This paper presents our recent work for participation in the Second International Chinese Word Segmentation Bakeoff. According to difficulties, we divide word segmentation into several sub-tasks, which are solved by mixed language models, so as to take advantage of each approach in addressing special problems. The experiment indicated that this system achieved 96.7% and 97.2% in F-measure in PKU and MSR open test respectively.

1 Introduction

Word is a logical semantic and syntactic unit in natural language. So word segmentation is the foundation of most Chinese NLP tasks. Though much progress has been made in the last two decades, there is no existing model that can solve all the problems perfectly at present. So we try to apply different language models to solve each special sub-task, due to "No Free Lunch Theorem" and "Ugly Duckling Theorem".

Our system participated in the Second International Chinese Word Segmentation Bakeoff (henceforce, the bakeoff) held in 2005. Recently, we have done more work in dealing with three main sub-tasks: (1) Segmentation disambiguation; (2) Named entities recognition; (3) New words[1] detection. We apply different approachs to solve above three problems, and all the modules are integrated into a pragmatic system (**ELUS**). Due to the limitation of available resource, some kinds of features, e.g. POS, have been erased in our participation system. This segmenter will be briefly describled in this paper.

[1] New words refer to this kind of out-of –vocabulary words that are neither recognized named entities or factoid words nor morphological words.

2 ELUS Segmenter

All the words are categorized into five types: Lexicon words (LW), Factoid words (FT), Morphologically derived words (MDW), Named entities (NE), and New words (NW). Accordingly, four main modules are included to identify each kind of words, as shown in Figure 1.

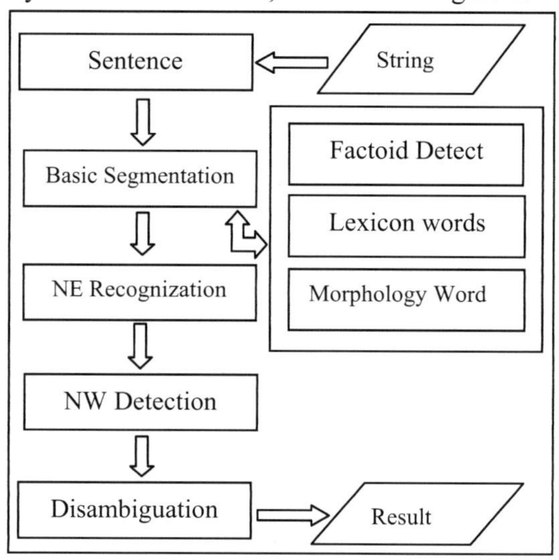

Figure 1 ELUS Segmenter

Class-based trigram model (Gao 2004) is adopted in the Basic Segmentation to convert the sentence into a word sequence. Let $\mathbf{w} = w_1 w_2 \ldots w_n$ be a word class sequence, then the most likely word class sequence w* in trigram is:

$$\mathbf{w}^* = \arg\max_{w_1 w_2 \cdots w_n} \prod_{i=1}^{n} P(w_i \mid w_{i-2} w_{i-1}),$$

where let $P(w_0|w_{-2}\ w_{-1})$ be $P(w_0)$ and let $P(w_1|w_{-1}\ w_0)$ be $P(w_1|w_0)$. And w_i represents LW or a type of FT or MDW. Viterbi algorithm is used to search the best candidate. Absolute smoothing algorithm is applied to overcome the data sparseness. Here, LW, FT and MDW are idendified (Zhao Yan 2005). All the Factoid words can be represented as regular expressions. As a result, the detection of factoid words can be archieved by Finite State Machines.

Four kinds of Named entities are detected, i.e. Chinese person name, foreign person name, location name and orgnization name. This is the most complicated module in ELUS.

Three kinds of models are applied here. HMM model (one order) is described as:

$$\mathbf{T}^{\#} = \arg\max_{T_1T_2\cdots T_n} \prod_{i=1}^{n} P(W_i \mid T_i)P(T_i \mid T_{i-1}),$$

where T_i represents the tag of current word, Viterbi algorithm is used to search the best path. Another model is Maximum Entropy (Zhao Jian 2005, Hai Leong Chieu 2002). Take Chinese person name as example. Firstly, we combine HMM and Maximum Entropy (ME) model to lable the person name tag, e.g. "姚/CPB 铜/CPI 梅/CPI" (Tongmei Yao); Secondly, the tagged name is merged by combining ME Model and Support Vector Machine (SVM) and some aided rules, e.g. merged into "姚/铜梅" in PKU test.

Some complex features are added into ME model (described in Zhao Jian 2005), in addition, we also collect more than 110,000 person names, and acquire the statistic about common name characters, these kinds of features are also fused into the ME model to detect NE. The other kinds of NE recognition adopt similar method, except for individual features.

New Words is another important kind of OOV words, especially in closed test. Take PKU test as example, we collect NW suffixes, such as "市"(city),"灯"(lamp). Those usually construct new words, e.g. "景观灯"(sighting lamp).

A variance-based method is used to collect suffixes. And three points need to be considered:(1) It is tail of many words;(2) It has large variance in constructing word;(3) It is seldom used alone. We acquire about 25 common suffixes in PKU training corpus by above method.

We use Local Maximum Entropy model, e.g. "黄冈/1 市/1"(Huanggang city), i.e. only the nearer characters are judged before the suffix "市" (city). By our approach, the training corpus can be generated via given PKU corpus in the bakeoff. The features come from the nearer context, besides, common single words and punctuations are not regarded as a part of New Word.

The last module is Word Disambiugation. Word segmentation ambiguities are usually classified into two classes: overlapping ambiguity and combination ambiguity. By evaluating ELUS, the most segmentation errors are one segmentation errors (about 95%). i.e. the two words on both sides of current segmentation errors are right. These include LW ambiguities and FT ambiguities etc. Here, we adopt Maximum Entropy model. The same as other modules, it is defined over H×T in segmentation disambiguation, where H is the set of possible contexts around target word that will be tagged, and T is the set of allowable tags. Then the model's conditional probability is defined as

$$p(t \mid h) = \frac{p(h,t)}{\sum_{t' \in T} p(h,t')},$$ where

$$p(h,t) = \pi\mu \prod_{j=1}^{k} \alpha_j^{f_j(h,t)}$$

where h is current context and t is one of the possible tags. The ambiguous words are mainly collected by evaluating our system.

In NE module and Word Disambiguation module, we introduce rough rule features, which are extracted by Rough Set (Wang Xiaolong 2004), e.g. "施展→才能"(display ability), "只有→才/能"(only→ can just), "记者+person+报道" (the reporter+person+report). Previous experiment had indicated word disambiguation could achieve better performance by applying Rough Set.

3 Performance and analysis

The performance of ELUS in the bakeoff is presented in Table 1 and Table 2 respectively, in terms of recall(R), precision(P) and F score in percentages.

Table 1 Closed test, in percentages (%)

Closed	R	P	F	OOV	R_{oov}	R_{iv}
PKU	95.4	92.7	94.1	5.8	51.8	98.1
MSR	97.3	94.5	95.9	2.6	32.3	99.1
CITYU	93.4	86.5	89.8	7.4	24.8	98.9
AS	94.3	89.5	91.8	4.3	13.7	97.9

Table 2 Open test, in percentages (%)

Open	R	P	F	OOV	R_{oov}	R_{iv}
PKU	96.8	96.6	96.7	5.8	82.6	97.7
MSR	98.0	96.5	97.2	2.6	59.0	99.0
CITYU	94.6	89.8	92.2	7.4	41.7	98.9
AS	95.2	92.0	93.6	4.3	35.4	97.9

Our system has good performance in terms of F-measure in simplified Chinese open test, including PKU and MSR open test. In addition, its IV word identification performance is remarkable, ranging from 97.7% to 99.1%, stands at the top or nearer the top in all the tests in which we have participated. This good performance owes to class-based trigram, absolute smoothing and word disambiguation module and rough rules.

There is almost the same IV performance between open test and closed test in MSR, CITYU and AS respectively, because we adopt the same Lexicon between open test and closed test respectively. While in open test of PKU, we adopt another Lexicon that comes from six-month corpora of Peoples' Daily (China) in 1998, which were also annotated by Peking University.

The OOV word identification performance seems uneven, compared with PKU, the other tests seem lower, due to the following reasons:

(1) Because of our resource limitation, NE training resource is six-month corpora of Peoples' Daily (China) in 1998, which came from Peking University, and some newspapers and web pages annotated by our laboratory;

(2) We have no traditional Chinese corpus, so the NE training resource for CITYU and AS is acquired via converting above corpora. Since these corpora are converted from simplified Chinese, they are not well suitable to traditional Chinese corpora;

(3) The different corpora have different criterions in NE detection, especially in location name and organization name, e.g. "崔村镇/香堂/猪场" (Cuicun Town Xiangtang Hogpen) in PKU and "崔村镇香堂猪场" in MSR criterion. Even if our system recognizes the "崔村镇/香/堂/猪场" as a orgnization name, we are not easily to regard "香堂" as one word in PKU, since "香堂" isn't a lexical word. However in MSR, that is easy, because its criterion regard the whole Orgnization as a word;

(4) We need do more to comply with the segmentation criterion, e.g. "露宿者"(outlier) in CITYU come from "露宿" + "者", while this kind of false segment is due to our bad understanding to CITYU criterion.

Though there are above problems, our system does well in regonization precision, since we adopt two steps in recognizing NE, especial in recognizing Chinese person name. And from the result of evalution in the bakeoff, we need to improve the NE recall in the future.

In order to make our New words comply with the criterion, we conservatively use New Word Detection module, in order to avoid having bad recognition result, since each corpus has its own New Word criterion.

4 Conclusion and Future work

We have briefly described our system based on mixed models. Different approachs are adopted to solve each special sub-task, since there is "No Free Lunch Theorem". And mixed models are used in NE detection. This sytem has a good performance in the simplified Chinese in the bakeoff.

The future work is mainly concentrating on two directions: finding effective features and delicately adjusting internal relations among different modules, in order to improve segmentation performance.

References

Fu Fuohong. 2000. Research on Statistical Methods of Chinese Syntactic Disambiguation. Ph.D. Thesis. Harbin Institute of Technology, China.

Hai Leong Chieu, Hwee Tou Ng. Named Entity. Recognition: A Maximum Entropy Approach Using Global. Information. Proceedings of the 19th International Conference. on Computational Linguistics, 2002.

Hua-Ping Zhang, Qun Liu etc. 2003. Chinese Lexical Analysis Using Hierarchical Hidden Markov Model, Second SIGHAN workshop affiliated with 4th ACL, Sapporo Japan, pp.63-70, July 2003.

Jianfeng Gao, Mu Li et al. 2004. Chinese Word Segmentation: A Pragmatic Approach. MSR-TR-2004-123, November 2004.

Wang Xiaolong, Chen Qingcai, and Daniel S.Yeung. 2004. Mining PinYin-to-Character Conversion Rules From Large-Scale Corpus: A Rough Set Approach, IEEE TRANSACTION ON SYSTEMS, MAN. AND CYBERNETICS-PART B:CYBERNETICS. VOL. 34, NO.2, APRIL.

Zhao Jian, Wang Xiao-long et al. 2005. Comparing Features Combination with Features Fusion in Chinese Named Entity Recognition. Computer Application. China.

Zhao Yan. 2005. Research on Chinese Morpheme Analysis Based on Statistic Language Model. Ph.D. Thesis. Harbin Institute of Technology, China.

Two-Phase LMR-RC Tagging for Chinese Word Segmentation

Tak Pang Lau and **Irwin King**
Department of Computer Science and Engineering
The Chinese University of Hong Kong
Shatin, N.T., Hong Kong
{tplau, king}@cse.cuhk.edu.hk

Abstract

In this paper we present a Two-Phase LMR-RC Tagging scheme to perform Chinese word segmentation. In the Regular Tagging phase, Chinese sentences are processed similar to the original LMR Tagging. Tagged sentences are then passed to the Correctional Tagging phase, in which the sentences are re-tagged using extra information from the first round tagging results. Two training methods, Separated Mode and Integrated Mode, are proposed to construct the models. Experimental results show that our scheme in Integrated Mode performs the best in terms of accuracy, where Separated Mode is more suitable under limited computational resources.

1 Introduction

The Chinese word segmentation is a non-trivial task because no explicit delimiters (like spaces in English) are used for word separation. As the task is an important precursor to many natural language processing systems, it receives a lot of attentions in the literature for the past decade (Wu and Tseng, 1993; Sproat et al., 1996). In this paper, we propose a statistical approach based on the works of (Xue and Shen, 2003), in which the Chinese word segmentation problem is first transformed into a tagging problem, then the Maximum Entropy classifier is applied to solve the problem. We further improve the scheme by introducing correctional treatments after first round tagging. Two different training methods are proposed to suit our scheme.

The paper is organized as follows. In Section 2, we briefly discuss the scheme proposed by (Xue and Shen, 2003), followed by our additional works to improve the performance. Experimental and bakeoff results are presented in Section 3. Finally, We conclude the paper in Section 4.

2 Our Proposed Approach

2.1 Chinese Word Segmentation as Tagging

One of the difficulties in Chinese word segmentation is that, Chinese characters can appear in different positions within a word (Xue and Shen, 2003), and *LMR Tagging* was proposed to solve the problem. The basic idea of LMR Tagging is to assign to each character, based on its contextual information, a tag which represents its relative position within the word. Note that the original tag set used by (Xue and Shen, 2003) is simplified and improved by (Ng and Low, 2004) . We shall then adopt and illustrate the simplified case here.

The tags and their meanings are summarized in Table 1. Tag *L*, *M*, and *R* correspond to the character at the beginning, in the middle, and at the end of the word respectively. Tag *S* means the character is a "single-character" word. Figure 1 illustrates a Chinese sentence segmented by spaces, and the corresponding tagging results.

After transforming the Chinese segmentation problem to the tagging problem, various solutions can be applied. *Maximum Entropy model* (MaxEnt) (Berger, S. A. Della Pietra, and

Original sentence:	大衛喜歡吃士多啤梨。
After segmentation:	大衛　喜歡　吃　士多啤梨　。
Tagging:	L R　L R　S　L M M R　S

Figure 1: Example of LMR Tagging.

V. J. Della Pietra, 1996; Ratnaparkhi, 1996) was proposed in the original work to solve the LMR Tagging problem. In order to make MaxEnt success in LMR Tagging, *feature templates* used in capturing useful contextual information must be carefully designed. Furthermore, it is unavoidable that invalid tag sequences will occur if we just assign the tag with the highest probability. In the next subsection, we describe the feature templates and measures used to correct the tagging.

Table 1: Tags used in LMR Tagging scheme.

Tag	Description
L	Character is at the beginning of the word (or the character is the leftmost character in the word)
M	Character is in the middle of the word
R	Character is at the end of the word (or the character is the rightmost character in the word)
S	Character is a "single-character" word

2.2 Two-Phase LMR-RC Tagging

In this section, we introduce our *Two-Phase LMR-RC Tagging* used to perform Chinese Text Segmentation. The first phase, *R*-phase, is called *Regular Tagging*, in which similar procedures as in the original LMR Tagging are performed. The difference in this phase as compared to the original one is that, we use extra feature templates to capture characteristics of Chinese word segmentation. The second phase, *C*-phase, is called *Correctional Tagging*, in which the sentences are re-tagged by incorporating the regular tagging results. We hope that tagging errors can be corrected under this way. The models used in both phases are trained using MaxEnt model.

Regular Tagging Phase

In this phase, each character is tagged similar to the original approach. In our scheme, given the contextual information (x) of current character, the tag (y^*) with highest probability will be assigned:

$$y^* = \arg\max_{y \in \{L,M,R,S\}} p(y|x).$$

The features describing the characteristics of Chinese segmentation problem are instantiations of the feature templates listed in Table 2. Note that feature templates only describe the forms of features, but not the actual features. So the number of features used is much larger than the number of templates.

Table 2: Feature templates used in *R*-phase. Example used is "32 個蘋果".

	Feature Type	Example – Features extracted of character "個"
1	Characters within window of ±2	C_{-2}="3", C_{-1}="2", C_0="個", C_1="蘋", C_2="果"
2	Two consecutive characters within window of ±2	$C_{-2}C_{-1}$="32", $C_{-1}C_0$="2個", C_0C_1="個蘋", C_1C_2="蘋果"
3	Previous and next characters	$C_{-1}C_1$="2蘋"
4	Current character is punctuation	–
5	ASCII characters within window of ±2	A_{-2}, A_{-1} (as "3" and "2" are ASCII)
6	Current and character in window ±1 belong to different types	D_{-1} (as "2" is digit, but "個" is letter)

Additional feature templates as compared to (Xue and Shen, 2003) and (Ng and Low, 2004) are template 5 and 6. Template 5 is used to handle documents with ASCII characters. For template 6, as it is quite common that word boundary occurs in between two characters with different types, this template is used to capture such characteristics.

Correctional Tagging Phase

In this phase, the sequence of characters is re-tagged by using the additional information of tagging results after *R*-phase. The tagging procedure is similar to the previous phase, except extra features (listed in Table 3) are used to assist the tagging.

Table 3: Additional feature templates used in *C*-phase. Example used is "32 個蘋果" with tagging results after *R*-phase as "SSLMR".

	Feature Type	Example – Features extracted of character "個"
7	Tags of characters within window of ± 2	T_{-2}="S", T_{-1}="S", T_0="L", T_1="M", T_2="R"
8	Two consecutive tags within window of ± 2	$T_{-2}T_{-1}$="SS", $T_{-1}T_0$="SL", T_0T_1="LM", T_1T_2="MR"
9	Previous and next tags	$T_{-1}T_1$="SM"

Training Method

Two training methods are proposed to construct models used in *R*- and *C*-phase: (1) *Separated Mode*, and (2) *Integrated Mode*. Separated Mode means the models used in two phases are separated. Model for *R*-phase is called *R*-model, and model for *C*-phase is called *C*-model. Integrated Mode means only one model, *I*-model is used in both phases.

The training methods are illustrated now. First of all, training data are divided into three parts, (1) Regular Training, (2) Correctional Training, and (3) Evaluation. Our method first trains using observations extracted from Part 1 (observation is simply the pair $(context, tag)$ of each character). The created model is used to process Part 2. After that, observations extracted from Part 2 (which include previous tagging results) are used to create the final model. The performance is then evaluated by processing Part 3.

Let O be the set of observations, with subscripts R or C indicating the sources of them. Let $TrainModel : O \rightarrow P$, where P is the set of models, be the "model generating" function. The two proposed training methods can be illustrated as follow:

1. Separated Mode

$$R - model = TrainModel(O_R),$$
$$C - model = TrainModel(O_C).$$

2. Integrated Mode

$$I - model = TrainModel(O_R \cup O_C).$$

The advantage of Separated Mode is that, it is easy to aggregate different sets of training data. It also provides a mean to handle large training data under limited resources, as we can divide the training data into several parts, and then use the similar idea to train each part. The drawback of this mode is that, it may lose the features' characteristics captured from Part 1 of training data, and Integrated Mode is proposed to address the problem, in which all the features' characteristics in both Part 1 and Part 2 are used to train the model.

3 Experimental Results and Discussion

We conducted closed track experiments on the Hong Kong City University (CityU) corpus in The Second International Chinese Word Segmentation Bakeoff to evaluate the proposed training and tagging methods. The training data were split into three portions. Part 1: 60% of the data is trained for *R*-phase; Part 2: 30% for *C*-phase training; and Part 3: the remaining 10% for evaluation. The evaluation part was further divided into six parts to simulate actual size of test document. The MaxEnt classifier was implemented using Java opennlp maximum entropy package from (Baldridge, Morton, and Bierner, 2004), and training was done with feature cutoff of 2 and 160 iterations. The experiments were run on an Intel Pentium4 3.0GHz machine with 3.0GB memory.

To evaluate our proposed scheme, we carried out four experiments for each evaluation data. For Experiment 1, data were processed with *R*-phase only. For Experiment 2, data were processed with both *R*- and *C*-phase, using Separated Mode as training method. For Experiment 3, data were processed similar to Experiment 2, except Integrated Mode was used. Finally for Experiment 4, data were processed similar to Experiment 1, with both Part 1 and Part 2 data were used for *R*-model training. The purpose of Experiment 4 is to determine whether the proposed scheme can perform better than just the single Regular Tagging under the same amount of training data. Table 4 summarizes the experimental results measured in F-measure (the harmonic mean of precision and recall).

From the results, we obtain the following observations.

1. Both Integrated and Separated Training modes

Table 4: Experimental results of CityU corpus measured in F-measure.

Data Set	Exp1	Exp2	Exp3	Exp4
1	0.918	0.943	**0.949**	0.947
2	0.913	0.939	**0.943**	**0.943**
3	0.912	0.935	**0.939**	0.937
4	0.914	0.940	**0.943**	0.942
5	0.921	0.942	**0.945**	**0.945**
6	0.914	0.941	**0.945**	0.942

in Two-Phase Tagging (Exp 2 and Exp 3) outperform single Regular Tagging (Exp 1). It is reasonable as more data are used in training.

2. Integrated Mode (Exp 3) still performs better than Exp 4, in which same amount of training data are used. This reflects that extra tagging information after *R*-phase helps in the scheme.
3. Separated Mode (Exp 2) performs worse than both Exp 3 and Exp 4. The reason is that the *C*-model cannot capture enough features' characteristics used for basic tagging. We believe that by adjusting the proportion of Part 1 and Part 2 of training data, performance can be increased.
4. Under limited computational resources, in which constructing single-model using all available data (as in Exp 3 and Exp 4) is not possible, Separated Mode shows its advantage in constructing and aggregating multi-models by dividing the training data into different portions.

The official BakeOff2005 results are summarized in Table 5. We have submitted multiple results for CityU, MSR and PKU corpora by applying different tagging methods described in the paper.

Table 5: Official BakeOff2005 results.
Keys:
F - Regular Tagging only, all training data are used
P1 - Regular Tagging only, 90% of training data are used
P2 - Regular Tagging only, 70% of training data are used
S - Regular and Correctional Tagging, Separated Mode
I - Regular and Correctional Tagging, Integrated Mode

Corpus	R	P	F	R_{OOV}	R_{IV}	Method
CityU	0.938	0.915	0.927	0.658	0.961	F
	0.936	0.913	0.925	0.656	0.959	P1
	0.925	0.896	0.910	0.639	0.948	P2
	0.937	0.922	0.929	0.698	0.956	I
MSR	0.946	0.933	0.939	0.587	0.956	F
	0.941	0.932	0.937	0.624	0.950	S
PKU	0.926	0.908	0.917	0.535	0.950	F
	0.917	0.903	0.910	0.600	0.937	P2
	0.918	0.915	0.917	0.621	0.936	I

4 Conclusion

We present a Two-Phase LMR-RC Tagging scheme to perform Chinese word segmentation. Correctional Tagging phase is introduced in addition to the original LMR Tagging technique, in which the Chinese sentences are re-tagged using extra information of first round tagging results. Two training methods, *Separated Mode* and *Integrated Mode*, are introduced to suit our scheme. Experimental results show that Integrated Mode achieve the highest accuracy in terms of F-measure, where Separated Mode shows its advantages in constructing and aggregating multi-models under limited resources.

Acknowledgements

The work described in this paper was fully supported by a grant from the Research Grants Council of the Hong Kong Special Administrative Region, China (Project No. CUHK4235/04E).

References

A. L. Berger, S. A. Della Pietra, and V. J. Della Pietra. 1996. A maximum entropy approach to natural language processing. *Computational Linguistics*, 22(1):39-71.

A. Ratnaparkhi. 1996. A maximum entropy model for part-of-speech tagging. In *Proceedings of the First Conference on Empirical Methods in Natural Language Processing*, pages 133-142.

H. T. Ng and J. K. Low. 2004. Chinese Part-of-Speech Tagging. One-at-a-Time or All-at-once? Word-Based or Character-Based? In *Proc. of EMNLP*.

J. Baldridge, T. Morton, and G. Bierner. 2004. The opennlp maxent package in Java. URL: *http://maxent.sourceforge.net* .

N. Xue and L. Shen. 2003. Chinese word segmentation as LMR Tagging. In *Proc. of SIGHAN Workshop*.

R. Sproat, C. Shih, W. Gale, and N. Chang. 1996. A stochastic finite-state word-segmentation algorithm for Chinese. *Computational Linguistics*, 22(3):377-404.

R. Sproat and T. Emerson. 2003. The first international Chinese word segmentation bakeoff. In *Proc. of SIGHAN Workshop*.

Z. Wu and G. Tseng. 1993. Chinese text segmentation for text retrieval: achievements and problems. *Journal of the American Society for Information Science*, 44(9):532-542.

Chinese Word Segmentation in ICT-NLP

ShuangLong Li
Institute of Computing Technology,Beijing
University of Science and Technology Beijing,Beijing
slli@ict.ac.cn

Abstract

Chinese word segmentation is always much accounted of in ICT-NLP. In this bakeoff, two different systems in ICT-NLP participated. The one is SYSTEM_#1 evaluated in three tracks -- PK-close, MSR-close and MSR-open, and SYSTEM_#2 PK-open. Through this bakeoff , the development of Chinese segmentation is learned and the problems are found in our systems.

1 System Description

Two different systems in ICT-NLP participated the second bakeoff.

1.1 SYSTEM_#1

The SYSTEM_#1 is implemented mainly based on the log-linear model CRFs(Conditional Random Fields). CRFs are arbitrary undirected graphical models trained to maximize the conditional probability of the desired outputs given the corresponding inputs. We cast the segmentation as one of sequence tagging.

The conditional probability for the tag sequence $T = t_1 t_2 ... t_n$ given a input Chinese sentence $C = c_1 c_2 ... c_n$ is defined by a linear-chain CRF with parameters $\lambda = \{\lambda_1 \lambda_2 ... \lambda_m\}$ to be

$$P_\Lambda(T \mid C) = \frac{1}{Z_c} \exp\left(\sum_{i=1}^{n} \sum_{m} \lambda_m f_m(t_{i-1}, t_i, C, i) \right)$$

Where Z_c is the per-input normalization that makes the probability of all state sequences sum to one. $f_m(t_{i-1}, t_i, C, i)$ is a feature function which is can be any real number.

The most probable tag sequence for an input C,

$$T^* = \arg\max_T P_\Lambda(T \mid C)$$

is determined using the Viterbi algorithm, An *N*-best list of tagging sequences is obtained using modi-fied Viterbi algorithm.

Six tags according to the different positions of one character in a word are used in this model, such as #START(beginning of one sentence), B(beginning of one word), M(middle of one word), E(end of one word), and #END(end of one sentence).

The feature templates used in this model are listed in Table 1.

Description	Feature
current state	t_i, c_i
current & previous states	t_{i-1}, t_i, c_i
current & two previous states	$t_{i-2}, t_{i-1}, t_i, c_i$
state transitions	t_{i-1}, t_i
second previous character	t_i, c_{i-2}
previous character	t_i, c_{i-1}
next character	t_i, c_{i+1}
second next character	t_i, c_{i+2}
previous two characters	t_i, c_{i-2}, c_{i-1}
next two characters	t_i, c_{i+1}, c_{i+2}
previous current & next character	$t_i, c_{i-1}, c_i, t_{i+1}$
current and previous character	t_i, c_{i-1}, c_i
current and next character	t_i, c_i, c_{i+1}
character types of current & two previous & two next characters	$t_i, T_{i-2}; T_{i-1}, T_i, T_{i+1}, T_{i+2}$

Table 1. Feature templates used in SYSTEM_#1

- Any Arabia number like “ 0 , 1 , 2 …” is replaced by mark #N;
- Some punctuation like “。 ,! ,? …” is replaced by mark #C;

- Any Chinese letter like "a, A ,b, B …" is replaced by mark #L;
- All the characters are classified to be 7 types, such as : number, letter, time-suffix, etc.

In this model, the parameters are estimated by one Perceptron Algorithm. The parameters can also be trained through the maximum entropy learning algorithms like GIS or IIS, but performed poorly in our tests.

1.2 SYSTEM_#2

The SYSTEM_#2 is mainly a HHMM-based Chinese segmentation system which has participated the 1st bakeoff in 2003. And the improvement has been made by some post processes. The system structure is shown in Figure 1

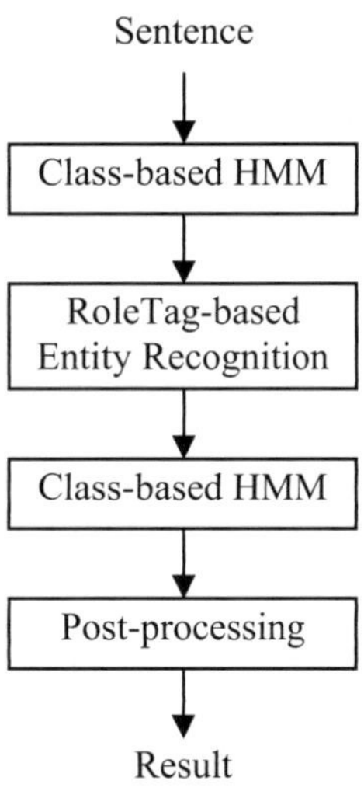

Figure 1 . SYSTEM_#2 structure

Details of the post-processing are listed below.

- TBL(Transformation Based Learning) is applied for adaptation to different segmentation standards.
- The repeating strings extracted in the test data using Accessor Variety correct the inconsistent segmentation.
- A filtering approach to find the unknown words in the single character strings is used.

2 Track

Here ,we introduce the operation of the different tracks. Table 2 gives the results of the tracks.

Tracks	SYSTEM_#1	SYSTEM_#2
PK-close	P: 0.942 R: 0.938 F: 0.940	--
PK-open	--	P: 0.961 R: 0.944 F: 0.952
MSR-close	P: 0.942 R: 0.948 F: 0.945	--
MSR-open	P: 0.933 R: 0.916 F: 0.924	--

Table 2 . The results of the tracks

2.1 Closed Tracks

Only the SYSTEM_#1 participated the closed tracks(PK and MSR) because SYSTEM_#2 must utilize the POS information in the entity recognition process.

All the features information used in the SYSTEM_#1 were trained automatic for one time.

We split the training randomly to two parts—80% used for training and 20% used for estimating the parameters.

2.2 Open Tracks

We participated two open tracks--SYSTEM_#1 MSR and SYSTEM_#2 PK.

For SYSTEM_#1, an external dictionary which contains 140,332 entries with POS is used. However, because of the standard conflict, the open result is weaker than the closed result.

For SYSTEM_#2, the system is trained on six-months tagged news corpus of People Daily 1998 and an external dictionary which contains 22,858 entries with POS.

3 Conclusion

The result in this bakeoff is not so satisfied as there are also many problems in our systems. Through this bakeoff, we learn more about the the development of Chinese segmentation. So the future research is needed to improve our work.

Towards a Hybrid Model for Chinese Word Segmentation

Xiaofei Lu
Department of Linguistics
The Ohio State University
Columbus, OH 43210, USA
xflu@ling.osu.edu

Abstract

This paper describes a hybrid Chinese word segmenter that is being developed as part of a larger Chinese unknown word resolution system. The segmenter consists of two components: a tagging component that uses the transformation-based learning algorithm to tag each character with its position in a word, and a merging component that transforms a tagged character sequence into a word-segmented sentence. In addition to the position-of-character tags assigned to the characters, the merging component makes use of a number of heuristics to handle non-Chinese characters, numeric type compounds, and long words. The segmenter achieved a 92.8% F-score and a 72.8% recall for OOV words in the closed track of the Peking University Corpus in the Second International Chinese Word Segmentation Bakeoff.

1 Introduction

This paper describes a hybrid Chinese word segmenter that participated in the closed track of the Peking University Corpus in the Second International Chinese Word Segmentation Bakeoff. This segmenter is still in its early stage of development and is being developed as part of a larger Chinese unknown word resolution system that performs the identification, part of speech guessing, and sense guessing of Chinese unknown words (Lu, 2005).

The segmenter consists of two major components. First, a tagging component tags each individual character in a sentence with a position-of-character (POC) tag that indicates the position of the character in a word. This could be one of the following four possibilities, i.e., the character is either a monosyllabic word or is in a word-initial, middle, or final position. This component is based on the transformation-based learning (TBL) algorithm (Brill, 1995), where a simple first-order HMM tagger (Charniak et al., 1993) is used to produce an initial tagging of a character sequence. Second, a merging component transforms the output of the tagging component, i.e., a POC-tagged character sequence, into a word-segmented sentence. Whereas this process relies largely on the POC tags assigned to the individual characters, it also takes advantage of a number of heuristics generalized from the training data to handle non-Chinese characters, numeric type compounds, and long words.

The approach adopted here is reminiscent of the line of research that employs the idea of character-based tagging for Chinese word segmentation and/or unknown word identification (Goh et al., 2003; Xue, 2003; Zhang et al., 2002). The notion of character-based tagging allows us to model the tendency for individual characters to combine with other characters to form words in different contexts. This property gives the model a good potential for improving the performance of Chinese unknown word identification, a major concern of the Chinese unknown word resolution system that the segmenter is a part of.

The rest of the paper is organized as follows. Section two describes the system architecture. Section three reports the results of the system in the bakeoff. Section four concludes the paper.

2 System Description

The overall architecture of the segmenter is described in Figure 1. An input sentence is first segmented into a character sequence, with a space inserted after each character. The segmented character sequence is then processed by the tagging component, where it is initially tagged by an HMM tagger, and then by a TBL tagger. Finally, the tagged character sequence is transformed into a word-segmented sentence by the merging component.

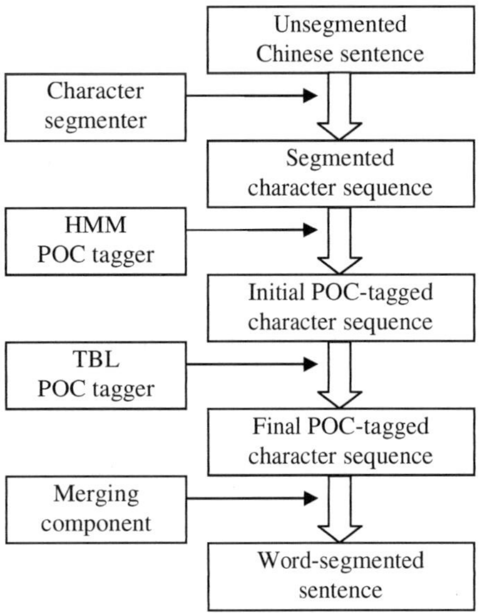

Figure 1: System Architecture.

2.1 The Tagging Component

The tagset used by the tagging component consists of the following four tags: *L*, *M*, *R*, and *W*, each of which indicates that the character is in a word-initial, word-middle, or word-final position or is a monosyllabic word respectively. The transformation-based error-driven learning algorithm is adopted as the backbone of the tagging component over other promising machine learning algorithms because, as Brill (1995) argued, it captures linguistic knowledge in a more explicit and direct fashion without compromising performance. This algorithm requires a gold standard, some initial tagging of the training corpus, and a set of rule templates. It then learns a set of rules that are ranked in terms of the number of tagging error reductions they can achieve.

A number of different initial tagging schemes can be used, e.g., tagging each character as a monosyllabic word or with its most probable POC tag. We used a simple first-order HMM tagger to produce an initial tagging. Specifically, we calculate

$$\arg\max_{t_1 \ldots t_n} \prod_{i=1}^{n} p(t_i | t_{i-1}) p(t_i | w_i) \qquad (1)$$

where t_i denotes the *i*th tag in the tag sequence and w_i denotes the *i*th character in the character sequence. The transition probabilities and lexical probabilities are estimated from the training data. The lexical probability for an unknown character, i.e., a character that is not found in the training data, is by default uniformly distributed among the four POC tags defined in the tagset. The Viterbi algorithm (Rabiner, 1989) is used to tag new texts.

The transformation-based tagger was implemented using fnTBL (Florian and Ngai, 2001). The rule templates used are the same as the contextual rule templates Brill (1995) defined for the POS tagging task. These templates basically transform the current tag into some other tag based on the current character/tag and the character/tag one to three positions before/after the current character. An example rule template is given below:

(1) Change tag *a* to tag *b* if the preceding character is tagged *z*.

The training process is iterative. At each iteration, the algorithm picks the instantiation of a rule template that achieves the greatest number of tagging error reductions. This rule is applied to the text, and the learning process repeats until no more rules reduce errors beyond a predefined threshold. The learned rules can then be applied to new texts that are tagged by the initial HMM tagger.

2.2 The Merging Component

The merging component transforms a POC-tagged character sequence into a word-segmented sentence. In general, the characters in a sequence are concatenated, and a space is inserted after each character tagged *R* (word-final position) or *W* (monosyllabic word).

In addition, two sets of heuristics are used in this process. One set (H1) is used to handle non-Chinese characters and numeric type compounds, e.g., numbers, time expressions, etc. A few patterns of non-Chinese characters and numeric type compounds are generalized from the training data. If the merging algorithm detects such a pattern in the character sequence, it groups the characters that are part of the pattern accordingly.

The second set of heuristics (H2) is used to handle words that three or more characters long. Our hypothesis is that long words tend to have less fluidity than shorter words and their behavior is more predictable (Lu, 2005). We extracted a wordlist from the training data. Based on our hypothesis, if the merging algorithm detects that a group of characters form a long word found in the wordlist, it groups these characters into one word.

3 Results

The segmenter was evaluated on the closed track of the Peking University Corpus in the bakeoff. In the development stage, we partitioned the official training data into two portions: the training set consists of 90% of the data, and the development set consists of the other 10%. The POC tagging accuracy on the development set is summarized in Table 1. The results indicate that the TBL tagger significantly improves the initial tagging produced by the HMM tagger.

	Accuracy
HMM tagger	0.814
TBL tagger	0.936

Table 1: Tagging Results on the Development Set.

The performance of the merging algorithm on the development set is summarized in Table 2. To understand whether and how much the heuristics contribute to improving segmentation, we evaluated four versions of the merging algorithm. The set of heuristics used to handle non-Chinese characters and numeric type compounds did not seem to improve segmentation results on the development set, suggesting that these characters are handled well by the tagging component. However, the second set of heuristics improved segmentation accuracy significantly. This seems to confirm our hypothesis that longer words tend to behave more stably.

Resources used	R	P	F
POC Tags only	0.928	0.926	0.927
+ H1	0.929	0.925	0.927
+ H2	0.938	0.959	0.948
+ H1 & H2	0.940	0.960	0.950

Table 2: Segmentation Results on the Development Set. H1 stands for the set of heuristics used to handle non-Chinese characters and numeric type compounds. H2 stands for the set of heuristics used to handle long words.

Corpus	R	P	F	R_{OOV}	R_{IV}
PKU	0.922	0.934	0.928	0.728	0.934

Table 3: Official Results in the Closed-Track of the Peking University Corpus.

The official results of the segmenter in the closed-track of the Peking University Corpus are summarized in Table 3. It is somewhat unexpected that the results on the official test data dropped over 2% compared with the results obtained on the development set. Compared with the other systems, the segmenter performed relatively well on OOV words.

Our preliminary error analysis indicates that this discrepancy in performance is partially attributable to two kinds of inconsistencies between the training and test datasets. One is that there are many ASCII numbers in the test set, but none in the training set. These numbers became unknown characters to the tagger and affected tagging accuracy. It is possible that this inconsistency affected our system more than other systems. Second, there are also a number of segmentation inconsistencies between the training and test sets, but these should have affected all systems more or less equally. The error analysis also indicates that the current segmenter performed poorly on transliterations of foreign names.

4 Conclusions

We described a hybrid Chinese word segmenter that combines the transformation-based learning algorithm for character-based tagging and linguistic heuristics for transforming tagged character sequences into word-segmented sentences.

As the segmenter is in its first stage of development and is far from mature, the bakeoff provided an especially valuable opportunity for evaluating its performance. The results suggest that:

1. Despite the lack of a separate mechanism for unknown word recognition, the segmenter performed relatively well on OOV words. This confirms our hypothesis that character-based tagging has a good potential for improving Chinese unknown word identification.
2. Using linguistic heuristics at the merging stage can help improve segmentation results.
3. There is much room for improvement for both the tagging algorithm and the merging algorithm. This is being undertaken.

References

Eric Brill. 1995. Transformation-based error-driven learning and natural language processing: A case study in part-of-speech tagging. *Computational Linguistics*, 21(4):543-565.

Eugene Charniak, Curtis Hendrickson, Neil Jacobson, and Mike Perkowitz. 1993. Equations for part-of-speech tagging. In *Proceedings of AAAI-1993*, pp. 784-789.

Chooi Ling Goh, Masayuki Asahara, and Yuji Matsumoto. 2003. Chinese unknown word identification using character-based tagging and chunking. In *Proceedings of ACL-2003 Interactive Posters and Demonstrations*, pp. 197-200.

Xiaofei Lu. 2005. Hybrid methods for POS guessing of Chinese unknown words. In *Proceedings of ACL-2005 Student Research Workshop*, pp. 1-6.

Grace Ngai and Radu Florian. 2001. Transformation-based learning in the fast lane. In *Proceedings of NAACL-2001*, pp. 40-47.

Lawrence R. Rabiner. 1989. A tutorial of hidden Markov models and selected applications in speech recognition. In *Proceedings of IEEE-1989*, pp. 257-286.

Nianwen Xue. 2003. Chinese word segmentation as character tagging. *International Journal of Computational Linguistics and Chinese Language Processing*, 8(1):29-48.

Kevin Zhang, Qin Liu, Hao Zhang, and Xue-Qi Cheng. 2002. Automatic recognition of Chinese unknown words based on roles tagging. In *Proceedings of the 1st SIGHAN Workshop on Chinese Language Processing*, pp. 71-78.

Chinese Word Segmentation Based On Direct Maximum Entropy Model

Wu-Guang Shi
Peking University, Beijing, 100871, China
shiwuguang@pku.edu.cn

Abstract

Chinese word segmentation is a fundamental and important issue in Chinese information processing. In order to find a unified approach for Chinese word segmentation, the author develop a Chinese lexical analyzer PCWS using direct maximum entropy model. The paper presents the general description of PCWS, as well as the result and analysis of its performance at the Second International Chinese Word Segmentation Bakeoff.

1 Introduction

Och and Ney(2002) present a framework based on direct maximum entropy model to construct the machine translation system. The model treats knowledge sources as feature functions, and allows the system to be extended easily by adding new feature functions. We think the model can be used to provide a unified approach for Chinese word segmentation. PCWS is the system based on this thinking.

2 System Description

PCWS consists of four components: Word generation, Disambiguation, Select the best word sequence and Output the result. They are described below.

2.1 Word Generation

The procedure of word generation involves two steps: (1) generation of the common words which are listed in the Dictionary. (2) generation of the unknown words. The unknown words handled by the system involve numeric expression, time expression, personal name, location name and organization name. PCWS can recognize the abbreviation of person name, and fail to find the abbreviation of location name and organization name.

PCWS constructs an integrated segmentation graph. The node in the graph is the minimal segmentation unit that cannot be split in any stage that follows. The unit consists of Chinese character, punctuation, Arabic numeral string and English character string. Every word that be generated is an edge in the graph.

Making the integrated segmentation graph is to avoid the blind spots in segmentation, but it brings the graph more complex, and make the system's speed slow.

Every word will belong to a class.

Given a word w_i, its class is defined by Figure 1.

$$c_i = \begin{cases} \text{Wi} & \text{iff } \mathbf{Wi} \text{ is listed in the segmentation lexicon.} \\ \text{PER} & \text{iff } \mathbf{Wi} \text{ is a person name} \\ \text{LOC} & \text{iff } \mathbf{Wi} \text{ is a location name} \\ \text{ORG} & \text{iff } \mathbf{Wi} \text{ is an organization name} \\ \text{NUM} & \text{iff } \mathbf{Wi} \text{ is a numeral expression} \\ \text{TIME} & \text{iff } \mathbf{Wi} \text{ is a time expression} \end{cases}$$

Figure 1: Class Definition of word **Wi**

2.2 Disambiguation

In constructing the graph, PCWS detect the ambiguities of the segmentation and classify the ambiguities into two classes: the false ambiguity and the true ambiguity. The former is simply solved by querying a table. The segmentation information around the true ambiguities will be collected and PCWS will give an estimate of each possible segmentation mode of the true ambiguities. These estimates will be used by selecting the best path.

2.3 Select the Best Word Sequence

The procedure of this part consists of two processes: generating the candidate word sequences and finding the best word sequence.

If **S** is a Chinese sentence which is a character sequence, **W** is the all possible word sequences given **S**, $W^\# = \{W_1, W_2, ..., W_N\}$ is a word sequence, $C=\{C_1, C_2, ..., C_N\}$ is a corresponding class sequence of $W^\#$. We use Viterbi algorithm to generate the candidate paths. In order to control the search space, all the paths will be ranked by a class mode score. The maximum number of the candidate paths generated by each node in the graph cannot be larger than a Number threshold we give.

The class mode score we used can be written as

$$\text{Score}(w^\#) = P_{\text{generate}}(w^\# \mid c) P_{\text{context}}(c)$$

The P(C) and P($W^\#$ | C) is similar to the one defined by Gao et al.(2003).

We use the direct maximum entropy model to find the best word sequence. If W^+ is the best path we need. **W*** is the candidate set.

Giving the direct maximum entropy model and neglecting its renormalization, we can obtain the following decision rule:

$$w^+ = \arg\max_{w^\# \in w^*} \left\{ \sum_{m=1}^{M} \lambda_m \mathrm{h}_m \left(w^\#, s \right) \right\}$$

hi ($W^\#$, S) is the feature function of the word sequence. The parameter λi is the power of the feature.

In PCWS, we define five feature functions:

1) Context feature

$$\mathrm{h}_1(w^\#, s) = -\log P_{\text{context}}(c)$$

2) Candidate person name feature

$$\mathrm{h}_2(w^\#,s) = \sum_{i==1}^{N} \text{genper}(w_i \mid c_i)$$

Here

$$\text{genper}(w_i|c_i) = \begin{cases} -\log P_{\text{generate}}(w_i|c_i) & \text{iff } c_i == \text{PER} \\ 0 & \text{else} \end{cases}$$

3) Candidate location name feature

$$\mathrm{h}_3(w^\#,s) = \sum_{i==1}^{N} \text{genloc}(w_i|c_i)$$

Here

$$\text{genloc}(w_i|c_i) = \begin{cases} -\log P_{\text{generate}}(w_i|c_i) & \text{iff } c_i == \text{LOC} \\ 0 & \text{else} \end{cases}$$

4) Candidate organization name feature

$$\mathrm{h}_4(w^\#,s) = \sum_{i==1}^{N} \text{genorg}(w_i|c_i)$$

Here

$$\text{genorg}(w_i|c_i) = \begin{cases} -\log P_{\text{generate}}(w_i|c_i) & \text{iff } c_i == \text{ORG} \\ 0 & \text{else} \end{cases}$$

5) The length of the path

$$\mathrm{h}_5(w^\#,s) = \text{Length}(c)$$

We realize the GIS algorithm which can handle any type of real-valued features to train the values of λ_1^5 .

2.4 Output the Result

The component outputs the best word sequence and adjusts the result form based on the standard of test corpora. In PCWS, we only adjust the form of the unknown words the system recognizes.

For example, in "１９９２年１１月", "１９９２年" and "１１月" will be recognized independently as unknown word. Base on the standard of Msr corpora, we combine the continuous words which belong to the class TIME."

2.5 System Overview

The overall architecture of our word segmentation system is presented in figure 2.

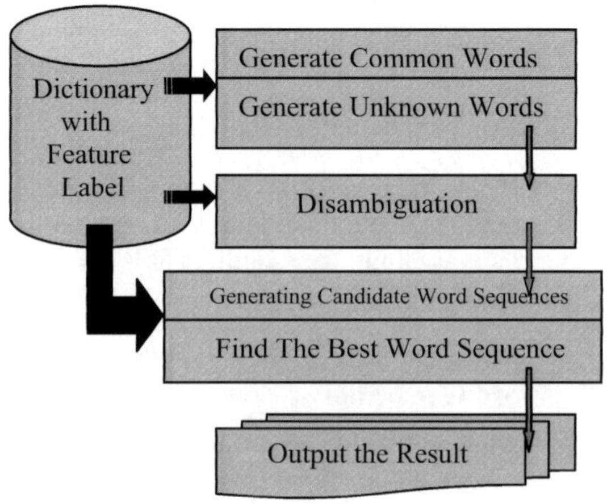

Figure 2: Overall architecture of PCWS

Track	TOTAL TRUE WORD COUNT	TOTAL TEST WORD COUNT	P	R	F	OOV	Roov	Riv
Msr_Open	106873	106624	0.913	0.915	0.914	0.026	0.725	0.918

Table 1: Test Result on Msr-open Track

3 Evaluation

Because of the bakeoff's rule and the limit of time, we only attend the track of Msr_open.
Table 1 is the result of PCWS in this bakeoff.
Form the table, we can know the system is remarkable in OOV recognize.
Due to only small named entity words are included in the PCWS's dictionary, most of named entity words are generated by the system. However, the system's overall performance is not in balance with its good Roov. We notice Riv of the result is low. The main reason causes Riv low is the difference between the segmentation standard of PKU training corpora and the segmentation standard of MSR test corpora. The difference is so distinctly even in the segmentation standard of common words. For instance:

Example 1
[Correct Result] "另外 旅游 、 侨汇 **也是** 经济 收入 的 重要 组成部分 ， 制造业 规模 相对 **较小** 。"
[PCWS Result] "另外 旅游 、 侨汇 **也 是** 经济 收入 的 重要 组成部分 ， 制造业 规模 相对 **较 小** 。"
The result's True Words Recall = 0.875, Test Words Precision = 0.778

Example 2
[Correct Result] "**在此** 之前 的 **回 购** 合同 继续 执行 完毕 。"
[PCWS Result] "**在 此** 之前 的 **回购** 合同 继续 执行 完毕 。"
The result's True Words Recall = 0.700, Test Words Precision = 0.700

Before we get the result, we neglected the problem. We put our attention in named entity recognize, which need the training corpora with the label information, so we use six month PKU corpora to construct our system and not use well the MSR training corpora in the bakeoff.

In order to know the influence of the problem, we test our system in PKU test corpora, Table 2 is the result of PCWS in the test.

Track	P	R	F
Pku_Open	0.973887	0.978405	0.976141

Table 2: Test Result on Pku_open

It's an excellent result and powerful proves our suppose.
We wish to make our system more adaptable to different standards in the near future.

4 Conclusion

We have presented our Chinese word segmentation system PCWS and its result for Msr_open track. We are glad to see its good performance of OOV recognize. In the course of the bakeoff, we find some problems in PCWS. We will try to select more useful feature functions into the existing segmentation model in future work. We are confident the system's performance will have a big progress next time.

5 Acknowledgement

Thank Prof. Hou-Feng Wang for his attention and aid. The author would especially express gratitude to his family, their encouragement and support make the author to hold the line.

References

Franz J. Och and Hermann Ney. 2002. Discriminative training and maximum entropy models for statistical machine translation. In Proceedings of the 40th Annual Meeting of the Association for Computational Linguistics (ACL), pages 295-302, Philadelphia, PA, July.

Gao, Jianfeng, Mu Li and Chang-Ning Huang. 2003. Improved source-channel model for Chinese word segmentation. In: ACL2003.

A Hybrid Approach to Chinese Word Segmentation around CRFs

ZHOU Jun-sheng[1, 2] **DAI Xin-yu**[1] **NI Rui-yu**[1] **CHEN Jia-jun**[1]
[1]Department of Computer Science and Technology, Nanjing University, Nanjing, 210093 CHINA
[2]Deptartment of Computer Science, Nanjing Normal University, Nanjing, 210097 CHINA
{Zhoujs, dxy, niry, chenjj}@nlp.nju.edu.cn

Abstract

In this paper, we present a Chinese word segmentation system which is consisted of four components, i.e. basic segmentation, named entity recognition, error-driven learner and new word detector. The basic segmentation and named entity recognition, implemented based on conditional random fields, are used to generate initial segmentation results. The other two components are used to refine the results. Our system participated in the tests on open and closed tracks of Beijing University (PKU) and Microsoft Research (MSR). The actual evaluation results show that our system performs very well in MSR open track, MSR closed track and PKU open track.

1 Introduction

Word segmentation is the first step in Chinese NLP, but segmentation of the Chinese text into words is a nontrivial task. Three difficult tasks, i.e. ambiguities resolution, named entity recognition and new word identification, are the key problems to word segmentation in Chinese.

In this paper, we report a Chinese word segmentation system using a hybrid strategy. In our system, texts are segmented in four steps: basic segmentation, named entity recognition, error-driven learning and new word detection. The implementations of basic segmentation component and named entity recognition component are both based on conditional random fields (CRFs) (Lafferty et al., 2001), while the Error-Driven learning component and new word detection component use statistical and rule methods. We will describe each of these steps in more details below.

2 System Description

2.1 Basic segmentation

We implemented the basic segmentation component with linear chain structure CRFs. CRFs are undirected graphical models that encode a conditional probability distribution using a given set of features. In the special case in which the designated output nodes of the graphical model are linked by edges in a linear chain, CRFs make a first-order Markov independence assumption among output nodes, and thus correspond to finite state machines (FSMs). CRFs define the conditional probability of a state sequence given an input sequence as

$$P_{\Lambda}(s \mid o) = \frac{1}{Z_o} \exp\left(\sum_{t=1}^{T} \sum_{k=1}^{K} \lambda_k f_k(s_{t-1}, s_t, o, t) \right)$$

Where $f_k(s_{t-1}, s_t, o, t)$ is an arbitrary feature function over its arguments, and λ_k is a learned weight for each feature function.

Based on CRFs model, we cast the segmentation problem as a sequence tagging problem. Different from (Peng et al., 2004), we represent the positions of a *hanzi* (Chinese character) with four different tags: B for a *hanzi* that starts a word, I for a *hanzi* that continues the word, F for a *hanzi* that ends the word, S for a *hanzi* that occurs as a single-character word. The basic segmentation is a process of labeling each *hanzi* with a tag given the features derived from its surrounding context. The features used in our experiment can be broken into two categories: character features and word features. The character features are instantiations of the following templates, similar to those described in (Ng and Jin, 2004), *C* refers to a Chinese *hanzi*.

(a) C_n $(n = -2,-1,0,1,2)$

(b) C_nC_{n+1} $(n = -2,-1,0,1)$

(c) $C_{-1}C_1$

(d) $Pu(C_0)$

In addition to the character features, we came up with another type word context feature which was found very useful in our experiments. The feature captures the relationship between the *hanzi* and the word which contains the *hanzi*. For a two-*hanzi* word, for example, the first *hanzi* "连" within the word "连续" will have the feature WC0=TWO_F set to 1, the second *hanzi* "续" within the same word "连续" will have the feature WC0=TWO_L set to 1. For the three-*hanzi* word, for example, the first *hanzi* "梳" within a word "梳妆镜" will have the feature WC0=TRI_F set to 1, the second *hanzi* "妆" within the same word "梳妆镜" will have the feature WC0=TRI_M set to 1, and the last *hanzi* "镜" within the same word "梳妆镜" will have the feature WC0=TRI_L set to 1. Similarly, the feature can be extended to a four-*hanzi* word.

2.2 Named Entity recognition

After basic segmentation, a great number of named entities in the text, such as personal names, location names and organization names, are not yet segmented and recognized properly. So the second step we take is named entity recognition based on CRFs. In contrast to Chinese personal names and location name, the recognition of Chinese organization names is a difficult task. Especially in Microsoft Research corpus, the whole organization name, such as "国际竹藤组织", "北京航空航天大学国家软件开发环境重点实验室" and so on, is regarded as a single word. In this section, we only present our approach for organization name recognition.

The important factor in applying CRFs model to organization name recognition is how to select the proper features set. The constitution of Chinese organization is very complicated, and most organization names do not have any common structural characteristics except for containing some feature words, such as 公司, 学校 and so on. But as a proper noun, the occurrence of an organization name has the specific context. The context information of organization name mainly includes the boundary words and some title words (e.g. 局长、董事长). By analyzing a large amount of organization name corpus, we find that the indicative intensity of different boundary words vary greatly. So we divide the left and right boundary words into two classes according to the indicative intensity. Accordingly we construct the four boundary words lexicons. To solve the problem of the selection and classification of boundary words, we make use of mutual Information *I(x, y)*. If there is a genuine association between x and y, then $I(x,y) >> 0$. If there is no interesting relationship between x and y, then $I(x,y) \approx 0$. If x and y are in complementary distribution, then $I(x,y) << 0$. By using mutual information, we compute the association between boundary word and the type of organization name, then select and classify the boundary words.

In order to increase the precision of organization name recognition, we still introduce the "forbidden word" feature that would prevent some words from being recognized as component of organization name.

For we know that some words, such as "当然", "即使", are impossible to occur in organization name, we collected these words to formed a "forbidden words" lexicon. Based on the consideration given in preceding section, we constructed a set of atomic feature patterns, listed in table 2. Additionally, we defined a set of conjunctive feature patterns, which could form effective feature conjunctions to express complicated contextual information.

2.3 Error-driven learning

As a method based on statistics, no matter how well a CRFs model is constructed, some obviously errors always occurred because of the sparseness of training data. For this reson, error-driven learning method (Brill, 1995) is adopted to refine the segmentation result in this bakeoff in three steps:

1) Based on CRFs model, we segment the *training data* which has been removed all the space between words. Based on the comparison of the segmentation result with the original training data, the difference between them will be extracted. If a difference occurs more than one time, an error-driven rule will be constructed. The rule is described as: $\alpha \rightarrow$ w1w2w3, w1w2w3 is the segmentation of α in training data. We named this rule set constructed by this step *CRF-Ruleset*.

2) Based on FMM&BMM, we segment the *training data* which has been removed all the space between words. As we know, overlapping ambiguity strings can be found through FMM&BMM, and the true segmentation of such *OASs* can be found in training data. If an OAS string has unique segmentation, a rule $\alpha \rightarrow$ w1w2w3 was constructed. We called the rule set constructed in this step *OAS-Ruleset*.

3) In the testing data, if there is the same string as α in *CRFs-Ruleset* or *OAS-Ruleset*, it will be segmented as w1w2w3 according to the rule $\alpha \rightarrow$ w1w2w3.

For example, in the PKU testing data, through error-driven learning, we can segment the string "邓小平理论" as "邓小平理论" while this string is always segmented wrong as "邓 小平 理论" segmented by CRFs model. In other words, error-driven learning can always can be seen as a consistency check. It assures the consistency of the segmentation of the training data and testing data when some strings such as "邓小平理论" occur in both.

2.4 New word detection

CRFs segmentation model can gives good performance on OOV words identification. But there are still some new words that have not been recognized. So an additive new words recognizer is adopted (Chen, 2003).

In-word probability of each character is used for new word detection. The in-word probability of a character is a probability that the character occurs as a part of a word of two or more characters. And the in-word probability of a character is trained from the training data and is calculated as follows:

$$P_{in-word}(C) = \frac{Number\ of\ C\ Occurrence\ in\ words}{Number\ of\ C\ Occurrence}.$$

The consecutive single characters are combined into a new word if the in-word probability of each single character is over a threshold. Obviously, the value of the threshold is the key to the performance of this new words recognizer. Same as (Chen, 2003), we divided the training data as training data and developing data to find an exactly value of the threshold. For this bakeoff, we set the threshold of PKU data as 0.86 and that of MSR data as 0.88. Some new words such as "车购费" "互致" "亚欧" were recognized by this recognizer.

3 Experimental results

We participated in the four GB tracks in the second international Chinese word segmentation bakeoff: PKU-open, PKU-closed, MSR-open, MSR-closed. In the closed tracks, we used the dictionary with the words appearing in the training corpus and didn't conduct the process of named entity recognition. In the open tracks, we employed a dictionary of 134,458 entries. The size of training data used in the open tracks is same as the closed tracks. Except for a dictionary with more vocabulary, we have not employed any other special resources in the open tracks. Table 1 shows the performance of our system in the bakeoff.

	PKU (open)	PKU (closed)	MSR (open)	MSR (closed)
Precision	0.970	0.950	0.971	0.956
Recall	0.964	0.941	0.959	0.959
F	0.967	0.946	0.965	0.957
OOV	0.058	0.058	0.026	0.026
Recall on OOV	0.864	0.813	0.785	0.496

Table 1: Official Bakeoff Outcome

It's a pity that we make a careless mistake (a program bug) which led to 752 left quotation marks concatenated to the words following it in the closed and open tracks on Microsoft research corpus. With the problem fixed, the actual results of the official test data are better than any other system, as shown in Table 2.

	MSR (open)	MSR (closed)
Precision	0.978	0.957
Recall	0.976	0.976
F	0.977	0.966
OOV	0.026	0.026
Recall on OOV	0.772	0.387
Recall on In-Voc	0.982	0.992

Table 2 Actual evaluation on MSR corpus

4 Conclusion

Our open and closed GB track experiments show that its performance is competitive. The most important advantage of our system is the ability to cope with the unknown words. Especially in the open track on the Microsoft research corpus, the recall on OOV of our system achieves 77.2%, higher than any other system. In future work, we would attempt to generalize the ideas of large-margin to CRFs model, leading to new optimal training algorithms with stronger guarantees against overfitting.

References

Eric Brill , 1995. Transformation Based Error Driven Learning and Natural Language Processing : A Case Study in Part of Speech Tagging , Computational Linguistics , V21. No. 4 ,

J. Lafferty, A. McCallum, and F. Pereira. 2001. Conditional random fields: Probabilistic models for segmenting and labeling sequence data. In Proc. ICML 01.

Aitao Chen. 2003. Chinese Word Segmentation Using Minimal Linguistic Knowledge. In *Proceedings of the Second SIGHAN Workshop on Chinese Language Processing.*

Ng, Hwee Tou and Jin Kiat Low. 2004. Chinese Part-of-Speech Taging: One-at-a-Time or All at Once? Word-based or Character based? In *Proceedings of the Conference on Empirical Methods in Natural Language Processing*, Spain.

Peng, Fuchun, Fangfang Feng, and Andrew McCallum. 2004. Chinese Segmentation and New Word Detection using Conditional Random Fields . In *Proceedings of the Twentith International Conference on Computaional Linguistics*, pages 562–568.

Author Index